THE
AMERICAN
MIDWEST

THE AMERICAN MIDWEST

Managing Change in Rural Transition

Edited by
Norman Walzer

M.E.Sharpe
Armonk, New York
London, England

Copyright © 2003 by M. E. Sharpe, Inc.

Library of Congress Cataloging-in-Publication Data

The American Midwest: managing change in rural transition / edited by Norman Walzer.
    p. cm.
    Includes bibliographical references and index.
    ISBN 0-7656-1121-X (hardcover: alk. paper)—ISBN 0-7656-1122-8 (hardcover: alk.
paper)
      1. Sociology, Rural—Middle West. 2. Middle West—Rural conditions. 3. Middle West—
Economic conditions. I. Walzer, Norman.

HN79.A14 A46 2003
307.72'0956—dc21   2002075888

Printed in the United States of America

The paper used in this publication meets the minimum requirements of
American National Standard for Information Sciences
Permanence of Paper for Printed Library Materials,
ANSI Z 39.48-1984.

BM (c) 10 9 8 7 6 5 4 3 2 1
BM (c) 10 9 8 7 6 5 4 3 2 1

To Emma Kathleen

Contents

List of Tables, Figures, and Maps

Tables

Figures

Maps

Preface

The recession in the early 1980s, followed by the longest-running economic expansion in U.S. history, and then what appears to be a shorter recession, but still with substantial increases in unemployment, has brought major changes in rural areas. While many parts of rural areas in the Midwest have participated very well in the economic expansion, others still face relatively high unemployment and population out-migration.

Advances in technology specifically, but other advances as well, have altered the basic economic structure in rural areas, especially in the Midwest. Production agriculture, long a major employer, now represents a much smaller proportion of the employment base and currently is experiencing significant competition from foreign producers. Industrialization of agriculture and more attention to preserving the identity of the commodities and tailored production will change the ways in which agriculture is managed, which will have an impact on small towns and the rural countryside.

This book examines major issues facing areas such as the Midwest that are undergoing a substantial transition in economic structure. Manufacturing plants in small towns have declined, eroding the employment base. Retail stores have been replaced by regional shopping centers and discount outlets. Population declines have threatened schools and other public services in some areas.

Though many population and economic trends have seemed adverse, opportunities also exist for economic revitalization. Value-added agriculture offers producers a chance to retain more of the value added to their commodities and livestock during the production process. Technology and telecommunication advances provide opportunities to access markets that were virtually unavailable even a few years ago. To reach these objectives, however, rural public officials, producers, and community leaders must adopt new and innovative strategies, some of which are described in this text.

Many people have contributed to this book. The editor gratefully acknowledges contributors who were willing to prepare their chapters under the usual tight deadlines. Second, the Illinois Council on Food and Agricultural Research, under a project managed by Raymond Lenzi, provided financial support. Third, Nancy Baird, Carol Harper, Karen Poncin, Lori Sutton, and Bill Westerhold from the Illinois Institute for Rural Affairs and the staff of the Curriculum Publications Clearinghouse at Western Illinois University helped manage the several drafts and prepare them for publication. Without their help, this project would not have been completed. As always, any errors belong to the editor.

Part I

Overview

NORMAN WALZER

Introduction and Overview

The national economic expansion during the 1990s brought relative prosperity to many regions—rural and urban alike—that had experienced significant distress in the previous decade. Population out-migration was reversed in some cases, and high unemployment rates were replaced by a need for a larger labor force to meet growing employment demands. Housing construction and higher spending were fueled by increased incomes resulting from better-paying jobs and overtime.

Rural areas, heavily dependent on natural resources and agriculture with employment declines, had experienced especially high unemployment, leading to a significant out-migration of people seeking better economic opportunities during the 1980s. This situation was compounded as mature industries, facing significant foreign and domestic competition, were ultimately forced to close.

Midwestern states[1] experiencing significant economic declines during the 1980s were termed the "Rust Belt" in contrast with states in the south and southwest which were denoted as the "Sun Belt." Losses in the Midwest were especially plagued by lower business birthrates (Testa, Klier, and Mattoon 1997) as businesses started operations in growing markets with lower labor and energy costs—two advantages offered by Sunbelt states.

The relative prosperity in the 1990s led investigators to write about a "rural rebound" and discuss the possibility of a return to the 1970s when rural areas grew more rapidly than did metropolitan (metro) regions. It also caused them to speculate whether the 1980s, rather than the 1970s, were, in fact, the atypical decade (Johnson, Beale, Gurwitt, and Taylor 1998).

Though rural areas have typically lagged behind metro areas, the rural economy of the Midwest by some measures responded reasonably well in the 1990s, although substantial economic changes occurred. Overall, nonmetro areas in the Midwest had a 16.8 percent increase in employment compared with an average of 17.3 percent for nonmetro areas in the United States; however, nonmetro manufacturing employment in the Midwest increased 13.6 percent compared with an overall U.S. growth of 4.1 percent in the same period (U.S. Department of Commerce 2001). These numbers partially reflect the fact that setbacks experienced by Midwestern states in the previous decade lowered the basis on which changes are compared.

The prosperity, however, was not evenly spread across the Midwest, and it varied with industrial structure, population characteristics, and other factors. Though manufacturing employment in nonmetro areas increased 44 percent in South Dakota, a small rural state, it increased only 1.4 percent in Illinois, a large industrial state. Relative to total employment, U.S. manufacturing went from 17.3 percent to 15.4 percent and from 16.9 percent to 16.5 percent in the nonmetro Midwest during the 1990s. The relative stability of manufacturing in the Midwest helped maintain rural incomes in many areas (Testa et al. 1997).

In contrast, farm employment in the Midwest declined 7.9 percent during the 1990s compared with only a 2.1 percent decline nationwide. Likewise, farm employment represented 8.1 percent of total employment in the Midwest in 1999, down from 10.2 percent in 1990. Nationwide, farm employment was 8.0 percent (1990) and 6.7 percent, respectively. These figures indicate the greater relative importance of farm employment in the Midwest but also the fact that the declines during the expansion of the 1990s were relatively greater in the Midwest.

The declines in farm employment, usually in sparsely populated rural areas, negatively impacted surrounding small towns and contributed to the population out-migration. Service and trade employment changes in the nonmetro Midwest (27.2% and 18.0%, respectively) were below the 31.1 percent and 20.2 percent experienced for nonmetro areas in the U.S. (U.S. Department of Commerce 2001). The growth in trade may have occurred disproportionately in larger cities containing shopping and discount centers, which tend to draw from surrounding small towns. In addition, the service sector that is attracted to remote rural areas often involves lower paid consumer services compared with higher paid business services located in larger centers (Crump and Walzer 1996).

Though, overall, the economic prosperity of the 1990s affected much of the United States, it is clear that not all regions participated equally in the process. Rural population growth often occurred in areas attractive to retirees and/or recreation users (Johnson et al. 1998). Unfortunately, the Midwest, with harsh winters and a relatively flat landscape, is not as attractive to retirees as the South and West with their warmer seasons and more scenic landscape.

The result, as shown by Paul Lasley and Margaret Hanson (chapter 2), is that during the 1990s the Midwestern states, as a group, did not grow in population as much as the United States, with wide differences among Midwestern states. North Dakota, for instance, gained only 0.5 percent population during the 1990s, whereas Minnesota had a population gain of 12.4 percent.

These major differences, of course, highlight the difficulties associated with trying to describe a region as complex and diverse as the Midwest.

Many forces are at work that will affect the future of the Midwest—some that threaten the current conditions and some that provide opportunities, if suitable adjustments can be made. Agriculture, a large employer in many Midwestern states, is experiencing unprecedented competition from other countries in marketing commodities. Lower land prices, along with techno-logical advances that have been incorporated into production methods in these countries, have significantly increased foreign productivity, making it more difficult for U.S. producers to compete for traditional markets. At the same time, technology, including the Internet, offers opportunities for agri-cultural producers to identify new markets both domestically and overseas, allowing them to compete in new arenas such as niche markets.

In the manufacturing sector, high wages, unionization, and high employee benefits, in some Midwestern states, have caused businesses to relocate off-shore in search of lower production costs. "Right-to-work" states, those with lower compensation costs, and others willing to provide tax-expenditure in-centives have competed effectively for new business investment. These ef-forts, combined with an attractive living environment and lower energy costs, make other regions more competitive as industrial locations. This is not to say that Midwestern states are totally unable to compete; rather, it is to sug-gest that the competition is fierce and the ability of other regions to attract businesses is evident.

Conversely, Midwestern states enjoy high-quality and well-educated labor forces. Some states have high levels of urbanization and technology advances, especially in metro regions, that could extend into rural areas. Proximity to large metro areas typically means access to business services and major mar-kets, especially in states with modern highway and rail systems.

While the 1990s brought population gains in rural areas, small communi-ties, even in states with population growth, face challenges. Downtown busi-nesses must compete with discount outlets and regional shopping centers. They also are threatened by catalogue and Internet sales. Many small towns do not have access to broadband technology, which is often essential for attracting businesses. Faced with population out-migration as well, these cities find it difficult to remain economically viable.

Theme of Book

This book explores major trends under way in twelve Midwestern states, identifies the types of issues faced, and then examines innovative approaches available to address these concerns. The main focus of the discussions is on rural areas; however, the strong linkages between metro and nonmetro areas are also recognized. For example, some rural residents, including farm families, often have jobs in nearby large communities and, in some instances, these jobs allow families to remain on the farm. In addition, residents living in small communities that have lost their main employment base must now commute to larger centers. At the same time, urban centers rely on the surrounding regions for their labor force.

It is hoped that a discussion of major issues facing the Midwest, along with insights into possible strategies, will help policymakers find and implement workable solutions. Understanding the factors determining the future of the rural Midwest involves a realization that two broad sets of issues are involved. First, statewide trends affect both metro and nonmetro areas in the state. The economic structure of the state, tax-expenditure policies, business climate, and other considerations are in this category and are affected by state policies or programs over which rural policymakers have little if any control.

Second, it is important to realize that, while rural areas in the past depended heavily on agriculture and manufacturing for employment, the recent growth has more often been in services. This trend is likely to continue and, because of the lower pay in the service industry, there is an adverse impact on rural economies. Likewise, businesses have been more prone to contract out some activities rather than to provide them in-house, thus avoiding the costs of benefits.

Not all the trends facing rural areas are negative, however. There is a growing concern in both urban and suburban areas about quality-of-life issues. Social concerns such as drugs and gangs are often mentioned. Rising housing costs in densely populated metro areas can also encourage families to seek rural locations (Deller, Tsai, Marcouiller, and American 2001; Dissart and Deller 2000; Halstead and Deller 1997; Rudzitis 1999).

Rural areas with high-speed access to the Internet can open worldwide markets for businesses even in these areas to serve customers in large and distant metro regions. Electronic telecommunications make it possible for professional services such as accounting, engineering, and even medical services to be provided efficiently from remote locations. Large metro areas in the past have benefited from the availability of specialized talent and access to specialized services; however, through the Internet, businesses in rural areas can obtain technical assistance and expertise from distant locations, and this is likely to continue in the future. Building on these options, however, takes a vision and a concerted effort by local development practitioners working with telecommunications providers to keep the community current with telecommunication advances (see Tom Bonnett, chapter 13).

This book has three intended audiences: (1) state policymakers, (2) students and scholars, and (3) local leaders. State policymakers who must seek solutions or remedies for rural issues will find the material especially useful because it describes strategies and alternatives that have been used successfully. It is hoped they will see the value of experimenting with these approaches. While many of the ideas tried elsewhere cannot be replicated immediately, most can be adapted to fit local conditions. They will at least provide a starting point.

Second, students and scholars interested in learning more about rural trends and their implications will discover that the material provides a basis for additional research and study. Contributors to this volume discuss implications of these trends and offer many ideas about approaches that can be used in the future to rebuild the local economies and stimulate rural development. They also review the literature on these topics and provide a base for additional research.

Third, after reviewing some of the examples presented, local leaders interested in solutions to current dilemmas will be encouraged to learn more about these approaches. They also will better understand the underlying factors contributing to local issues. Communities are unique in the issues to be addressed, but effective solutions must start with local groups attempting to find ways to address their concerns. In subsequent presentations, contributors demonstrate the importance of local decisions and the ability to manage a changing environment.

Organization and Overview of the Book

The American Midwest has two main perspectives. The next five chapters describe and document major trends affecting rural areas and especially the Midwest. Lasley and Hanson (chapter 2) review population changes experienced by Midwestern states in recent years and point out that rural areas represent two very different cultures—one that is closely tied to agriculture and the other that is linked more closely to metro regions. Agricultural dependent areas may continue to lag behind in population and income growth, whereas those linked to metro areas find that the rural hinterland is a good place to live but residents will continue to shop and work in the nearby metro centers. Agriculture will continue to shrink as an employment source for rural areas, and youth will leave the region for higher-paying employment.

Changes in U.S. policies toward rural areas will be necessary for rural areas to prosper. Several researchers, including Lasley and Hanson, note that past rural policies focused on agriculture with insufficient recognition that the term *rural* is broader than *agriculture*. This view has also been expressed elsewhere (Drabonstott 2001). For rural areas to prosper, federal programs must lead to increased job opportunities allowing people to return to these areas.

While many counties in the Midwest lost population, this was by no means true for all. Andrew Sofranko and Mohamed Samy (Chapter 3) show that immigration, mainly Hispanics, is an important factor and, in some instances, this meant the difference between population growth and population decline; however, these increases may reflect low-paying jobs in the meat-processing or other industries. Immigration can impose costs on rural areas ill-equipped to provide needed support services such as extra education programs for recent immigrants. Another major finding is that Hispanics now locate in smaller communities rather than in large metro centers.

Preliminary census estimates also show that the elderly are another important population group to be considered in rural settings. These residents may require additional health care, public transportation, nursing home facilities, and other services. Without access to these services, elderly residents are often forced to relocate to larger communities. Thus, in order to retain them in small rural settings, a serious investment in health and transportation services must be made.

Much of the employment base in rural areas, of course, is no longer in agriculture; instead, manufacturing and service industries have become more important as an employment source. Thomas Johnson and James Scott (Chapter 4) point out that technology increases have substituted capital for labor in many production processes, reducing the local employment needed to reach the same level of production. The switch to a service economy has downplayed the comparative advantage of rural areas, with a greater reliance on commodity production, and increased the importance of connectivity through the Internet.

Services can be provided over a long distance using the Internet, making it all the more important for rural areas to have high-speed access. At the same time, low population densities in rural areas make technology improvements more expensive and, left to private sector decisions, many of the services will not be provided. In such cases, the impetus for modernization upgrades rests with local initiatives by public officials and community leaders. Rural residents must see the importance of these improvements and understand how they can benefit from their use. These will be major issues that must be addressed in rural areas.

Recent declines in farm employment, a major industry, have had a significant impact on many rural communities, and these changes are likely to continue. Burton Swanson, Mohamed Samy, and Andrew Sofranko (Chapter 5) describe the implications of the "new agriculture." Farms have been consolidated, and producers are paying more attention to specialty crops that offer higher prices. While large capital investments, on the one hand, have reduced the on-farm employment, producers turning to specialty crops may spend more time on these activities, which, in turn, provide opportunities for other new business ventures in rural areas.

Overall, producers will be forced to move toward greater product-identity preservation if they are to access and retain new markets. They must form alliances with processors and customers to remain competitive. The suitability of a region to grow specific specialty crops will also partially determine the continued profitability or even viability of local agriculture. Competition from countries such as Brazil or Argentina during the next decade will have a major impact on the U.S. agricultural industry.

Although agriculture is a major employment source in many, if not most, rural areas, the linkage between agriculture and local economic development is not as clear as one might think. Kimberly Zeuli and Steven Deller (chapter 6) show that one major impact of agriculture on local economies results from federal payments to landowners. Their analysis suggests that counties relying heavily on production agriculture are more likely to have slower growth in income. They also find a positive connection between farms that provide more on-farm employment (usually larger farms) and local economic expansion.

The second major section of the book addresses possible remedies for issues facing the rural Midwest. Many of the proposed approaches pertain to rural areas in other sections of the country as well. When possible, examples of innovative adaptations of identified strategies are provided with special attention paid to Midwestern examples.

Christopher Merrett and Norman Walzer (Chapter 7) describe the trends leading to the growth of new generation cooperatives (NGCs) in the Midwest and how they have helped farm producers increase incomes. The benefits of these business ventures are not limited to producers, however; rather, they also generate local employment in the surrounding area partly because a high percentage of the inputs are purchased locally (McGrahan and Gale 2000). For this reason, it makes sense for local developers to work with producer groups to organize and start NGCs.

Using NGCs as a local development approach offers several advantages. Producers may be willing to invest in these ventures and, therefore, provide a source of investment capital. The NGCs typically purchase inputs (commodities) locally, causing producers to receive higher incomes and, in turn, spend at least a portion of the funds locally, thus, generating additional income. Locally owned businesses are more likely to stay in the region and provide a stable employment source. At the same time, however, any business that uses farm commodities and/or livestock may encounter environmental problems and, in these cases, may face resistance from population groups. Merrett and Walzer examine the economic development impacts from several NGCs and estimate the local multipliers involved.

Business incubator programs have been used to foster small business development in urban areas for many years with varying degrees of success. The underlying theory is that if several small entrepreneurs are in close proximity, they can share resources, expertise, and facilities, and, thus, save costs and increase their probability of success. Proximity is the important factor in these cases.

Expanding on this idea, Lee Munnich and Greg Schrock (Chapter 8) ask whether there are concentrations of rural knowledge businesses that might foster economic growth and development. Though they might not be in close proximity, the context in which they are located may foster growth and development. Could rural knowledge clusters be a suitable economic development approach in some regions?

After examining three case studies in rural Minnesota, Munnich and Schrock suggest that innovative companies are affected by their environment and that sharing common ties can aid in the enterprises' growth and development. They also conclude that the same knowledge base can drive several companies. The importance of linkages between educational institutions and industry was also confirmed by the experiences in rural Minnesota.

The importance of providing a local environment in which businesses can start and prosper is confirmed by Brian Dabson (Chapter 9) in an analysis of the role entrepreneurship can play in enhancing local economic development. In comparing Midwestern states according to various measures of entrepreneurial environment and the extent to which urban and rural portions of each state vary, Dabson notes that, overall, the Midwest does not compare favorably with other parts of the United States. While specific measures differ, Midwestern states are below average on many indices reflecting small business growth and other characteristics.

Based on several analyses of entrepreneurial environment and business trends, Dabson suggests several directions. Rural entrepreneurship must place higher on the federal policy agenda and must receive more recognition for its role in stimulating local economic development. Current federal policy for rural areas is still primarily focused on agricultural programs, a view also shared by Lasley and Hanson. The increased importance assigned to rural areas in federal policy must be reflected in additional funding for rural entrepreneurship programs. Local institutions that can support innovation and entrepreneurship must be strengthened, and they should build on existing programs.

The fact that employment levels in production agriculture, commodity prices, and farm incomes are lagging behind and that producing commodities in the future may be headed for even more competition means that alternative approaches to enhancing producer incomes and stimulating local employment must be found. One approach has been for farmers to join to-gether in collaborative ventures to retain ownership of a product as it moves up the value-chain.

For a variety of reasons, including their relative remoteness from markets, producers in Minnesota, North Dakota, South Dakota, and Wisconsin have led the way in forming value-added ventures. New generation cooperatives (NGCs) have increased in popularity in the past twenty years as producers have tried novel approaches to raise their incomes. As with any small busi-ness ventures, NGCs involve risk; however, when successful, they offer op-portunities for producers to obtain higher prices for commodities and share in the value-added generated in the production of final products.

Though agriculture is a major employer in many rural areas, it does not account for a majority of employment, as was noted earlier (Gale 1999). Manu-facturing, retail, health care, education, and other institutions employ a large number of rural residents. With the growth of technology, the Internet, and other telecommunication advances, new opportunities exist for businesses in rural areas. John Leatherman (Chapter 10) examines the opportunities avail-able to Internet-based businesses. The opportunities are not limited to selling merchandise over the Internet; rather, rural businesses can access technical in-formation and support, purchase supplies and merchandise, obtain services, and participate in technical industry discussions that may reduce operating costs.

For rural businesses to use the Internet effectively, however, high-speed access must be available. Successfully enhancing access usually involves local officials, community leaders, and other groups actively engaged in tech-nology planning. As noted earlier by Johnson and Scott (Chapter 4), this involvement may require a cultural change, which would entail more ag-gressive pursuit of technological updates as well as a commitment to take advantage of the opportunities offered.

Most discussions of local economic development sooner or later turn to finding the resources to start businesses, expand infrastructure, or promote revitalization efforts in other ways. While numerous agencies and programs that finance businesses exist, inadequate capital is still one of the most fre-quently cited causes of small business failure. Entrepreneurs may underesti-mate the amount of capital needed to start operations or they may have insufficient funds to continue operations when unexpected costs arise. Fi-nancial institutions, especially in rural areas, may be relatively unfamiliar with lending to business ventures or it may be that potential entrepreneurs have not worked out a detailed business plan.

Raymond Lenzi (Chapter 11) examines issues involved in financing busi-ness ventures in the rural Midwest. In particular, he notes that situations may arise in slow economies where intervention by public agencies is needed to help finance local development projects. In recent years, several approaches have been especially useful. Some areas have created local or regional foundations to provide seed money to businesses. These foundations can augment funds available through local financial institutions and state or federal agencies that provide low-cost funds. Many local governments have revolving loan funds to assist with gap financing for business start-ups.

Another major source of business capital involves venture capital funds in which investors take an ownership position in the business. In rural areas, venture capital funds are relatively rare, making it difficult for potential entrepreneurs to access this funding source. An alternative approach is to use nontraditional venture capital sources (Markley 2001). These programs involve industries and sectors not normally served by regular venture capital sources. Investors usually expect a lower rate of return from the business venture. Often, they operate in a narrower region or area and have a dual focus. They expect a social as well as a financial return. These programs have succeeded in many states, including some in the Midwest, and their record suggests that they should be seriously considered in other regions.

While several contributors report that effective remedies for the issues facing the Midwest will require significant local initiative, many rural policymakers are inexperienced with programs available and approaches that might be needed to undertake these efforts. This situation is worse in small governments without an experienced or full-time staff.

John Gruidl and Ronald Hustedde (Chapter 12) make the case that the learning organization approach can help communities more effectively formulate and implement changes. The learning community approach involves creating a situation in which local leaders continually increase their capacity to generate the types of actions needed to produce the desired results.

Rather than focusing on a specific problem facing their community, leaders work to build trust among various population segments and create an environment that ultimately leads to more effective decisions and a higher quality of life. Gruidl and Hustedde identify six practices that communities can follow in implementing this approach, including engaging a diversity of population groups in the decision-making process and causing them to think systematically. Helping residents to consider the assets of the community rather than to focus on deficiencies is also important, as is providing residents with the opportunities to share what they have learned and to reflect on accomplishments. Agreeing on basic principles and sharing a common vision will also empower local leaders to move the community ahead in resolving local issues.

This approach to planning and decision making should result in a different management style. Rather than a pyramid structure, multiple leadership centers may exist with community development decisions and practices made by a very different cast of players from across the community. Gruidl and Hustedde cite several examples of communities that have taken this approach with at least some success. By engaging more population groups in these communities, they have been able to bring new ideas and approaches to the table and gain a consensus about promoting local development or revitalization.

While it is clear that a major impetus for solutions must come from local officials, if issues facing the rural Midwest are to be solved, state governments also must play a supporting role, especially regarding issues that extend beyond the jurisdiction of a single local government. Several contributors cited technology as having a major impact on rural areas and offering substantial opportunities for local expansion. At the same time, however, technology issues typically are resolved at least on a regional basis. Private companies may not consider the high fixed investment in sparsely populated areas as profitable, and state incentives or investment may be necessary to guarantee access to modern facilities in rural areas.

Tom Bonnett (Chapter 13) traces the history of state investment strategies and asks whether states should support the expansion of telecommunications infrastructure in rural areas. While a strong case can be made for these investments, much can also be learned from past state involvement in local issues. Additional state support can bring more state control and, to some extent, loss of local decision making, which ultimately may be key to finding a new future for rural areas. The opportunities currently available to rural regions differ from those in the past, and it may be difficult to address these concerns using traditional approaches.

At the same time, issues facing local governments now and in the near future involve coordinating the policies implemented with other governments. Using a regional approach will be important whether they involve public transportation, technology, job creation, or environmental issues. Effective state policies and solutions will be essential, even though the main impetus must start with local officials and community leaders.

Conclusions

Rural areas in the Midwest clearly are responding to a variety of pressures. In many areas, commodity prices are low and the employment base is shifting from manufacturing to lower-paying services. Some counties continue to experience the population out-migration of the 1980s. Retail shopping patterns are moving toward regional shopping and discount centers at the expense of merchants in small towns.

At the same time, however, opportunities exist for rural areas to respond in innovative ways. Technology offers access to much broader domestic, and even international, markets for specialty goods. Agricultural producers who can target specific markets for identity-preserved products may capture higher returns. Other producers may be able to invest in NGCs to capture more of the value-added during the production process and, thus, achieve higher incomes.

Several common themes run through the chapters in this volume. First, for rural areas to prosper, there must be a broadening of the federal policy for rural communities beyond farm programs. Though agriculture remains an important component of the rural economy, especially in terms of the impact of support payments, many other industries employ more residents and offer opportunities for growth.

An emphasis must be placed both on investing in the capacity of rural areas to participate in the information economy and on providing modern telecommunications infrastructure. If left to private decision makers, low-density rural areas may not be profitable enough to obtain modern communications facilities. Without these facilities, remote rural areas will be at a decided disadvantage.

Second, the rural areas that will achieve the greatest success will be those in which local policymakers and residents take a lead in identifying issues and initiating action. The time when state and federal governments brought solutions to rural areas has passed. Instead, local leaders must organize their constituents, undergo a long-term planning process, create an action plan, and then follow through.

Third, attitudes and approaches adopted by rural leaders and residents must change. A community learning environment that involves more residents, broadens the leadership pool, achieves a common vision, and gains a commitment to action is needed in some communities. Business leaders and residents must also recognize the potential of technology and find ways to incorporate this tool in development efforts.

Fourth, rural areas must recognize that innovative economic development approaches offer decided advantages. For instance, the importance of industrial clusters is becoming better understood, and the environment in which companies locate affects the innovation potential. Sharing the specialized talent and knowledge base and having access to educational institutions have both been of substantial importance to small businesses as shown by the case studies of rural areas in Minnesota.

Fifth, business financing opportunities have also changed. Traditional sources such as banks and other financial institutions may not be adequate to encourage and finance business start-ups in rural areas. Some type of venture capital may be needed. In these cases, however, venture capitalists may have to accept lower rates of return and be willing to accept a social benefit as part of the profit incentive.

The rural Midwest will undergo many changes in the next several years depending on unique local considerations and the national economy. What finally happens, however, will depend on local actions and, by necessity, these effective initiatives will be crucial. Opportunities will arise to participate in new ventures and development activities. Those communities that can participate in these efforts will do well; others may continue to face stagnation or decline. The ability to identify and implement innovative strategies will be vital to the future of many rural areas.

Note

1. In this book, the twelve Midwestern states are the traditional Census Midwest (East North Central and the West North Central states), which includes Illinois, Indiana, Iowa, Kansas, Michigan, Minnesota, Missouri, Nebraska, North Dakota, Ohio, South Dakota, and Wisconsin.

References

Crump, Jeff, and Norman Walzer. 1996. *Producer Service Workers in the Nonmetropolitan Midwest* (Number RE-2). Chicago: Federal Reserve Bank of Chicago.

Deller, Steven C., T. Tsai, David W. Marcouiller, and D.W. American. 2001. The role of amenities and quality of life in rural economic growth. *Journal of Agricultural Economics* 83(2): 352–365.

Dissart, J.C., and Steven C. Deller. 2000. Quality of life in the planning literature. *Journal of Planning Literature* 15: 135–161.

Drabonstott, Mark. 2001. New policies for a new rural America. *International Regional Science Review* 24(1): 3–15.

Gale, Fred. 1999. Value-added manufacturing has strong local linkages. *Rural Conditions and Trends* 8(3): 23–26.

Halstead, John M., and Steven C. Deller. 1997. Public infrastructure in economic development and growth: Evidence from rural manufacturers. *Journal of Community Development Society* 28(2): 149–169.

Johnson, Kenneth M., Calvin L. Beale, R. Gurwitt, and F. Taylor. 1998. The revival of rural America: Defying all predictions, rural America is coming back. What's behind the sudden influx of people and businesses, and will it ruin the very things the newcomers cherish most? *The Wilson Quarterly* 22(2): 15–42.

Markley, Deborah M. 2001. Financing the new rural economy. In *Exploring Policy Options for a New Rural America*, 69–80. Kansas City, MO: Federal Reserve Bank.

McGrahan, David, and Fred Gale. 2000. *Rural Industry: Is Rural America Being Left Behind in the New Economy?* Washington, DC: U.S. Department of Agriculture–Economic Research Service. Available on-line: <www.ers.usda.gov/briefing/industry/neweconomy>.

Rudzitis, G. 1999. Amenities increasingly draw people to the rural west. *Rural Development Perspectives* 14: 23–28.

Testa, William A., T.H. Klier, and R.H. Mattoon. 1997. *Assessing the Midwest Economy: Report of Findings*. Chicago: Federal Reserve Bank of Chicago.

U.S. Department of Commerce, Economics and Statistics Administration, Bureau of Economic Analysis. 2001. *REIS, Regional Economic Information System, 1969–99* (CD-ROM). Washington, DC: Bureau of Economic Analysis.

2

PAUL LASLEY AND MARGARET HANSON

The Changing Population of the Midwest

A Reflection on Opportunities

This chapter explores the most recent population shifts within the North Central Region, which have resulted from the lack of opportunities because of the contraction of farming. Population decline in rural counties and increased urbanization within the region reflect the severity of the farm crisis of the 1980s. As farm families reduced expenditures to cope with lost incomes and profits, the farm crisis soon infected the economies of rural communities, resulting in much economic stress on small town businesses. The failure of the farm economy to rebound in the decade of the 1990s has extended the farm crisis into a chronic rural problem. The rural restructuring triggered by the collapse of the farm economy in the 1980s continues to threaten the viability of many rural social institutions such as churches and schools.

It may be argued that farming and agriculture, which were historically the major building blocks for much of the Midwest economy, have failed to provide adequate opportunities to support population growth equal to the rest of the nation in the past decade. Recent population shifts highlight the ongoing forces of economic restructuring within farming and rural industries (Lasley, Leistritz, Lobao, and Meyer 1995; Lobao 1990). The failure to restore prosperity to the farm economy has resulted in continued population decline, especially in small, agriculturally dependent counties. Population decline is a natural response to what has been described as the worst period of modern history for farm families and farm-dependent communities since the Great Depression (Davidson 1990; Harl 1990; Lasley et al. 1995). This chapter discusses population shifts in the dozen states that constitute the North Central Region, often referred to as the "breadbasket of the world."

Social and economic changes are not neutral concepts, for they generally produce gains for some and losses for others. Nowhere are the differential consequences of social and economic change more evident than in the Midwest following a decade of economic hardship and record number of business failures stemming from the farm crisis. The rapidly changing landscape throughout the Midwest shows gains for some communities and losses for others. Recent census data confirm that the restructuring of rural America challenges the basic understanding of these trends and poses difficult policy choices about the future of the region, especially in those counties defined as totally rural and heavily dependent upon farming. Although historically there have been considerable variations in the population distributions and economic bases of this region, the forces of the last two decades have widened the gap between rural counties. Though viewed by some as so unimportant as to only be referred to as the "fly-over" zone, the trends in the Midwest reflect some of the most profound and disconcerting rural trends since the Great Depression.

The twelve states that make up the North Central Region show considerable diversity in terms of population growth between 1990 and 2000 (Map 2.1). North Dakota, the least populated state in the region, also had the slowest growth rate of 0.5 percent. South Dakota, also a sparsely settled state, had a growth rate of 8.5 percent. Minnesota's growth rate, the highest in the region, was 12.4 percent. Even so, the growth rate in all of the twelve states in the region was well below the national average of 13.2 percent. The differential growth rates among the dozen states in the region deserve attention. For example, North Dakota has the lowest population growth in the region, and Minnesota has the highest. Even though these two states share a common border and similar histories, it is evident that their trajectories in terms of population are quite distinct. Likewise, what accounts for Iowa having only a 5.4 percent population growth rate, yet each of its neighboring states having growth rates that are three percentage points higher? Asked differently, what are the higher-growth states doing that the slower growth states are not?

The Setting

The historic U.S. development model was closely tied to natural resources that were discovered in the new land. For the Midwest, the riches of the soil provided the foundation for agricultural development. Similarly, in the Northwest Territories, lumbering developed; and in the coal-laden mountains of Appalachia, and later in the West, mining towns took root. Population growth was a function of natural resource development and the employment opportunities that these industries provided.

Several important political decisions set the course of events that led to the development of the Midwest and determined the future of the region. The Homestead Act of 1862 provided land in small parcels to immigrant families wanting to gain a foothold in achieving the American dream. The Home-

Map 2.1   **Population and Percent Change in Population, North Central Region, 1990–2000**

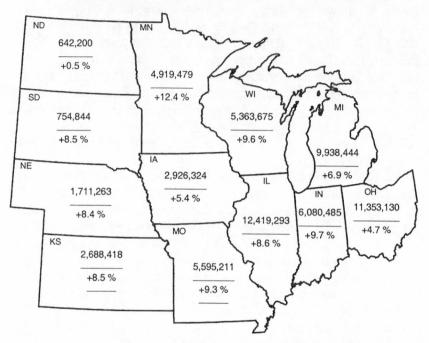

Source: U.S. Bureau of the Census. *U.S. Census 2000.* Available on-line: <www.census.gov/main/cen2000.html>.

stead Act was intended in part to ensure continuation of family farms and an extension of the democratic thesis espoused by small-farm advocates. Under this land disposal act, families could receive 160 acres under the most generous terms. The creation of a large number of small family farms ensured a dispersed agriculture and a rural culture composed of small towns and an agrarian democracy. This rural culture, which was created by the large number of first- and second-generation European settlers acquiring small parcels of land and living within the confines of small and rather homogeneous communities, remained pretty much intact until the Great Depression.

The Great Depression (1929 to 1934) challenged the notion that agrarian living and a rural culture were superior to urban life. The struggles of farm families from the crash of farm prices in 1918 at the end of World War I (WWI) and continuing throughout the 1930s called into question the assumptions that a nation of family farmers and rural communities would provide economic and social stability. As Richard Kirkendall (1991) and others have noted, this crisis, which lasted for nearly two decades, had enormous consequences on political thought and economic policy. It led to heavy governmental involvement in agriculture, providing fuel for the New Deal era and the justification for what Kirkendall calls the "Great American Agricultural Revolution."

Pervasive poverty throughout much of rural America at that time provided the rationale for New Deal programs such as the Resettlement Administration and the Farm Security Administration; however, some historians such as William Cochrane (1993) argue that the outbreak of World War II (WWII) did more to improve rural conditions than the combined effects of the New Deal programs. In response to new jobs and opportunities being created in the cities and the chronic economic hardships on farms, many farm families joined one of the largest migration streams of American history—the rural to urban migration.

Throughout the remainder of the twentieth century, the Midwest struggled with the forces set in motion by WWII. The failure to achieve the promised rural prosperity resulted in several attempts to modernize and strengthen rural life, including the mechanization of agriculture, the adoption of commercial fertilizers, and the utilization of hybrid seeds that greatly improved yields. While these developments contributed to increased farm productivity, they soon resulted in chronic surpluses, low prices, low farm incomes, and stagnating rural conditions.

The history of communities based on extractive industries is well known. Extractive industries, including farming, are highly dependent upon available natural resources. Transitions occur when the natural resource base is depleted. Coal mines shut down as coal deposits are exhausted; lumber mills close when logs are no longer readily available; and fishing boats and canneries sit idle when the fisheries are depleted. In each of these cases, people either move to other regions where they can ply their skills or find a new line of work.

Once the natural resource base is depleted, unless there is a concerted effort to diversify the community's economic base, the community falls on hard times. Without this effort, community decline is evidenced by high rates of unemployment, increased rates of dependency, out-migration, and economic stagnation. Communities that were once thriving places to live and work wither as natural resources are exhausted. Osha Davidson (1990) describes this process as the formation of rural ghettos. The continued lack of adequate incomes and investment capital further contributes to higher rates of substandard housing, poor nutrition, inadequate health care, and inferior education. It is under these conditions that the next generation born into poverty conditions fuels an increasingly chronic situation. Janet Fitchen's (1981) case study in upstate New York captures this downward spiral:

What all of the chronically poor nonfarm people in the rural areas have in common today, then, is that their parents or grandparents made an unsatisfactory transition from agriculture or agriculture-related occupations, in which insufficient resources, unfortunate timing, and large-scale economic trends all worked against their making an advantageous adaptation to nonagricultural pursuits. (56–57)

Structural Changes in the Midwest

Many books, census reports, and government findings have documented the structural changes in farming and agriculture during the past sixty years. Increased farm surpluses and resulting low prices, combined with ever-larger capital requirements, have contributed to the declining number of farms. From 1945 to 1997, farm numbers in the Midwest dropped from nearly two million to 749,000—a 62 percent decline. This post-WWII transformation mirrors the national decline, from 5.8 million to 1.9 million—a 67 percent change (Table 2.1). The consolidation of farms into ever-larger units as families left farming has contributed to much restructuring beyond farming. The decline in farm numbers and the accompanying loss of farm population is visible throughout much of the countryside as well as in trade center towns in which existence depended on serving the needs of farm families.

What these data often fail to show is the level of personal and community hardship resulting from this long-term adjustment. Throughout the past two decades, various books and documentary films have called attention to the social costs of the restructuring of farming (Conger and Elder 1994; Harl 1990; Lasley et al. 1995).

Population Trends in the Midwest

Since 1960, the nation's population has increased from 179 million to 281 million, or about 57 percent (Table 2.2). Much of this growth has occurred in the Southern states, which posted an 82 percent gain, and in the Western states, which grew 125 percent from 1960 to 2000. During this same period, the Midwest population increased only 25 percent, and the Northeast grew 20 percent—less than one-half of the national growth rate. These differential population growth rates during the past forty years pose important questions about why some regions are growing and others are not, and what measures state and federal government might implement to stimulate growth. In slow growing regions, questions about how to ensure adequate and affordable services are paramount; yet in high growth areas, important issues such as how to accommodate the needs of new residents and the related need for new investments in infrastructure improvements are present.

Table 2.1
Total Number of Farms in North Central Region, 1945–1997

State	1945	1950	1954	1959	1964	1969	1974	1978	1982	1987	1992	1997
Illinois	204,239	195,268	175,543	154,644	132,822	123,565	111,049	109,924	98,483	88,786	77,610	73,051
Indiana	175,970	166,627	153,593	128,160	108,082	101,479	87,915	88,427	77,180	70,506	62,778	57,916
Iowa	208,934	203,159	192,933	174,707	154,162	140,354	126,104	126,456	115,413	105,180	96,543	90,792
Kansas	141,192	131,394	120,167	104,347	92,440	86,057	79,188	77,129	73,315	68,579	63,278	61,593
Michigan	175,268	155,589	138,922	111,817	93,504	77,946	64,094	68,237	58,661	51,172	46,562	46,027
Minnesota	188,952	179,101	165,225	145,662	131,163	110,747	98,537	102,963	94,382	85,079	75,079	73,367
Missouri	242,934	230,045	201,614	168,672	147,315	137,067	115,711	121,955	112,447	106,105	98,082	98,860
Nebraska	111,756	107,183	100,846	90,475	80,163	72,257	67,597	65,916	60,243	60,502	52,923	51,454
North Dakota	69,520	65,401	61,943	54,928	48,836	46,381	42,710	41,169	36,431	35,289	31,123	30,504
Ohio	220,575	199,359	177,074	140,353	120,381	111,332	92,158	95,937	86,934	79,277	70,711	68,591
South Dakota	68,705	66,452	62,520	55,727	49,703	45,726	42,825	39,665	37,148	36,376	34,057	31,284
Wisconsin	177,745	168,561	153,558	131,215	118,816	98,973	89,479	89,945	82,199	75,131	67,959	65,602
Total NCR	1,985,790	1,868,139	1,703,938	1,460,707	1,277,387	1,151,884	1,017,367	1,027,723	932,836	861,982	776,705	749,041
U.S.	5,859,169	5,388,437	4,782,416	3,710,503	3,157,857	2,730,250	2,314,013	2,478,642	2,240,976	2,087,759	1,925,300	1,911,859

Source: Compiled from selected Census of Agriculture reports, U.S. Summary and State Data, USDA, National Agricultural Statistics Service.

Table 2.2
Population and Change by Region, 1960–2000

	Population (in thousands)					Percent Change in Population				
	1960	1970	1980	1990	2000	1960–1970	1970–1980	1980–1990	1990–2000	1960–2000
U.S.	179,323	203,302	226,546	248,710	281,422	13.4	11.4	9.8	13.2	56.9
Northeast	44,678	49,061	49,135	50,809	53,594	9.8	0.2	3.4	5.5	20.0
Midwest	51,619	56,589	58,866	59,669	64,393	9.6	4.0	1.4	7.9	24.7
South	54,973	62,812	75,372	85,446	100,237	14.3	20.0	13.4	17.3	82.3
West	28,053	34,838	43,172	52,786	63,198	24.2	23.9	22.3	19.7	125.3

Source: http://eire.census.gov/popest/archives/state/st_stts.php

Map 2.2   **Population Change in North Central Region, 1990–2000**

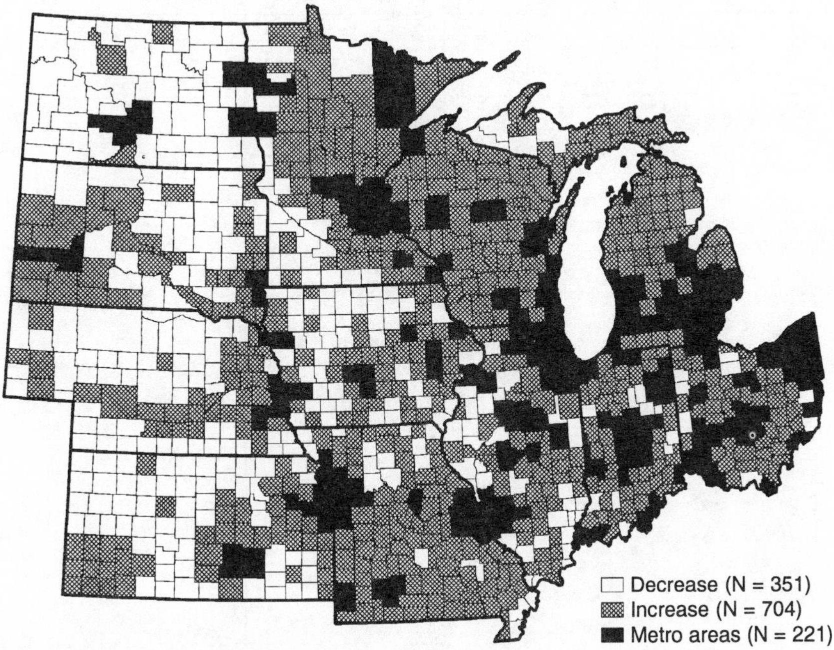

☐ Decrease (N = 351)
▨ Increase (N = 704)
■ Metro areas (N = 221)

Source: U.S. Bureau of the Census. *U.S. Census 2000.* Available on-line: <www.census.gov/main/cen2000.html>.

Between 1990 and 2000, the nation's population rose by 13.2 percent, although the growth was concentrated in the Southern and Western states (Table 2.2). Looking at population growth in the Midwest between 1990 and 2000, proximity to metropolitan areas appears to be a significant driving force. Among the 1,055 counties in the region, 704 experienced a population increase between 1990 and 2000. Of the 351 counties that lost population, the loss tended to occur in those counties nonadjacent to metro counties or beyond the commuter zone to metro areas (Map 2.2).

In addition to the slow rate of population growth, it might be asked why there is so much variation in population growth between these states? Looking for a single answer has proven difficult because the fact that many factors influence population growth and decline. Our first task was to assess population distribution within the region. Even though the region has historically been defined as heavily dependent upon agriculture (Bender et al. 1985), it is also evident that the process of urbanization has resulted in a concentration of population in or near metropolitan areas.

Using the Urban Influence County codes to classify counties (Ghelfi and

Table 2.3
Urban Influence County Codes in North Central Region

Code	Number of Counties	Percent of Total Population	Percent Change in Population 1990-2000
Metropolitan Counties			
1 Counties in large metropolitan areas of 1 million or more residents	88	46.3	9.4
2 Counties in small metropolitan areas of 250,000 to 999,999 residents	133	27.5	7.7
Subtotal	**221**	**73.8**	
Urban or Metro Adjacent Counties			
3 Counties adjacent to large metro area and contain all or part of their own cities of 10,000 or more residents	23	2.2	9.2
4 Counties adjacent to large metro area and do not contain any part of a city of 10,000 or more residents	43	1.4	10.1
5 Counties adjacent to a small metro area and contain all or part of their own cities of 10,000 or more residents	59	4.7	4.8
6 Counties adjacent to a small metro area and do not contain any part of a city of 10,000 or more residents	184	5.8	7.8
7 Counties not adjacent to a metro area and contain all or part of their own cities of 10,000 or more residents	89	5.1	4.4
Subtotal	**398**	**19.2**	
Rural Counties			
8 Counties not adjacent to a metro area and contain all or part of their own towns of 2,500 to 9,999	191	4.7	4.0
9 Counties not adjacent to a metro area and do not contain any part of a town of 2,500 or more residents	245	2.3	3.1
Subtotal	**436**	**7.0**	
Total	**1,055**	**100.0**	

Source: USDA-ERS Briefing Room. 2002. *Measuring Rurality, Urban Influence Codes*.
Available on-line:<www.ers.usda.gov/briefing/rurality/urbaninf/>.

Parker 1997), we examine the types of counties within the North Central Region (Table 2.3). Of the 1,055 counties in the region, 221 (20.9%) are defined as metropolitan counties (Codes 1 and 2); these counties are where nearly 74 percent of the region's population resides. Urban counties or metropolitan-adjacent counties (Codes 3–7) account for 398 counties (37.7%) and almost one-fifth of the region's population. Together, these two sets of counties represent 59 percent of counties in the region, but are home to 93 percent of the total population. Rural counties (Codes 8 and 9), on the other

Map 2.3 **Source of Population Change, North Central Region, 1990–2000**

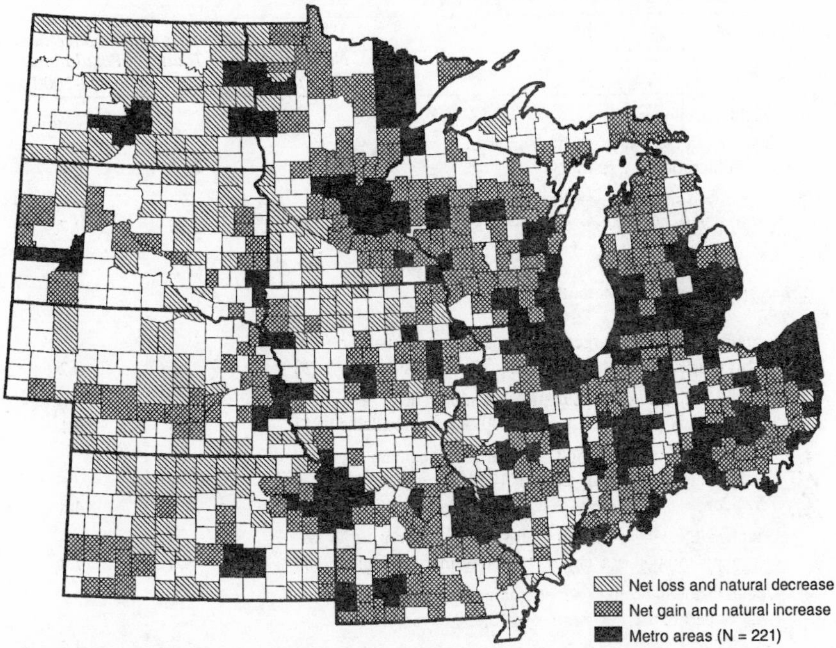

Net loss and natural decrease
Net gain and natural increase
Metro areas (N = 221)

Source: U.S. Bureau of the Census. *U.S. Census 2000.* Available on-line:
<www.census.gov/main/cen2000.html>.

hand, make up over 40 percent of the region's counties, but account for only 7 percent of the region's population.

The two components of population change are natural change (births versus deaths) and migration (people moving in versus people moving out) (Map 2.3 and Table 2.4). Among the 1,055 counties in the North Central Region, 703 (67%) experienced a population increase between 1990 and 2000. Of those counties that increased in population, 97 grew through natural change only, 131 increased because of net migration, and two-thirds grew from both natural change and net migration. In contrast, 352 counties in the region (33%) lost population between 1990 and 2000. Among those counties losing population, 76 counties had more deaths than births, 119 counties experienced more people moving out than in, and 156 counties had both natural loss and out-migration.

Among the 221 metro counties in the region, 89 percent (196 counties) gained population in the 1990s. Among the growing metro counties, the population growth was the result of both natural change and net migration. There were 25 metro counties (11%) that lost population during the 1990s, and most of this loss was the result of natural change.

Table 2.4

Population Change and Source of Population Change by County Type in the North Central Region, 1990–1999

	Total Counties (N = 1,055)		Metropolitan Counties (N = 221)		Urban Counties (N = 398)		Rural Counties (N = 436)	
	Number	Percent	Number	Percent	Number	Percent	Number	Percent
Population increase	703	67	196	89	313	79	194	44
Population increase due to . . .		100		100		100		100
Natural change only	97	14	28	14	42	13	27	14
Net migration only	131	19	1	—	48	15	82	42
Both natural change and net migration	475	68	167	85	223	71	85	44
Population decrease	352	33	25	11	85	21	242	55
Population decrease due to . . .		100		100		100		100
Natural change only	76	22	23	92	10	12	43	18
Net migration only	119	34	1	4	46	54	72	30
Both natural change and net migration	156	44	1	4	29	34	127	52

Source: http://eire.census.gov/popset/archives/county/cd-99-4/99c4_00.txt

In the 398 urban counties, nearly eight out of ten gained population during the past decade. Their growth tended to be attributable to both natural change and net migration. Twenty-one percent of the urban counties lost population during this period, and for these counties, migration was the dominant reason.

Rural counties in the region had the poorest performance in terms of population growth throughout the decade of the 1990s. Of the 436 counties defined as rural, only 44 percent (194) recorded population growth. Only 14 percent of this growth resulted from natural change. This reflects the higher concentration of elderly population in rural counties. Rural county population growth was usually the result of net migration. Eighty-two percent of the rural counties that gained population during the decade had net in-migration.

Fifty-five percent of the rural counties in the region (242) lost population during the 1990s. The population loss in rural counties is accounted for by natural change (18%) and net out-migration (30%). About one-half of the rural counties losing population during the 1990s experienced both natural change and out-migration.

Population growth in rural counties provides some curious patterns, as shown in Map 2.3. We observe a concentration of rural counties that gained population in northern Michigan, much of rural Wisconsin, northern Minnesota, and southern Missouri. Whereas each of these areas was historically based upon extractive industries, such as farming, mining, fisheries, and lumbering, these regions have sought development in new industries or sectors. Much of the growth in these regions appears to be related to amenities of rural life, including rural recreation, enjoyment of the natural environment, and places to retire. Generally speaking, these areas are within 100 miles of a major metropolitan population center, and they have sought to maximize their natural resource advantages by developing rural tourism and recreation activities. In these counties, the land is frequently marginal for large-scale farming, but the topography affords scenic views and lakes or river recreation.

Even so, it seems that areas with some of the most productive agricultural lands have been slow to change to the new economy. Throughout vast expanses of the Midwest, where large-scale agriculture is still practiced, the need to shift to a new model of rural development has generally not been viewed as urgent. Ironically, those areas with the best farmland have experienced some of the highest out-migration and contraction of the local economies. A windshield survey of the region confirms what the data suggest. While driving through agricultural counties endowed with some of the best farmland in the country, towering grain silos and agribusiness firms are seen and attest to the importance of agriculture; however, more often than not, nearly abandoned Main streets lead to these important symbols of farm country. Establishments that provided goods and services to people, such as clothing, hardware, and general merchandise stores, have closed, often leaving the community with little beyond the grain elevator, perhaps a feed mill, and a convenience store or tavern.

As agriculture contracted, farms consolidated, and employment opportunities dwindled, the loss of farm population and declines in retail sales resulted in Main Street business failures. Failing to adjust to the new economy, farm-dependent communities have become the modern-day version of Western ghost towns. While these villages and communities generally still exist, their viability as trade centers has nearly evaporated. Often the home of retired local farmers and persons with deep ties to the community, these places are increasingly experiencing out-migration as young people leave and the age structure becomes skewed to an increasingly elderly population. Zeuli and Deller explore these trends in more detail later in Chapter 6 and describe the effects of farm reorganization on income change.

Large numbers of rural counties have experienced population decline throughout the western portion of the region. Moving westward across the 98th meridian from an imaginary line that passes through eastern Nebraska discloses an area where farming has historically proven to be quite difficult. Arid conditions and a hostile farming environment make farming almost impossible unless there is an opportunity for irrigation. As the underground aquifers are pumped down, making irrigation more expensive, the long-term sustainability of row-crop agriculture in this region becomes problematic.

What Accounts for the Disparate Growth Rates?

Population growth reflects opportunities. Whereas economic developers tend to emphasize job creation, we believe that employment opportunities are but one factor stimulating population shifts. People move to areas where they perceive that there are more opportunities for self-improvement and an enhanced quality of life (Sofranko and Williams 1980). For some it may be the attraction of better jobs, higher salaries, and economic security; however, others are motivated by quality of life considerations such as the opportunity to buy a home, to enjoy the out-of-doors, or to enhance some other lifestyle dimension. Still others seek places where they can escape the pressures of urban life, crime, traffic, and congestion. We argue that high growth counties provide opportunities for residents that maximize their personal preferences and, thus, counties losing population are not providing adequate opportunities.

Rural areas that have increased in population have sought to diversify the local economy. It appears that rural living, enjoyment of the out-of-doors, and rural recreation hold a strong attraction for many urban dwellers. Communities that have discovered the benefits of rural tourism, of arts and crafts, and of vacation homes, resorts, and retreats that cater to those seeking new experiences are enjoying somewhat of a rebirth. As an increased number of people choose to work at home through access to high-speed, broadband Internet connections, they have more choices about where they live. While property ownership, such as farms and family-owned businesses, tends to give people roots in the community, workforce changes causing increased numbers to be employees rather than employers have increased the mobility of the workforce. Better-educated youth, who are not trapped by property-ownership in homes or businesses, are often the first to leave.

The Emergence of Two Rural Midwest Cultures

The dominant population growth pattern in the Midwest from 1990 to 2000 was associated with being adjacent or close to metro counties. Conversely, rural, isolated counties tended to lose population or grow at slower rates. The exceptions, primarily in northern Minnesota, much of rural Wisconsin, and southern Missouri, offer lifestyle amenities such as outdoor recreational experiences and are viewed as places for retirement and/or second homes. In the main, rural population growth is closely associated with proximity to urban areas. Rural communities within commuter belts around metro areas have gained population by providing, in many cases, lower-cost housing; a perceived higher quality of life; a sense of community or belonging; or, perhaps, a safer, less hectic lifestyle. Beyond those commuter belts, however, the situation is much different.

If not addressed, these trends will result in two rural Americas. One will consist of rural, isolated counties with sparse populations. The low populations will make the provision of services more expensive, contributing to the counties being even less desirable places to live. Institutional consolidation has occurred and more is projected to occur—school closings, churches, hospitals, and local units of government that are already struggling to survive will be further jeopardized. Though somewhat dated, the President's National Advisory Commission on Rural Poverty's (1967) publication, *The People Left Behind,* may accurately describe the emerging situation in many rural areas. Fitchen (1981) and Davidson (1990) provide a glimpse of what may lie ahead if nothing is done to create new opportunities to arrest this population decline. These counties struggle with population loss due mainly to the out-migration of young adults, reflecting the lack of opportunities. The continued consolidation of farms and the corporatization of agribusinesses as discussed by William Heffernan and Douglas Constance (1994) have contributed to dwindling opportunities in farming communities. The changing occupational structure that has accompanied the restructuring of farming has often resulted in farmers becoming employees rather than owner-operators; Linda Lobao (1990) has summarized this rather large literature.

The second "rural America" will include those rural places within commuter zones of metro areas. These areas will increasingly become miniaturized versions of urban places. Outlet chains, minimalls, and convenience stores will cater to the needs of this population. In those satellite communities, residents have the amenities of rural or small town living while at the same time enjoying the benefits of urban employment, health care, entertainment, and so on.

The most pressing problem seems to lie beyond the commuter belts where economic conditions lag behind the rest of the region. In the most rural, isolated counties, the lack of good-paying jobs, diminished public and institutional services, and perceptions that "it's a great place to visit, but a poor place to live" serve to discourage the best and brightest young people from returning after completion of their education. As a result of selective migration of young people, the age structure shifts to increased proportions of elderly often living on fixed incomes, which serves to further erode the taxing capacity of the community.

The second rural culture emerging in the Midwest is increasingly tied to metro areas. Rural culture is rapidly giving way to "urbanized rural culture" in counties adjacent to or within commuter distances to metro areas. In this set of counties, new residents are often refugees escaping city life. The proliferation of rural nonfarm residences, mobile home parks, rural housing subdivisions, and bedroom communities in these counties are indicators of their links to urban centers. In many of these metro-adjacent counties, residents commute to the city for employment, shopping, and recreation. Managing urban sprawl and the need for zoning are often high on the public agenda in these fast growing counties. Unlike the truly rural counties, those adjacent to metro centers face a much different set of issues about how to direct growth and how to provide services to the growing population. It is on the metro fringe where some of the important clashes between cultures occur. Issues of location of livestock facilities, adequacy and the need for rural services, and land use planning and zoning are often points of contention between agricultural interests and their new rural neighbors (Diaz and Green 2001).

Consequences of Trends

The emergence of two rural Americas in the Midwest is distressing. Despite more than $42 billion in farm program payments between 1996 and 2000, most agriculturally dependent rural counties lost population. Though it could be argued that funds dispersed under the Freedom to Farm program kept some farmers in business, it appears that it did not translate into attracting new opportunities for new farmers or for the bulk of rural residents. More attention should be directed toward how these federal funds might be better used to stimulate economic development and create new opportunities to attract or retain rural populations.

If there are virtues in keeping the rural population dispersed, then rural development should be about creating opportunities that will attract and maintain rural populations. The aftereffects of the September 11, 2001, terrorist bombing of the World Trade Center and the Pentagon may offer some hope for the future of rural areas. It is possible that our nation is entering into an era where urban areas are viewed as unsafe and vulnerable to attack. This may motivate people to seek places they perceive as safer. This could be similar to the urban to rural migration of the 1970s in which civil unrest spurred movement beyond the suburbs; perhaps a resumption of that urban to rural migration will occur because of the September 11 attack.

A second ray of hope may be that of new migrants to the region. It appears that Hispanics are moving into rural areas where there has been substantial population loss. Much of this migration is due to the jobs offered by meatpacking and other agricultural enterprises. The immigration to rural America is controversial in some communities, but many of the issues about assimilation of newcomers were present in the mid-nineteenth century when the immigration floodgates were opened wide.

A third potential trend is the mounting evidence that telecommunications may serve as the interstate highway system of the future. Geographically isolated places may be able to participate in the electronic age with the development of high-speed broadband capacity. Recent developments such as the wireless Internet may help bridge the digital divide. As technology makes it possible to be electronically connected independent of geography in an information-based economy, there are opportunities to decentralize the American workforce.

It is evident that the opportunity structure has a profound influence on population growth. Opportunities for employment, education, recreation, health care, home ownership, sense of community, and overall quality of life are important dimensions in attracting and retaining population. It is unlikely that state economies already reeling from the economic slump will be able to finance the infrastructure improvements needed to make rural areas more attractive. The population loss in the region is symptomatic of stagnating rural conditions. Many students seeking postsecondary degrees often express a wish to return to their home communities after college, but they often admit they likely will not be able to because of the lack of opportunities. Other students recount stories of older siblings or neighbors or, in some cases, even of parents who have struggled to keep a business or farm afloat. As a result of these experiences they have decided to seek careers outside of agriculture or rural places.

The farm crisis that gripped the Midwest throughout the 1980s has evolved into a chronic condition that now enters into its third decade. It seems that the solution to this set of issues does not lie in traditional responses of increased farm production or efficiency such as improving yields or rate of gain. Rural counties must develop the capacity to look beyond farming to solve the rural crisis. Conditions described in this chapter suggest the need for an aggressive rural-development agenda that is broader than shoring up farm incomes.

An Alternative Proposal: A Rural Resettlement Agenda

There is an urgent need to protect the most productive agricultural lands; however, within the Midwest, many areas of marginal agricultural land do not lend themselves to large-scale intensive agricultural cultivation. These regions could become areas of innovative rural development programs to diversify the economic bases of rural, isolated counties. Programs to finance affordable housing, by providing public utilities such as water systems, telecommunications systems, roads, and other public utilities, could breathe new life into many rural areas that have failed to grow in the past decade. Renewed attention to conservation programs designed to protect the environment while at the same time providing opportunities for local residents is needed. Conversion of marginal agricultural land to rural homesteads, rural retreats and resorts, scenic waterways, bike trails, and tourist destination areas may create new employment opportunities in service sectors in counties facing significant contraction of opportunities in agriculture.

The conversion of agricultural land to nonfarm uses is a problem in many of the metro counties. Many of the metro areas and urban centers are located at the confluence of major rivers. Urban sprawl takes out thousands of acres of prime farmland each year in these counties; this is not a major issue in many rural, isolated counties where some of the less productive agricultural lands are located. A national rural development policy to encourage rural nonfarm development in those regions where marginal agricultural lands exist should be considered.

Recent public interest in organic foods has triggered considerable enthusiasm for alternative food systems. Local food systems that rely upon local producers and locally available inputs such as community-supported agriculture may serve to create new opportunities for those wanting to start farming. While truck gardening is not a panacea to the long-term chronic problems of commodity surpluses, it is an option worthy of additional investigation. Critics of alternative agriculture, including farmers' markets, community supported agriculture (CSAs), and organic farming, often claim these systems are neither practical nor profitable. The profitability critiques have become muted in the last few years because conventional, large-scale capital-intensive agriculture must receive heavy infusions of government subsidies to keep them afloat. Perhaps if subsidies were directed toward conservation efforts or wage subsidies rather than bushels of corn or soybeans, these alternative enterprises would be more profitable.

Selective targeting of federal expenditures is needed. Just as targeting of conservation programs to areas of highest need has shown positive outcomes, federal expenditures for rural economic development must be targeted to areas that have fallen behind. High on the priority list for rural development would be those counties in the most rural, isolated areas. It makes little sense for government policy and expenditures to continue to encourage urbanization in the most densely settled counties. One only need look at Mexico and other developing nations where substantial rural–urban differences exist to see the unintended consequences of depopulating the countryside. Major social issues such as the overcrowding of the cities, the negative environmental impacts of uncontrolled urban growth, and stretching the capacity of urban infrastructures are the result of unbridled rural to urban migration.

Just as the Homestead Act of 1862 was a courageous policy action to attract people to the Midwest, we need an equally bold effort to once again attract new residents to rural America. While it is tempting to view the Homestead Act as only a land-disposal action, it can be more broadly viewed as a policy to create opportunities. This legislation created opportunities for a new class of farmers and businesses to start. Many Midwestern families can trace their family roots back to this period when their ancestors were lured to the region because of the opportunities created by the Homestead Act. An equally bold rural development policy in the twenty-first century will likely not involve farmland, but it would certainly involve using the power of government to create opportunities in areas that have not enjoyed the benefits of the new economy.

In Ireland and other Western European countries, agro-tourism and rural aesthetic protection are important parts of the rural development strategy. Bed and breakfast establishments, farmhouse restoration, castle protection, and rural walking paths and trails have created new opportunities for rural residents. There are some initial efforts in Iowa along these lines, including the Iowa Barn Again Foundation to protect the agricultural heritage of old barns; Silos and Smokestacks; Rural Heritage Foundation; and ongoing discussions about creating new national parks as examples of ways to diversify local economies.

The renewed attention toward sustainable agriculture may provide new opportunities for some to begin farming. Efforts such as the Leopold Center for Sustainable Agriculture at Iowa State University have been at the forefront of diversifying agricultural production while at the same time creating additional opportunities in small communities in such activities as farmers' markets, value-added processing, and niche markets. Other Midwest states have similar efforts underway to diversify the economies of rural counties, but often state funds are limited, and too often the pressing needs of urban areas overshadow the needs of rural counties in state legislatures.

Examples of rural development efforts exist in disadvantaged areas where there have been major efforts to build a new economic base when the natural resources base was exhausted. Mining communities have become tourist attractions, and fishing villages have refocused their energies on tourism and beach property development. In other cases, communities have successfully attracted new forms of industrial recruitment, such as light manufacturing, or service sector employment; however, these efforts tend to pale in comparison to the large need that is presented.

Throughout the last half-century, chronic agricultural surpluses and low commodity prices have become a persistent feature of agriculture. Through various government programs, farmers have become increasingly dependent on government payments. Despite attempts to reduce farm dependence on government aid, it appears that farmers are now more dependent than ever before. Various proposals have been made to limit production, promote new uses, or add value to existing crops; developing new markets have generally been ineffective in stabilizing the decline in farm numbers. Despite record levels of farm program payments, these seem to have had a minimal effect on stabilizing out-migration and creating new opportunities in agricultural-dependent communities.

Each of these programs has failed to address the underlying problem that there is simply too much land devoted to farming. In the settlement period, it made sense to take advantage of these seemingly inexhaustible land resources, but with the application of technology and the concomitant improved yields, farmers are able to produce more than the market demands; hence, low prices have persisted despite sixty years of federal farm programs. With the application of new biotechnologies, the problem is likely to get worse as new generations of seeds become available. It makes sense, perhaps, to retire permanently some land from agricultural production.

Farm policy advocates argue that the federal subsidies are needed to keep family farmers viable, yet the growing evidence is that these policies may have worked against the small operators and have yielded modest gains for most rural places. If it is a national goal to maintain the viability of rural areas, then we need to address what is necessary to create opportunities for the residents of these rural places beyond family-operated farms. Few question the need for federal expenditures for metropolitan infrastructure—airports, highways, police protection, hospitals, schools, and so forth—yet there is a reluctance to make the same type of investments in rural areas to keep them viable. People are being forced out of rural places because of a lack of jobs, but the more basic issue is the lack of opportunities for self-improvement.

In some states, the continued out-migration of the best and brightest young people, often referred to as the "brain drain," has resulted in shortages in certain professional occupations such as physicians, nurses, teachers, clergy, and others. Some states have offered tuition loan forgiveness and other options to students willing to serve in underserved communities. It would seem reasonable that other such incentive programs to retain young people in professions and careers in their home states should be considered.

Some Midwestern states have offered beginning farmer loan programs to assist young people entering agriculture. Other programs attempt to match retiring farmers without heirs or successors by identifying young persons wanting to farm. While these farm transfer programs have had modest success, it would seem reasonable that these programs could be expanded across other occupations. Programs that would assist family-owned businesses on Main Street as well as family farms should be expanded so that deserving young people could start in business.

Many states offer economic development packages to large businesses in the form of direct loans or grants, tax deferrals, and other incentives to attract them to relocate. Most evidence is that smokestack chasing does not result in long-term benefits to the community (Effland 1993; Reid 1993). Others have argued that business retention and expansion programs directed toward the needs of small businesses are far more likely to succeed (Flora, Green, Gale, Schmidt, and Flora 1992; Green, Flora, Flora, and Schmidt 1990). Small-business development grants to low- and moderate-income young people should be expanded.

As tuition costs for postsecondary education continue to escalate, shutting out many deserving low-income students, educational assistance programs must be expanded to prepare future workers. Many retiring workers were able to pursue postsecondary education through Veterans Affairs (VA) benefits for military service, and they are quick to admit that the VA program was critical to their educational achievement. Equally bold state programs are needed to ensure the adequacy of tomorrow's workforce.

Other options to retain or attract new residents would be low-interest loans for homes or businesses. Home ownership and the opportunity to own your own business are still deeply held American values. States should consider creative ways to finance home ownership for first-time buyers.

Conversely, other state policies should focus on making rural counties more attractive to newcomers. In some cases, various forms of unwelcome development have marred attempts to create desirable places to live. Confined animal feeding operations, which have polluted rivers and streams, created troublesome odors, and paid such low wages as to only perpetuate poverty, in many cases have made rural areas unattractive. Unfortunately, many Midwestern states, desperate for job creation, have failed to focus on quality jobs. In too many instances, low-paying jobs have brought about significant social and community problems because full-time employment still allows families to qualify for social service assistance, such as subsidized school lunches, low-income housing, and energy assistance programs. Creation of low-paying jobs is not sustainable development and may, in fact, contribute to community decline.

References

Bender, Lloyd D., Bernal Green, Thomas Hady, John Kuehn, Marlys Nelson, Leon Perkinson, and Peggy Ross. 1985. *The Diverse Social and Economic Structure of Nonmetropolitan America* (USDA–ERS Rural Development Research Report Number 49). Washington, DC: U.S. Department of Agriculture–Economic Research Service.

Cochrane, William W. 1993. *The Development of American Agriculture: A Historical Analysis.* Minneapolis: University of Minnesota Press.

Conger, Rand, and Glen Elder. 1994. *Families in Troubled Times: Adapting to Change in Rural America.* New York: Aldine de Gruyter.

Davidson, Osha G. 1990. *Broken Heartland: The Rise of America's Rural Ghetto.* New York: The Free Press.

Diaz, Daniel, and Gary Green. 2001. Growth management of agriculture: An examination of local efforts to manage growth and preserve farmland in Wisconsin cities, villages, and towns. *Rural Sociology* 66(3): 317–341.

Effland, Anne B.W. 1993. Federal rural development policy since 1972. *Rural Development Perspectives* 9(1) (October): 8–14.

Fitchen, Janet. 1981. *Poverty in Rural America: A Case Study.* Boulder, CO: Westview Press.

Flora, Jan L., Gary P. Green, Edward A. Gale, Frederick E. Schmidt, and Cornelia Flora. 1992. Self-development: A viable rural development option? *Policy Studies Journal* 20(2): 276–288.

Ghelfi, Linda M., and Timothy S. Parker. 1997. A county-level measure of urban influence (ERS Staff Paper No. 9702). Washington, DC: U.S. Department of Agriculture–Economic Research Service, Rural Economy Division.

Green, Gary P., Jan L. Flora, Cornelia B. Flora, and Frederick Schmidt. 1990. Local self-development strategies: National survey results. *Journal of Community Development Society* 21(2): 3–15.

Harl, Neil. 1990. *The Farm Debt Crisis of the 1980s.* Ames: Iowa State University Press.

Heffernan, William D., and Douglas Constance. 1994. Transnational corporations and the global food system. In *From Columbus to ConAgra: The Globalization of Agriculture and Food,* ed. A. Bonanno, L. Busch, W.H. Friedland, L. Gouveia, and E. Mingione, 29–51. Lawrence: University Press of Kansas.

Kirkendall, Richard S. 1991. A history of American agriculture from Jefferson to revolution to crisis. In *Social Science Agricultural Agendas and Strategies,* ed. G.L. Johnson and J.T. Bonnen with D. Fineup, C.L. Quance, and N. Schaller, 114–123. East Lansing: Michigan State University Press.

Lasley, Paul F., Larry Leistritz, Linda Lobao, and Katherine Meyer. 1995. *Beyond the Amber Waves of Grain.* Boulder, CO: Westview Press.

Lobao, Linda. 1990. *Locality and Inequality: Farm and Industry Structure and Socioeconomic Conditions.* Albany: State University of New York Press.

The President's National Advisory Commission on Rural Poverty. 1967. *The People Left Behind.* Washington, DC: Superintendent of Documents.

Reid, J. Norman. 1993. Building national strategies for rural economic development. *Rural Development Perspectives* 9(1) (October): 24–27.

Sofranko, Andrew J., and James D. Williams. 1980. Motivations and migration decisions. In *Rebirth of Rural America.* Ed. Andrew J. Sofranko and James D. Williams, chapter 3. Ames: North Central Regional Center for Rural Development, Iowa State University.

Part II

Major Issues and Concerns

3

ANDREW J. SOFRANKO AND MOHAMED M. SAMY

Growth, Diversity, and Aging in the Midwest

An Examination of County Trends, 1990–2000

Capturing the totality of social change in rural America is especially diffi-cult. Speculating on how rural America tomorrow will differ from today is virtually impossible. These difficulties stem from its elusive and indefinable diversity. Swanson (2001) correctly notes that "rural America is extraordinarily diverse in its geography, social and economic activities, variegated ethnic composition, and cultures . . . ; it defies efforts to demonstrate its singularity" (102). Consequently, rural areas have had mixed economic and demographic experiences. At the same time, rural America's future is clouded by the fact that the larger society is changing to such an extent "that the society of 2030 will be very different from that of today and bear little resemblance to that predicted by today's best-selling futurists" (Drucker 2001, 20). This "next society," as Drucker terms it, is being shaped by the growing number of older persons, a decline in the number of young people, and "immigration to maintain the population and workforce."

There has been no shortage of attempts to describe the types of changes taking place in the rural communities and areas of this country, or to identify the economic, political, and demographic driving forces behind these changes (cf. Thomas Johnson 2001). This chapter focuses on selected aspects of broader demographic forces affecting the rural Midwest.[1] It looks briefly at recent population trends, then shifts to an examination of the Hispanic and elderly components of population change. Immigration and growth in the Hispanic population and aging are two of the current century's master trends. Their implications for rural areas have not been well documented. Over the past decade, the older population (65 and over) grew by 3.5 million and now totals nearly 35 million people (*New York Times Almanac* 2002, 274). Proportionally, older Americans have gone from 12.5 to 12.6 percent of the population. The Hispanic population grew by 58 percent overall between 1990 and 2000, an increase of nearly 13 million. Of these, 1.4 million settled in the Midwest, which at 8.8 percent is the U.S. region with the lowest proportion of Hispanics. That figure belies what is occurring within the Midwest.

An Overview of Recent Rural Trends

Economic and demographic trends in rural America during the last several decades have been described as the equivalent of being on a roller coaster, as "a striking mix of the best and worst of times" (Drabenstott 2001, 15). Farm losses, rural community decline, and net out-migration have been the norm throughout much of the past half century, yet these trends have been interspersed with periods of net in-migration, employment growth equaling or bettering that of urban areas, higher farm income, and selective rural revitalization. More than a few rural places have performed well enough to be reclassified by the Census as "urban" or, in Andrew Isserman's (2001) terminology, as "Formerly Rural." Clearly, not all rural areas and places have experienced identical fates. For many, however, employment and population losses, aging populations, and the loss of local institutions and services have been the order of the day. And, contrary to previous periods, these trends have been accompanied by a growing realization that there is little governments can do to reverse long-term economic trends or their underlying forces (Giertz 1992).

Farming and Rural America

There is also a growing realization, if not a consensus, that relatively few counties' fortunes are linked to agriculture. Whatever their origins, rural places were once intimately linked to agriculture and the land. No longer. The economic bases of rural areas have become considerably more diverse. A healthy agriculture no longer assures a healthy rural America (Drabenstott 2001), and economic assistance to agriculture is no longer seen as being synonymous with rural development. Still, the farm financial crises during periods of the 1980s and 1990s, current low farm prices, and the changing structure of agriculture are seen as more than benign forces affecting rural communities and economies (Lobao and Meyer 2001). Rural localities still compete with one another in attracting "mega-farms" and agricultural processing plants. And Midwest farmers are showing interest in value-added investments and opportunities in the hope of improving their income while creating off-farm employment, which has become the mainstay of farm family well-being.

The Old and the "New" Rural America

Space and time dimensions are, of course, critical to any description of rural conditions. The decline in lower-skilled manufacturing employment and the loss of jobs to other regions and countries have diminished the attractiveness of many rural Midwest places. The loss of human capital in the form of young and educated people moving out is reflected in the "aging" of rural areas and in their loss of "voice" in political matters. At the same time, more than a few rural economies have become diversified by attracting retirees and immigrants; by service employment growth associated with transportation, recreation, and incarceration; and by forging linkages with community colleges (Rubin 2001). Some, the "connected rural communities" (Thomas Johnson 2001, 34), have inadvertently become implicated in a different broad-based rural trend—"urban sprawl"—which is overtaking many rural places and turning some into "suburbs."

Even those places still defined as "rural" are no longer as far outside the mainstream of modern society as they once were. There has been a "reworking of the American countryside" (Purdy 1999). Urban mass culture has penetrated and transformed small towns and rural existence, and vice versa (Wright 2000). Unquestionably, residents of once remote and isolated rural areas have a greatly improved quality of life, thanks to interstate highways, cable systems, satellite dishes, and branches of urban-based businesses that have brought services and choice within the reach of many rural residents. "Rural" no longer implies backward, poor, or bucolic. In fact, many of the wealthiest communities in the country are technically rural communities. One of the interesting histories of the twentieth century is the transformation of rural and farm life by "investing rural life with an urban character. . . . Good roads, rural free delivery of mail, the telephone, the automobile, and electricity were the agents of change" (Kline 2000, 7).

Growth, Aging, and Migration

Overall perceptions of how rural areas are faring have been shaped by population trends. Population loss and growth have been the yardstick against which the vitality and future prospects of rural areas were measured. "More people" has typically meant stronger communities and a brighter economic future; population loss evoked terms such as "decline" and "dying." Population has not always been a good measure, however. High rates of growth over time often entail change, disruption, and loss, and these growth rates shift many rural counties and places into "urban" and "metro" categories. The composition of growth is an important factor as are other conditions such as whether growth stems from young people deciding to stay in their home communities, from college graduates returning to rural areas, from wealthy elderly in-migrants, from immigrants revitalizing local economies by taking jobs that long-term residents would not, or from poor families attracted to rural areas by lower-cost housing. Not all types of growth are viewed equally in terms of their attractiveness and potential for community stability and integration.

Amidst the discussion of rural growth and migration over the past few decades there were a few constants that received little more than perfunctory attention. One was that many small towns and rural areas were aging. In fact, many already had an age structure unlikely to be seen in the nation within the next twenty years. The expectation that age structure will affect rural areas stems from a considerable body of research that has examined the effects of age on community behaviors (Li and McLean 1989).

More recently, a new "wild card" emerged on the rural demographic scene—growth by immigration. In literally dozens of places across the Midwest, immigration has "made a difference." In Frey's (2002, 18) view, immigrants "revitalize the economy of the region they move to and enrich them culturally with their tastes in music, food, and entertainment." In some places, jobs opened up around economic enterprises seeking a cheap labor pool. In scattered locations, immigrants have undergirded a modest "comeback" from decline by starting small businesses and spending locally. The impact and implications of immigration are beginning to surface in more than a few areas of the region. A major goal of this chapter is to document the growth and location of growth in both the older population and the Hispanic population.

Overall population growth and migration have varied over the last several decades. Less than thirty years ago, demographers identified a surprising countertrend; rural counties across the country were growing, and more people were moving into rural areas than were leaving. This "population turnaround" hinted at a "rural renaissance" in the making. Major questions revolved around the continuation of the trend and its compositional and cultural impacts. While it was noted that not all rural areas benefited from in-migration, enough did to provide a modicum of hope that rural areas had finally solved the problem of decline. The decade of the 1970s was portrayed as the decade of "rural revival," a period of population and employment decentralization (Roseman, Sofranko, and Williams 1981).

During the 1980s, however, the historically dominant trend of net out-migration and rural loss had reasserted itself. The "turnaround" had, in fact, turned around. Urban areas were once again attracting more people than were rural areas, and residential preference surveys were documenting a more favorable attitude toward cities and places near large cities (Brown, Fugitt, Heaton, and Waseem 1997). Rural areas lost jobs to foreign locations and youth to the cities of the nation. The optimism of the decade reverted back to a more languid view reminiscent of previous decades.

To complete this picture, data from the early 1990s provided new grounds for hope. Rural areas had, apparently, staged a demographic comeback, this time described as a "rural rebound." Not only were people once again moving into rural areas, but those making such moves were often younger and better educated. Once more, rural areas were enjoying a faster rate of job and population growth than were metro areas, leading Johnson and Beale (1998) to conclude, "The rebound is for real" (17). A more definitive picture of this rebound is seen in current population survey data, which temper early 1990s data. According to John Cromartie (2001), in the period 1999 to 2000, more people were moving from nonmetro areas than to them, a "turnaround" from the previous nine years. Furthermore, he concludes, without immigration from abroad, nonmetro areas would have lost population during the 1990s.

Census 2000: What Have We Learned So Far?

Data from the 2000 Census are revealing interesting trends that have the potential for affecting rural growth and population composition. The nation grew by nearly 33 million people (13.2%) in the last decade, the largest census-to-census increase in U.S. history. It counted several million more than were expected. An additional seven million to eleven million people were "uncounted." The Midwest grew by a more modest rate, 7.9 percent, but higher than the 5.5 percent in the slowest growing Northeast (Wellner 2002). Every state in the nation grew, with many of the more rural western areas of the nation having the largest growth. North Dakota had the lowest population growth, 0.5 percent, but this was a reversal of the previous decade.

Much of this national growth was fueled by immigration and higher fertility rates among recent immigrants (*New York Times Almanac* 2002). Of note, however, is the modest expansion away from immigrant concentration in the nation's large metro ("gateway") centers, which have absorbed most of the nation's newcomers. Many of the more recent immigrants are spreading out to smaller places, and to widely scattered parts of the country. Hispanic growth, for example, has ceased being a regional phenomenon. At the same time, the 2000 Census showed that population is spreading out from urban centers, and workers are exhibiting a willingness to spend more time commuting. Fueled largely by the cost of housing in large urban areas and the desire for less dense living, urban sprawl into many rural areas has become a political issue. Overall, however, the nation is becoming more urban, with more than 80 percent of the population now living in metro areas. The nation also continued to "age" as the population of those sixty-five and over grew 12 percent, about 3.5 million people during the decade, even as its share of the nation's population changed only negligibly, from 12.5 to 12.6 percent. For the first time in history, those sixty-five and over grew at a lower rate than the overall population (*The World Almanac and Book of Facts* 2002). Still, the median age of America's population increased 2.7 years to 35.7. Finally, the nation has become more diverse; 2.4 percent or about seven million Americans identified themselves as "multiracial." Nearly seventy million Americans identify themselves as something other than white alone (Wellner 2002, S5).

With the previous material as prologue, the remainder of this chapter will concentrate mainly on recently released Census data and will examine growth in the Hispanic and elderly populations in both metro and nonmetro counties. The focus is mainly on counties in a subset of eight Midwest states, the eastern part of the North Central Region. The following section, however, provides a brief overview of population growth in the entire North Central Region, first for the four western states in the region and then for the eight states that are the focus of later analyses.

Midwest Demographic Changes

The following sections examine recently released population data for the Midwestern counties, 1990 and 2000. A distinction is made between nonmetro adjacent and nonadjacent counties in order to establish whether or not rural growth might be attributable to "extended suburbanization" or "urban sprawl." The metro areas are those defined by the Office of Management and Budget in 1996 (by the U.S. Bureau of the Census in 1998). The nonmetro, nonadjacent counties are expected to be the most rural, given that they have neither a population center of the size to qualify them for metro status nor are located next to such a county. The nonmetro, adjacent group of counties are the rural counties most likely to benefit from their location and are, therefore, most likely to reflect population spillover from metro centers. They are also likely to attract people who prefer living nearer, but not in, a large urban center. In a sense, this categorization is a rough approximation of a rural–urban continuum of counties: metro; nonmetro, adjacent; and nonmetro, nonadjacent.

There are two parts to the analysis. The first focuses specifically on the four westernmost states in the North Central Region. This analysis is considerably shorter than the second part, mainly for reasons discussed below. The second part will examine the remainder of the region, an eight-state area that is, in many respects, different from the four more western states. In both cases, the primary emphasis will be on changes in Hispanic and elderly population trends since population change across the region has been covered by Lasley and Swanson (Chapter 2).

Figure 3.1   **Distribution of Counties, Metro–Nonmetro Status**

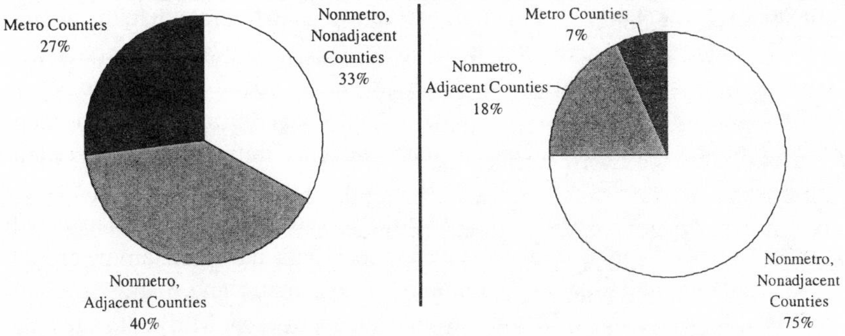

Source: U.S. Bureau of the Census. *U.S. Census 2000.* Available on-line: <www.census.gov/main/www/cen2000.html>.

Western Part of the Midwest

For census purposes, the Midwest geographic region includes twelve states, which we have collapsed into two groups: (1) North and South Dakota, Kansas, and Nebraska, and (2) the remaining eight states. A major difference between these two sets of states is seen in Figure 3.1. The four western states include 317 counties, three-fourths of which are in the most rural (nonmetro, nonadjacent) category. Only 7 percent of the western states' counties are classified as metro, compared to 27 percent for the eight-state region. The proportion of counties that are metro in the four states ranges from 8.6 percent (n = 9) in Kansas to 4.5 percent (n = 3) in South Dakota. By including the four western states in a single, broader region, the number of metro counties would increase by 11 percent, while the number of the most rural counties (nonmetro, nonadjacent) would nearly double (98%). In North and South Dakota, the metro counties accounted for large portions of the population increases between 1990 and 2000, virtually all of the growth in North Dakota and nearly 70 percent in South Dakota. In North Dakota, three cities (Bismarck, Fargo, and Mandan) grew by 31,152, while the state overall grew by 3,563. In Kansas, 89 percent of the growth was in metro areas, and in Nebraska, 85 percent of the growth was. Slightly more than half of the counties in South Dakota (52%) grew, whereas only 11 percent of those in North Dakota grew between 1990 and 2000. Fewer than half of the counties in Kansas (45%) grew, as did only 38 percent of Nebraska's counties. All four states were well below the 80 percent level seen in the counties of the eight-state region.

The trends of most interest in this chapter are presented for the four western states in the North Central Region in an abbreviated table using the same indicators included in the eight-state region (Table 3.1). In all four states, the metro counties grew by more than 10 percent and, as a whole, these state's metro counties grew by 14.3 percent. With the exception of North Dakota, the counties adjacent to metro counties grew, but at a much lower rate than the metro counties. In North Dakota, the adjacent counties as a group lost population. The most rural counties lost population in three of the four states. The exception is South Dakota, where the most rural counties grew by slightly more than 2 percent. The Hispanic population grew substantially in the metro counties in each of the four states; for the four-state area, the Hispanic population more than doubled (from 140,600 to 301,400). The Hispanic population also more than doubled in the two categories of rural counties—by 112.6 percent in the most rural, or from 55,700 to 123,200. In the nonmetro, adjacent counties, the Hispanic population increased from 9,893 to 16,726 (69%). The pattern of growth in the older population mirrors, in general, what is seen across the twelve-state region: sizable growth among older persons in the metro counties (15.5%) and losses in the other nonmetro counties. The four states contain nearly ten thousand fewer older persons in rural counties than in 1990, a trend seen across the entire Midwest.

Eastern Eight-State Area of the Midwest

The eight-state area examined in greater detail covers 738 counties. Of these, 198 (27%) are classified as metro counties; 296 (40%) as nonmetro, adjacent counties; and 244 (33%) as nonmetro, nonadjacent counties. States with the largest number of metro counties are Ohio (40) and Indiana (36). The states with the largest numbers of nonmetro, adjacent counties are, again, Ohio (45) and Indiana (45), while Missouri (55) and Iowa (50) have the largest numbers of nonmetro, nonadjacent counties. These latter counties are scattered across the Midwest, but they cluster in several broad areas. One such area includes the upper portions of Michigan and Wisconsin. Another cluster forms over eight western Illinois counties and continues across Missouri and into southern Iowa. A third major cluster cuts across fifteen or so southern Illinois counties and continues through the southeastern Ozarks area of Missouri. Finally, a fourth cluster encompasses western Iowa and several adjoining Minnesota counties (Map 3.1).

Most of the counties in the eight-state region (81%) gained population between 1990 and 2000. The only concentrations of counties with population losses were western and southern Illinois, parts of Missouri and Iowa, and northwest Minnesota. There was considerable variability in county popu-

Table 3.1
Hispanic, Elderly, and Total Population Growth in Four Western States of the North Central Region 1990-2000, by Metro-Nonmetro Status

	Metro Counties Percent Change			Nonmetro, Adjacent Counties Percent Change			Nonmetro, Nonadjacent Counties Percent Change		
	Population	Hispanic	Elderly	Population	Hispanic	Elderly	Population	Hispanic	Elderly
Kansas	14.1	103.7	13.5	4.6	35.9	-3.0	1.1	109.2	-4.0
Nebraska	14.3	149.3	11.9	4.2	296.6	-1.1	2.2	153.5	-1.9
North Dakota	10.3	60.4	18.0	-6.4	78.3	-3.3	-5.9	69.3	-1.2
South Dakota	18.3	132.7	18.5	6.7	41.1	-0.9	3.0	118.4	2.1
Total	**14.2**	**115.6**	**13.9**	**2.9**	**68.8**	**-2.3**	**0.9**	**121.0**	**-2.0**

Sources: U.S. Bureau of the Census, U.S. Census 1990 and U.S. Census 2000. Available on-line:<www.census.gov/main/www/cen2000.html> and <http://homer.ssd.census.gov/cdrom/lookup/999805720>.

Map 3.1 **Distribution of Midwestern Counties by Metro–Nonmetro Status**

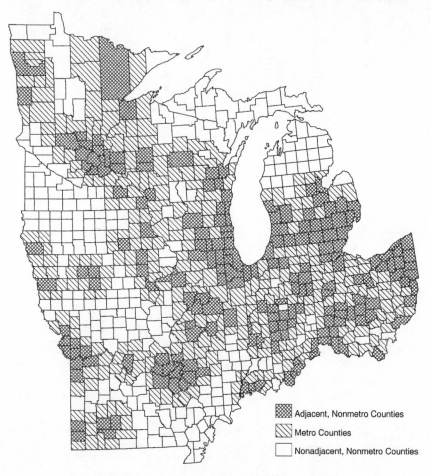

Adjacent, Nonmetro Counties

Metro Counties

Nonadjacent, Nonmetro Counties

Sources: U.S. Bureau of the Census. *U.S. Census 1990* and *U.S. Census 2000.*
Available on-line: <www.census.gov/main/www/cen2000.html>.

lation loss across the eight states. In Iowa, for example, 45 percent of all
counties lost population and in Illinois 30 percent of all counties lost population. At the other end of the continuum, two counties in Wisconsin and only
6 percent of the counties in Michigan lost population in this time period.

Population losses were seen mainly in the most rural (nonmetro, nonadjacent) counties. Thirty-eight percent of these types of counties lost population
or, to state it another way, two-thirds of all counties that experienced population losses were those that were most rural. In Iowa (69%) and Minnesota

(53%), a majority of the most rural counties lost population, whereas none in Ohio and Wisconsin lost population. Altogether, only 23 of the 244 most rural counties had sizable population growth (of 20% or more), and 14 of these were in Michigan. The remainder were nonmetro, adjacent counties, with one exception (Milwaukee County).

Hispanic Population Growth

The worldwide movement of people beyond their countries of birth is a dominant demographic trend. By some estimates, the number of such migrants is about 125 million (Kane 1995). Millions of immigrants, refugees, and asylum-seekers are crossing national boundaries in search of jobs, to reunify family members, or for security and a better life. The migration reflects a wide range of "push" and "pull" factors. Some moves are involuntary, resulting from civil strife; some are from population pressure and resource depletion. Others are voluntary and directed toward the richer nations, where migrants expect to obtain employment and improve their standard of living. While about half of all international migrants have gone from one poor country to another, the component of the trend attracting the most attention is the shift of population from the poorer to the more developed nations.

The United States has been a major destination of international migrants, averaging between 700,000 and a million or more arrivals per year during the past decade (Martin and Midgley 1999). As Simon and Cannon (2001) point out, "The beginning and end of the century were both marked by huge numbers of immigrants flocking to the United States, separated from old communities and old ways in search of better opportunities or refuge from political turmoil or religious strife" (13). One result is that America has become a more ethnically and racially diverse nation, due largely to "the ongoing process of immigration of races and peoples from all quarters of the globe" (Glazer 2001, 3). A little more than a third of the nation's population growth during the 1990s was due to immigration.

A major change between earlier immigration and this "new immigration" is reflected in immigrants' countries of origin. Instead of being European, as in the early years of the last century, more recent immigrants are Hispanics, mainly from Mexico but also from other parts of Latin America. Over the past decade alone the Hispanic population grew by 58 percent and is now 12.5 percent of the country's overall population. The Hispanic population has grown to 35.3 million. Of the thirteen million Hispanics added to the U.S. population, seven million were from Mexico. As a result, Hispanics are at parity with blacks as the nation's largest minority.

This large increase in Hispanic population was one of the surprises in the

2000 Census. Most Hispanics are from Mexico, and most are concentrated in major urban centers of the West and Southwest, along with New York, Chicago, and a few other large cities. In the West, the Hispanic population is nearly 25 percent of the total, or twice their level in the United States as a whole (*The World Almanac and Book of Facts* 2002).

Though much of the Hispanic immigrant population has been concentrated in a few states and in metro centers, "one of the surprising demographic stories of the decade has been the dispersion of Hispanics out of these areas to smaller cities and even rural areas of the Midwest, South and Northeast" (Kent, Pollard, Haaga, and Mather 2001, 16). Some came directly from their native countries, while others have been displaced from their original places of residence by later immigrants. The more subjective indicators for this particular type of spreading out into more rural locations are seen in signs printed in different languages, local ads promoting a variety of ethnic events, and new ethnic-owned and -oriented businesses opening up in the downtown business districts of smaller towns. Increasingly, Hispanic immigrants are taking up residence in rural areas, often in conjunction with low-wage employment in meatpacking, farming, horticulture, and the leisure–recreation sectors. Although many immigrants are attracted by jobs, others are attracted as well by the slower pace of life in small community environments, to communities without a "rush-rush lifestyle" (Yeoman 2000), where they are "seeking the same things that generations of native-born Americans have found in small-town life: a place where their children could go to school without fear of gangs or violence and where they could plant their own feet on the ground" (Gurwitt 1998, 36). In scattered locations around the Midwest, recent Hispanic immigrants are increasingly being seen as a means of keeping and attracting new economic activity, and of stabilizing population in lagging and bypassed rural areas. As we will see later, there are in fact rural counties where Hispanic growth has meant the difference between a growing and declining county population. This trend has not been without consequences, though, as tensions surface and cultural clashes emerge (Flora, Flora, and Tapp 2000).

The Hispanic population grew in virtually every county in the eight-state area. Only twenty counties (2.7%) had fewer Hispanics in 2000 than ten years earlier—for example, Koochichin (MN), Atchison (MO), and Marquette (MI) Counties. Over 90 percent of the counties in the Midwest had more than 20 percent Hispanic population growth. In twenty-nine counties, Hispanic population growth was sufficient to shift the counties from the "loss" to "growth" columns for the decade (Map 3.2). Still, in most cases, Hispanic population growth was not sufficient to turn counties from population losers to gainers; 163 counties lost population despite Hispanic population growth.

Map 3.2   **Non-Hispanic and Hispanic Population Growth by County, 1990–2000**

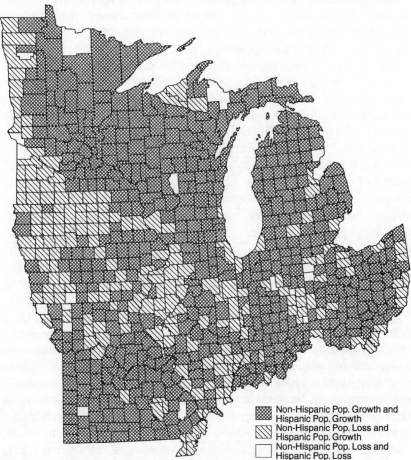

Non-Hispanic Pop. Growth and Hispanic Pop. Growth
Non-Hispanic Pop. Loss and Hispanic Pop. Growth
Non-Hispanic Pop. Loss and Hispanic Pop. Loss

Sources: U.S. Bureau of the Census. *U.S. Census 1990* and *U.S. Census 2000.*
Available on-line: <www.census.gov/main/www/cen2000.html> and <http://homer.ssd.census.gov/cdrom/lookup/999805720>.

A closer look at Hispanic population gains, by metro and nonmetro status and by state, is provided in Figures 3.2 and 3.3. Figure 3.2 illustrates that the vast majority of Hispanics in the eight states live in metro counties, with only 3.4 percent in the most rural. For the eight-state region, Hispanic population grew by 1.24 million, a 75 percent increase over 1990. At the same time, population growth overall was 4.3 million, a 7.9 percent increase. The Hispanic population of the region went from 2.9 percent of the total to 4.8 percent. Most of the gains in Hispanic population occurred in metro counties

Figure 3.2 **Distribution of Hispanic Population Growth, 1990–2000, by Type of County**

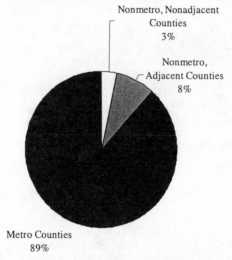

Nonmetro, Nonadjacent
Counties
3%

Nonmetro,
Adjacent Counties
8%

Metro Counties
89%

Source: U.S. Bureau of the Census. *U.S. Census 2000.* Available on-line:
<www.census.gov/main/www/cen2000.html>

(Figure 3.2). Only 3.4 percent of the overall Hispanic growth occurred in the most rural counties. Much of the Hispanic gain also took place in one state, Illinois, with a gain of slightly over 54 percent (Figure 3.3). The state with the next largest gain was Michigan at 11.2 percent.

Considerable variation exists across states and among metro and nonmetro counties, as shown in Table 3.2 (page 56). More than half (54.2%) of all Hispanic growth in the eight states' metro counties was in Illinois (i.e., more than a half million persons). Chicago is 26 percent Hispanic, with more than 700,000 Latin residents. Michigan is some distance behind, with a gain of slightly over 100,000 in the state's metro counties. Of all the Midwest states, Iowa had the smallest gain in metro Hispanic population, a little over 25,000; however, Iowa had the largest Hispanic growth in metro counties of the eight states during the past decade—168 percent. Altogether, four states more than doubled their metro Hispanic population. For the region, Hispanic growth in metro counties was 75 percent. This level of growth was lower, however, than that of Hispanics in nonmetro counties, both of which more than doubled their Hispanic populations over the decade. For example, in absolute numbers the most rural (nonmetro, nonadjacent) counties gained 42,263 Hispanics. Still, that placed the total Hispanic population in these counties at only 73,600, or 1.57 percent of the population. It is nevertheless noteworthy because many of these counties were losing population and, as

Figure 3.3 **Regional Distribution of Hispanic Population Growth, 1990–2000**

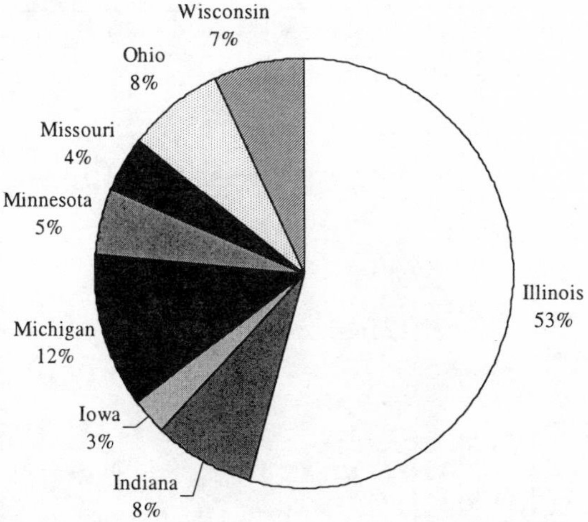

Source: U.S. Bureau of the Census. *U.S. Census 2000.* Available on-line: <www.census.gov/main/www/cen2000.html>.

noted earlier, would have lost population had it not been for Hispanic growth.

Most of the rural Hispanic gains occurred in Iowa and Minnesota, which together accounted for 56 percent of the Hispanic growth in the most rural counties in the eight states. In every state in our analysis, the Hispanic growth rate in the most rural counties was greater than in the metro counties. This is somewhat expected given the base from which the growth took place. Despite the recent trend toward repopulation of rural areas, data continue to point out that the Hispanic growth is occurring mainly in metro counties and in other select areas of the eight-state region.

Impacts of Hispanic Growth

It would be surprising if immigration and the growth of the Hispanic population had no impact on rural areas. The magnitude of that impact, and its desirability, will depend on the number of immigrant newcomers and their characteristics. Beyond the obvious implication of adding a million or so people to the nation's population annually, the impacts are debated and contentious. It should be pointed out that despite the high growth of Hispanics in the most rural counties, their share of the population remains low—1.6 percent in 2000. Their share in the metro counties of the eight states rose to 5.9 percent; and for the eight states, the share grew from 3 percent to 4.9 percent (Figure 3.4).

Table 3.2
Hispanic Population Change 1990–2000, by State and Metro–Nonmetro Status

	Metro Counties			Nonmetro, Adjacent Counties			Nonmetro, Nonadjacent Counties		
	1990	2000	Pct Change	1990	2000	Pct Change	1990	2000	Pct Change
Illinois	881,657	1,491,405	69.16	17,872	29,347	64.21	4,917	9,510	93.41
Indiana	85,318	176,995	107.45	12,210	34,385	181.61	1,260	3,156	150.48
Iowa	15,266	41,031	168.77	11,548	22,646	96.10	5,833	18,796	222.24
Michigan	182,939	290,367	58.72	12,727	22,541	77.11	5,930	10,969	84.97
Minnesota	42,313	108,049	155.36	5,878	18,898	221.50	5,693	16,435	188.69
Missouri	50,421	90,785	80.05	5,131	16,239	216.49	6,150	11,568	88.10
Ohio	115,855	184,445	59.20	23,675	32,325	36.54	166	353	112.65
Wisconsin	81,201	164,028	102.00	10,596	26,071	146.05	1,397	2,822	102.00
Region	**1,454,970**	**2,547,105**	**75.06**	**99,637**	**202,452**	**103.19**	**31,346**	**73,609**	**134.83**

Sources: U.S. Bureau of the Census, U.S. Census 1990 and U.S. Census 2000. Available online: <www.census.gov/main/www/cen2000.html> and <http://homer.ssd.census.gov/cdrom/lookup/999805720>.

Figure 3.4 **Hispanic Share of Population in Metro and Nonmetro Counties, 1990–2000**

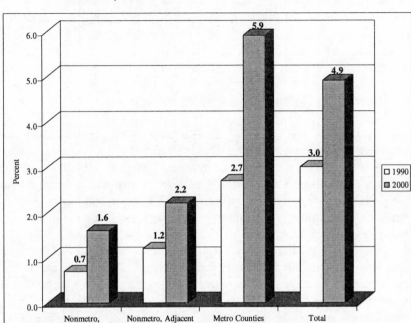

Source: U.S. Bureau of the Census. *U.S. Census 2000.* Available on-line: <www.census.gov/main/www/cen2000.html>.

Census data on Hispanic population growth across counties of the Midwest are more suggestive than revealing about the implications of this trend. In all types of counties examined, Hispanic growth greatly exceeded non-Hispanic growth, although in most counties Hispanic populations make up a small portion of the county's total population. Still, changes in population composition have effects on *places* of destination; people bring characteristics with them. The impacts that accompanied previous Hispanic population growth occurred mainly in a small number of large metro areas, and they contributed greatly to city growth; however, the 2000 Census data show a broadening of the trend even into more rural counties; very few have not experienced Hispanic growth.

The impacts of Hispanic growth will vary depending on volume, compositional differences between Hispanic newcomers and natives, the spatial concentration of newcomers, the types of employment they take, and the overall economic conditions in the areas experiencing growth from immigration. These factors will likely be mediated by whether immigrants are moving from other residences in the United States or from abroad, their ability to speak English, and whether they create jobs or simply take less desirable employment. Insights into these types of issues will come not from aggregate census data, but more likely from locality-specific research, at the county and community levels. A body of evidence along these lines is accumulating.

Growth and Distribution of the Elderly Population

The United States and other high-income nations are experiencing an unprecedented "graying" of the population. Since 1950, both the size and the relative share of the older population have steadily increased, and during the next three decades, the nation's "65–and-over" population will more than double to seventy million (Peter Peterson 1999). This trend has its roots in currently low fertility, historically high fertility in the baby-boom era, and improvements in life expectations due to medical advances and economic changes. The aging of the "baby-boom" generation will be one of the more significant demographic forces in American society, affecting social and economic institutions, the consumer market, employment patterns, and political issues (DeVita 1996). The effects of an aging population will be seen in the need for new service-delivery systems, shifts in the tax base, proposals for reform of entitlements based on age, and in a host of other areas.

The nation's elderly population, now at nearly thirty-five million, grew by 3.5 million over the past decade; however, the growth was 12 percent, the lowest rate in many decades, and for the first time in history the older population had a lower level of growth than the population as a whole (*The World Almanac and Book of Facts* 2002, 374). As a result of overall population growth, and growth due to immigration in particular, the elderly are roughly the same proportion of the population they were in 1990 (12.5 vs. 12.6%). In the eight-state portion of the Midwest covered in this chapter, the older population grew by 6.8 percent over the decade, with most of the increase (80%) taking place in metro counties. This level of growth was considerably lower than that of the nation. In the most rural subset of counties, there were 26,329 more older people in 2000 than there were in 1990, which reflects an older age structure, natural decrease, and out-migration from these types of counties. State variations exist across the region. Excluding Ohio, Michigan, and Wisconsin, metro counties in every state had large increases in the elderly population. The most rural counties typically had low rates of elderly population growth, and in Illinois and Iowa there are actually fewer older people in the most rural counties than there were a decade ago (Table 3.3). Subsequent releases of census data will show more precisely the sources of this decline.

Table 3.3

Elderly Population Change 1990–2000, by State and Metro–Nonmetro Status

	Metro Counties			Nonmetro, Adjacent Counties			Nonmetro, Nonadjacent Counties		
	1990	2000	Pct Change	1990	2000	Pct Change	1990	2000	Pct Change
Illinois	1,120,976	1,187,834	5.96	194,727	192,318	-1.24	120,842	118,269	-2.13
Indiana	469,672	513,768	9.39	184,537	196,473	6.47	41,987	42,469	1.15
Iowa	121,198	131,535	8.53	150,780	153,777	1.99	154,128	150,641	-2.26
Michigan	876,902	955,645	8.98	93,090	104,770	12.55	138,469	159,493	15.18
Minnesota	312,461	350,876	12.29	127,564	134,509	5.44	106,909	109,283	2.22
Missouri	441,635	472,251	6.93	126,905	130,835	3.10	149,141	152,292	2.11
Ohio	1,141,893	1,224,585	7.24	256,803	275,871	7.43	8,265	8,731	5.64
Wisconsin	401,611	434,339	8.15	205,533	218,269	6.20	44,077	48,959	11.08
Region	**4,886,348**	**5,270,833**	**7.87**	**1,339,939**	**1,406,822**	**4.99**	**763,818**	**790,137**	**3.45**

Sources: U.S. Bureau of the Census, U.S. Census 1990, and U.S. Census 2000. Available online: <www.census.gov/main/www/cen2000.html> and <http://homer.ssd.census.gov/cdrom/lookup/999805720>.

Map 3.3   **Change in Population 65 and Over, 1990–2000**

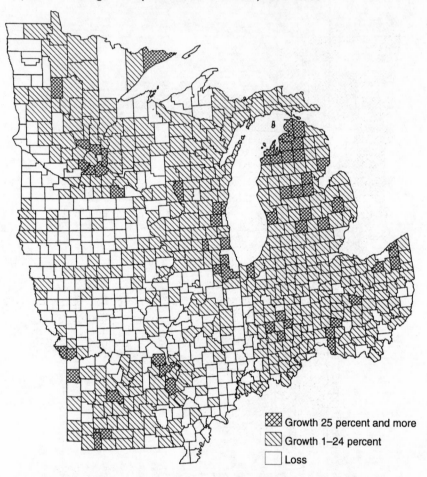

Growth 25 percent and more
Growth 1–24 percent
Loss

Source: U.S. Bureau of the Census. *U.S. Census* 1990 and *U.S. Census* 2000.
Available on-line: <www.census.gov/main/www/cen2000.html >.and <http://
homer.ssd.census.gov/cdrom/lookup/999805720>.

The state with the largest gain in metro elderly (12.3%) was Minnesota.
Michigan and Minnesota had the highest growth of older persons in the most
rural counties. Undoubtedly, much of this is attributable to retirement migration. Still, to keep a perspective on these trends, while the most rural counties in Wisconsin and Michigan grew significantly, this involved fewer than
26,000 people. In the same period, their metro areas alone gained 111,471
older persons.

Map 3.3 shows the change in the elderly population across counties of

Map 3.4   **Percent of Population 65 and Over, 2000**

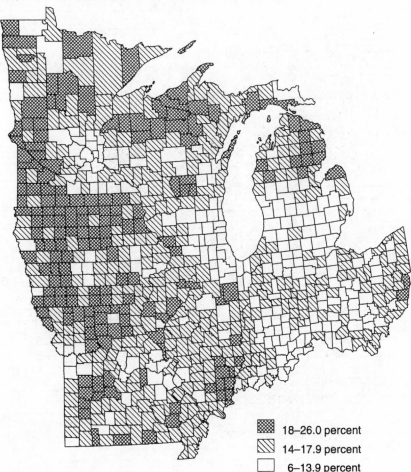

18–26.0 percent

14–17.9 percent

6–13.9 percent

Source: U.S. Bureau of the Census. *U.S. Census 2000.* Available on-line:
<www.census.gov/main/www/cen2000.html>.

the eight-state area. Quite a few counties have fewer older persons now than
a decade ago. Most of the counties losing elderly population are in the
westernmost portion of the eight-state region where the gains in elderly population occurred mainly in metro and their surrounding counties; however,
these rural areas still have relatively high proportions of older persons in the
population. Map 3.4 shows the elderly share of the population by county.

Finally, Figure 3.5 shows the redistribution of elderly persons across
county types in the last decade. These data continue to show, although slightly

Figure 3.5   **Elderly Share of Population in Metro and Nonmetro Counties, 1990–2000**

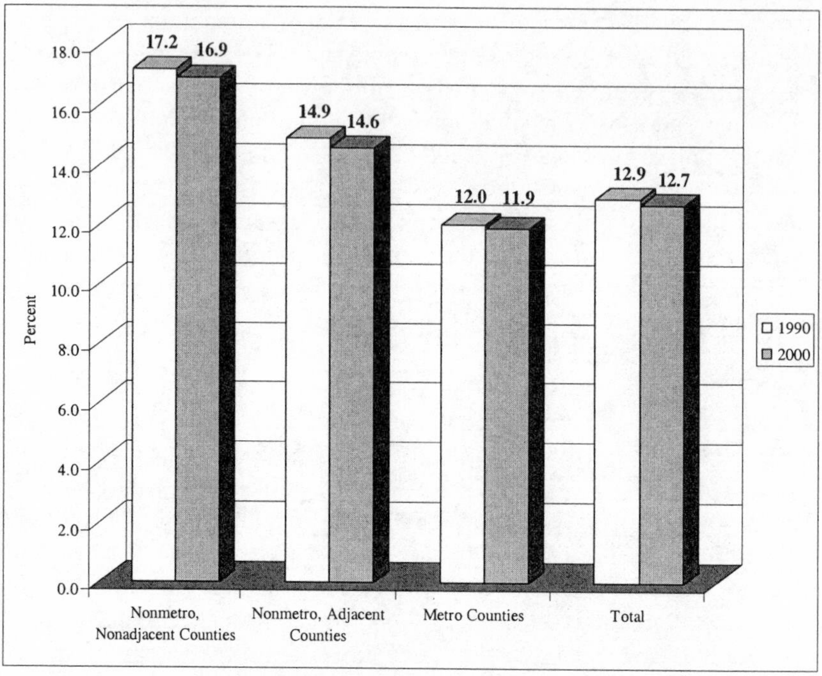

Source: U.S. Bureau of the Census. *U.S. Census 2000.* Available on-line: <www.census.gov/main/www/cen2000.html>.

decreased, a higher population of older people in the rural counties of the eight-state region.

Implications of an Aging Population

Aging will be one of the more important demographic forces in American society. William Peterson (2001) notes that, along with gender, age is one of the most important classifications in demography, as "almost all behavior patterns diverge along these two dimensions" (46). Because age structure is an important explanatory factor, an aging population will affect many of society's basic institutions. Research studies in rural areas have begun to look at some of the rural implications of a changing age structure, especially its effects on local economies, funding for schools, community involvement, and local taxing capacity (Rice and Miller 1999). Age structure has been invoked as an explanation for lower crime rates, voting patterns, availability of housing, employment opportunities provided to newcomers, passage of school-related tax increases, housing upkeep, and overall attractiveness of the community. Age structure is one factor, and an important one, one that interacts with a host of other demographic and economic factors.

The age structure of rural areas results from decades of out-migration of younger persons from small towns and communities and the continued "aging-in-place" of older residents. Consequently, more than a few smaller towns will have surpassed the levels of elderly in the population projected for the state during the next quarter century. In many respects, then, these places provide a "window on the future" for a broad set of communities. Clearly, any discussion of rural improvement and small town viability must confront the reality of disproportionately large elderly populations.

Among those researchers who have examined the effects of age structure, Lee Cuba (1992) has shown that aging populations have the potential for affecting community life: older people *do* alter the demand for services, the political climate, and the propensity for community development and change. Cuba also notes a differential effect associated with being an "old newcomer" versus being an older lifelong resident. S.J. South (1991), similarly, has examined the influence of age structure on the allocation of public expenditures for children. It does have an influence, through a "covariation of age structure with income per capita" (672). In other research, a change in the number of elderly was shown to have an effect on the variety of services available in rural areas, but an older population was also shown to contribute to community economic viability and local retail sales (Li and McLean 1989) as elderly residents tend to patronize local services and businesses.

Along similar lines, Pinkerton, Hassinger, and O'Brien (1995) found that, owing to limited mobility, "older persons spend a larger share of their resources in the local community" (475). This "in-shopping" contributes to community economic viability; however, older persons' greater use of local businesses and services is related to their longer length of residence, degree of community integration, and higher level of community satisfaction (Brown 1993; Lee and Whitbeck 1987; Sofranko and Fliegel 1984). Older community residents tend to be more satisfied with the way things are and are more likely to stay put. As Salamon, Farmsworth, and Rendziak (1998) point out, they do not even worry much about pollution. Sara Rimer (1998) presents evidence that older residents' contributions may extend further than sustaining the local economy—to volunteering, helping others, and "being good neighbors," especially in small towns where older persons are more involved in local activities.

More than a few researchers have pointed out that the role and contribution of older persons will undoubtedly vary, depending on the number of years they have resided in their rural locations, whether or not they are recent newcomers, and their stage in the life cycle. All of these factors may have an effect on older residents' community integration, satisfaction, and attachment (cf. Beggs, Hurlbert, and Haines 1996; Goudy 1990; Stinner, Van Loon, and Seh-Woong et al. 1990). Thus, existing research illustrates that there is a body of findings pointing to age structure, and specifically the presence of elderly persons, as an important influence in small communities and rural areas.

Implications of Age Structure for Agriculture

One of the fertile areas for research on the importance of age structure is agriculture. The following data present a few insights into how older farmers differ from younger ones and suggest a few ways in which they influence farming. Surprisingly, the implications of age structure for agriculture have been overlooked, despite the fact that a large proportion of farmers are at or beyond retirement age. Their median age is nearly twenty years higher than that of the general population, and many farmers pay scant attention to what society defines as the "retirement age."

Over the past century, the proportion of men sixty-five and over who are still in the labor force declined by nearly 75 percent. In 2001, the proportion of sixty-five-year-old males still working was about 14 percent. There are not comparable national figures for farmers, but an Illinois survey suggests that at age sixty-five their employment rate is nearly twice that of nonfarmers. The median age of Illinois farmers, fifty-three years, is typical of farmers in the country. Yudelman and Kealy (2001) report the average age of farmers as fifty-seven years old, which is nineteen years older on average than the civilian labor force. In the United States, for example, where the proportion of farmers sixty-five and over went from 17 percent to 25 percent over the last three decades, the ratio of farmers over sixty-five to those under thirty-five is 3 : 1 (Halweil 2000). The average age of farm operators increased by one year between the agricultural census of 1992 and 1997 (*U.S. Agricultural Census* 1997).

The following section, which focuses on older farmers in Illinois, addresses two broad issues: (1) whether age structure is related to farmers' level of involvement in agriculture and off-farm work and (2) whether it has an effect on their adoption of recent innovations. Data for this analysis derive from a survey of all farmers in Illinois; a total of 11,079 farmers provided responses, which is about 15 percent of all of the farmers in the state.

Involvement in Farming

Our research on Illinois farmers shows that not only is there a sizable proportion of producers sixty-five and over (27%), but that many continue to farm

Table 3.4
Age Structure and Agriculture

| | Age | | |
	45 or less	*46-64*	*65 and older*
Size of farm (acres)	712	678	393
Off-farm employment	61%	52%	21%
Spouse, off-farm employment	59%	59%	18%
Operate sideline business (excluding farming)	29%	25%	14%

Source: U.S. Bureau of the Census, U.S. Census 1990 and U.S. Census 2000.
Available online: <www.census.gov/main/www/cen2000.html> and
<http://homer.ssd.census.gov/cdrom/lookup/999805720>.

well beyond age sixty-five. The average age of "65-and-over" farmers is seventy-three; however, farmers' involvement in farming and off-farm work changes with age. Many reduce the size of their operations, and older farmers and their spouses greatly reduce their off-farm work. Nor are older operators as likely to operate a side business to supplement their income (Table 3.4). These businesses range from selling dogs, to consulting, to operating a small manufacturing operation, to giving music lessons.

Age and Innovation

The effect of age structure on the adoption of agricultural innovations is not a new topic among researchers. Its precise effects are, however, uncertain. A review of research on the effects of age concludes that there is no consistent pattern, given that age is confounded with stage of life cycle, education, debt, social and residential mobility potential, and, perhaps most importantly in the case of farming, the availability of a successor. We found, for example, that nearly half of the older farmers (48%) did not have a family member to take over the farm operation. Our purpose here is not to untangle these effects but simply to look at the influence of age on the utilization of three relatively recent agricultural innovations: (1) use of the Internet in agriculture, (2) use of GPS (Global Positioning System) technology, and (3) value-enhanced crop production. All three are recent in the sense that they are viewed as important improvements with respect to making farming decisions and improving producer income.

Figure 3.6 shows the relationship between age and adoption of the three innovations described above. Age is presented in ten equal groups of farmers. Each contains 10 percent of the farmers, ranked in age. The range of ages represented in each group appears at the bottom of Figure 3.6. The graph

Figure 3.6 **Age Structure and Adoption of Recent Agricultural Innovations**

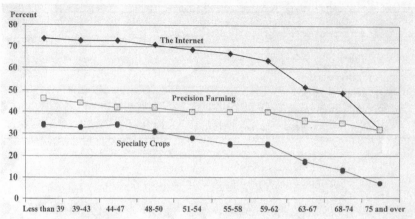

Source: Illinois Farm Survey, *Improve Farm Incomes and Rural Communities Through Value-added Agriculture* Project, 2000, University of Illinois, Urbana–Champaign.

illustrates a gradual decline in utilization of the three innovations across the ten age groups, although the decline in use of these innovations is more pronounced for the Internet and production of value-enhanced crops than for use of GPS, precision farming technology. These types of relationships serve to point out that age structure does influence farmers' behavior. They suggest that the presence of a large number of older farmers is shaping the scale of agriculture and the adoption of innovations.

Summary

The only data released so far from the 2000 Census has been from the Short Form, which went to all American households. It contained information asked on six questions: age, gender, race, Hispanic origin, household relationship, and owner/renter status (Kent et al. 2001). This chapter looked mainly at three types of data: (1) population growth, (2) growth in Hispanic population, and (3) changes in the ólder population (persons sixty-five and over). Counties were classified by metro–nonmetro status for all dozen states of the North Central Region. Most of the text and data focused on the eight easternmost states in the region.

Overall, like the nation, much of the region's growth has taken place in metropolitan counties; however, nonmetro counties also grew, although at a lower level than did metro counties. Growth rates varied considerably across the states covered in this study and also by metro–nonmetro status. In a few states, the more rural, nonmetro counties grew faster than did those located adjacent to metro counties, and, in some cases, the more rural counties grew faster than the metro counties. Migration data and the characteristics of migrants in and out of these counties will be established in later census releases.

The Hispanic population grew substantially and much faster than anticipated. Data for the region highlight the dominance of Chicago and Illinois as centers of Hispanic growth, however. Most of the Hispanic growth in the region took place in Chicago and in metro areas in general. A very large proportion of the Hispanic population in the region currently resides in metro counties. Again, as national trends show, Hispanic growth is beginning to take place outside metro areas. Although the numbers are still low, the growth rates for Hispanics in nonmetro counties are higher than in the metro counties. In many cases, however, the growth rates reflect the low base from which the change is occurring. Finally, while there have been significant changes in Hispanic population across Midwest counties, the Hispanic share of the population remains low, especially in the most rural counties.

The older population also grew—mainly in metropolitan counties—counties with both high numerical growth and proportional growth. The trend of the past decade has virtually eliminated metro–nonmetro differences in proportions of elderly in the population. This likely reflects both the movement of older persons and the age structure of the more rural counties of the region.

Note

1. Support for this research has been provided by a C-FAR SRI, "The Value Project: Improving Farm Incomes and Rural Communities Through Value-Added Agriculture," and by HATCH funding from the University of Illinois Agricultural Experiment Station.

References

Beggs, John J., Jeanne S. Hurlbert, and Valerie A. Haines. 1996. Community attachment in a rural setting: A refinement and empirical test of the systemic model. *Rural Sociology* 61 (Fall): 407–426.

Brown, David L., Glenn V. Fugitt, Tim B. Heaton, and Saba Waseem. 1997. Continuities in size of place preferences in the United States, 1972–92. *Rural Sociology* 62 (Winter): 408–428.

Brown, Ralph B. 1993. Rural community satisfaction and attachment in mass consumer society. *Rural Sociology* 58 (Fall): 387–403.

Cromartie, John B. 2001. Nonmetro out-migration exceeds in-migration for the first time in a decade. *Rural America* 16 (Summer): 35–37.

Cuba, Lee. 1992. Aging places: Perspectives on change in a Cape Code community. *Journal of Applied Gerontology* 11(1): 64–83.

DeVita, Carol J. 1996. The United States at mid-decade. *Population Bulletin* (Population Reference Bureau) 50(4): 2–44.

Drabenstott, Mark. 2001. New policies for a new rural America. *International Regional Science Review* 24(1): 3–15.

Drucker, Peter. 2001. The next society. *The Economist* 3 (November): 1–20.

Flora, Cornelia Butler, Jan L. Flora, and Ruben J. Tapp. 2000. Meat, meth and Mexicans: Community responses to increasing ethnic diversity. *Journal of the Community Development Society* 31(2): 277–299.

Frey, William H. 2002. Migration swings. *American Demographics* (February): 18–21.

Giertz, J. Fred. 1992. Public intervention for economic development. *Illinois Research* 34 (Fall): 20.

Glazer, Nathan. 2001. American diversity and the 2000 census. *The Public Interest* 144 (Summer): 3–18.

Goudy, Willis J. 1990. Community attachment in a rural region. *Rural Sociology* 55 (Spring): 178–198.

Gurwitt, Rob. 1998. Keeping the heart in the heartland. *Wilson Quarterly* 22 (Spring): 28–36.

Halweil, Brian. 2000. Where have all the farmers gone? *World Watch* 13 (September/October): 12–28.

Isserman, Andrew M. 2001. Competitive advantages of rural America in the next century. *International Regional Science Review* 24(1): 38–58.

Johnson, Kenneth M., and Calvin L. Beale. 1998. The rural rebound. *Wilson Quarterly* 22 (Spring): 16–27.

Johnson, Thomas G. 2001. The rural economy in a new century. *International Regional Science Review* 24 (January): 21–37.

Kane, Hal. 1995. Leaving home. *Society* 32 (May/June): 16–25.

Kent, Mary M., Kelvin M. Pollard, John Haaga, and Mark Mather. 2001. First glimpses from the U.S. census. *Population Bulletin* (Population Reference Bureau) 56 (June): 3–39.

Kline, Ronald R. 2000. *Consumers in the Country: Technology and Social Change in Rural America.* Baltimore, MD: Johns Hopkins University Press.

Lee, Gary R., and Les B. Whitbeck. 1987. Residential location and social relations among older persons. *Rural Sociology* 52 (Spring): 89–97.

Li, Peter S., and Brian D. McLean. 1989. Changes in rural elderly population and their effect on the small town economy: The case of Saskatchewan, 1971–86. *Rural Sociology* 54 (Summer): 213–226.

Lobao, Linda, and Katherine Meyer. 2001. The great agricultural transition: Crisis, change and social consequences of twentieth-century U.S. farming. *Annual Review of Sociology* 27: 103–124.

Martin, Philip, and Elizabeth Midgley. 1999. Immigration to the United States. *Population Bulletin* (Population Reference Bureau) 54(2): 1–44.

New York Times Almanac. 2002. New York: Penguin Books.

Peterson, Peter G. 1999. *Gray Dawn.* New York: Random House.

Peterson, William. 2001. Age and sex. *Society* 38 (May–June): 46–52.

Pinkerton, James R., Edward W. Hassinger, and David J. O'Brien. 1995. Inshopping by residents of small communities. *Rural Sociology* 60 (Fall): 467–480.

Purdy, Jedediah. 1999. The new culture of rural America. *The American Prospect* (December 20): 26–31.

Rice, Tom W., and Douglas N. Miller. 1999. The correlates of small town upkeep. *Environment and Behavior* 31 (November): 821–837.

Rimer, Sara. 1998. Rural elderly create vital communities as young leave void. *New York Times* (February 2): 1, 14.

Roseman, Curtis C., Andrew J. Sofranko, and James D. Williams, eds. 1981. *Population Redistribution in the Midwest.* Ames: Iowa State University.

Rubin, Sarah. 2001. Rural colleges as catalysts for community change. *Rural America* 16(2): 12–19.

Salamon, Sonya, Richard Farmsworth, and Jody A. Rendziak. 1998. Is locally led conservation planning working? A farm town case study. *Rural Sociology* 63 (2): 214–234.

Simon, Roger, and Angie Cannon. 2001. An amazing journey. *U.S. News and World Report* (August 6): 10–18.

Sofranko, Andrew J., and Frederick C. Fliegel. 1984. Dissatisfaction with satisfaction. *Rural Sociology* 48 (Fall): 353–373.

South, S.J. 1991. Age structure and public expenditures on children. *Social Science Quarterly* 71 (7): 661–675.

Stinner, William F., Mollie Van Loon, and Chung Seh-Woong et al. 1990. Community size, individual social position, and community attachment. *Rural Sociology* 55 (Winter): 494–521.

Swanson, Louis E. 2001. Rural opportunities: Minimalist policy and community based experimentation. *Policy Studies Journal* 29(1): 96–107.

U.S. Agricultural Census. 1997. Available on-line: <www.nass.usda.gov/census/census97/volume1/us-51/us1_01.pdf>.

U.S. Department of Agriculture-Economic Research Service (USDA–ERS). 1998. Precision agriculture for improved resource use. *Agricultural Outlook* (April): 19–23.

Wellner, Alison S. 2002. The census report. *American Demographics* (January): 5-3–5-6.

The World Almanac and Book of Facts. 2002. New York: World Almanac Books.

Wright, James D. 2000. Small towns, mass society and the 21st century. *Society* 38(1): 3–10.

Yeoman, Barry. 2000. Hispanic diaspora. *Mother Jones* (July/August): 35–41, 76–77.

Yudelman, Montague, and Laura J.M. Kealy. 2001. The graying of farmers. Available on-line: <www.prb.org/pt/2000/mayjune2000/graying_farmers.html>.

4

Thomas G. Johnson and James K. Scott

Population Trends and Impact on Viability

This chapter examines the economic status of rural regions in the Midwest (and many other parts of the world) at the Millennium. It focuses on the current status of rural areas and the incipient forces that will change life in these areas through the early twenty-first century. It also explores the changing role of the rural Midwest within the larger U.S. economy.

What is meant by "rural and urban"? Throughout this chapter, we will refer to comparisons between metropolitan (metro) and nonmetropolitan (nonmetro) counties and their equivalents. Metro (or urban) places have a core city with at least 50,000 residents and an area population of at least 100,000 residents in the most recent census. Nonmetro (rural) counties are all other counties. It is important to point out that this census-based definition of nonmetro includes some distinctly rural areas that happen to fall in the shadow of cities. It also means that many nonmetro residents live in small cities.

At the dawn of the twenty-first century, rural America faces unprecedented change; however, for at least the last half-century, many rural Midwestern communities have experienced slow but steady demographic and economic decline. The decline is evident from (1) out-migration of workers and their families leaving agriculture employment in the West and Southwest; (2) concentration of retail, services, and other economic activity in larger regional trade centers; (3) loss of tax base; (4) consolidation of schools and reduction in public services; and (5) a population aging in place. Certainly, many rural communities in the Midwest did not experience this decline. Nevertheless, general shifts in culture, technology, and economic and political institutions since 1950 have made the future of the rural Midwest more difficult to envision.

From 1950 to 1975, the status and role of rural America within the larger economy was somewhat clearer (at least in retrospect) than it has been in the last quarter century. In general, urban areas produced goods in the early stages of the product cycle, while rural areas generated raw materials; food and energy; and, in some regions, provided low-cost labor for the production of goods in the mature stage of their product cycle. Rural communities depended on the income and employment generated by farms, farm policy, and farm families. Average farm size increased while farm numbers declined. Excess labor from farm families joined the local or urban labor markets. Manufacturing firms chose to locate in least-cost locations (increasingly in the Sunbelt regions of the South and West). The labor force followed jobs, which, in turn, followed inexpensive inputs, markets, and business climate.

As traditional rural industries became more capital intensive, rural employment bases shrank and populations declined. At the least, rural communities could still count on the linkages between their agriculture, mining, and manufacturing sectors and financial, trade, and service sectors. New economic activities, when they occurred, had significant and predictable multiplier effects on the rest of the local economy. Economic development strategies for rural areas, while often of limited success, were simple (e.g., support agriculture, forestry, and mining, and attract manufacturing). These basic economic engines would then generate multiplier effects in the service sectors. They would also generate the tax base needed to run local government. The economic fortunes of individual rural communities, though not especially good, were closer to that of the average community than they have been since.

Local government itself was relatively simple—collect taxes and provide a rather static array of public services. The more aggressive local governments were actively involved in industrial attraction.

Then, new forces began to influence rural areas. In the 1970s, the population turnaround meant growth for many rural areas for the first time in many decades. The outflow of rural youth and the most employable members of the labor force declined but, more importantly, a significant number of people choose to migrate to rural areas and a rural lifestyle.

The return to population decline in the 1980s seemed to mark the end of the population turnaround. In retrospect, it now seems more likely that the 1980s were just a short setback in a fundamental change in settlement patterns in the United States. So many fundamental forces affecting rural areas—deregulation, the dismantling of community safety net programs, the globalization of economic relationships, and technology—had changed that the economies of rural areas were altered forever. There was also a fundamental transformation in the sectoral structure of rural areas. The basic economic rules were different from when the short-lived population turnaround began. Some communities used the experiences and resources gained during

Map 4.1   **Nonmetro Population Change, 1990–2000**

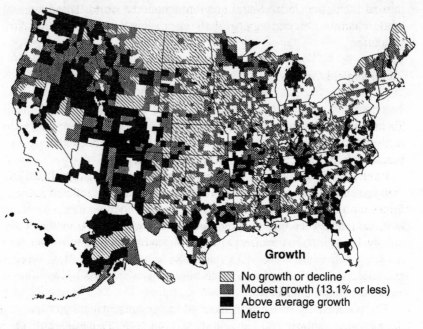

Source: U.S. Bureau of the Census.

the 1970s to free themselves from the downward economic spiral. Other communities fell back into decline.

In the final decade of the twentieth century, population growth returned to many rural communities in America, yet the mixed experience of rural communities in the 1980s remains. Despite the fact that growth is occurring in rural communities in every region of America, many rural communities continue to lose population. One-quarter of all rural communities continue to decline, and three-quarters of all nonmetro growth occurred in just one-third of nonmetro counties. Almost all of the declining counties are in the Plains region from North Dakota to Texas as shown by U.S. Department of Agriculture–Economic Research Service (USDA-ERS) data (Map 4.1). Rural areas are increasingly attractive to new residents but not in all regions. Most growth is in areas adjacent to the larger cities, whereas peripheral areas continue to decline.

The Changing Rural Economy

Obviously, one cannot understand the changes occurring in rural communities without understanding the changes, mostly global, occurring in the broader economy. Several forces have combined and are causing significant changes in rural life in the United States and throughout the world. These forces include changing technology, globalization, localization, and industrial structure.

Technological Change

Technological change is so ubiquitous that it heads most lists of change. Technological change is nothing new to economies dependent on agriculture, mining, forestry, or manufacturing. No sector has been affected more fundamentally by technological change than agriculture.

From a rural community's perspective, technological change affects more than just employment patterns. In production, the most significant economic forces are the rising importance of information, communication, robotics, artificial intelligence, genetic engineering, and other embodiments of technology. In addition to the direct effects of technology on employment, it has led to increased use of services (particularly information-related services) and reduced use of goods (especially raw materials) in the production processes of other manufacturers.

The productivity of labor in most goods-producing industries has risen dramatically—almost 260 percent since 1948 (U.S. Department of Labor n.d., Table 1). The productivity of labor in services, on the other hand, has increased considerably less—about 25 percent. These increases have been accomplished by combining increasingly greater amounts of capital with each unit of labor. Because the demands for many goods have risen only modestly, the growth of employment in these industries has been relatively meager. Some of the new capital has been introduced to take advantage of the emerging technologies discussed above, while other capital has been substituted for high cost labor. It is important to note that as this trend progresses, the cost of labor becomes less and less important in location and investment decisions because it represents a declining portion of total costs. This process, then, can have positive effects on income, job security, and so on, even while it reduces employment.

As a consequence of technological change, goods production and employment have become decoupled. Production has increased while employment has decreased. Intersectoral linkages have replaced intrasectoral linkages. In addition, the product cycle has been broken, at least from the perspective of domestic rural economies. Rural areas are losing some of their comparative advantage in standardized goods (commodity)-producing industries that use labor extensively.

Technological advances also affect the relationship that people share with each other, with their communities, and with their governments. People are more mobile, more flexible in their choices of employment and residence, and have greater access to information. Information and communication technology (ICT), especially, has changed the nature of distance. Distance has been made less important by technology, but that same technology has increased the importance of being connected and connected to the right places. As Edward Malecki (1996) points out,

> For people in local places, it is important, perhaps crucial, to have links to the global networks of large firms where information, commerce, and decisions are centered. Links to global networks no longer require proximity, but they do require having links and using them to obtain and exchange information. The "links" are those of individuals' personal networks and the business networks of highly competitive firms with their suppliers, customers, and other sources of knowledge. The cost of being unconnected or remote is a higher cost of operation, usually in the form of a time penalty.

The linkage between productive activity and distribution of income has changed. The substitution of capital for labor affects the functional distribution of income by shifting returns from the owners of human capital to the owners of physical capital. Between 1959 and 1999, wages and salaries declined as a percent of personal income, from 66 percent to 57 percent. At the same time, dividends, rent, and interest increased from 13 percent to 19 percent of personal income (Figure 4.1).

In the case of agriculture, this capitalization has resulted in larger farms, shrinking farm population, and declining labor income. These changes are not nearly as dramatic as those occurring in some mining, forestry, and manufacturing-dependent communities. Unlike agriculture, where the owners of the physical capital are much like the owners of the human capital and labor that they are displacing, the owners of physical capital in mining, forestry, and related manufacturing industries are very different from the displaced labor. In addition, the so-called Wal-Mart effect, in which independent, locally owned retail businesses and service establishments are replaced by large, often international, chain stores, is changing the ownership of physical capital as well.

These new owners of rural physical capital are frequently very affluent, and they are usually not residents of the community in which their investments are made. They tend to spend their income outside the community, which leads to lower employment and income multipliers in the community. The income tends to be distributed more unevenly and be more variable in these communities (Bernat 1985).

Figure 4.1   **Wages and Salaries Versus Dividends, Rent, and Interest as Proportions of Personal Income, U.S. 1959–1999**

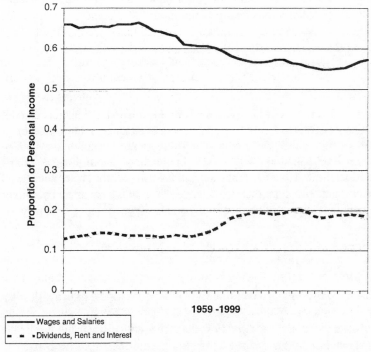

Source: Bureau of Economic Analysis.

Globalization

The "globalization" of the economy is so frequently cited as an important economic force that it has become a cliché. Increased trade and global competition among firms is usually the assumed consequence of this globalization. Of greater significance to communities, however, is the movement of information, technology, capital, and people. In addition to the competition in markets for goods and services, then, is the heightened competition among communities around the world for jobs, residents, and finances.

As Malecki (1996) and others have pointed out, globalization and technological change, especially the changes in ICT, are closely related forces. Information and communication technology has allowed firms to decentralize in a spatial sense while centralizing in an information sense. Firms in many industries, especially producer and consumer services, have distributed activities worldwide and overcome distance with ICT:

In the retailing sector, Wal-Mart Stores uses a leased satellite transponder to link its 1,700 stores to its Bentonville, Arkansas, headquarters and 14 distribution centers, in order to track every item sold at each checkout and to play the same background music in each store.

Firms also use ICT to link with each other in order to coordinate and to achieve logistical advantages. Gateway Computers has extended the concept to the point that United Parcel Service (UPS) now essentially assembles computer systems in its warehouses. Gateway directs components from its various sources directly to UPS, which packages and delivers systems to Gateway's customers.

Globalization has left many rural communities unsure of their best strategies. Very different spatial features attract employers than in the past. Traditional industrialization incentive programs are very risky and, when successful, attract employers of a type that can as easily be lured away again by another community with an attractive incentive offer.

Localization

"Localization" is the growing role of local conditions and local choices to determine the prosperity of a community. The reasons for the growing primacy of local circumstances include technological change, changing social and political attitudes, increasing returns to scale in many industries, and, ironically, the globalization that has opened competition with the world. Robert Reich (1991), in *The Work of Nations*, describes how global competition means that we as a nation are no longer in the same boat. The prosperity of our community depends on whether we are competing with the rest of the world as routine producers or whether our economy is based on the work of symbolic analysts. Rural communities, then, depend on how well their economic base fares.

As we saw above in the discussion of globalization, there is a growing freedom of all industries, but most strikingly of services, to behave like footloose industries and to decentralize different functions spatially. The declining role of goods, especially raw materials, in production has provided both traditionally factor-oriented and market-oriented industries with a wider array of potential locations. Many factor-oriented manufacturing industries choose to transport their raw materials to areas closer to their markets, where amenities are higher, or where factors other than raw products cost less. Conversely, the growing role of information exchanges, ICT, and computers allows many services and otherwise market-oriented industries to locate at a distance from their markets. Newspapers need no longer be local. National newspapers exploit economies of size without compromising quality. Satellite and fiber optic technologies allow instantaneous audio, video, and information transmissions over long distances. This allows financial, insurance, real estate, educational, business management, accounting, legal, and many other services to centralize some functions and decentralize others but, in general, it frees them from locating strictly according to the location of their clients. Indeed, many of these services can be, and are being, provided in international markets just as goods have always been. Retailing will become increasingly footloose as consumer acceptance of mail order and e-commerce rises. New service industries, yet unimagined, will arise to take advantage of the new technologies.

Overall, we observe an emerging economy in which the definitions of economic base, services, public and private enterprise, competition, and even sectors themselves have become blurred. We see an economy in which trusted linkages—linkages between production growth and employment growth, between base and nonbase industries, between activity and place—have been severed. We see an economy in which linkages have become more numerous but more decentralized, and where distance becomes a resource rather than a cost or constraint.

Rural areas face potential disadvantages when compared to the localization forces of urban areas. Perhaps the greatest disadvantage is lower population density. Low density increases the cost of infrastructure, limits the size and complexity of the labor market, and reduces the size of markets. In a world of significant economies of scale in many sectors, low population density is a decided disadvantage. In addition, low density means that rural areas will always be last to receive the benefits of technological change.

An oft-cited disadvantage is distance from population centers; however, as several researchers have shown, transportation costs related to distance can be a centrifugal force. Ironically, technology is tending to erode the decentralizing effects of transportation costs. An obvious example of this is the centralizing effects of e-commerce.

Industrial Structure

The structure of all industries and the relationships between firms are changing everywhere. In rural areas, a fundamental restructuring is underway. The emergence of industrialized agriculture, farmer alliances, new generation cooperatives (NGCs), and other elements of supply chains is precipitated by changes in technology, growing globalization, and the existence of economies of size. The supply chain revolution in agriculture is having a wrenching effect on rural communities as well (Drabenstott 1999). For one thing, the spatial concentration of agricultural products and firms is growing. This affects the stability of these emerging "commodity communities" (Drabenstott 1999, 3) and increases their dependency on particular firms.

Similar patterns are also occurring in some rural manufacturing activities. Over the past thirty years, the emergence of "just in time" (JIT) manufacturing and other management changes have provided new employment opportunities for some rural communities—especially those in close proximity to larger assembly plants such as in the auto industry. Rural firms—and communities—that produce component parts for larger manufacturing firms are increasingly dependent on these firms, and they are under significant pressure to reduce costs, ensure quality, and respond to rapidly changing production levels.

Changing Demographics

Migration to Rural Communities

As pointed out at the beginning of this chapter, many rural communities, especially those in the mountain and coastal regions, are experiencing significant inflows of new residents. This internal migration consists primarily of older adults who are, or who expect to be, retired, and of telecommuters or businesspeople no longer tied to particular locations. An important dimension of this internal migration is the rising demand for amenities. David McGranahan (1999) identified six climatic and topographic rural amenities. The amenities were used to generate an index (Map 4.2). Using statistical methods, McGranahan found that the index explains at least one-quarter of the variance in rural growth rates.

The resurgence of some rural communities obviously brings new investment and income to selected places. Migrants often bring entrepreneurial talents, experience, market knowledge, and capital to their new communities. Return migrants (natives to the community who had left to pursue employment opportunities) combine these characteristics with an understanding of their new locales.

Population increases in smaller, rural areas that are not accustomed to new residents can also lead to economic and social conflict between the "from-heres" and the "come-heres." In addition, in-migration puts significant new demands on private and public services, and this can lead to rapid increases in prices for housing and other real property.

According to McGranahan's (1999) analysis, the rural Midwest offers fewer amenities to prospective in-migrants (see Map 4.2), yet even here there are exceptions in small cities and in recreational and tourism areas, as well as in communities that provide outstanding educational and other public services.

Map 4.2   **Rural Amenity Index Scores by County**

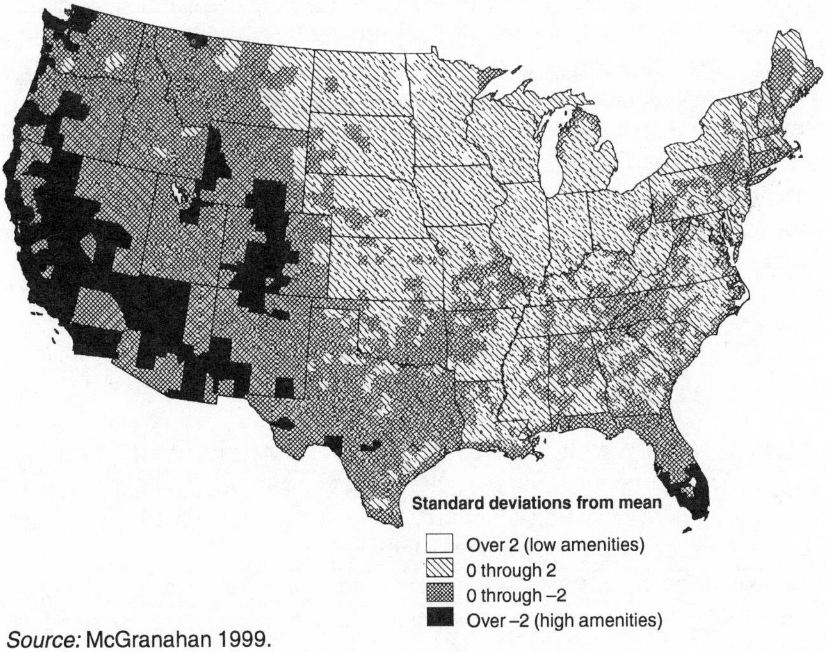

Standard deviations from mean

☐ Over 2 (low amenities)
▨ 0 through 2
▦ 0 through −2
■ Over −2 (high amenities)

Source: McGranahan 1999.

Settlement Patterns

In addition to the more macro phenomena of growing rural populations, communities are being changed by a trend toward more dispersed settlement patterns. Increasingly, people are interested in fleeing the congestion and high cost of suburban life for the quieter, safer, and more affordable surroundings of the metropolitan fringe. This is a continuation and acceleration of urban sprawl into the suburbs and rural areas.

In many places, small jurisdictions lack the planning resources and the physical infrastructure to respond to this kind of growth. Growth then exacerbates existing fiscal constraints for local governments and, in some cases, contributes to problems with water quality and other key natural resources.

Aging of the Population

As the baby boom generation begins to turn fifty, and as life expectancy continues to rise, the overall population is becoming older. Many of the baby boomers who are now entering their retirement years have accumulated wealth. These households are increasingly choosing nonmetropolitan communities as their retirement destination (Rogers 2000). Because the poorer elderly may not migrate as readily as those who are wealthier, declining communities may experience rising poverty and increased demands for social services. Growing rural communities will face increased demands for other public services and amenities. As residents in rural communities age, more people will receive direct and indirect income from federal transfer payments (e.g., pensions, Medicare, etc.).

New Governance

Devolution

Throughout the world, communities are faced with the prospect of making more decisions of greater importance than ever before. For rural local governments, this is often a tall order given their small staffs and resources, and limited experience with many of the new areas of responsibility, each of which creates its own problems. In the area of economic development, communities, often neighboring communities, find themselves pitted against each other in competition for migrating employers.

Devolution has become a commonly used term to describe the changing relationship between central and local governments. In recent years, the Scots, Welsh, and Irish have all opted for their own legislative assemblies—a concept referred to as "devolution" by the British government. In Europe, the concept of "subsidiarity" means that responsibility for public issues is assumed to be the role of the lowest possible level of government. In the United States, "devolution" refers to the process of shifting policy responsibility from the federal government to local and state governments.

"New governance" is a larger trend than just devolution, however. It includes a fundamental rethinking of how policy decisions are made and how public services are delivered. The European Union (1997) has adopted a policy called the "Civil Society" in which the democratic process is being broadened. The concept of Civil Society goes beyond formal government institutions to encourage public participation in decision making; new forms of public–private partnerships; and more flexible, responsive governance.

Reinventing Government

In many parts of the world, all levels of government are transforming in the face of changing technology, economics, and global realities. Market-oriented, entrepreneurial, competitive, and results-oriented—these are some of the descriptors that David Osborne and Ted Gaebler (1992) use to describe the effective government of the future in their book *Reinventing Government.* Reinvented governments are balancing their budgets and overhauling taxes. They are financing services with user fees and other market mechanisms. They are privatizing, outsourcing,[1] and forming strategic alliances[2] with other governments and with the private sector. They are becoming performance-based.

Performance-based government is designed to target limited public resources for maximum impact, to provide incentives for government units to improve the delivery of public services, and to hold government more accountable to specific measurable objectives. This trend is seen in a variety of policy contexts. At the community level, states such as Oregon and Minnesota have initiated the development of key performance indicators and specific short- and long-term quantitative targets for each of these measures, identified through a grassroots process at the local level. Performance against these targets will, in part, determine local government assistance from state funds.

This trend places even more importance on the capacity of rural communities to manage information and to develop strategies to interact with that information in ways that help them achieve measurable improvements in the delivery of public services.

Decentralization of Decision Making

The most fundamental aspect of new governance is the tendency toward greater decentralization in the decision-making process itself. Throughout the world, community residents are demanding more direct influence over the decisions they care about and that affect their communities. This type of public involvement can be a high risk, high stakes issue for local governance. It often takes place in the midst of conflict and highly politicized tactical relationships (Forester 1999). It is a broad category, including public meetings, task forces, collaborative research, community-based planning, deliberation, and conflict resolution. For public administrators, public involvement means sharing decision making with other stakeholders. It means conducting stakeholder analysis and knowing why public involvement is or is not called for in a rapidly changing environment. Public involvement requires new skills, new roles, new responsibilities, new institutional support, and significant investment of public resources; however, it can also lead to new perspectives, new alternatives, new relationships, and significant new community learning.

The ITC infrastructure offers great potential to support this decentralization process by reducing the transaction costs involved in becoming informed. It also facilitates the process of achieving agreement by reducing the transaction costs involved in communication.[3] Rural local governments usually have less capacity and fewer resources to respond to these changes in governance than do their metropolitan counterparts.

The Rural Midwest: Ironies and Paradoxes

Taken together, the economic, technological, demographic, and political shifts described thus far are creating much more diversity in rural Midwestern communities, and they are creating many new challenges for policymakers. In the face of this uncertainty, we observe the following important ironies and paradoxes.

Farms Depend More on Rural Communities Than Rural Communities Do on Farms

Farms and their communities, both the small towns nearby and the regional shopping centers, are interdependent. The argument is often made that "the best rural development policy is a good agriculture policy." The belief underlying this statement is that rural communities are highly dependent on local farms for their prosperity and viability; however, the reverse is much more the case—that the viability of a vast majority of farms is highly dependent on the prosperity and viability of their communities.

Nationwide, farm income represents less than 2 percent of total income. Most studies of the contribution of farming to local and state economies find that even including farm input suppliers, agricultural value-added processing, distribution of food and fiber, and the multiplier effects of income earned in all of these activities, agriculture still contributes less than 20 percent to the gross domestic product (GDP)of their state. Much of this contribution by agriculture actually occurs in urban, not rural, communities.

At the local level, even the most farm-dependent communities depend on agriculture for a fraction of their income. Map 4.3 shows the 556 U.S. Department of Agriculture (USDA)-defined farming-dependent counties in 1989. Farming-dependent counties are those in which at least 20 percent of total labor and proprietor income derives from farming. Given strong growth in nonfarm income and very weak growth in farm income over the last decade, this number is likely to be smaller today. Even with the multiplier effects of farm income, the contribution of farming to all but a few communities is likely to be considerably less than 50 percent.

In contrast, in 1997, the average census farm family had net earnings of just under $6,000 from all farming activities (down from almost $8,000 the previous year). In the same year, the average farm family earned over $46,000 from off-farm sources, for a total of over $52,000. Thus, the average farm family depended on off-farm jobs, dividends, interest, and transfers for over 88 percent of its income. On average, 54 percent of this income came from off-farm jobs in their localities.

Map 4.3   **Nonmetro Farming-Dependent Counties, 1989**

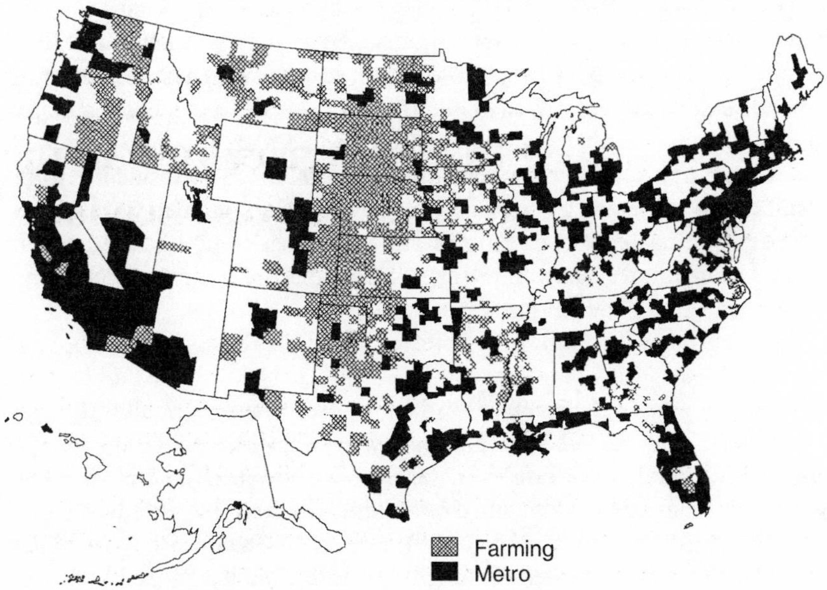

Source: USDA–ERS, Rural Economy Division, using data from the Bureau of Economic Analysis.

Overall, it is quite clear that farms depend more on their communities for income and quality of life than communities depend on farms for their economic base. Farms and farm families rely on their communities to provide them with public and private services, roads and marketing opportunities, good education, and so on. Farm families also depend on their communities to provide off-farm employment for the operator and for family members. Because of the physical tie of farm families to the location of their farms, farm families are especially sensitive to the location of these nonfarm jobs— they cannot relocate to improve their access to employment opportunities without also giving up their farms.

Nonfarm Rural Residents Are Often in Conflict with Farms and Agricultural Policy

In general, rural communities benefit when local agriculture prospers. Most nonfarm residents have an interest in the health of the agricultural sector; however, structural changes in agriculture seem to be eroding some of these common interests. Increased industrialization of agriculture appears to be weakening the ties between farms and their communities. Researchers (Allen, Filkins, Cordes, and Jarecki 1998) found that concerns with industrial agriculture and meatpacking plants were greater among rural residents who lived in smaller towns or who lived closer to these farms and plants than those more distant from the farms and plants. Other anecdotal evidence indicates growing feelings of mistrust, more serious land-use conflicts, and increasing environmental conflicts between farm and nonfarm rural residents. Rural residents do not seem to view new larger farms as community residents. Furthermore, in many communities and states, agriculture has effectively limited its exposure to local property taxes, further reducing the interest that nonfarm residents have in the sector.

What concerns do nonfarm rural residents have about agricultural policy? Rural residents, other than farm families and those closely tied to the farm economy, seem to have many of the same concerns with agricultural policy as does the general public—food safety, food prices, environmental issues, and federal fiscal effects of farm policy. Ironically, rural residents have additional interests that might trigger more conflicts with farms than do urban residents. For example, rural residents have concerns about local environmental effects—odors, threats to water quality, noise, and truck traffic. In addition, rural residents are often concerned about tax limitations and the impact of in-migration to fill low-wage agricultural value-added jobs.

Agricultural Policy Is Not Rural Policy

If the economies of rural communities are not particularly dependent on farms is it possible that agricultural policy can serve as our rural policy? Federal expenditures for agriculture (approximately $10 billion in 1999) are important stimulants to rural economies. The stabilizing and reassuring effects of agricultural policy are also possible; however, other federal agencies, notably the Department of Transportation (DOT), the Department of Education, the Social Security Administration, Department of Health and Human Services, Department of Housing and Urban Development (HUD), the Small Business Administration (SBA), and the Department of Commerce–Economic Development Administration (EDA), contribute significantly to rural economies as well. The USDA estimates that almost $6 billion of DOT expenditures and $6.6 billion of HUD expenditures benefit rural areas directly. Social Security, Medicare, and Medicaid are huge sources of income in many rural communities. Furthermore, many of these expenditures tend to have indirect impacts on quality of life in rural areas and the well-being of a broad array of rural residents.

Small Businesses Locate in Large Places and Large Businesses Locate in Small Places

The increasing economic returns believed to exist in so many industries lead to a potential paradox. The imperative of scale is leading to larger and larger firms and more complex agglomerations of businesses. In urban areas, small to medium firms can cluster to capture the benefits of agglomeration economies —savings due to proximity to a diverse labor force, specialized producer services, and high-quality public services. In rural areas, economies of scale are more likely to be achieved internally to firms. Companies must become, and increasingly are becoming, larger and larger. In agriculture, the emergence of supply chains is evidence of this trend. In other sectors, the location of large wholesale facilities, assembly plants, waste facilities, and prisons are examples of large, self-contained enterprises. The consequences of this trend are that rural areas will increasingly depend on the fortunes (and whims) of one or a few companies.

Where Are We Headed?

It is one thing to chronicle the current situation and speculate on the underlying trends. It is quite another matter to predict where these trends are taking us. In this section, we assume that major policies remain unchanged and that current trends continue for another generation. Under these conditions, how will rural America look in the next decade or so?

In the aggregate, population and income growth rates in rural America may equal or even exceed those in urban America. Metropolitan Statistical Areas will expand in each of the decennial censuses, incorporating some of the highest income and most rapidly growing nonmetropolitan counties, officially leaving the remaining rural areas poorer and slower growing. This average prosperity will obscure the bifurcation of rural communities, however. The range between the least and most successful communities will continue to widen. Some rural communities will experience significant prosperity and will be quite viable. Others, largely in the Midwest and in the most remote regions of the East and West will continue to decline, with many becoming nonviable as effective communities.

Two types of rural experience will stand out—the growing connected rural community and the isolated rural community.

The Connected Rural Community

Connected rural communities will have high levels of natural and manmade amenities. Because of higher than average income, education, and population growth, each new generation of telecommunications infrastructure will be provided at an early stage, encouraging private investment and growth. Most of these communities will have good commercial air service, health care, and high-quality public education.

A majority of the farms within the labor-sheds and retail areas of connected rural communities will be relatively small, many operated by part-time and hobby farmers. Some farms will produce high-valued products targeted at local niche markets—horticultural crops, U-pick farms, and so on. Industrial agriculture will have largely exited these communities in search of lower land costs and fewer land-use conflicts. Land values will be too high, and the transaction costs of developing a viable business in these areas will have become prohibitive for low valued, high-volume production.

Connected rural communities will face what they have come to consider serious land-use issues. In many cases, the rural character of the local towns has been displaced by more suburban characteristics. Traffic will overwhelm the local roads, and much of the rural "farmscape" will have been replaced by large-lot residential development, campus-style industrial and commercial development, and strip malls. In short, the connected rural community will become less and less rural and more and more suburban.

The Isolated Rural Community

Isolated rural communities will generally exist at considerable distances from urban centers. These communities will be those that have survived a period of significant rural consolidation—that is, the decline of some and the stabilization of others. Most of these communities will be in the Upper Plains and western regions, although pockets of isolation will exist in all regions. Population will be stable or declining. Income levels will be significantly lower, and income growth will lag behind the national average. These communities will have telecommunications infrastructure, but it will typically be at least one generation behind that of urban and growing rural areas, and it will be more expensive. Nowhere will the digital divide be more striking than in the isolated rural community.

Farms will be large and technologically cutting-edge. These regions will be the home to a majority of the largest Confined Animal Feeding Operations (CAFOs). Some counties and states will have found legislative or regulatory means of limiting industrial agriculture. In most cases, the economies in these counties and states will struggle even more than in those that admit industrial agriculture.

Residents have few local entertainment and retail alternatives. Those that can afford to be connected depend on the Internet for entertainment, shopping, investing, and education. Farms and manufacturers almost totally depend on the Internet for marketing, sales, and purchases of inputs.

Local public services, especially education, will be minimal. Both the property and retail sales tax bases will have dropped significantly since the turn of the twenty-first century, leaving many rural counties and school districts without adequate financing.

These communities will rival inner cities as the primary destination of international immigrants. These immigrants will largely work at close to minimum wages for value-added agriculture processing or other manufacturing firms.

Conclusions

The rural Midwest is at a crossroads. During the twentieth century, technology eroded the employment base of most rural communities, depressed incomes, and made out-migration the only recourse for millions. In the twenty-first century, technology may reverse that bias and, instead, favor rural localities and rural residents. Rural communities face a number of hurdles before these forces will work to its advantage rather than disadvantage.

The fortunes of rural America are diverging. Some are continuing to face traditional economic hardships and decline. Others are trying to cope with rapid growth in jobs and population, land-use conflicts, and a growing demand for public services. With a continuation of current policies, there is little reason to expect this process of divergence to ease.

Conversely, economic and technological trends are reducing the cost of distance and increasing the value of space. Technology is reducing the need for labor, especially proximate labor. Demand for the lifestyles available in rural communities is growing. There are reasons to be cautiously optimistic, and certainly reasons to explore the potential for business growth and to search for new engines of rural growth. With new, effective policies, rural communities can contribute much more to the vitality of the national economy.

Notes

1. *Outsourcing* refers to the practice of going outside the firm for services that were traditionally provided internally.

2. *Strategic alliances* refer to the practice of co-venturing and contracting vertically with suppliers and clients, and horizontally with competitors.

3. ICT can facilitate decentralization of public decisions by improving information quality, enhancing information access, and developing capacity for community decision support (O'Dubhchair, Scott, and Johnson 2001).

References

Allen, John C., Rebecca Filkins, Sam Cordes, and Eric J. Jarecki. 1998. *Nebraska's Changing Agriculture: Perceptions About the Swine Industry.* Lincoln: University of Nebraska–Lincoln, Institute of Agriculture and Natural Resources. Available on-line: <www.ianr.unl.edu/rural/98porkpaper.pdf>.

Bernat, G. Andrew, Jr. 1985. *Income Distribution in Virginia: The Effect of Intersectoral Linkages on the Short-Run Size Distribution of Income in Small Regions.* Unpublished Ph.D. dissertation, Department of Agricultural Economics, Virginia Polytechnic Institute and State University.

Drabenstott, Mark. 1999. *An Introduction to the Center for the Study of Rural America.* Washington, DC: National Press Club. Available on-line: <www.kc.frb.org/RuralCenter/speeches/centerintro.htm>.

European Union. 1997. *Cohesion and the Information Society.* Communication from the Commission to the European Parliament, the Council, the Committee of the Regions, and the Economic and Social Committee (COM [97] 7/3).

Forester, John. 1999. *The Deliberative Practitioner: Encouraging Participatory Planning Processes.* Cambridge, MA: MIT Press.

Malecki, Edward J. 1996. *Telecommunications Technology and American Rural Development in the Twenty-First Century.* Paper prepared for TVA Rural Studies. Available on-line: <www.rural.org/workshops/rural_telecom/malecki>. Downloaded January 2002.

McGranahan, David J. 1999. *Natural Amenities Drive Rural Population Change* (Agricultural Economic Report No. 781). Washington, DC: U.S. Department of Agriculture.

O'Dubhchair, Kate, James K. Scott, and Thomas G. Johnson. 2001. Building a knowledge infrastructure for learning communities. *The Electronic Journal of Information Systems in Developing Countries* 4(4). Available on-line: <www.is.cityu.edu.hk/ejisdc/vol4/v4r4.pdf>.

Osborne, David, and Ted Gaebler. 1992. *Reinventing Government: How the Entrepreneurial Spirit Is Transforming the Public Sector.* Reading, MA: Addison-Wesley.

Reich, Robert B. 1991. *The Work of Nations: Preparing Ourselves for 21st Century Capitalism.* Boston: Addison-Wesley.

Rogers, Carolyn. 2000. Changes in the older population and implications for rural areas. *USDA–ERS Briefing Room.* Available on-line: <www.ers.usda.gov/Publications/rdrr90/index.htm>.

U.S. Department of Agriculture–Economic Research Service (USDA–ERS). 1999. *Rural Conditions and Trends* 9(2). Available on-line: <www.ers.usda.gov/epubs/pdf/rcat/rcat92/>.

U.S. Department of Labor. n.d. *Multifactor Productivity Trends.* Available on-line: <www.bls.gov/newsrelease/prod3.toc.htm>.

5

Burton E. Swanson, Mohamed M. Samy,
and Andrew J. Sofranko

Global Challenges and Opportunities
for Midwest Farmers

Change is endemic to agriculture. It has been changing for decades, centuries, and millennia. What is different about the present-day transformation is the widespread belief that agriculture is in a state of rapid evolution, and that the technologies and market forces that have changed other industries are reshaping it into a qualitatively different enterprise. Its essential characteristics are being altered, giving rise in the process to a "new agriculture," which, in turn, produces "new products" for better-informed and more demanding "new consumers." The dilemma associated with this transformation stems from its providing new opportunities for some Midwestern farmers while simultaneously contributing to the "exit" of others from farming.

This contemporary transformation is summarized in a variety of terms: the "industrialization of agriculture," "globalization," "trade liberalization," and "customized/value-enhanced production." They all reflect the fact that Midwestern farmers are, increasingly, turning from the production of bulk commodities to more specialized products, competing with other producers around the world, and utilizing biotechnologies in the production of genetically modified crops. New partnerships are emerging along the food chain as companies and farmers alike pursue new efficiencies. Many farmers are crossing over into the information age, others are exploring new ways of organizing themselves, and many agricultural enterprises are seeking novel pockets of knowledge and attempting to turn them into new or differentiated products. In addition, new national and multinational players in the production and trade of agricultural products are appearing on the international scene. The present situation is dynamic and fraught with both risks and opportunities.

The combination of agricultural industrialization, globalization, and trade liberalization is having a dramatic impact on the world food system. Structural change is rapidly occurring in the agricultural sector, including the vertical integration of the input supply, production, marketing, and processing subsectors. The progressive removal of domestic and international impediments to competition is resulting in the globalization of many sectors of the agricultural economy, which, according to Jerome Siebert (2001), has not participated as fully as the other sectors in the new market economy.

In the first part of this chapter, we briefly sketch out two major trends in U.S. and Midwestern agriculture. We focus mainly on the "industrialization of agriculture" and on "globalization and trade liberalization." The second part briefly outlines the challenges and implications of this emerging global market economy for Midwestern farmers, especially with the emergence of Brazil and Argentina as major competitors for global soybean, corn, beef, and pork markets. The chapter identifies possible strategies for producers, while in the process recognizing some of the imperatives of the "new agriculture" and the new opportunities inherent in it.

The final section outlines the experience of the University of Illinois' Value Project in helping Illinois farmers meet some of these challenges by identifying market opportunities and by determining the comparative advantage for different value-enhanced commodities. It discusses a unique set of activities designed to bridge the gap for Illinois farmers between present-day agriculture and the opportunities in the "new agriculture." The strategy outlined in this part of the chapter focuses on area and producer attributes, the identification of new types of crops and their profitability, locating new markets, and the assessment of producer interest in organizing into cooperative activity.

Industrialization of Agriculture

Change in American agriculture has been described in terms of its shifting structure, its technological sophistication, commercialization, specialization, energy-intensiveness, and a host of similar concepts. These and other newly emerging trends have been subsumed under the rubric of "the industrialization of agriculture," a term signaling the advent of a "new agriculture" with major implications for the way farming is carried out.

In broad terms, "industrialization" refers to the concentration of production on large operations (Albrecht 1997), the increasing integration of each step in the food production system (Urban 1991, 4), higher levels of market differentiation made possible by biotechnology research, and the introduction of unique crops and genetically altered old crops by agriculture-related corporations (Pollan and Levine 1998). Industrialization entails the shift away from smaller units linked by decentralized markets to a system of larger units increasingly linked by contracts and negotiated relationships among input suppliers, processors, distributors, and retailers (Castle 1998). It refers to the "transformation of agriculture from an industry that raises commodities to one that manufactures goods" (Boehlje and Schrader 1996, 335). It involves large production units, the rationalization of production, use of capital-intensive technology, and loss of producer independence. It is shifting from "production driven technologies of suppliers to the consumer driven requirements of processors" (Coffey 1993, 1132).

Industrial agriculture thus encompasses a range of structural and operational changes in farming, ranging from large-scale confinement operations, which function much like a factory, to explicit contractual relations and vertical integration (Rhodes 1993). Perhaps the most visible examples of "industrial agriculture" are the assembly-line "mega-farms" and large confinement operations. Less visible, but also burgeoning, is the number of farmers entering into contracts for a wide variety of specialty crops and farm products, drawn by premiums offered for producing more exacting products and by the prospects of assured markets and higher income.

Underlying Forces

Technological innovation, resulting from the shift from public sector to private sector funding (Huffman 1998), has played a role in industrialization. Recently, a more rapid pace of technological change has been ushered in with the granting of intellectual property rights for new plant varieties, new life-forms, and computer software. Biotechnology is contributing to significant improvements in agricultural plants and animals through genetic engineering for insect, weed, and disease control, along with growth stimulants and reproductive technologies. These newer technologies require changes in the production process and higher-quality management; many require greater inputs of human capital and investment by the producer. Less educated farmers with limited capital resources are at a disadvantage in adopting new computer, biological, and genetically based technologies. As in the past, those with technical and financial resources will ride the wave with the result that the gap between the capital-rich and the capital-limited will widen ("Innovation in Industry" 1999).

A more discriminating consumer, one concerned with convenience, safety, nutrition, and taste, is another influence on the food system, as are a host of demographic and lifestyle trends. Higher incomes, ethnic diversity, an aging population, changing household composition in terms of size, age distribution, and marital status, as well as changes in employment and the perceived value of time all contribute to a "manufacturing approach to creating specific products for unique end-users" (Boehlje and Schrader 1996, 335).

There is also greater information and concern for food safety, health, and food labeling (Kinsey 1994). "Health food" purchases are increasing dramatically. Organic products are no longer a niche market, but have been mainstreamed in major supermarkets (Halweil 2000), as has "customized" production based on consumer needs and preferences for product presentation (Gilmore and Pine 1997). Pressures from restaurants, fast-food franchises, and processors who want more reliable, more uniform, and better-quality products are contributing to greater control over the food production process.

Finally, pressures originating in research and development firms have enhanced the capacity for producing "new" products with new traits, and for exploring nonagricultural uses for agricultural products (Behling 1998). Together, these pressures are promoting a more vertically integrated food system, along with producer contracts and greater market coordination.

Implications for Midwestern Producers

What has been of historical interest to social scientists are the implications of industrialization beyond the accompanying structural changes. The broad forces that are producing a more "industrial" type of agriculture have resulted in a growing receptivity among farmers for improving their income through diversification and expansion of production into areas that once might have been viewed as "marginal" to commercial agriculture. In the Midwest, where agriculture has been characterized as large scale and commercial, many farmers now pursue new opportunities by producing limited quantities of products requiring skilled labor and management, producing crops once thought to be too specialized, and/or by producing value-enhanced commodities that will allow farmers to shift from one end-use market to another.

The types of enterprises emerging from these opportunities are quite diverse. They range from vertically integrated production to value-added production arrangements between producers and market representatives, to farmers growing organic or pesticide-free grain, fruits, or vegetables for regional or international markets, to farmers producing for local community markets, and to producer alliances and new generation cooperatives that promise to give farmers greater access to specialty markets and more economic leverage. These enterprises vary in terms of structure and levels of coordination, producer autonomy, and the degree to which they take farmers away from their traditional production routines.

A prominent aspect of the trends currently underway in Midwestern agriculture is the growing differentiation of markets, described by one observer as just the "tip of the iceberg" ("Brazil Hopes to Grow . . ." 1998). Although a market still exists for bulk commodities and standardized agricultural products, there has also been a shift to smaller and more customized markets stemming from changes in consumer demands and processor/input suppliers' ability to modify crops to provide a better fit with an expansion of end-uses. Consumers are, increasingly, being matched with "finely tuned products" that reflect new uses and preferences. The results of this fragmentation and diversification have been captured in the terms "specialty crops" and "high-value products." It is expected that as agriculture becomes more attuned to what end-users want and need, more farmers will produce specialty crops that embody distinct attributes for specific end-users. Increasingly, they will be paid on the basis of how they perform in providing products that meet the specific needs of end-users.

Boehlje and Schrader (1996) have alluded to a social–psychological aspect of industrial agriculture. They refer to it as a "manufacturing mentality," one of the imperatives of the new "manufacturing paradigm." As part of the initiative to achieve greater control over the production process, and to direct production to what end-users want, farmers will be required to routinize production at a higher and more precise level. There will be pressures to perform tasks at a higher level of specification, and there will be pressures to improve scheduling and coordinate technology use so as to gain greater control over the production process.

A related aspect of an emerging "marketing mentality" may be the need among producers to form new partnerships and alliances via contracting to obtain resources and services. In effect, farmers will be taken "off the farm" by purchasing agents, their negotiations with contractors, and their need for capital in order to expand. Whatever the dimensions of industrial agriculture, larger-scale contract production will be a part of the "total system focus" (Boehlje and Schrader 1996), which is quite different from a more traditional system of commodity production. It will also give rise to a "new farmer," who is highly skilled in financial management and responsive to new opportunities for raising income and reducing risk.

Current agricultural trends have also revived interest in the need for more organized and cooperative action on the part of commercial Midwestern farmers. This interest in "group action institutions" is being fueled by a combination of conditions and trends, among them the growing importance of differentiated specialty grains, niche markets, and value-added activities (cf. Coffey 1993; Welsh 1997). Interest in a more organized mode of agricultural production is reflected in farm media coverage of farmers entertaining ideas of partnering, starting cooperative ventures, and entering into alliances that would permit them to adapt to value-added opportunities and negotiate with buyers from a position of greater economic power (cf. Cook 1995; Husar 1999).

Some experts view the renewed interest of farmers in cooperative-type activities and their participation in "downstream" activities as a new "social movement of independent farm operators" (Torgerson, Reynolds, and Gray 1997, 3). The joint activities are being promoted as institutional mechanisms to counter the economic power of input and marketing firms, and to provide producers with greater leverage in emerging specialty markets and value-added activities. More than a few farmers appear to be willing to relinquish some of this traditional autonomy so as to gain access to new markets and improve their incomes.

Globalization and Agricultural Trade Liberalization

The world economy has undergone considerable change as international trade followed the removal of national border barriers, such as tariffs and exchange controls, as well as internal restrictions, such as directed credit, subsidies, and preferential purchasing. International institutions, including the World Trade Organization (WTO), the European Union (EU), the North American Free Trade Agreement (NAFTA), the Free Trade Area of the Americas (FTAA), and the World Bank, have underpinned cooperation among nations and helped promote global integration and cross-border trading (Wolf 2001). Still, major trading nations have continued to protect their farmers from the brunt of global market forces through subsidies, agriculture support payments, farm aid quotas, and tariffs. As WTO rules are implemented, the role of government policy in maintaining domestic food security and protecting inefficient producers will gradually diminish. The result may be important shifts in agricultural production within and between countries, and greater exposure of products and producers to competition across different eco-regions, states, and nations.

The move toward trade liberalization and the globalization of agricultural production has been facilitated by advances in technology and infrastructure improvements, which reduced the costs of transportation and communication between different parts of the world. During the last fifty years, technical revolutions have occurred in the collection and dissemination of technical information and in the cost of moving physical objects (Buelens 1999). The diminishing costs of communication and transport are increasing the pace of international economic integration. Opportunities represented in these trends are having a profound impact on agricultural development, in both the industrially developed and less developed countries.

New agricultural technologies have also permitted agribusiness firms to change production and marketing methods and, in turn, increase their profit margins. New information and management technologies allow firms to identify market opportunities and integrate production technology into market demands (Siebert 2001). For example, biotechnology has encouraged firms to produce for health and nutrition niche markets and to reduce costs. ("Niche" markets are geared toward handling differentiated and specialized products. They are also smaller as opposed to mass commodity markets, in which most most producers sell.) Biotechnology and other breakthroughs in agricultural technology have combined with information and transportation technologies to commercialize new products across a growing number of global niche markets. As a result, farmers in different parts of the world are now taking advantage of new genetic, mechanical, chemical, and information technologies, which until twenty or thirty years ago were largely available only to American farmers. These new technologies have allowed farmers worldwide to aggressively compete with U.S. farmers not only in traditional commodity markets but also in new niche markets.

The growing pace of foreign competition and the declining role of government have, simultaneously, exposed farmers to new sets of risk factors. Biotechnological innovations and the ascendance of input suppliers and processors as "more powerful decision makers now than in the past" (Gilles and Dalecki 1988, 40) have changed farmers' perceptions of their role in what is increasingly becoming accepted as an industrialized agriculture.

Today, American farmers live and function in a global economy. When consumers of U.S. agricultural exports lose purchasing power, as happened in Asia, Russia, and Mexico, agriculture is the first to feel the effect (Klechner, 1999). In addition, world output of food per capita has increased while prices of most agricultural commodities are steadily falling in real terms. Figures 5.1 and 5.2 illustrate how corn and soybean prices have steadily eroded over the past five years. This has given larger, more integrated producers a distinct competitive advantage in integrating production and marketing, and in supplying large end-use processors and/or major urban markets.

The ability of American agriculture to maintain global market share will depend on several factors, including its ability to produce products with unique identities and values in new and open export markets, and to forge linkages with the other sectors in supply chains beyond domestic markets (Siebert 2001). Global food demand is still expanding, with 95 percent of the world's consumers living outside U.S. borders (Klechner 1999). Thus, maintaining exports is vital to the future of Midwestern agriculture.

Diversification and Specialization of Agricultural Production

Developments within the global market economy offer new growth opportunities for Midwestern agriculture. As market forces strengthen, there will be increased demand by end-use processors and more demanding consumers for highly specialized products with unique identities and values. Many pro-

Figure 5.1 **Global Corn Production and Price Trends, 1995–2000**

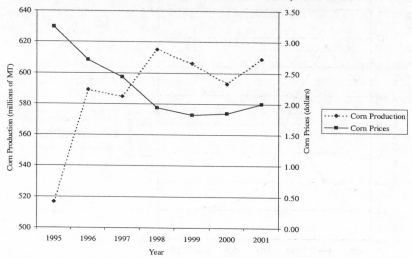

Source: FAO Statistical Database, 2002 and National Agricultural Statistical Service, 2002. Available on-line: <www.apps.fao.org/default.htm and www.usda.gov/nass/>.

cessors are already demanding farm products with specific traits of consistent quality, and they are requiring timely delivery to increase their production and/or processing efficiency. Farmers may be able to achieve higher returns through product differentiation and by exploiting their possible "comparative advantage" within an eco-region. This is a primary factor driving the current trend toward value-enhanced commodity production in the Midwest. In addition, food safety and quality control management, both of which require product traceability, are becoming important features of this emerging food system. More efficient farmers will be able to spread these new "identity preservation" (IP) and traceability costs over a greater production base and, thereby, have a comparative advantage in the production and marketing of value-enhanced commodities.

Another important aspect of the shift toward farm products with unique identities and values is the direct link to consumer demand for farm products with different traits and values. Our research on meat products shows that many well-educated, high-income consumers are more discerning and willing to pay substantially higher prices for food products with particular traits and modes of presentation. These "new consumers" are being defined through changing lifestyles, and demographics, as well as dietary and health concerns (Siebert 2001). For example, consumers in several areas of the world are concerned with food safety issues and are demonstrating a willingness to pay more for organic and "naturally grown" food products, products cultivated without the use of chemi-

Figure 5.2 **Global Soybean Production and Price Trends, 1995–2000**

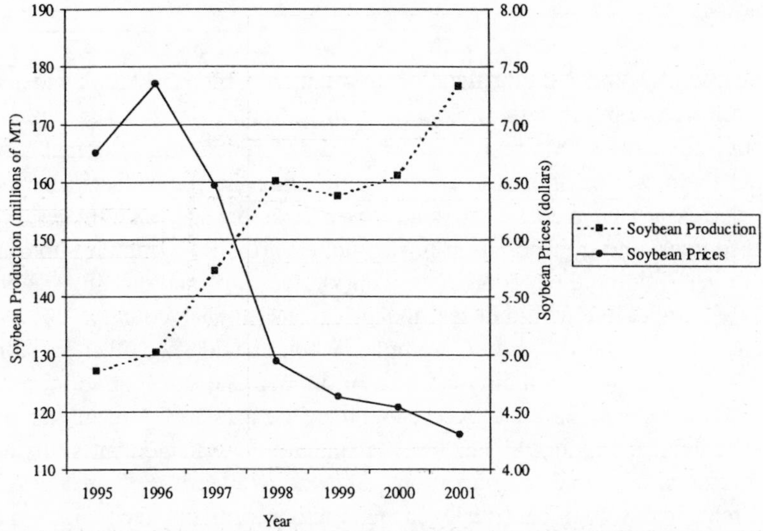

Source: <FAO Statistical Database, 2002, and National Agricultural Statistical Service, 2002. Available on-line: <www.appe.fao.org/default.htm> and<www.usda.gov/nass/>.

cals, hormones, or antibiotics, and uncontaminated by genetically modified organisms (GMOs). Because of consumer demands, some governments are keeping unapproved GMO crops out of the national food system. The question here is not whether these organic or naturally produced food products are safer; the issue is whether a growing number of consumers will pay a premium sufficient to increase the production, marketing, and processing of specialized farm products that meet their demands. Trends in Europe and Japan, and emerging trends in North America, suggest that the demand for high-quality, naturally produced and organic food products will continue to increase during the foreseeable future. These trends could open new specialized opportunities for small- and medium-scale producers.

As the structure of demand diversifies, the older *commodity production strategy* of treating agricultural goods as homogenous products, which dominated U.S. agriculture during the last century, is being replaced by a new *differentiated goods and services strategy*. This appears to be a classic paradigm shift in which old business models, institutions, and management practices have declining relevance as new approaches and management tools are developed and implemented. If the trend toward increasing product diversification continues, the important question among Midwestern farmers becomes: How are we to prepare for and compete in this changing global agricultural economy? This issue will be examined briefly in the remainder of this chapter.

Implications of the Global Marketplace for Midwestern Farmers

Trade liberalization and globalization are impacting the world food and agricultural system by, in effect, picking "winners and losers" based on comparative advantage. Different countries, and different agro-ecological zones within them, are beginning to specialize in agricultural products in which they currently have a comparative advantage. Factors such as climate, natural resources, and transportation infrastructure are all playing an important role in determining the predominant crop(s), livestock, and farming systems that are competitive within different eco-regions[1] of each country.

The situation becomes more complex when considering other variables such as factor costs, including land, labor, inputs, and transportation; proximity to local, regional, and export markets; the availability of human and social capital, including higher-level technical and management skills and the presence of farmer organizations; and the availability of or access to research and development (R&D) capacity and information technology (IT). Within the WTO framework, national agricultural policy may mitigate the relative impact of these factors as countries seek to maintain some level of food security and protect their farmers while taking advantage of new trade opportunities. As noted in *The Economist* ("Agriculture and Technology" 2000, 10), however, "there is a fine line between protection and protectionism." All of these variables will affect the mix of crop and livestock systems that can operate profitably within different eco-regions of individual countries.

Opportunities and Competition from Mexico

These underlying conditions and various governments' responses to them will have major implications for farmers in both industrially developed and less developed countries. A brief comparison of white, food-grade maize (corn) production in Mexico and the United States highlights some of these forthcoming challenges and opportunities. First, white maize is the primary food staple crop throughout most of Mexico; however, due to agronomic conditions, seed quality, input costs, management skills, and other production factors, maize production costs are about 25 percent higher in Mexico than in the United States. Even with the passage of NAFTA, Mexico has been able to restrict white maize imports through the use of quotas and tariffs to protect domestic producers and the subsistence income of small farm households. Under NAFTA, however, white maize tariffs will be incrementally phased out; however, until 2008, imports are being limited to the gap between domestic production and consumption.

After the year 2008, Mexican *campesinos* (farmers) will be forced to compete directly with highly efficient American farmers for the Mexican tortilla market. Without further government intervention, the market will determine the "winners and losers" for this important market. Though commercial farmers in Mexico may not have an advantage in producing white maize, they may have a competitive advantage over farmers in California and Florida in producing vegetables and fruit for the "high value" winter market in the United States. To illustrate further the complexity of trade, Mexican growers will have to become more efficient and consumer sensitive if they are to stay competitive with the well-organized Chilean farmers who have already gained considerable market share in the United States.

Competition from Brazil

Perhaps the most serious competition Midwestern farmers face is from Brazilian farmers, especially for the global soybean market. Brazil, a country of 174 million people, has the largest economy in Latin America and ranks sixth largest in the world. It is the world's largest producer of coffee and sugar, the second largest producer of soybeans, and the third largest of corn. It also has the world's largest cattle herd, with 170 million head ("Brazil May Export Beef . . ." 2000).

The Brazilian economy, led by foreign investment and exports, was projected to expand by 4.5 percent in 2001. Despite the rapid pace of industrialization, agriculture and agribusiness remain very important to the Brazilian economy, accounting for 35 percent of GDP and 25 percent of total employment. The growth of the agricultural sector has been impressive. During the 1990s, total agricultural output (measured in constant prices) increased by nearly 40 percent. Rapid growth in the poultry, milk, pork, soybean meal and oil, coffee, and sugar industries reflects increasing demands from export markets. The official Brazilian forecast predicted that the 2001 soybean harvest would be the largest in history, up 19 percent from 2000 ("Agriculture, Horticulture . . ." 2001)

As part of broader economic reforms adopted in the early 1990s, Brazil unilaterally implemented a series of economic reforms to open domestic markets and liberalize agricultural trade, most notably the abolition of export controls and the elimination of export taxes. These reform measures have enhanced Brazil's growth prospects and significantly contributed to the doubling of agricultural exports since 1990. For example, in 2000, agriculture accounted for 35 percent of all exports, which totaled $16.7 billion. In 2001, Brazilian soybean exports alone were expected to be valued at $2.5 billion, while beef exports were projected to be about $800 million.

Brazil is also actively engaged in international trade policy initiatives, both in conjunction with membership in the Mercosur Custom Union with Argentina, Uruguay, and Paraguay, and as a key member of the Cairns Group. In addition, Brazil is playing a critical role in negotiations over the formation of the FTAA.

Brazil's ambitions as a competitor in global markets have led to an aggressive policy of investment in infrastructure to support the expansion of agricultural exports. Most of this investment has come from the private sector, including multinational companies. During the 1990s, ADM, Cargill, and Bunge substantially improved Brazil's agribusiness infrastructure, and Pioneer and Monsanto have served as a primary conduit for the introduction of new technologies. A considerable investment is being made in new transportation networks, including a combination of water and rail systems. The goal is to link new production areas, such as in the Mato Grosso, to the Amazon River and a new railroad stretching more than 2,200 miles (AgLink 2001). These investments will reduce the cost of transporting food and agricultural products to foreign markets. In addition, the Brazilian government offers incentives for people to move into unoccupied *cerrado* areas where there are now eight million acres of soybeans under cultivation in the Mato Grosso alone. Brazil's national agricultural research organization, Embrapa, estimates that there are another 250 million acres in the *cerrado*[2] region that can be brought into modern mechanized crop production.

The opening of the Brazilian domestic economy in the early 1990s sparked a race to introduce modern technology to increase agricultural productivity and cut production costs. Brazil now has a continuing supply of new technology from both the public (Embrapa) and private sector (e.g., Monsanto and Cargill) with which to increase its competitive advantage in export markets. American companies and banks are the most important investors in Brazil; U.S. direct foreign investment in Brazil has increased from less than $19 billion in 1994 to an estimated $35 billion through 2000 (U.S. Department of State 2001).

A good example of U.S. interest in Brazilian agriculture is Cargill, which has become Brazil's leading agribusiness and food company, with $600 million in physical assets and annual revenues of $2.3 billion (Cargill website n.d.). Other multinational companies include Doux (France) in the poultry sector, and the Vestery Group and Unilever (Britain) in production and food processing. By purchasing Manah, the largest fertilizer business in Latin America, Bunge subsidiaries now have a 28 percent share of the fertilizer market in Brazil. Bunge describes Brazil as the world's fourth-largest fertilizer market and claims it possesses some of the greatest expansion potential of any area in the world (Ray and the Agricultural Policy Analysis 2000).

Brazilian agriculture is characterized by high land concentration, where 1 percent of the farm operators own 50 percent of the total agricultural land. These large-scale farmers operate capital- and machinery-intensive production systems. Following a strategy of agricultural diversification, the production of cereals and oilseeds has grown consistently, especially for soybeans, but also for corn and wheat. The rapid growth in area planted to soybeans since the 1970s and increasing productivity have made Brazil the world's second largest soybean producer. Soybean yields in the central-west (Mato Grosso) are unsurpassed. According to *AGWEEK Online* (AgLink 2001), typical soybean yields are equivalent to 44.5 bushels/acre or about 16 percent higher than average U.S. yields. In addition, land in the state of Mato Grosso costs as little as $200 an acre—less than one-tenth the cost of comparable farmland in the Midwest.

The Brazilian government has decreed that growth in the soybean sector will be an officially designated "locomotive" of the country's industrial development for the next decade. As noted earlier, ADM, Cargill, and Bunge—the top three soybean processors in Brazil—have played a major role by investing heavily in Brazil's soybean industry. During the last ten years, ADM alone has marketed about 20 percent of Brazil's export soybeans (Ray and the Agricultural Policy Analysis 2000). Brazil has become the world's largest exporter of soybean meal, one of the top four countries in soybean oil exports, and second in the export of whole soybeans. Brazil is destined to replace the United States as the world's leading soybean producer and exporter. According to John Gordley, a spokesman for the American Soybean Association, "There is no question the U.S. will be in a tightly competitive situation with Brazil in the years to come" (AgLink 2001). Paradoxically, the stimulus for the soybean boom in Brazil came largely from the United States. In 1980, after President Jimmy Carter banned agricultural sales to Russia, Brazilian farmers began switching to soybeans to meet the new world demand (Rich 2001).

Brazilian agriculture is making rapid progress, but it still faces major problems that will affect its future growth. One problem is the lack of adequate storage and transportation infrastructure, which contributes to high wastage levels. Another problem is that most *cerrado* soils are highly acidic and have low fertility levels; therefore, they require high limestone and fertilizer inputs. Even so, with its high yield potential, a favorable climate, cheap labor, and an untapped land potential of upwards of 250 million acres, Brazil has the comparative advantage to become the world's largest soybean and cotton exporter. In addition, it is already expanding into industrial-scale pork, beef, and poultry operations. In short, during the next two decades, Brazil appears positioned to become the world's dominant exporter of low-cost soybeans, cotton, pork, beef, and poultry.

Implications for Midwestern Farmers

Recent developments in Brazil illustrate the types of impacts that trade liberalization will have on the world's food and agricultural system, and especially on Midwestern agriculture. As a result, Midwestern farmers are already pursuing value-enhanced crops where they may have a comparative advantage over producers in other states and countries, including Brazil. At the same time, some Midwestern farmers are buying inexpensive land in Brazil and Argentina.

The role of government policy in maintaining domestic food security and protecting inefficient producers will be gradually phased out as WTO rules are implemented. As a result, important shifts in agricultural production within and between countries may occur as Midwestern agricultural products are exposed to intense competition from different eco-regions, states, and countries. Only by establishing longer-term strategic alliances with end-users—both processors and consumers—can producers avoid some of the price volatility and manage the risk associated with these dynamic market changes. In the process, the global market economy will identify those farmers and production areas that can supply high-quality products for the lowest cost. In the final analysis, it will be the urban consumers, especially in the industrialized North, who will gain the most from globalization and trade liberalization.

Agricultural Diversification and Specialization in the Midwest

Since the mid-1970s, there has been a slow but growing trend in Illinois and elsewhere in the Midwest toward the production and marketing of value-enhanced farm products. Examples of value-enhanced crops include white and yellow food-grade corn, clear hilum food-grade soybeans for soymilk and tofu, waxy and high amylose corn for industrial uses, and high oil corn as a natural, high energy livestock feed. These crops are directed toward smaller, more demanding markets, which pay farmers a premium over and above what conventional markets pay. Also, as seed companies become more closely integrated with agricultural processing firms, private-sector plant breeders are developing new hybrids/varieties for specific end-use markets. Examples are value-enhanced soybeans, such as high oil, high protein, low saturated fat, high sucrose, low linolenic, high oleic, and high isoflavone soybeans.

Similar changes are under way within the livestock industry, but the pace of change is somewhat slower owing to the time, complexity, and expense involved in farmers shifting from standardized to customized livestock production. Some examples of value-enhanced livestock in the United States include Berkshire Gold pork (for export to Japan), Certified Angus Beef, Niman Ranch pork, and Laura's Lean Beef. Again, each of these products is destined for a targeted segment of the consumer market in major cities, with the prospect of higher prices for producers. Both Niman Ranch and Laura's Lean certify that their meat products are produced without the use of hormones or antibiotics. Also, some of these "branded meat products" require that animals be produced using humane and sustainable production methods. These value-enhanced livestock production systems have considerable potential for medium-scale farmers but, because of space and data limitations, only value-enhanced crops will be discussed in the remainder of this chapter.

An additional trend is seen in the groups of Illinois farmers who are pursuing new business models and practices, organizing into producer alliances and new generation cooperatives (NGCs) to market these value-enhanced crops and pursuing value-added processing. Through this trend, farmers who are interested in these new opportunities are becoming more "demand" rather than "supply" driven. If these current trends continue, both domestic and global markets will demand and contract for a growing array of differentiated agricultural products. Those producers or groups of producers who can identify these markets early, and who have a comparative advantage in producing and marketing these specialized farm products, will be able to capture and hold onto these new and emerging markets.

Bridging the Old and "New" Agriculture: The Illinois Value Project

Both the transformation of agriculture by global competition and the "industrialization" of farming have shifted the balance of advantage to producers who understand the "new consumer" and changing end-user demands. The movement toward value-enhanced crops and livestock is challenging Illinois producers to discover new ways of creating value within a rapidly changing agricultural structure. To assist them in this process, the Illinois Council for Food and Agricultural Research (C-FAR) created a special research initiative (SRI) to investigate alternative crops and other means of improving farm incomes and strengthening rural communities.

One of four projects funded under this SRI was the Value Project, which was designed to investigate the production and marketing of value-enhanced commodities and explore value-added processing opportunities. This project was begun in October 1998, with four basic components: (1) specialty crop marketing, (2) specialty crop technology, (3) pilot projects to develop and field-test an intervention strategy, and (4) assessment of producer network/

alliance possibilities. A fifth component, centered on value-enhanced live-stock, was initiated during the second year of the project. Using primary and secondary data sources, the project seeks to expand the development of value-enhanced production and marketing systems for Illinois farmers. The research approach and intervention strategy utilized by the Value Project is briefly described here.

Value-Enhanced Crop Market Identification

The first element examines market opportunities for producers of value-en-hanced crops. This involves identifying the types of value-enhanced crops available for planting in the state and identifying the markets that deal with various value-enhanced crops. The project's marketing component began by identifying markets across Illinois that were handling value-enhanced crops. A telephone survey was carried out among 1,100 Illinois grain handlers (firms or cooperatives) to identify the value-enhanced crops they were handling, the premiums paid, the additional costs of handling specialty grain, and the final market destination for each value-enhanced crop.

This survey, completed by 95 percent of the grain handlers contacted, revealed the scope of value-enhanced crop marketing in the state and the location of these markets. To increase the transparency of the value-enhanced crops marketing system, a specialty crop-marketing directory, *Illinois Specialty Corn and Soybean Handlers Directory—2000* (Good and Bender 2000), and a comprehensive marketing report, *Marketing Practices of Illinois Specialty Corn and Soybean Handlers* (Good and Bender 2001), were published and distributed to farmers and grain handlers. The directory lists markets, by county and type of value-enhanced crop. Before publication of this informa-tion, farmers either had to search out markets on their own or they had to rely on selling directly to a contractor. Given the highly dynamic nature of these markets, the location of specialty corn and soybean handlers is being up-dated annually. This information is published on the Internet at <http://web.aces.uiuc.edu/value/>, and it includes a searchable database. Maps 5.1 and 5.2 illustrate the types of maps that have been developed to show where a range of value-enhanced corn and soybean markets are located in the state.

Bridging the Knowledge Gap

Once the markets had been identified, the next step was to assess the farm-ers' knowledge about and experiences with these different crops. A survey of all farmers in five pilot project counties was carried out during the winter of 1999. It revealed that about 15–16 percent of farmers produced value-

Map 5.1 Value-Enhanced Corn Handlers in Illinois, 2001

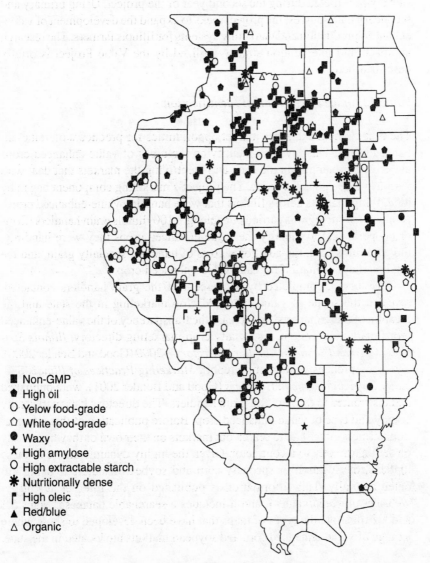

■ Non-GMP
⬟ High oil
○ Yelow food-grade
⌂ White food-grade
● Waxy
★ High amylose
○ High extractable starch
✳ Nutritionally dense
⌐ High oleic
▲ Red/blue
△ Organic

enhanced crops, but fewer than 5 percent of all respondents believed they had "sufficient information" on most value-enhanced crops (except for high-oil corn). Moreover, the vast majority said they wanted more information on specific value-enhanced crops. The next step was to develop and distribute a set of "fact sheets" on each type of value-enhanced corn and soybean.

When the Value Project was initiated, very little was known within the

Map 5.2   **Value-Enhanced Soybean Handlers in Illinois, 2001**

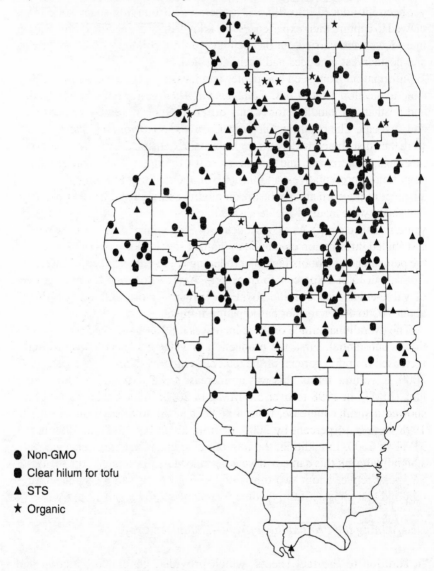

● Non-GMO
▮ Clear hilum for tofu
▲ STS
★ Organic

public research and extension systems about value-enhanced corn and soy-beans in Illinois or the Midwest. Providing this basic information became a high priority; therefore, the Value Project team compiled information from a variety of sources, mainly from private seed companies that were selling different types of value-enhanced crop seed and from innovative farmers who were already growing these crops. Because some of these crops had not yet been introduced into Illinois, farmers in surrounding states were interviewed to capture their experiences and knowledge for specific crops. Farmer interviews were carried out on each crop until a common set of production and postharvest practices had been identified.

Information from seed companies and farmers' experiences made it possible to develop a set of *best management practices* for both the production and postharvest handling for twenty different types of value-enhanced corn and soybean. The resulting *Specialty Corn and Soybean Fact Sheets* (2000) were then distributed widely through normal Extension Service channels (i.e., meetings, conferences, and the mass media), through commercial seed company field representatives, and through direct mailings to farmers under the auspices of the corn and soybean commodity associations. In addition, these fact sheets were made available via the Internet (see http://web.aces.uiuc.edu/value/Factsheets.pdf). As a consequence of expanding markets and the widely distributed information contained in the fact sheets, between 1998 and 2000 the percentage of Illinois farmers producing value-enhanced crops increased from about 15 or 16 percent to 24 percent. At the same time, the average area of value-enhanced corn and soybeans per farm more than doubled, from about 200 to 400 acres per participating farmer.

The overall magnitude of these increases in value-enhanced crop production is substantial. First, the production of value-enhanced corn in Illinois increased from 5.5 percent of the total crop in 1998 to about 15.5 percent in 2000. In volume terms, this was an increase from about 2.1 million metric tons (MMT) in 1998 to over 5.8 MMT in 2000. Value-enhanced soybeans showed a similar increase, from 4 percent of the total soybean acreage in 1998 to over 14 percent by 2000, or from about 0.7 MMT in 1998 to 2.3 MMT in 2000. In addition, the mix of value-enhanced crops changed substantially during this same two-year period. Most important, from the farmers' perspective, about two-thirds of those growing value-enhanced crops reported that their net farm income was increased by about 12 percent.

Determining the Profitability of Value-Enhanced Crops

In addition to the fact sheets, which provided general production and postharvest management information on each type of value-enhanced crop, it was important to determine the actual performance and profitability of these different crops relative to conventional elite hybrids, or varieties. Determining performance and profitability became the third element in the overall project. These comparisons were made by conducting a series of on-farm research trials in various eco-regions of the state. By design, these trials were to be farmer-managed strip plots "spatially replicated" within different eco-regions of Illinois. During 1999, nineteen trials were successfully completed, primarily in the west-central part of the state. In both 2000 and 2001, this number was increased to about seventy trials that covered those parts of Illinois that are best suited for value-enhanced corn and soybean production.

The results of these on-farm trials revealed that some value-enhanced crops are more profitable than conventional crops and some are less profitable, with significant eco-regional differences. These findings were displayed on the project's website (see http://web.aces.uiuc.edu/value/on-farm/default.htm), and current and prospective value-enhanced crop producers and grain handlers are using the results.

Integrating Data Using an Asset Mapping Methodology

The project team developed a unique "asset mapping" methodology to determine the comparative advantage of different eco-regions within the state for producing and marketing different types of value-enhanced crops. This analytical framework is based on the "SWOT analysis" (Strengths, Weaknesses, Opportunities, and Threats) technique that is commonly used in strategic planning. The first part of the SWOT analysis is to identify the important strengths and weaknesses in each eco-region of the state with respect to value-enhanced crop and livestock production. In general, we refer to these strengths as "strategic assets." These factors include agronomic conditions, proximity to existing markets, transportation infrastructure, on-farm resources (e.g., storage, low temperature drying capacity), human capital, and so forth. Weaknesses, in contrast, imply the absence of specific assets or conditions, which might be considered "strategic liabilities." For example, the on-farm research program has determined that food-grade corn productivity and profitability are much higher in central and southern Illinois in contrast with northern Illinois. The converse is true for food-grade soybeans grown for soymilk and tofu.

Identifying Strategic Opportunities in Domestic and International Markets

The second part of the analysis examined strategic opportunities (and threats) to current and potential value-enhanced markets. Initially, the research team identified market opportunities for each eco-region within the state by contacting the local grain handlers; however, given the growing impact of trade liberalization and the changing structure of agriculture, this part of the analysis is being expanded to include global opportunities in Asia, Europe, and Latin America for Illinois farmers, as well as the threats from growing competition for global markets currently being posed by countries such as Brazil and Argentina.

This expanded focus on both global market opportunities and threats will be a primary research thrust during the final years of the project. When examining strategic opportunities, the research team will identify specific quality traits or grain attributes that would be required by manufacturing firms or other end-users to increase processing efficiency and/or to improve food quality. In most cases, the primary focus will be to identify and assess the needs of small- to medium-scale processors in both domestic and international markets, especially those firms that might be interested in developing a strategic partnership with one or more producer groups, cooperatives, or alliances.

A second area of research will concentrate on a supply chain analysis that would consider the cost and capacity of alternative modes of transportation channels and the capacity of producers and grain handlers to provide identity preservation (IP) and product traceability. In both types of analysis, the goal is to make the demand for different types of value-enhanced farm products more transparent, while systematically detailing the most cost-efficient and effective means of transporting value-enhanced farm products from producers in different eco-regions within the state to end-users, both in the United States and overseas. In many cases, the combination of productivity and the efficiency of different transportation systems can determine comparative advantage.

Social Capital Formation: Getting Farmers Organized

Serving different niche markets for value-enhanced farm products in a timely and expeditious manner may entail the organization of producers into some type of cooperative or marketing alliance. One way of mobilizing farmers within an eco-region that has comparative advantage for particular types of value-enhanced products is to work through an experienced manager of a grain cooperative or group of cooperatives that have the facilities and capacity to consolidate and transport value-enhanced grain.

The imperative of producing value-enhanced crops to specification in a more coordinated way will likely require greater involvement and commitment on the part of the producers themselves. Getting them organized within an eco-region to serve specific markets can help to motivate, educate, and mobilize farmers to play a more active role in supplying end-use markets with high-quality, value-enhanced farm products. In short, if producers expect to capture more value from their farm products, they may have to play a more active role in producing what the market demands, in marketing their products, in reducing transaction costs, and in "shortening the value chain."

To capture more value from specialty farm products, farmers must relinquish some autonomy they now have in producing what they want and in the quality they choose. They will rely more on producer networks and alliances rather than on private grain merchandizing firms to look out for their economic interests. Though this will undoubtedly go against their customary way of operating the farm enterprise, many farmers in the Illinois Farm Survey have expressed an intellectual understanding of the need to produce for specific markets by "getting together with other farmers." The farmers' share of the "value" residing in value-enhanced farm products is likely to hinge on their working together as a buffer against the growing power of the large marketing firms and on their tailoring production to emerging needs.

Conclusion

Trade liberalization and free market economic policies have created a relatively new phenomenon commonly referred to as "globalization." It has and will continue to have a major effect on agriculture in most countries. Simultaneously, the structure of agriculture in the United States is changing as input suppliers, producers, and processors become more integrated. These trends are having a major impact on the agricultural economies of most nations.

Traditionally, farmers have produced for local markets and have not been concerned about where their crops or livestock products were eventually used or consumed; however, new market opportunities are emerging based on the specific demand requirements of consumers and/or end-use processors. These expanding "niche markets," both domestic and international, provide opportunities for many family-size farmers to exploit new comparative advantages in producing value-enhanced products to specification and for specific markets.

To take advantage of these new opportunities, farmers must become more active participants in the value chain. First, they need to know what products are needed, including products' specific quality traits and attributes. Second, they must know whether they have an inherent comparative advantage in producing these products relative to other potential suppliers. Third, they should learn the most efficient and effective means of supplying these niche markets. Fourth, they must obtain economies of scale by organizing into some type of marketing alliance or working through existing cooperatives, which can provide processors or consumers with a consistent supply of high-quality products.

Public research and extension can play a more active role in assisting farmers to participate more effectively in the emerging global economy. Research and extension teams can help to identify and assess the relative comparative advantage that different regions in the state and various types of farmers might have in supplying value-enhanced products for niche markets. To carry out this analysis, teams should systematically assess the strategic assets that farmers in different eco-regions may have in producing different value-enhanced crop and livestock products; and they must assess emerging market opportunities for value-enhanced farm products. Where research and extension organizations take on these new responsibilities and challenges, they will be able to play an instrumental role in making farmers more competitive in the emerging global economy and, in the process, will improve farmers' prospects for higher farm income.

Notes

1. Eco-regions reflect both the *eco*logical or agronomic conditions in different parts of the state that affect the productivity of different value-enhanced crops, plus the *eco*nomic factors (e.g., existing markets, processors, transportation costs, and so forth) that affect the market demand and profitability of different value-enhanced crops or enterprises.

2. *Cerrado* is the Brazilian Portuguese word for "closed, inaccessible wasteland." According to AgBrazil (2002), "Until the early 1970s that was a good description; the cerrado was literally an inaccessible, useless wasteland. Brazil's cerrado is considered the largest virgin landmass on earth."

References

AgBrazil, LLC. 2002. *Brazil's frontier.* Available on-line: <www.agbrazil.com/the_vast_wasteland.htm >. Downloaded: April 2, 2002.

AgLink. 2001. Creating a "new Midwest." *AGWEEK Online.* Available on-line: <www.agweek.com>.

Agricultural and technology. 2000. *The Economist* (March 25): 3–16.

Agriculture, horticulture and fisheries market in Brazil. 2001. *Brazilian Profile.* Available on-line: <www.tradepartners.gov.uk/agriculrture/brazil/profile/overview.shtml>.

Albrecht, Don E. 1997. The changing structure of U.S. agriculture: Dualism out, industrialism in. *Rural Sociology* 62: 474–490.

Behling, Ann. 1998. Commodity clips. *Soybean Digest* (August/September): 51.

Boehlje, Michael, and Lee Schrader. 1996. Agriculture in the 21st century. *Journal of Production Agriculture* 9(3): 335–341.

Brazil hopes to grow pork numbers, exports. 1998. *Successful Farming Online.* Available on-line: <www.agriculture.com/sfonline/sf/1998/march>.

Brazil may export beef to the U.S. in 2000. 2000. *Feed Lot Magazine Online VII*(6). Available on-line: <www.feedlotmagazine.com/issues/199911>.

Buelens, Frans. 1999. Globalisation and the nation-state: An introduction. In *Globalisation and the Nation-State,* ed. Frans Buelens. Cheltenham, UK: Edward Elgar.

Cargill website. n.d. Available on-line: <www.cargill.com/prodserv/country/bbrazil.htm>.

Castle, Emery. 1998. *Agricultural Industrialization in the American Countryside..* Greenbelt, MD: Henry Wallace Institute. Available on-line: <www.hawiaa.org/psprll.htm>.

Coffey, Joseph. 1993. Implications for farm supply cooperatives on industrialization of agriculture. *American Journal of Agricultural Economics* 75 (December): 1132–1136.

Cook, Michael. 1995. The future of agricultural cooperatives: A neo-institutional approach. *American Journal of Agricultural Economics* 77 (December): 1153–1159.

Gilles, Jere Lee, and Michael Dalecki. 1988. Rural well-being and agricultural change in two farming regions. *Rural Sociology* 53 (Spring): 40–55.

Gilmore, James H., and B. Joseph Pine III. 1997. The four-faces of mass customization. *Harvard Business Review* 75 (January–February): 91–101.

Good, Darrel, and Karen Bender. 2000. *Illinois Specialty Corn and Soybean Handlers Directory* (AE-4734). Urbana-Champaign: Department of Agricultural and Consumer Economics, College of Agricultural, Consumer and Environmental Sciences, University of Illinois at Urbana-Champaign.

————. 2001. *Marketing Practices of Illinois Specialty Corn and Soybean Handlers* (AE 4743). Urbana–Champaign: Department of Agricultural and Consumer Economics, College of Agricultural, Consumer, and Environmental Sciences, University of Illinois at Urbana–Champaign.

Halweil, Brian. 2000. Where have all the farmers gone? *World Watch* 13 (September/October): 12–28.

Huffman, Wallace. 1998. Modernizing agriculture: A continuing process. *Daedalus* 4: 159–186.

Husar, Deborah Gertz. 1999. Area farmers gaining new ally? *The Quincy Herald Whig* (March 15): 1A–2A.

Innovation in industry. 1999. *The Economist* (February 20): 5–27

Kinsey, Jean. 1994. Changes in food consumption from mass markets to niche markets. In *Food and Agricultural Markets: The Quiet Revolution* (NPA Report No. 270). Ed. Lyle Schertz and Lynn Daft. Washington, DC: National Planning Association.

Klechner, Dean. 1999. The importance of a new trade round for America's farmers. *Economic Perspectives* (USIA Electronic Journal) 4(2).

Pollan, Stephen, and Mark Levine. 1998. *Die Broke: A Radical, Four-Part Financial Plan.* New York: Harper Business.

Ray, Daryll, and the Agricultural Policy Analysis. 2000. *Are Multinationals Now the Stealth of Brazil's Agricultural Expansion?* Knoxville: Agricultural Policy Analysis, University of Tennessee. Available on-line: <http://agpolicy.org/WeeklyCols/020–BrazilSoybeans3Stealth.htm>.

Rhodes, James. 1993. Industrialization of agriculture: Discussion. *American Journal of Agricultural Economics* 5: 1137–1139.

Rich, Jennifer. 2001. U.S. farmers look back . . . and see soy growers in Brazil shadowing them. *New York Times* (July 10): Sec. C, 1.

Siebert, Jerome. 2001. *The Role of Bargaining Cooperatives in a Global Market Economy* (Working Paper Series, 10). Davis: University of California Center for Co-op.

Specialty Corn and Soybean Fact Sheets (AD-4736). 2000. Urbana–Champaign: Department of Agricultural and Consumer Economics, College of Agricultural, Consumer, and Environmental Sciences, University of Illinois at Urbana-Champaign.

Torgerson, Randall C., Bruce J. Reynolds, and Thomas W. Gray. 1997. Evolution of cooperative thought, theory, and purpose. In *Cooperatives: Their Importance in the Future Food and Agricultural System*, ed. Michael Cook, Randall Torgerson, Tom Sporleder, and Dan Padberg, 3–20. Gainesville: University of Florida.

U.S. Department of State. 2001. *Background note: Brazil, Bureau of Western Hemisphere Affairs*. Available on-line: <www.state.gov/r/pa/bgnindex.cfm?docid=1972>.

Urban, Thomas. 1991. Agricultural industrialization: It's inevitable. *Choices* (4th quarter): 4–6.

Welsh, Rick. 1997. Vertical coordination, producer response, and the locus of control over agricultural production decisions. *Rural Sociology* 64(2): 491–507.

Wolf, Martin. 2001. Will the nation-state survive globalization. *Foreign Affairs* (January/February): 178–190.

6

KIMBERLY A. ZEULI AND STEVEN C. DELLER

The Role of Agriculture in the Midwest Economy

Agriculture continues to play an important, albeit no longer dominant, role in the Midwest economy. Structural change in the U.S. economy in general, and in rural America in particular, has clearly minimized the economic significance of production agriculture, although the extent of this decline has not yet been fully measured (Walzer and Deller 1996). This chapter explores the connection between agriculture and local economic growth in the Midwest, attempting, where possible, to quantify that relationship. A current and accurate accounting of the changing impact that agriculture has on local rural economies is essential for understanding where agriculture and rural towns are headed and for choosing appropriate local development policies.

On average, production agriculture now accounts for a relatively marginal percentage of local economic activity in most Midwestern counties (see chapter 2). Care must be taken, however, in interpreting this result. Economic dependence on agriculture varies greatly across counties. Although aggregate trends and average statistics are important, they can hide the realities experienced by specific local economies. Indeed, the social and economic diversity of rural America has been well-documented (Bender et al. 1985).

The chapter begins with an analysis of agricultural and local economic growth trends across the Midwest, exploring the variations in results apparent at the county, state, and regional levels. Building on the work of a team of researchers organized by the Rural Policy Research Institute (RUPRI) at the University of Missouri, we drew a sample of Midwestern counties to examine in this chapter. The larger RUPRI project on which some of the work in this chapter is based is designed to provide local case studies that document the impact of alternative policy options being discussed in the current national Farm Bill debate. It is important to note that some of the counties were selected to include federal representatives directly engaged in the construction of the Farm Bill. Although one could argue that the sample of counties is not truly random, the diversity of the counties analyzed is sufficient to draw several important observations (see Tables 6.3 through 6.5, pages 122–124, for a listing of the counties used for this chapter).

The accompanying discussion centers on whether the declining relative share of agriculture in local economic activity can be interpreted as a consequence of growth in other sectors. In other words, has the actual impact of agriculture been, in fact, stagnant, or even growing slowly, or has it just been surpassed by other rapidly expanding sectors such as recreational services?

A snapshot account of agriculture's direct and indirect economic impact in the Midwest during 1998 provides greater insight into the current link between agriculture and local economic growth. Social accounting matrices were constructed for the sample of Midwestern counties using 1998 IMPLAN data sets. The results for household income, value-added income, and gross output (or industry sales) are analyzed. The social accounting analysis does not, however, convey the significance of the substantial federal dollars that agriculture brings into local economies. This issue is addressed in a separate and subsequent section.

Predictions for agriculture's role in future economic growth complete the chapter. These forecasts are made within a broader discussion of the impact of structural change within the agricultural sector. Once supported by numerous small-scale family farms, most rural counties now house relatively few agricultural enterprises; a few large commercial farms coexist with some small, off-farm income-dependent operations. Walter Goldschmidt's (1947) pioneering research suggested that the demise of the family farm doomed rural towns. Fifty years later, the data are inconclusive. This issue is revisited throughout the chapter.

Trends in Agriculture and Local Economic Growth

The health of the rural economy has been very cyclical during the past thirty years. Periods of vitality in the 1970s and 1990s bookmarked a decade of decline starting in the late 1970s through the farm crises of the 1980s. Rural areas were generally vibrant as they headed into the twenty-first century and were able to retain rural residents. The total population in the Midwest has risen fairly steadily since 1958, although not as great as in the nation as a whole. As Lasley and Hanson point out in chapter 2, rural areas lag behind urban areas in terms of population growth.

Population growth in Midwestern states varied widely during the past four decades. North Dakota and Iowa have realized very little growth (6% and 8%, respectively), while Oklahoma and Minnesota were more on par with the nation (52% and 49%, respectively). Population statistics for the sample

Table 6.1
Trends in Income for the Midwest

	1960	1965	1970	1975	1980	1985	1990	1995	2000
				As Share of Total Income					
Farm Income	4.5	4.3	3.2	3.7	0.9	1.3	1.	0.5	0.7
Food and Kindred Product Income	2.9	2.4	2.2	1.9	1.8	1.4	1.3	1.3	1.1
				In Real Dollars					
Per Capita Income Growth Index	100.8	119.3	134.5	149.1	170.2	186.4	207.9	224.4	256.4
Total Income Growth Index	103.1	127.9	150.7	171.1	199.5	219.1	247.5	279.2	329.8
Farm Income Growth Index	78.3	94.1	81.2	107.4	29.2	48.4	54.4	25.0	38.7
Food and Kindred Product Growth Index	99.0	103.8	112.2	109.0	117.1	104.8	109.3	117.0	124.6

Source: USDC, Bureau of Economic Analysis, Regional Economic Information System.

of Midwestern counties reveal a more mixed picture regarding total population growth. Between 1969 and 2000, ten counties reported population declines, with Decatur County, Kansas, reporting the most significant decline at 31.5 percent. The remaining counties showed population growth, with some more than doubling their population (e.g., Platte County, Missouri, and Finney County, Kansas).

Trends in income for the Midwest during roughly the same period are summarized in Table 6.1. Per capita and total incomes in the Midwest have been steadily growing in real terms since 1960 (the base year is actually 1958). Real per capita income has more than doubled, while total income has more than tripled. Income derived from food and kindred products has also achieved steady, but slow, growth, whereas growth of farm income has been highly variable, peaking in 1973 but slowing to a crawl in 1983.

Clearly, as a share of total income, farm income and food and kindred product income have both steadily decreased over time. It is interesting to note, however, that even in 1960, farm income accounted for less than 5 percent of total income, suggesting that, relatively speaking, agriculture has not been a significant factor in rural economic growth for several decades.

In actuality, the regional statistics hide important state variations in farm income dependence and decline (space limitations prevent reporting data for

Table 6.2
Employment Statistics for Select Midwestern Counties, 1999

	Percent of Employment	
County, State	Farming and Agricultural Services	Total Employment Increase 1969–1999
Audubon, Iowa	22.1	(15.4)
Fayette, Iowa	13.5	13.7
Webster, Iowa	4.4	8.3
Decatur, Kansas	27.0	(13.3)
Finney, Kansas	5.6	205.1
Sumner, Kansas	10.6	31.5
Macon, Missouri	15.6	27.9
McDonald, Missouri	16.8	92.4
Pemiscot, Missouri	8.2	(5.7)
Platte, Missouri	3.5	260.0
Saline, Missouri	8.8	19.3
Custer, Nebraska	27.9	3.7
Scots Bluff, Nebraska	6.4	37.8
Thurston, Nebraska	14.7	13.5
York, Nebraska	7.6	87.1
Darke, Ohio	9.4	53.8
Fulton, Ohio	4.3	70.7
Morgan, Ohio	11.1	26.1
Wayne, Ohio	5.3	73.4
Bryan, Oklahoma	10.4	119.5
Jackson, Oklahoma	9.4	14.5
Washita, Oklahoma	25.1	(38.8)
Dane, Wisconsin	2.3	28.9
Lincoln, Wisconsin	4.0	70.5
St. Croix, Wisconsin	6.1	196.9
United States	3.2	79.8

Source: USDC, Bureau of Economic Analysis, Regional Economic Information System

individual states). For instance, in 1960, farm income as a percentage of total income was roughly 24 percent and 22 percent, respectively, in South Dakota and North Dakota. By 2000, these ratios had tumbled to 6 percent and 4 percent, respectively, with extreme declines occurring between 1975 and 1980. Still, the farm income to total income ratio in those two states, as well as in Iowa, Kansas, Nebraska, and Oklahoma, remains higher today than for the entire region (less than 1 percent).

Employment statistics for the sample counties generally reveal total employment growth between 1969 and 1999, but with relatively few jobs remaining in farming and agricultural services by 1999 (Table 6.2). Again, these trends vary greatly among the counties. Dramatic increases in total

Map 6.1 **Estimate of the Number of Farms by County, Based on the 1997 Agricultural Census**

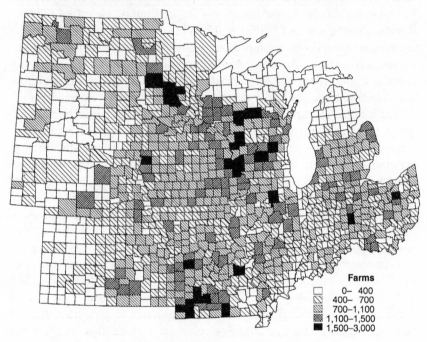

Source: U.S. Consolidated Federal Funds Report, Fiscal Year 2000.

employment growth (more than 100%) occurred in several counties. Platte County, Missouri, for example, experienced a 260 percent increase in employment. Other counties reported a declining employment; Washita County, Oklahoma, for instance, lost nearly 40 percent. By comparison, national employment growth during that period was not quite 80 percent.

Although a county-by-county discussion of why some sample counties grew while others declined is beyond the scope of this chapter, a discussion of this sample may provide some insight into the changing structure of the rural Midwest. St. Croix County, Wisconsin, for example, is located on the Wisconsin–Minnesota border and has historically been considered a farming region. Starting about twenty years ago, the growth of the Minneapolis–St. Paul area encroached into the western part of St. Croix County. Once considered on the far outer fringes of the Twin Cities, St. Croix County is now part of the Twin Cities metropolitan area. Though the vast majority of land area in eastern and central St. Croix County remains in production agriculture, the economic growth associated with the suburbanization of western St. Croix County has dominated the overall structure of the county's economy.

Dividing employment into major sectors shows that farming and agricultural services represent a relatively small proportion in nearly all of the counties (see Table 6.2). A few counties—Custer County, Nebraska (27.9%); Decatur County, Kansas (27.0%); and Washita County, Oklahoma (25.1%)—are notable exceptions. Washita County is especially interesting because it experienced such a substantial decline in total employment; this may suggest that it was always heavily dependent on agricultural jobs and, therefore, was significantly impacted by declines in the agricultural sector.

The national average for employment dependency on production agriculture is 3.2 percent, lower than every county in the sample except Dane County, Wisconsin, which is home to the state government and the University of Wisconsin–Madison. Even with the state capital and the university, Dane County remains one of the largest agricultural production counties in the United States. In 1997, it ranked number 74 of 3,076 U.S. counties for total value of agricultural products sold and in the top 20 for livestock sales. As in many Midwestern counties, however, a viable agricultural sector is overshadowed by other economic activities.

Farm numbers in the Midwest and the United States continue to decline. In 1999, numerous Midwestern counties had fewer than 400 farms (Map 6.1). Counties with more than 1,500 farms were, and are becoming increasingly, scarce. The consolidation and industrialization of agriculture has not, however, resulted in a disruption of commodity production levels, which have remained fairly constant with some commodity production actually increasing. Sales and earnings on a per farm basis have also grown during the past thirty years (Figure 6.1 on page 120), demonstrating that fewer farms are generating more sales and income.[1]

This trend raises the old Goldschmidt (1947) question, "Do fewer farms matter in terms of rural economic health?" Mapping simple growth indices for total employment, farm employment, nonfarm employment, and number of farm proprietors (a proxy for number of farms) for all rural areas in the United States shows a weak link between a declining farm sector and rural economic growth (Figure 6.2 on page 121).

In a majority of the thirty years examined, the farm and nonfarm rural economy appear to have moved in opposite directions, at least in terms of employment growth. The divide is most apparent and persistent from about 1983 to 2001. The idea of a weak relationship between agriculture and rural economic growth is further supported by the declining, and currently very small, farm income to total income ratio in the Midwest. Although this issue will be addressed more fully in a later section, the analysis presented thus far suggests that declining farm numbers may have little negative economic impact on rural areas.

Figure 6.1   **Sales and Earnings per Farm, 1969–1998**

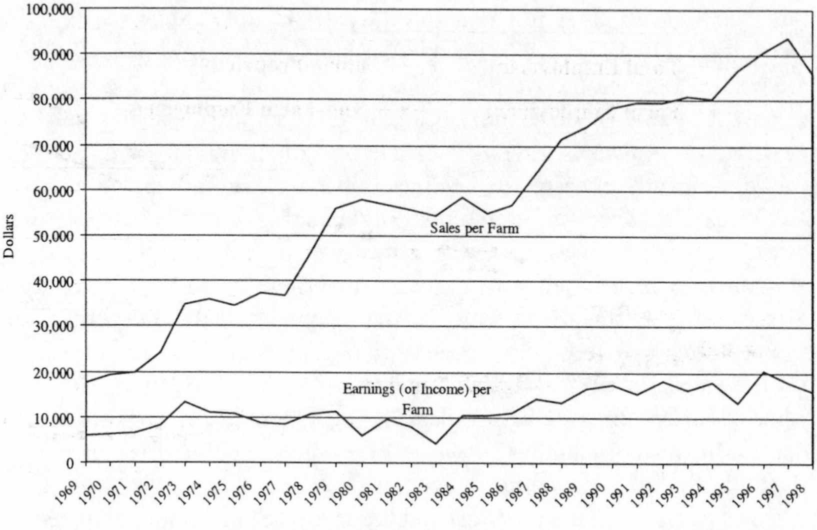

Source: USDC, Bureau of Economic Analysis, Regional Economic Information System.

Agriculture's Economic Impact

Agriculture impacts local economies directly through sales, wages, and employment, and indirectly when this money cycles through the economy. Money flowing directly from agriculture can be used to purchase goods and services from local businesses, which, in turn, spend their profits, perpetuating the cycle. These economic transactions can be tracked using a social accounting matrix (SAM); SAMs were constructed and analyzed for the sample counties using 1998 IMPLAN data sets. Using the SAM framework not only identifies the direct contributions of production agriculture to the local economy but also the indirect effects associated with economic multipliers.

The results for three measures of economic activity—(1) household income, (2) value-added income, which is akin to gross domestic product (GDP) at the local level, and (3) gross output or industry sales—are presented in Tables 6.3 through 6.5. The results correspond to the impacts from the county's transactions with local and nonlocal entities—the sale of locally produced goods and services to entities inside and outside the county and the nonlocal income received by households within the county.

Figure 6.2 **Rural Employment Growth Index Comparison, 1969–1998**

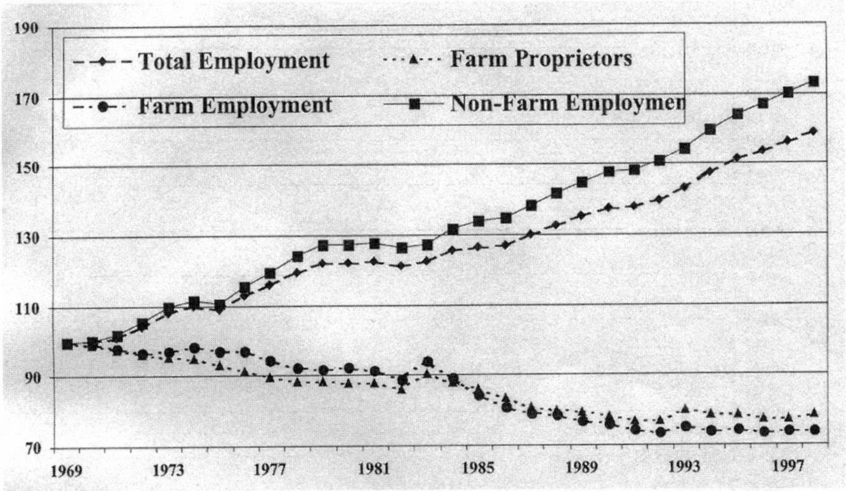

Source: USDC, Bureau of Economic Analysis, Regional Economic Information System.

Value-added, or GDP, represents the sum of employee compensation, proprietors' income, other property income, and indirect business taxes generated exclusively through economic activity within the county. Gross output, or sales, corresponds to the sales in the county associated with nonlocal consumers (i.e., nonlocal demand) as well as the income received by county households from nonlocal sources.

Each table (or measure) contains four sources for income and output: (1) production agriculture, (2) other goods producing, (3) service producing, and (4) nonlocal. *Other goods producing* includes construction and manufacturing industries (manufacturing includes food processing). *Service producing* accounts for government industries; services; finance, insurance, and real estate industries; trade and transportation; communications; and public utilities. The *nonlocal* category consists of income from government transfers (e.g., Social Security benefits and pensions), nonlocal government employee earnings, dividends from investments, and income from commuters.

On average for the entire sample, production agriculture represents 7 percent of the total household income generated in each county; nonlocal sales of

Table 6.3
Sources of Household Income for Select Midwestern Counties, 2000

County, State	Production Agriculture	Other Goods Producing	Service Producing	Nonlocal
	Percent of Household Income			
Audubon, Iowa	23.2	8.8	19.3	48.7
Fayette, Iowa	15.5	15.5	16.6	52.4
Webster, Iowa	5.3	29.2	23.0	42.5
Decatur, Kansas	22.5	4.4	17.4	55.8
Finney, Kansas	1.8	41.2	22.2	34.9
Sumner, Kansas	5.1	15.4	14.4	65.1
Macon, Missouri	5.4	21.5	22.5	50.6
McDonald, Missouri	0.7	35.1	9.7	54.6
Pemiscot, Missouri	5.0	9.4	21.0	64.6
Platte, Missouri	0.8	13.7	40.0	45.5
Saline, Missouri	3.0	26.7	17.0	53.4
Custer, Nebraska	26.3	10.3	13.6	49.8
Scots Bluff, Nebraska	6.2	17.4	28.1	48.4
Thurston, Nebraska	13.5	12.1	26.8	47.6
York, Nebraska	10.3	21.5	28.6	39.5
Darke, Ohio	4.6	31.1	14.1	50.3
Fulton, Ohio	2.5	49.2	14.8	33.5
Morgan, Ohio	3.5	31.9	21.5	43.1
Wayne, Ohio	1.8	42.8	17.8	37.6
Bryan, Oklahoma	2.1	14.8	22.2	60.9
Jackson, Oklahoma	3.0	10.0	47.3	39.7
Washita, Oklahoma	10.7	10.0	17.4	61.9
Dane, Wisconsin	0.8	20.8	48.0	30.3
Lincoln, Wisconsin	1.3	36.0	19.7	43.0
St. Croix, Wisconsin	1.5	25.1	13.3	60.2
Average for Sample	**7.0**	**22.2**	**22.2**	**48.6**

Source: USDC, Bureau of Economic Analysis, Regional Economic Information System

county-produced agricultural products account for roughly 13 percent of each county's value-added income and about 16 percent of the local economy's gross output. Production agriculture is a fairly minor source of household income, which is primarily derived from nonlocal sources (49%); other goods and services share the remaining income stream with about 20 percent each.

Within value-added income, production agriculture and nonlocal sources account for roughly the same percentage (13% and 15%, respectively), with the other two categories again accounting for equal parts of the remaining income. The story is similar for gross output, although with this measure, other goods production (e.g., mining, construction, and manufacturing) represents the lion's share of income (about 48%).

Table 6.4
Sources of Value-Added Income (Gross Domestic Product) for Select Midwestern Counties, 2000

| County, State | Percent of Value-Added Income | | | |
	Production Agriculture	Other Goods Producing	Service Producing	Nonlocal
Audubon, Iowa	40.0	14.9	33.0	12.1
Fayette, Iowa	26.4	27.1	28.8	17.7
Webster, Iowa	8.1	44.9	33.5	13.5
Decatur, Kansas	43.1	7.8	31.5	17.6
Finney, Kansas	2.7	56.8	30.3	10.2
Sumner, Kansas	13.7	32.7	32.5	21.0
Macon, Missouri	9.4	39.2	38.7	12.7
McDonald, Missouri	1.4	65.9	18.4	14.3
Pemiscot, Missouri	12.4	20.7	46.6	20.2
Platte, Missouri	1.3	21.2	65.1	12.4
Saline, Missouri	5.6	48.3	29.0	17.1
Custer, Nebraska	44.8	16.9	22.8	15.5
Scots Bluff, Nebraska	9.6	27.0	45.7	17.8
Thurston, Nebraska	24.9	21.3	43.2	10.6
York, Nebraska	15.5	30.4	43.2	10.9
Darke, Ohio	7.8	52.8	24.4	15.0
Fulton, Ohio	3.6	67.8	20.9	7.7
Morgan, Ohio	4.4	47.9	42.0	5.8
Wayne, Ohio	2.4	61.7	25.5	10.4
Bryan, Oklahoma	3.9	29.1	42.3	24.7
Jackson, Oklahoma	4.3	15.0	71.3	9.4
Washita, Oklahoma	22.3	21.2	34.8	21.7
Dane, Wisconsin	1.2	26.4	63.0	9.4
Lincoln, Wisconsin	2.6	54.4	31.0	11.9
St. Croix, Wisconsin	3.5	48.1	26.4	22.1
Average for Sample	**12.6**	**36.0**	**37.0**	**14.5**

Perhaps more important than the average level of economic activity created via production agriculture is the significant variation in the importance of agriculture across the sample of Midwestern counties. For instance, the impact of production agriculture is most significant in Custer County, Nebraska (26% of household income, 45% of value-added income, and 56% of gross output; see Tables 6.3 through 6.5); however, production agriculture has little impact in places such as McDonald County, Missouri, and Finney County, Kansas. Production agriculture in each of these two counties contributes 2 percent of household income, 3 percent of value-added income, and 4 percent of gross output.

The rural Midwest is no longer composed of homogeneous farming. In some

Table 6.5
Sources of Gross Output (Industry Sales) for Select Midwestern Counties, 2000

	Percent of Gross Output			
County, State	Production Agriculture	Other Goods Producing	Service Producing	Nonlocal
Audubon, Iowa	47.5	20.4	23.3	8.8
Fayette, Iowa	27.8	38.0	20.8	13.5
Webster, Iowa	7.8	59.3	23.3	9.5
Decatur, Kansas	55.3	9.6	22.1	13.0
Finney, Kansas	3.3	79.3	12.8	4.6
Sumner, Kansas	13.0	44.8	25.4	16.8
Macon, Missouri	9.1	52.6	28.1	10.1
McDonald, Missouri	2.7	81.2	8.7	7.4
Pemiscot, Missouri	19.6	32.3	33.4	14.8
Platte, Missouri	1.6	27.5	59.4	11.5
Saline, Missouri	7.0	66.1	16.5	10.4
Custer, Nebraska	56.0	19.7	14.7	9.6
Scots Bluff, Nebraska	13.6	39.4	34.1	12.9
Thurston, Nebraska	29.9	34.7	28.3	7.1
York, Nebraska	20.9	37.6	33.4	8.1
Darke, Ohio	11.8	62.1	15.8	10.3
Fulton, Ohio	4.2	76.7	13.5	5.6
Morgan, Ohio	2.3	69.1	24.9	3.7
Wayne, Ohio	3.0	73.7	16.1	7.3
Bryan, Oklahoma	3.3	47.1	30.6	18.9
Jackson, Oklahoma	7.0	31.1	53.1	8.7
Washita, Oklahoma	33.5	26.2	24.5	15.8
Dane, Wisconsin	2.1	36.4	52.7	8.8
Lincoln, Wisconsin	4.5	63.5	22.8	9.2
St. Croix, Wisconsin	5.8	59.5	19.0	15.7
Average for Sample	**15.7**	**47.5**	**26.3**	**10.5**

counties, such as Dane County, Wisconsin, significant agricultural production is overshadowed by other economic activities. In other counties, production agriculture remains the backbone of the local economy. The blanket statement that rural areas should no longer be equated with production agriculture obviously cannot be used in reference to all rural counties in the Midwest; however, of the Midwestern counties examined here, only seven received more than 10 percent of total household income from production agriculture.

The Impact of Federal Funds

Regardless of the measure of economic activity examined, agriculture may retain its local economic significance because of the substantial federal dollars

Figure 6.3 **Federal Government Payment Patterns to Farmers, 1969–1998**

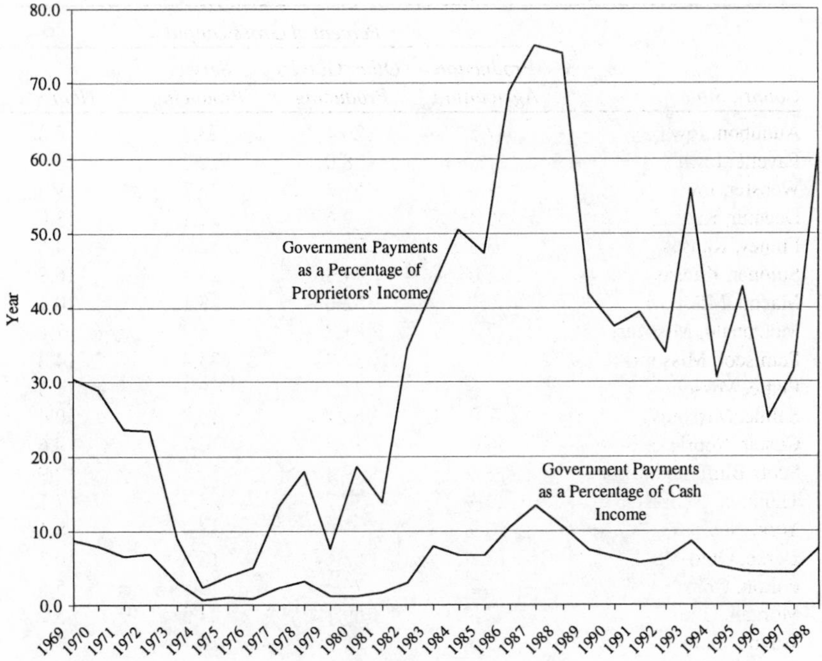

Source: USDC, Bureau of Economic Analysis, Regional Economic Information System.

spent on it. Traditional community economic development policy states that in addition to the promotion of export-based industries, such as production agriculture, strategies aimed at attracting dollars taxed away by higher units of government should be considered. These strategies range from the attraction of retirees to seeking investments in state and federal projects. Production agriculture is uniquely positioned to pursue this standard economic development policy.

For decades, a range of federal price support and tax programs aimed at keeping farming profitable has created an additional income source for farmers. Regardless of the specific program, direct and indirect payments to farmers usually result. Although many of these programs have been greatly scaled back or completely eliminated during the past decade, government transfer payments to farmers were nearly as great in 1998 as during the farm crisis of the 1980s (Figure 6.3). Many of these programs, including today's political tendency to move to direct subsidies, have been widely criticized as favoring larger farms at the expense of small, family farms (Gardner 2000; Gebremedhin and Christy 1996).

Map 6.2 **USDA Fiscal Year 2000 Total Direct Aid and Grants, County Totals**

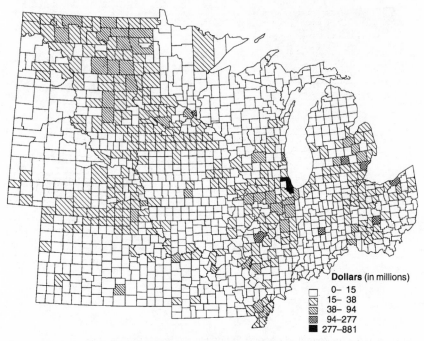

Source: U.S. Consolidated Federal Funds Report, Fiscal Year 2000.

A snapshot of U.S. Department of Agriculture (USDA) direct payments and grants in the Midwest by county for FY 2000 is provided in Maps 6.2 and 6.3. Direct spending includes payments to individuals, institutions, and enterprises. There are three major categories of direct payments: (1) farm-related (e.g., production stabilization, disaster payments, loan deficiency payments, etc.), (2) nutrition and family assistance (e.g., food stamps, school nutrition programs, etc.), and (3) all other USDA payments (e.g., rural housing, infrastructure, research, etc.) (Swenson and Eathington 2001). Direct payments do not include government loans.

In FY 2000, the USDA made $54.7 billion in direct payments and grants (Swenson and Eathington 2001). Of this total, 40 percent ($21.9 billion) of the payments were farm-related, 55 percent ($29.8 billion) supported nutrition and family assistance, and 5 percent ($2.97 billion) went for all other types of USDA programs. The average amount of farm-related payments to each farm in the Midwest is significant by any measure for several counties. The highest per farm payments ($51,000 to $220,000) were concentrated in North Dakota counties. Most counties across the Midwest received payments of less than

Map 6.3 **USDA Direct Aid and Grants to Farms, per Farm, Fiscal Year 2000**

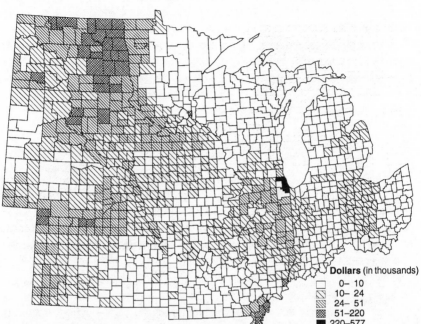

Dollars (in thousands)
- 0– 10
- 10– 24
- 24– 51
- 51–220
- 220–577

Source: U.S. Consolidated Federal Funds Report, Fiscal Year 2000.

$10,000 per farm. The per farm, county-level average for the entire United States was slightly less than $13,500 (Swenson and Eathington 2001).

Although USDA payments to local residents can represent significant injections of new dollars into the local economy, these programs introduce certain difficulties from the perspective of the local economy. First, the payments are seldom stable from one year to the next and, to a great extent, depend on the politics of Washington, D.C. During the mid- to late-1990s, the popular notion of "Freedom to Farm" greatly reduced the number of dollars flowing back into rural areas. Political pressure to reduce the federal deficit, coupled with a strong agricultural economy during the discussion of the 1995 Farm Bill, set the stage for significant reductions in support programs. Today, however, there is significant political pressure to turn the clock back on the notion of Freedom to Farm and return to traditional commodity support programs.

In addition to the instability introduced by these federal payments into the local economy, these payments also create uncertainty within the farming community. Sound business decisions require that business owners identify risks and minimize the uncertainties associated with those risks; however, unstable federal programs introduce a large degree of uncertainty, making sound long-term business decisions at the farm level difficult. Finally, to what extent do these federal payments to individual farms introduce market distortions and encourage marginal farm business enterprises to remain in operation? From an economic efficiency perspective, should all marginal farms remain in operation due to "random" federal policies? Federal programs administered through the USDA can represent significant economic gain for many rural communities, but the question remains, at what cost?

Agriculture's Role in Future Economic Growth

The continued restructuring of U.S. agricultural production will clearly impact the growth paths of rural counties. To gain further insight into the role of production agriculture in local economic growth, a simple neoclassical model of economic growth is specified and estimated. We pose the question within the broader regional economic debate surrounding the issue of convergence (Barro and Sala-i-Martin 1992).

The neoclassical theory of regional economic growth suggests that diverse regions should tend to converge over time. The growth of poorer regions should be sufficiently higher than richer regions, causing poorer regions to catch up to richer regions. In other words, over time, differences in economic well-being across regions should diminish and regions should converge. Based on the extensive work of Barro and others, the prevailing empirical evidence suggests that the predictions of neoclassical growth theory are valid for the United States and many other developed nations.

The empirical test for convergence within the framework of neoclassical growth theory is relatively straightforward. Regression analysis is typically used, with the measure of convergence being the growth rate in per capita income from one period (e.g., year) to the next. The key independent variable is lagged per capita income, or per capita income at the beginning of the period.

Typically, other independent variables of interest include economic structure, socioeconomic characteristics of the local government, and government policy measures. If the regression coefficient on lagged per capita income is negative and statistically significant, then the analysis is said to support the central hypothesis of convergence. In other words, regions with higher per capita income levels at the beginning of the time period examined tend to have slower growth rates. Poorer regions, as measured by per capita income, tend to grow faster, hence, catching up to richer regions.

In this analysis, we ask three basic questions within the structure of the neoclassical economic growth model: (1) Are regions (counties) in the Midwest converging over time as predicted by the theory of neoclassical growth? (2) Does local economic dependency on farming affect the levels of economic growth as measured by per capita income? (3) Does the size and type of farm enterprises influence economic growth? This latter question goes to the idea that the transition of small "family farms" to larger farms hinders the economic growth of rural areas.

Data to estimate the model of economic growth come from the BEA-REIS (San Diego Economic Information and Modeling Project 2002). Annual economic data for all Midwestern counties from 1969 to 1998 was combined into a pooled-time series sample of 27,462 observations. Six simple regression models were estimated, one for each measure of agricultural production. The dependent variable in each model is the annual growth rate in county per capita income over all counties in the Midwest region. Each regression included the following independent variables: lagged per capita income, lagged population (to capture scale effects), a binomial dividing the data into two time periods (pre- and post-1980, a recognized short-term shift in convergence patterns in the United States occurred at that time), and a binomial dividing the data into metro and nonmetro counties.

The regressions vary by the inclusion of six different farm measures (each introduced individually into the base model and each lagged): (1) share of farm employment, (2) share of farm income, (3) value-added per farm, (4) cash income per farm, (5) hired labor expenditure per farm, and (6) hired labor expenditure as a share of cash income. The share of total income and employment from farming is intended to measure the overall dependency of the local (county) economy on production agriculture.

Farm size is proxied by value-added and cash income per farm. If the broadly interpreted Goldschmidt (1947) hypothesis is correct, larger farms should dampen economic growth. Hired labor expenditures per farm and as a share of cash income are also intended to proxy larger farm structures. Larger "corporate" farms tend to have a higher share of their work conducted by hired labor as opposed to members of the farm family.

The regression analysis results provide significant insight into our central policy questions (Table 6.6). First, the negative and statistically significant coefficient on lagged per capita income confirms the neoclassical prediction of convergence. In other words, Midwestern counties are converging to a systemwide average.

Second, the results on the measures of farming dependency are consistent and provide strong statistical evidence that greater local dependency on production agriculture will reduce overall growth rates in per capita income. These more rigorous results support the casual observation made in the discussion of Table 6.2 above.

Table 6.6

Production Agriculture and Annual Growth in per Capita Income for the Midwest

Variable	Model A	Model B	Model C	Model D	Model E	Model F
Intercept	0.1068	0.1058	0.0905	0.1045	0.1066	0.1004
(Average annual growth rate is 0.065)	(45.53)	(55.39)	(45.62)	(52.45)	(52.97)	(48.97)
Lagged Log Per Capita Income	−0.0039	-0.0027	-0.0014	-0.0040	−0.0043	−0.0040
	(28.26)	(20.35)	(9.83)	(27.71)	(28.94)	(29.97)
Lagged Population	6.61E-09	1.29E-09	9.87E-09	7.55E-09	4.03E-09	4.73E-10
	(2.68)	(0.55)	(4.13)	(3.08)	(1.62)	(0.18)
Time Dummy (prior 1980)	0.0052	0.0357	0.0227	0.0047	0.0035	0.0039
	(3.17)	(21.11)	(13.56)	(2.86)	(2.10)	(2.366)
Metro Dummy	0.0051	-0.0134	-.0010	0.0071	0.0071	0.0050
	(3.71)	(10.49)	(0.82)	(5.56)	(5.59)	(3.91)
Lagged Share of Employment in Farms	−0.0105	—	—	—	—	—
	(2.04)					
Lagged Share of Income in Farms	—	-0.2501	—	—	—	—
		(10.49)				
Lagged Value Added per Farm	—	—	-0.0015	—	—	—
			(36.29)			
Lagged Cash Income per Farm	—	—	—	2.78E-05	—	—
				(3.59)		
Lagged Hired Labor Expenditures per Farm	—	—	—	—	0.0010	—
					(7.72)	
Lagged Hired Labor Expenditures as a Share of Cash Income	—	—	—	—	—	0.1134
						(7.99)
F-Statistic	45.820	969.32	736.01	453.71	463.82	464.73
Adjusted R^2	0.0759	0.1499	0.1180	0.0761	0.0777	0.0780

Absolute value of t-statistic in parentheses.
Sample size is 27,462.

Third, the results for aggregate farm size are mixed and somewhat contradictory. Higher value added per farm places downward pressure on per capita income growth rates, lending some support to the broader Goldschmidt (1947) hypothesis. Yet higher levels of cash income per farm seems to be associated with faster growth rates in per capita income, refuting the Goldschmidt hypothesis. The reasons for these apparent contradictory results are not clear. The fact that value-added per farm includes government support payments while cash income tends to be independent of government aid may, in part, explain the apparent contradictory results.

Finally, regions in the Midwest containing farms with a higher dependency on hired labor also tend to experience faster rates of growth in per capita income. Contrary to what might be expected in light of the Goldschmidt (1947) hypothesis, regions with larger farms (or at least higher cash income per farm) with more hired labor grow faster than do regions with smaller farms that use little hired labor.

The implication for policy is clear and straightforward. If the policy goal is to enhance the economic growth of local economies, regions should diversify away from agriculture. This is not to say that agriculture should be abandoned. Rather, the results suggest that from a purely economic perspective, a transition to larger farms that are in a position to offer on-farm employment opportunities may enhance economic growth.

Conclusion

Should agriculture continue to be considered a vehicle for rural economic growth or should it be considered two completely independent enterprises? Rural development policy debates at the national level may again be asked to recognize the interdependence of farm and nonfarm sectors in rural economies (Smith 1995) after a decade or more of being convinced that a healthy agricultural sector did not imply healthy rural towns. Steven Hastings and Gerald Cole (1995) warn, however, that the diversity of rural America implies that a "one size fits all" prescription for rural development would be inappropriate. Each rural area will have its own comparative advantage—for some, this will be related to agriculture; for others, it will not.

The results of the analysis presented here also provide some guidance for local development efforts. For instance, local policies should not be limited to a production agriculture focus. The evidence strongly suggests that heavy dependency on farming will result in slower overall rates of economic growth. Policies aimed at promoting a more diverse local economy will enhance the overall performance of the local economy.

Furthermore, serious consideration should be given to exploring the pros and cons of larger scale farm enterprises. Contrary to the broadly interpreted Goldschmidt (1947) hypothesis, the movement to larger farm enterprises is not necessarily detrimental to the overall local economy. From a narrow economic perspective, would a community be better off with many smaller farms offering lower household income or fewer and larger farms offering on-farm employment opportunities? The results presented here suggest that the latter situation may offer greater economic payoff for the community.

Note

1. There is an important distinction to be made between farm income and farm sales. Farm income, as used in this chapter, includes wages, salaries, and profits paid to farm workers and proprietors. Farm sales refer to the flow of money to the farm from the sale of commodities.

References

Barro, Robert J., and Xavier Sala-i-Martin. 1992. Converge. *Journal of Political Economy* 100(2): 223–251.

Bender, Lloyd D., Bernal L. Green, Thomas F. Hady, John A. Kuehn, Marlys K. Nelson, Leon B. Perkinson, and Peggy J. Ross. 1985. *The Diverse Social and Economic Structure of Rural America* (Rural Development Research Report No. 49). Washington, DC: USDA–ERS.

Gardner, Bruce L. 2000. Economic growth and low incomes in agriculture. *American Journal of Agricultural Economics* 82(5): 1059–1074.

Gebremedhin, Tesfa G., and Ralph D. Christy. 1996. Structural changes in U.S. agriculture: Implications for small farms. *Journal of Agricultural and Applied Economics* 28(1): 57–66.

Goldschmidt, Walter. 1947. *As You Sow.* Glencoe, IL: The Free Press.

Hastings, Steven E., and Gerald L. Cole. 1995. The changing rural policy context: Discussion. *Agricultural and Resource Economics Review* (October): 146–148.

San Diego Economic Information and Modeling Project. 2002. *Index of Data Sources on Web.* Available on-line: <http://typhoon.sdsu.edu/SDEIMP/IndexofRegData.htm>.

Smith, Stephen. 1995. The changing rural policy context. *Agricultural and Resource Economics Review* (October): 139–145.

Swenson, David, and Liesl Eathington. 2001. *USDA Direct Payments and Grants in the United States, Fiscal Year 2000.* Ames: Iowa State University, Department of Economics.

Walzer, Norman, and Steven Deller. 1996. Rural issues and trends: Role of visioning programs. In *Community Visioning Programs: Practices and Experiences*, ed. Norman Walzer, 1–19. Westport, CT: Praeger Press.

Part III

Possible Remedies

7

CHRISTOPHER D. MERRETT AND NORMAN WALZER

Making the Case for Value-Added Agriculture in Economic Development

During the 1990s, the United States experienced an economic boom and added more people to its overall population than at any other time in its history. Despite this, many rural counties in the Midwest experienced population declines and economic stagnation (see chapter 2). The fact that rural economic and population trends in these areas are moving in a direction opposite to the United States as a whole prompts us to explore other options for development building on local resources.

Many development strategies have been tried in rural communities, including the promotion of small business start-ups, business retention and expansion (BR&E) programs, tourism, and new firm recruitment (Falk and Lyson 1991). These strategies have succeeded, but as recent statistics show, other rural communities in the Midwest have experienced economic and demographic decline (U.S. Census 2000a).

To stabilize economic conditions, we argue that community leaders, especially in rural areas, might rethink the role of agriculture in promoting local economic growth as these communities have a competitive advantage in agricultural resources. Rather than exporting commodities to be processed elsewhere, farmers and businesses could process the commodities locally and export a product with much higher value. If the producers own part of the business, then they will gain some of the income generated from the value-added. This chapter argues that this approach can increase local jobs, while also increasing on-farm incomes in rural regions.

A single producer faces enormous obstacles in processing commodities or livestock. Processing facilities can cost millions of dollars to build, and projects of this size have inherent economic and technical problems that no farmer can resolve independently; however, by cooperating with other farmers and rural groups, the necessary capital can be raised to finance and manage such a value-added cooperative enterprise. Though this approach offers no guarantees of success, its viability is confirmed in a recent survey of 80 so-called New Generation Cooperatives (NGCs) in the United States (Merrett and Walzer 2001). Successful NGCs have increased incomes of farm families while improving local economic conditions because of the jobs created.

The purpose of this chapter is twofold. First, it explains why farmers and businesses in rural communities have an increased interest in collaborative business strategies. Low commodity prices, concentrated ownership among agricultural processors, and increasing market pressures have prompted farmers to explore new production and marketing strategies. The second purpose is to estimate the potential contribution that NGCs can make to the local and regional economies.

This chapter addresses these issues in the following manner. The next section, complementing the work of other chapters in this book (e.g., chapter 4), examines the rural economy, explaining why the number of family farms have decreased in Midwestern states. This leads to the third section, which summarizes rural economic development strategies and how farmers and rural leaders can collaborate around value-added agriculture, especially as manifested in producer cooperatives. This discussion is then followed by an input–output analysis to examine the economic impact that three NGCs have on their host communities.

Agricultural Restructuring and Rural Economic Decline

The outward manifestations of rural decline are easy to see. Where businesses once thrived, empty storefronts reflect economic deterioration. Local churches report declining attendance, and communities struggle to maintain vital services despite a shrinking local tax base. In agriculture, the number of farms has declined, with a disproportionate decline among family farms (Lobao and Lasley 1995). The impact of economic decline ripples across the rural landscape, causing one to speculate why this has happened and how it may be reversed.

Rural communities continue to languish because of the structural changes affecting agriculture during the past two decades (Buttel 1997). The challenge, then, is to understand the dynamics of agricultural change, with a specific emphasis on the plight of family farms. Why focus on the role of family farms in rural communities? According to Linda Lobao and Paul Lasley (1995, 1), the family farm, defined as independently operated enterprises providing the main source of income for the family, once served as the economic and social foundation for rural communities.

The USDA-sponsored National Commission on Small Farms agrees with this view (USDA 1998). Survey research in the 1970s showed how "middle-class" family farmers were more involved in community activities and had a higher degree of community attachment than did other farmers. In addition to providing social capital to sustain local community institutions, they also served as a dependable clientele for local businesses (Heffernan 1999; Lobao and Lasley 1995; Putnam 2000). (See Chapter 6 in this volume for further discussion and debate of this issue.)

Whereas the number of total farms has declined since World War II, family farms declined precipitously and disproportionately during the farm crisis of the 1980s. For example, between 1974 and 1997, the number of farms declined from 2.3 million to 1.9 million (USDA 1997a, 10); and the proportion of all farmers who declared farming as their primary occupation declined from 61.7 percent to 50 percent of all farms.

Regionally, the Midwest, as defined by the U.S. Census Bureau, had the largest number of family farms in 1992 and 1997 (USDA 1997b; see also Chapter 2 in this volume). During the 1990s, this region experienced the greatest loss in absolute numbers (almost 60,000) and percentage (12%) of its family farms. Given the importance of family farms, these declines adversely affected the economic and social viability of rural communities because fewer farm families resided in rural areas. Of course, the small towns also were adversely affected by shifts in purchases of rural residents to shopping malls and discount stores. The challenge then is twofold: (1) to explain why the number of farms, in general, and family farms, especially, are declining, and (2) to identify ways to sustain family farms and revitalize rural economies.

At least four different, yet interrelated, factors contribute to declines in the number of family farms in the United States. These factors include (1) technological change, (2) low commodity prices, (3) the vertical integration of production and market concentration, and (4) globalization and free trade. These factors work synergistically to force farm consolidation. Any strategy to revitalize the rural economy must specifically redress the impact of these factors.

The mechanization of agriculture in the late nineteenth century prompted the first wave of farm consolidation. Farms had to grow in size to amortize the costs of increasingly more expensive equipment and other farm inputs. This technological change continues to affect rural communities in the twenty-first century with the use of more complex equipment and genetically modified organisms (GMOs)—crop species that have been genetically altered to enhance specific traits (e.g., resistance to disease, or nutrient content)—further increasing productivity.

Distinct consequences derive for farmers and rural towns when productivity rises. In theory, as American farmers become more productive, they

Figure 7.1   **Simplified Value Chain for Grain and Oilseed Production and Processing**

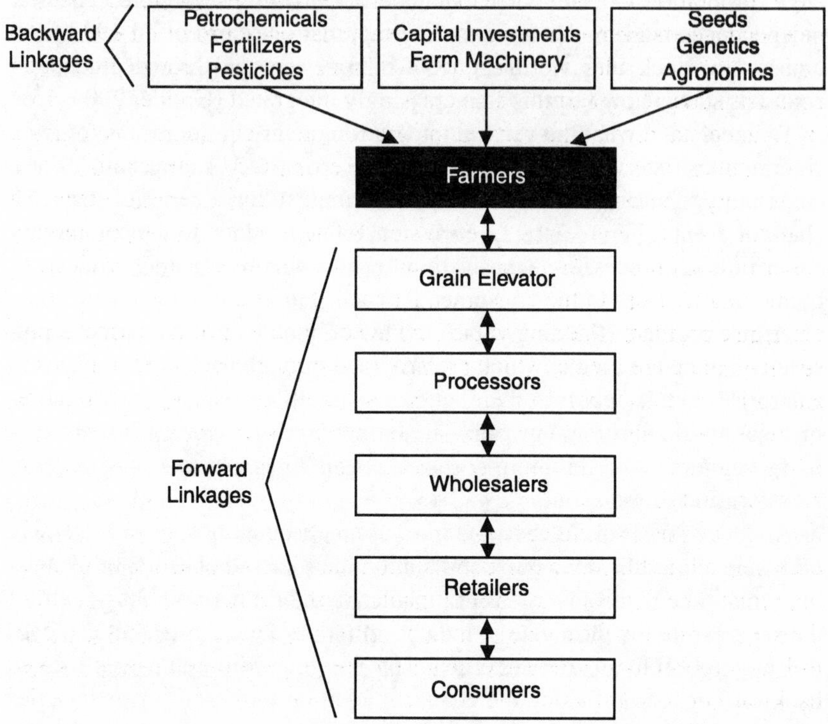

Source: Adapted from Fulton and Andreson 2001, 134.

can sell their crops in the global market at lower prices, undercutting international competition. Unfortunately, export-oriented farm policy has not succeeded as planned. Over the past thirty years, the United States has lost market share in global grain trade as countries such as Brazil expand production (Greider 2000; Rich 2001). Because the supply of commodities increased more rapidly than did demand, commodity prices dropped. To this point, the primary response by farmers to low prices has been to increase productivity. The idea is that increasing the volume of commodities produced can offset increasingly slim profit margins—a strategy that only exacerbates the market glut, bankrupting marginal farmers (Cochrane 2000).

The problem of low commodity prices is key for both quantitative and qualitative reasons. Quantitatively, it reduces the number of farmers by forcing the least successful ones out of business (McMichael 1993). There is a qualitative impact, too. Low commodity prices have prompted surviving farmers to become contract producers—selling crops to large processors under fixed price contracts (Kristof 2000). Farmers are becoming "franchisees" of large corporations—an outcome that undermines the sense of entrepreneurial independence held by the farmers. The fact that one-third of all 1997 farm crop and livestock sales, worth about $60 billion, were sold through production contracts shows how farming is increasingly integrated (Greider 2000, 15).

To understand what the vertical integration of agriculture means for rural communities, one must understand the concept of the "value chain." For a commodity to reach the consumer's plate, it must follow a series of steps in a chain of events (Figure 7.1). At each step, value is added to the commodity either through processing, transforming it into a more valuable product, or by moving it closer to the consumer. At each step in this value chain, some enterprise profits by "adding value" to the commodity. From a farmer's perspective, there are inputs, which are provided through backward linkages to enterprises that supply fertilizers, farm machinery, seeds, and other requirements for agricultural production. The farmer produces commodities or outputs, which are sold through forward linkages to enterprises such as grain elevators and processors.

An ideal world would have a market of independent buyers and sellers at each step along the value chain. In reality, the system is becoming increasingly integrated with just a few companies controlling several, if not all, of the steps "from the farm gate to the consumer's plate." Companies can control large portions of the value chain by merging with companies located backward or forward along the chain. In addition to these formal strategies of control, firms can also enter into strategic alliances or joint ventures as a way to reach back or forward along the value chain (Lehman and Krebs 1996). The recent actions of agribusiness giants such as ConAgra and Cargill illustrate this process, as they exert increasing control over the value chain— controlling companies selling inputs to, and buying outputs from, farmers. The impact of low commodity prices and agribusiness consolidation on family farms has prompted a *New York Times* reporter to ask, "Is the sun setting on [independent] farmers?" (Barboza 1999, 1).

A more important question is: Why is integration occurring to the extent that it is? It is occurring in response to free trade (Tweeten and Flora 2001, 1–13). Firms such as Cargill are expanding vertically to increase productivity through economies of scale. With lower unit costs of production, firms can compete better in the global marketplace. Concerns for quality control also drive consolidation. The global food market is increasingly segmented, with increased demands for specialty food products. It is easier for a food processor to deliver a specialty product if—by being part of a value chain—it can track where the food comes from and how it is handled. The bi-directional arrows

Figure 7.2 **Price Spread Between Farm Value and Consumer Prices,
1952–1999**

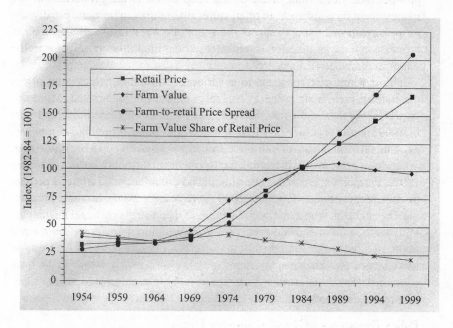

Source: USDA–ERS 2000.

between the value-chain links underscore the fact that information flows in
both directions (see Figure 7.1).

These interrelated processes have profound implications for farmers. First,
farmers are accepting lower prices in exchange for the ability to sell commodities into a predictable market. Because farmers are price takers, they
face intensified pressures to increase on-farm efficiencies to remain profitable. This imperative to become more efficient drives farmers to increase the
scale of their operations. Hence, the concentration of processors in the value
chain increases the pressure for farm consolidation. The increased drive toward farm consolidation increases productivity, further increasing output and
suppressing commodity prices.

While recent prices for commodities such as corn and soybeans have
dropped to their lowest in decades, the price for final products such as breakfast cereal has not. A comparison of four related factors helps explain why
(Figure 7.2). Farm value represents what farmers receive once the commod-

ity reaches the consumer. The retail price is what consumers pay for the final product. The farm value share of the food dollar is the proportion of the money spent by consumers in retail stores that returns to farmers. Finally, the farm-to-retail price spread shows the spread between farm value—what the farmer receives, and the retail price—what the final product sells for in the retail marketplace (Elitzak 1999).

The indexed data for these four variables show that, while retail prices have steadily risen since the 1970s, farm values have stagnated. More importantly, the data show that the farm value share of the retail price is lower in 1999 than it was in 1952. Rising retail prices and dropping farm values explain why the farm-to-retail price spread has risen since 1970. While food prices have gone up, in real terms, the payments to farmers have not (Barboza 1999). Farmers' share of the consumer food dollar declined from 37 percent to 20 percent between 1954 and 2000 (USDA-ERS 2000). Storage, processing, distribution, wholesaling, marketing, and retailing firms earn an increasingly large share of the value generated from agricultural markets. The overall impact has been rural depopulation and economic stagnation. The question is: What policies have been implemented to counter these trends in the rural economy? The next section discusses rural economic development strategies and their effectiveness.

Policy Responses to Rural Economic Decline

Traditional Approaches

Prior to the 1990s, there was minimal dialogue between agricultural policymakers and rural economic developers. The consequence was that plans for rural development assumed a small role for agriculture as farms consolidated. Instead, policies targeted the recruitment of new nonagricultural firms or business retention and expansion. For example, the National Rural Economic Developers Association (2000) clearly prioritizes nonagricultural industry when it states that a firm benefits by locating in a rural, rather than an urban, place, because of lower labor costs, taxes, crime rates, and real estate costs, among other attributes. A compilation of resources devoted to economic development by the W.K. Kellogg Foundation (1997) includes more than 280 references. Only twenty-four (8%) of the references directly mention that agriculture might play a central role in rural economic development.

More often, policy experts recommend economic development based on tourism or continued focus on nonagricultural manufacturing (Malecki 1991). These recommendations can actually conflict with agriculture. As farm operations increase in size, animal waste and odor also increase. This is especially true with confinement operations, which raise large numbers of livestock in close quarters. These noxious side effects can hurt rural tourism operations, as a recent case in Iowa reveals (Hupp and Beeman 2001). Some family farmers have ventured into agri-tourism, providing urban dwellers with a taste of the (sometimes idealized) farm life. Large factory farms undermine this form of rural tourism.

A focus on nonagricultural manufacturing in rural areas also has its limits. Overall, manufacturing plays a proportionately smaller role in the American economy, being replaced by service industries. For example, between 1990 and 1999, manufacturing jobs declined from 17.4 to 14.4 percent of the American workforce, while the contribution made by manufacturing to the U.S. gross domestic product (GDP) declined from 17.9 percent in 1990 to 16.4 percent in 1998 (U.S. Census 2000b, 2001). At the same time, there is increased competition among communities to recruit manufacturing firms, mainly because manufacturing has traditionally paid higher wages. Communities successfully attract businesses based on their specific attributes such as local wage levels, land costs, taxes and incentives, and quality of local workforce (Eisenger 1988, quoted in Flora et al. 1992). In general, rural communities offer a set of attributes different from urban areas, resulting in a qualitatively different type of manufacturing enterprise locating in each place.

The deindustrialization of the American economy has prompted economic developers to pay more attention to the service sector. Dissatisfied with the impact of branch plants, rural communities compete to attract gambling casinos, prisons, and retail businesses (Beale 1996; Dunlap 2001; Long, Clark, and Liston, 1994). One researcher describes this shift in rural communities toward the service sector as the rise of "The Wal-Mart Frontier" (Shelley 1993). Unfortunately, this shift ignores family farms. At the same time, agricultural policy has focused on farms and farmers—with scant attention paid to rural communities or economic development (see chapters 2 and 6 in this volume). The inattention to rural economic development policy is apparent as farm policy has evolved through the twentieth century.

According to Anne Effland (2000), government intervention was the hallmark of American farm policy between the 1930s and the 1980s. Low commodity prices during the Great Depression devastated farmers. The inability of markets to correct the crisis prompted President Franklin Roosevelt to usher in a New Deal for farmers by providing price supports and supply management. The farm crisis of the 1980s prompted Congress to rethink federal agricultural policy by embracing free markets and smaller government. During the early 1990s, farm policy began to reflect this philosophical change as farm supports were lowered, farmers were given more flexibility to plant different crops, and the United States joined the North American Free Trade Agreement (NAFTA). The market orientation of farm policy became fully manifest in the 1996 Farm Bill, popularly known as the Freedom to Farm Act. This legislation reduced subsidies and price supports, while greatly increasing the freedom for farmers to plant the crops they decided would be most profitable.

It was during this period of increasing market uncertainty that we can see increasing calls for developers and farmers to work together to promote rural economic development. Investigators cautioned against forsaking agriculture in local economic development strategies (Darling 1990; Walzer, Merrett, and Holmes 1999). Other reports argued that agriculture contributes a significant amount to the rural economic base, especially in the Midwestern and Great Plains states and, hence, should play an integral part in any rural economic development strategy (Golz, Thompson, and Leistritz 1992; Leistritz and Sell 2001b; Song, Doeksen, Woods, and Schreiner 1990). Though these reports justify why farmers should work with neighboring communities, little is said about how a farmer might engage in value-added agriculture. The following section describes how producer cooperatives can help farmers and communities revitalize or rebuild local economies.

Producer Cooperatives as an Economic Development Alternative

Many farmers have a few strategies for coping with growing market pressures: (1) They can contract with large processors to lock in market access, but lose independence in the process; (2) they can seek off-farm employment to sustain the farmstead, if they have not already done so; and (3) they can sell the farm and move into another line of work. For some farmers, a fourth option exists—to participate in a value-adding agricultural enterprise. The economic justification for farmers is simple. As commodity growers, farmers can expect to earn a 4 or 5 percent return on their investment (Morehart 1999; Roland 2000). Food processors can earn investment returns approaching 20 percent (Ridgeway 1999). By reaching up the value chain, farmers can earn higher returns on their investments.

Ascending the value chain is simple in theory, in reality, starting a commodity processing facility presents a daunting set of hurdles. A processing facility costs millions of dollars to build. Few individual farmers have the start-up capital to finance a processing facility. Furthermore, many steps must be completed before construction on the facility can even begin. A feasibility study must be done to identify markets and potential obstacles (Cropp 2001). If the feasibility study identifies potential for business success, proponents of the new processing facility must then address a series of financial, legal, engineering, environmental, and managerial issues that are beyond the scope of most farm operators (Hanson 2001).

Many enterprising farmers have overcome these obstacles by forming producer cooperatives to achieve, as a group, goals they could not achieve as individuals. By forming a cooperative, farmers can more easily raise equity to cover start-up costs and hire professional managers, lawyers, and engineers to move a project forward. Through combined efforts, farmers can more easily raise equity among themselves, but they can then approach banks, government agencies, and other institutions for loans and grants to help defray start-up costs. A cooperative also spreads the risk of starting a new business.

Cooperatives as a business model contain an inherent set of problems that hinder their profitability. Traditional producer cooperatives have faltered because, among a range of issues, they suffer from the so-called free-rider problem and the horizon problem (Fulton 2001; Fulton and Andreson 2001). The free-rider problem occurs whenever a good or service paid for by one group of persons cannot be excluded from those who have not paid for it (Krugman 1997). There is an incentive for individuals to use the good without paying, as long as others pay. In the case of a traditional producer cooperative, a member may sell commodities to the cooperative (co-op) for processing if the price offered by the co-op is sufficiently high; however, if a privately held processor offers a higher price, the co-op member may abandon the cooperative and sell to this processor, resulting in less revenue for the cooperative.

On the consumer side, individuals may form a co-op to lower costs by purchasing large quantities of goods; however, some members of the cooperative may go outside the cooperative if lower prices can be found. Again, this undermines the co-op by limiting its volume of sales. The point is that free riders can cause undercapitalization in cooperatives. Members will only invest in a co-op to the level required to patronize the cooperative. There is no incentive to invest further or to do business with the cooperative if prices are better elsewhere. Inadequate investment capital means that co-ops have difficulty upgrading facilities to compete with investor-owned firms.

The horizon problem also causes cooperatives to be undercapitalized (Fulton 2001). In a traditional co-op, membership is open to anyone willing to pay the membership fee. A member receives investment returns in the form of patronage refunds in proportion to the amount of business transacted with the cooperative. Some investments may mature over a time horizon beyond which the member is willing to consider (Fulton and Andreson 2001, 140). Hence, co-op members tend to prioritize investments that "maximize short-term rather than long-term returns" (Fulton 2001, 19).

The NGC (new generation cooperatives) approach resolves both the free rider and horizon problems (Fulton 2001). Unlike traditional cooperatives with open membership, NGCs are closed cooperatives, only extending membership to farmers willing to purchase shares in the co-op. Furthermore, the investment in the NGC creates obligations for both the farmers and the cooperative. By selling the shares, the NGC guarantees that it will purchase commodities from the farmer in proportion to the shares owned by the farmer.

By purchasing shares, a farmer agrees to sell commodities to the NGC for processing in proportion to shares owned. If a farmer is unable to sell the commodity from his or her own harvest, a farmer must purchase the commodity on the open market and deliver it to the NGC. In addition, members are required to sell commodities to the co-op at the contract price, even if better prices are available elsewhere; however, when the NGC pays less for commodities than the market, farmer-members still have a chance of receiving a higher return in terms of a value-added dividend at the end of the year. The problem of membership (dis)loyalty disappears under the NGC model. The horizon problem also disappears because, unlike the traditional co-op in which farmer equity is locked in, an NGC member owns tradable shares that provide more flexibility for increasing or decreasing investment in the NGC (Fulton 2001).

An organizational variant of the NGC, the limited liability company (LLC), allows venture capitalists and local nonfarm investors to purchase stock in the enterprise (Brown and Merrett 2000). Though not a legally recognized business form in every state, the LLC business model can provide further opportunity for collaboration between farm and nonfarm residents to promote rural economic development. We might think of LLCs and NGCs as new versions of a BR&E (business retention and expansion) policy, helping existing farmers to survive and even flourish in the community—this is especially true when local governments and nonfarm investors become involved with value-added agriculture.

Many examples of NGCs and LLCs exist in the United States, largely in the Great Plains and Midwest. According to a recent study, there are about eighty NGCs in operation (Merrett, Holmes, and Waner 1999), and they process a wide range of commodities. For example, South Dakota Soybean Processors converts soybeans into edible oil products, industrial lubricants, and soybean meal for animal feeds (Fink 2001). Renville, Minnesota, claims to be the "cooperative capital" of the United States because this farming community hosts nine cooperatives, five of which are NGCs (City of Renville n.d.).

Local NGCs include ValAdCo, whose members add value to corn by feeding it to hogs owned by the cooperative. Golden Oval NGC members add value to corn by feeding it to chickens. The eggs laid by the chickens are sold in liquid form to large food companies, including McDonald's and Pillsbury (Buschette 2001; Looker 1999). Two NGCs, MinAqua Fisheries Cooperative and Southern Minnesota Beet Sugar Cooperative, operate symbiotically.

Southern Minnesota Beet Sugar Cooperative converts sugarbeets into sugar. Warm water is one of the by-products. Instead of releasing the water as waste into the environment, the water is piped to MinAqua, a nearby aquaculture cooperative. The heat energy contained in the waste water is used by MinAqua to warm the water used to raise Tilapia, a soybean-fed tropical fish (Morrison 1998). The fish are then sold to Asian food markets in Toronto, Vancouver, Minneapolis, New York, and Chicago, and to smaller niche markets elsewhere (Cataldo 2001).

In Carrington, North Dakota, members of the Dakota Growers NGC add value to wheat by processing it into pasta products. This producer cooperative is now the third largest producer of pasta products in the United States (Dakota Growers 2001). In Kansas, the Twenty-first Century Alliance group of cooperatives process pinto beans, milk, and wheat into a range of products destined for American and Mexican markets (Williams and Merrett 2001). Other successful NGCs produce beef, wine, and turkey as well as other products. Some farm groups propose converting crop residue into fiberboard and paper products.

This apparent diversity, however, masks the fact that the most common type of NGC or LLC converts corn into ethanol (Merrett and Walzer 2001). Ethanol processors are the most common NGC because ethanol can be burned as a fuel in cars. Although ethanol is currently more expensive per gallon than gasoline, state subsidies, and the banning of the gas additive MTBE (methyl tertiary-butyl ether) as a known carcinogen, have created a growing market for biofuels such as ethanol. Since 1979, MTBE has been used to increase octane levels in gasoline; it replaced lead, to reduce "engine knock" (EPA 2001). Also, MTBE helps gasoline to burn more completely, thereby lowering car emissions. Several alternative additives to MTBE exist, including ethanol—the most likely replacement.

From a geographical perspective, North Dakota and Minnesota host a majority of NGCs, but farmers in Iowa, Kansas, Nebraska, Wisconsin, Illinois, Missouri, and Michigan, among other states, also belong to value-adding cooperatives (Merrett and Walzer 2001). The estimated number of eighty NGCs changes from year to year because, like any economic sector, new firms start up, while others close down. The NGCs are a relatively recent phenomenon—about three-quarters of them began operations within the last decade.

Reports suggest that farmers in successful NGCs earn a 12 to 20 percent return on investment depending upon the commodity processed (Carter 2000a; Pates 2001). In a 1999 survey of NGCs, boards of directors from eighty NGCs were asked about the viability of NGCs as a business model. Of the thirty-four NGCs that answered this question, eight reported that it was premature to report on profitability. Of the remaining twenty-six respondents, twenty reported they were operating profitably or at the break-even point after being in business for an average of nine years (Merrett and Walzer 2001, 108). This survival rate compares favorably for new business start-ups for which studies show a 50 percent failure rate for firms after only five years (Merrett and Gruidl 2000).

The question is, can NGCs and LLCs help the communities in which they operate? Do producer cooperatives provide a measurable economic impact in communities beyond the farm gates of NGC members? The next section addresses these questions.

Measuring the Local Economic Impact of New Generation Cooperatives

When a firm starts conducting business in a community, economic benefits usually accrue to the region. A new business hires employees and purchases inputs, which may be bought locally. If the number of jobs in a community increases, local businesses also benefit as workers spend their wages on housing, food, and other amenities. As business owners earn higher profits because new employees spend wages, existing businesses, in turn, may expand their operations or purchase more goods and services.

The impact of a business start-up or closure within a host community or region is referred to as the "multiplier effect" and is captured through an input–output analysis (Malecki 1991). This procedure acknowledges that any economy includes many sectors such as motor vehicles, food processing, agriculture, and others. The assumption is that in any regional economy, firms buy inputs from, and sell outputs to, other firms in other sectors. An input–output analysis tracks these exchanges to determine how change in one economic sector affects businesses in other sectors (Malecki 1991; Oser and Brue 1988).

Economic developers are interested in the direct impacts, indirect impacts, induced impacts, and total impacts. The *direct* impact is the number of people hired by a new establishment or expansions in existing companies. *Indirect* effects include employment increases resulting from purchases made by the expanding business. Strong evidence shows that value-added manufacturing can have a larger local impact than other manufacturing firms because they tend to purchase more local inputs. Fred Gale (1999) shows that, in 1995, nonmetro value-added plants in the forestry and dairy industrial classifications purchased 50 percent or more of their inputs locally, depending on the industry. Gale also reported that the local spending per job was substantial. Firms with backward or forward linkages to the new factory are affected.

The economic impact does not end here, because employees spend their higher disposable incomes and thereby create jobs in other sectors. This impact is called the *induced* effect. The total number of jobs created includes the direct, indirect, and induced jobs linked to the new firm. Data to conduct an input–output analysis are collected by government agencies such as the U.S. Bureau of Economic Analysis, the Bureau of Labor Statistics, and the Census Bureau (IMPLAN 1998). Current models use data representing 528 industrial sectors. The U.S. Forest Service (2001) was an early leader in developing the IMPLAN (IMpact analysis for PLANing software used for input–output analysis). Subsequently, proprietary firms such as the Minnesota IMPLAN Group have built on the software and have organized the data to facilitate input–output analyses.

There is substantial precedent for using input–output analysis to study the economic impacts of value-added agriculture (Darling 1990; Song et al. 1990). Less common are studies that focus specifically on NGCs. A series of recent studies have shown that NGCs, while imperfect, can have a positive economic impact on rural communities. These studies demonstrate that NGCs have raised incomes for farmers while creating new jobs and generating tax revenue for communities (Coon and Leistritz 2001; Leistritz and Sell 2000, 2001a, 2001b).

Building on this work, the remainder of this section will summarize the local economic impacts of three NGCs. A short vignette and results of an input–output analysis are presented for (1) Golden Oval NGC in Renville, Minnesota; (2) South Dakota Soybean Processors (SDSP) in Volga, South Dakota; and (3) West Liberty Foods in Muscatine, Iowa.

Golden Oval Cooperative

Golden Oval NGC adds value to corn by converting it into liquid egg material. Co-op members feed the corn they grow to chickens, which are also owned by the co-op. According to Patricia Buschette (2001), the idea to start this NGC evolved from concerns by the managers of Co-op Country Farmers Elevator, a traditional marketing cooperative. When examining the capital flows and age structure of the membership, they realized that a growing number of members were approaching age seventy-two, a time when farmers can withdraw a portion of their equity. Threatened by this potential capital shortfall, a perennial problem for traditional co-ops, the managers realized a need to develop a "profit center" to sustain their operations.

After investigating several options, Co-op Country decided to start a poultry-egg operation that used corn grown by co-op members as feed. The new producer cooperative was incorporated in 1994 and began operations in 1995, with the financial support of 411 producer members who contributed $4 million in start-up equity. The city of Renville, Minnesota, also supported Golden Oval by providing a forty-acre site in the local industrial park, which was part of a TIF (tax-increment financing) district.

Golden Oval experienced thirty straight profitable months between 1995 and August 1998 (Buschette 2001). Managers estimate that Golden Oval provides $14 million annually in payments to workers, shareholders, and to input suppliers (Golden Oval Eggs 2002a). While these achievements are certainly important to farmers and investors, the broader question is the extent to which NGCs contribute to the regional economy.

Using IMPLAN software with 1998 data, an input–output analysis indicates that Golden Oval had a positive multiplier impact in Renville (Table 7.1). Not only did it generate direct jobs, it also created indirect and induced jobs. While Golden Oval generated significant job growth, its impact on the population of the region is mixed. The city of Renville saw a small net population increase of eight people between 1990 and 2000, while Renville County experienced a population decline during the same time period (U.S. Census 2000c). More disconcerting is that, according to 1998 estimates, eight other co-ops operate in Renville employing 467 workers (IMPLAN 1998). This raises the question of what it would take to significantly increase the local population. Different commodities generate larger or smaller multipliers, depending on current market conditions and local linkages for that commodity (Gale 1999).

And yet, for the residents of Renville, the economic impacts are noticeable. Main Street is thriving. A new golf course began operations in 1999. The success of Golden Oval has prompted an expansion of operations. The modestly positive demographic impact that co-ops have had in Renville might be interpreted more optimistically in light of regional demographics in west central Minnesota. Renville County and the surrounding rural nonadjacent counties, including Brown, Chippewa, Redwood, and Yellow Medicine, experienced average population declines of about 2.4 percent between 1990 and 2000 (U.S. Census 2000a). From this perspective, the modest population gains experienced by the town of Renville, attributable in part to the co-ops, look more significant.

South Dakota Soybean Processors

Soybean farmers in South Dakota struggled to make a profit during the 1980s because of the distance to major markets (Fink 2001). South Dakota Soybean Processors (SDSP) (1998) traces its origins to a feasibility study conducted by the South Dakota Soybean Research and Promotion Council in 1992. The original plan was to attract a firm from outside the region to locate a processing facility in South Dakota. With no takers, the farmers involved in the study decided to undertake the project. A membership and equity drive eventually attracted 2,100 members and $21 million in equity toward the $32.5 million

Table 7.1

Demographic and Input–Output Analysis of New Generation Cooperatives (1988)

Criteria	Golden Oval, Renville, MN	South Dakota Soybean Processors, Volga	West Liberty Foods, IA
	Value-Added Impact ($)		
Direct Impact	$51,035,200	$5,142,514	$194,696,608
Indirect Impact	8,228,889	11,523,192	56,064,059
Induced Impact	1,160,982	2,207,578	12,258,212
Total Impact	60,425,073	18,873,284*	263,018,890
	Employment Impact (Jobs Created)		
Direct Impact	85	64.0	1,350
Indirect Impact	125	207.2	402.1
Induced Impact	21.1	67.1	232.7
Total Impact	231.1	338.3	1,984
	Population		
Town 2000	1,323	1,435	3,332
Town 1990	1,315	1,263	2,935
County 2000	17,154	28,220	41,722
County 1990	17,683	25,207	39,907

* We have used a conservative multiplier in this instance because of the unrealistic assumptions the
  IMPLAN model uses to evaluate the indirect impact of commodity processing firms on their host
  communities.

Source: U.S. Census 2000a and 2000c; IMPLAN 1998.

start-up costs. Since beginning operations in 1996, SDSP has distributed more than $9.2 million in patronage funds to co-op members (Fink 2001).

The input–output analysis shows that SDSP has had a major impact on the town of Volga and on Brookings County: SDSP employs sixty-four workers directly at the processing facility; however, the indirect and induced jobs linked to SDSP generate another 274 jobs in the community (see Table 7.1). Furthermore, the IMPLAN model estimates that the SDSP facility helps generate more than $18.9 million in Brookings County. This economic catalyst helps to explain, at least partially, explain the 200-person population increase in Volga and the addition of 3,000 people in Brookings County.[1]

West Liberty Foods

The final vignette examines a turkey-processing facility located in the eastern Iowa town of West Liberty. Unlike Golden Oval Eggs and SDSP, West

Liberty Foods was not a new business. According to Mary Holmes and Daniel Curry (2001), Louis Rich moved a processing plant to West Liberty in 1943. By 1949, the plant concentrated on turkey processing. Until 1996, the Louis Rich plant was the primary component in the local economic base. In 1996, Kraft Foods acquired the Rich company. Corporate managers reviewed the performance and location of each newly acquired plant. They decided that the West Liberty facility was in a marginal location, with minimal potential for expansion. They announced in May 1996 that the plant would close within six months.

The announced plant closing shocked the community. Local turkey growers, feed suppliers, and surrounding communities struggled to keep the plant open. They searched for new buyers, including Farmland, but no buyer emerged. Faced with an imminent plant closure, the turkey growers investigated raising equity to start an NGC. Local farmers contributed $2.4 million. Farmer equity, plus grants and forgivable loans from the Iowa Department of Economic Development, Iowa Corn Promotion Board, Muscatine County, the city of West Liberty, Iowa Farm Bureau, and the Iowa Turkey Federation, financed the operations. The USDA provided a key component of the financial package when it agreed to guarantee 70 percent of a $7 million loan approved by NorWest Bank (Holmes and Curry 2001). With the financial package in place, the NGC took ownership of the cooperative in December 1996.

The local economic impacts of West Liberty Foods are shown in at least two ways. Before its acquisition in 1996, the Louis Rich facility employed fewer than 500 workers; however, in a town of no more than 3,000 residents, the loss of 500 jobs would have been devastating. Thus, one could easily envision the negative effects created by a plant closing.

By 2001, the co-op not only survived the transition from investor-owned firm to co-op, but also expanded to employ 1,350 workers. The impact of this agricultural turnaround has been impressive as the jobs directly connected to West Liberty Foods generated another 634 indirect and induced jobs in the community (IMPLAN 1998). The populations of West Liberty and Muscatine County have both grown—bucking the downward demographic trend affecting rural counties in the Midwest (see Table 7.1).

Conclusion

This chapter set out to accomplish two goals. First, it attempted to show how economic and technological changes have worked against many family farmers. Increasingly complex production technology and the vertical integration of large processors are both a cause and consequence of low commodity prices. The trend has been toward farm consolidation and concomitant rural depopulation.

The second purpose of the chapter was to argue that the roots of rural revival can be found, at least in part, in reconceptualizing the role agriculture can play in economic development. Traditionally, farmers and economic developers largely ignored each other. Economic developers in rural communities concentrated their efforts on the traditional rural business development approach—recruiting a large nonagricultural manufacturer or high-tech company that would pay high wages, while contributing to the local tax base. The reality is that many, if not most, manufacturers attracted to rural communities are branch plants that have located in a rural community to take advantage of nonunion, low-skill, and low-wage workers.

Farmers were largely concerned about increasing crop yields, finding new ways to market existing crops, new crop hybrids, or federal farm policy; however, the continuing decline in the number of family farms combined with low commodity prices and the rise in contract farming prompted progressive farmers to consider alternative methods of farming. These two seemingly disparate groups came together around the concept of the NGC in the 1980s and early 1990s. This approach has proven a successful strategy for dozens of co-ops representing thousands of farmers across the Midwest and Great Plains.

We must be careful not to portray NGCs as a panacea for all the problems affecting the rural economy. Some critics rightfully argue that NGCs generate jobs that pay low wages, that they can cause environmental problems, and that recent NGC business failures raise questions about the viability of the closed cooperative business model. These are valid concerns deserving closer scrutiny. Wages paid by an NGC processor may not be any higher than wages paid by investor-owned firms such as Excel or IBP. The Iowa Department of Economic Development (IDED) attempted to address the issue of low wages by requiring firms using IDED loans to pay workers at least $9.66 per hour—a policy other states could follow to ensure that jobs created in rural communities pay a decent wage (Holmes and Curry 2001).

The NGCs are businesses that can cause environmental problems. The South Dakota State Department of Environment and Natural Resources (2001) cited SDSP for emitting waste by-products that exceeded both air- and water-quality standards. Consequently, SDSP installed new waste-management equipment and paid $53,000 in civil penalties for these infractions.

ValAdCo, the hog-processing cooperative located in Renville, Minnesota, was cited for air pollution and odor violations (Losure 1999). Acrimony within a community caused by pollution can undermine the benefits created by the cooperative—even forcing some co-ops to the brink of insolvency. Cooperatives, an embodiment of egalitarian business control and forward thinking, should extend their progressive ideals to recognize adverse effects on the environment—the foundation of family farms—a point made by Golden Oval Eggs (2002b) on its Web site.

The issue of insolvency is related to the third problem. Many examples of failed NGCs exist, including Southwest Iowa Soybean Cooperative and Ranchers' Choice Cooperative (Carter 2000b; Walzer and Holmes 2001). Furthermore, some poorly performing NGCs have sold shares to some of the agribusiness giants they were trying to avoid so as to preserve investor equity. Archer Daniels Midland controls 30 percent of Minnesota Corn Processors, an ethanol cooperative (Steil 2000). ProGold, another ethanol cooperative, is leasing its processing facilities to Cargill (1997) as part of a survival strategy.

It is with guarded optimism that NGCs are recommended for the potential role they can play in rural economic revitalization. When NGCs succeed, they provide incentives for farmers to patronize the co-op while obtaining a higher return on their investments. The local multiplier effect generated by NGCs can be significant, as the Golden Oval Eggs, SDSP, and West Liberty Foods examples show; however, the higher returns may be because of higher risks involved. NGCs are a business—designed first and foremost to increase producer income. As in any business, failure is possibility. These are important caveats for farmers or investors planning to invest in an NGC. The bottom line is that rural communities cannot remain complacent as market pressures threaten their existence. The NGC represents one approach among an array of ideas that can help rural communities survive and even flourish in the twenty-first century.

Note

1. IMPLAN makes assumptions about the availability of inputs that are not realistic in this instance. Consequently, we have chosen to report a more conservative set of values for the employment and value-added impact.

References

Barboza, David. 1999. Is the sun setting on farmers? *New York Times* (November 28): Sec. 3, 1.

Beale, Calvin. 1996. Rural prisons: An update. *Rural Development Perspectives* 11(2): 25–28.

Brown, Roger, and Christopher D. Merrett. 2000. The limited liability company versus new generation cooperatives: Alternative business forms for rural economic development. *Rural Research Report* 11(7). Macomb: Illinois Institute for Rural Affairs.

Buschette, Patricia. 2001. Golden Oval. In *New Generation Cooperatives: Case Studies, Expanded 2001*, ed. Mary Holmes, Norman Walzer, and Christopher D. Merrett, 33–42. Macomb: Illinois Institute for Rural Affairs.

Buttel, Frederick. 1997. Some observations on agro-food change and the future of agricultural sustainability movements. In *Globalising Food: Agrarian Questions and Global Restructuring*, ed. David Goodman and Michael Watts, 344–365. New York: Routledge.

Cargill. 1997. *Cargill to Operate ProGold Corn Wet Milling Plant.* [Press Release]. Available on-line: <www.cargill.com/today/releases/10021997.htm>.

Carter, David. 2000a. Going against the grain: The story of Mountain View Harvest Cooperative. In *New Generation Cooperatives: Case Studies*, ed. Mary Holmes, Norman Walzer, and Christopher D. Merrett, 43–54. Macomb: Illinois Institute for Rural Affairs. Available online: <www.value-added.org>.

———. 2000b. *Hard Choices: The Birth and Death of Ranchers' Choice Cooperative.* Macomb: Illinois Institute for Rural Affairs, 198. Available on-line: <www.value-added.org.>

Cataldo, Rosie. 2001. Fishing for diversity: Aquaculture in the Ninth District. *Fedgazette: Federal Reserve Bank of Minneapolis* 13(6). Available on-line: <http://minneapolisfed.org/pubs/fedgaz/01–11/index.html>.

City of Renville. n.d. *Co-op Capital of the United States.* Available on-line: <www.ci.renville.mn.us/coopcap/page1.htm>.

Cochrane, Willard. 2000. American agriculture in an uncertain global economy. *Agricultural Economist Newsletter* 700 (Spring). Available on-line: <www.extension. umn.edu/newsletters/ageconomist/components/ag237–700a.html>.

Coon, Randal, and F. Larry Leistritz. 2001. *Economic Contribution North Dakota Cooperatives Make to the State Economy* (Agricultural Economics Staff Paper No. AE01002). Fargo: Department of Agribusiness and Applied Economics, North Dakota State University.

Cropp, Bob. 2001. Starting a new generation cooperative. In *A Cooperative Approach to Local Economic Development*, ed. Christopher D. Merrett and Norman Walzer, 25–40. Westport, CT: Quorum Press.

Dakota Growers. 2001. Webpage for Dakota Growers Pasta Co. Available on-line: <www.dakotagrowers.com/index.shtml>.

Darling, David. 1990. *Estimating the Role of Production Agriculture in a County's Economy* (No. L-813, Revised Version). Manhattan: Kansas State University Cooperative Extension Service. Available on-line: <www.oznet.ksu.edu/library/agec2/l813.pdf>.

Dunlap, Angela. 2001. Princeton readopts ordinance supporting Wal-Mart. *Peoria Journal Star* (October 16). Available on-line: <www.pjstar.com/news/topnews/g63559a.html>.

Effland, Anne. 2000. U.S. farm policy: The first 200 years. *Agricultural Outlook* 269 (March): 21–25. Washington, DC: USDA–ERS. Available on-line: <www.ers.usda.gov/publications/agoutlook/mar2000/ao269g.pdf>.

Eisenger, Peter. 1988. *The Rise of the Entrepreneurial State: State and Local Economic Development Policy in the United States.* Madison: University of Wisconsin Press.

Elitzak, Howard. 1999. *Food Cost Review, 1950–97* (Economic Research Service, Agricultural Economic Report No. 780). Washington, DC: USDA–ERS.

Environmental Protection Agency (EPA). 2001. *EPA MTBE FAQS Gasoline.* Available on-line: <www.epa.gov/mtbe/gas.htm>.

Falk, William, and Thomas Lyson. 1991. Rural America and the industrial policy debate. In *Rural Policies in the 1990s*, ed. Cornelia Flora and James Christenson, 8–21. Boulder, CO: Westview Press.

Fink, Rodney. 2001. South Dakota Soybean Processors. In *New Generation Cooperatives: Case Studies, Expanded 2001*, ed. Mary Holmes, Norman Walzer, and Christopher D. Merrett, 151–166. Macomb: Illinois Institute for Rural Affairs.

Flora, Cornelia, Jan Flora, Jacqueline Spears, Louis Swanson, with Mark Lapping and Mark Weinberg. 1992. *Rural Communities: Legacy and Change*. Boulder, CO: Westview Press.

Fulton, Joan, and Kevin Andreson. 2001. Value-added enterprises in the rural community. In *A Cooperative Approach to Local Economic Development*, ed. Christopher D. Merrett and Norman Walzer, 129–146. Westport, CT: Quorum Press.

Fulton, Murray. 2001. Traditional versus new generation cooperatives. In *A Cooperative Approach to Local Economic Development*, ed. Christopher D. Merrett and Norman Walzer, 11–24. Westport, CT: Quorum Press.

Gale, Fred. 1999. Value-added manufacturing has strong local linkages. *Rural Conditions and Trends* 8(3): 23–26.

Golden Oval Eggs. 2002a. *Economic Impact in Renville, Minnesota*. Available on-line: <www.goldenovaleggs.com/economicimpact.htm>.

———. 2002b. *The Environmental Philosophy and Practices of Golden Oval Eggs*. Available on-line: <www.goldenovaleggs.com/environment.htm>.

Golz, Theresa, JoAnn Thompson, and F. Larry Leistritz. 1992. *North Dakota Agricultural Trends: A Statewide/Regional Perspective* (Agricultural Economics Statistical Series, No. 51). Fargo: North Dakota State University.

Greider, William. 2000. The last farm crisis. *The Nation* 271 (November 20): 11–18.

Hanson, Mark. 2001. Cooperative organization for value-added agribusiness. In *A Cooperative Approach to Local Economic Development*, ed. Christopher D. Merrett and Norman Walzer, 41–54. Westport, CT: Quorum Press.

Heffernan, William. 1999. *Consolidation in the Food and Agriculture System: Report to the National Farmers Union*. Washington, DC: National Farmers Union.

Holmes, Mary Swalla, and Daniel Curry. 2001. Iowa turkey growers and West Liberty Foods. In *New Generation Cooperatives: Case Studies, Expanded 2001*, ed. Mary Holmes, Norman Walzer, and Christopher D. Merrett, 167–178. Macomb: Illinois Institute for Rural Affairs. Available on-line: <www.value-added.org>.

Hupp, Staci, and Perry Beeman. 2001. Tourism and hog farms clash. *The Des Moines Register* (November 11). Available on-line: <www.DesMoinesRegister.com/news/stories.c4789013/16447909.html>.

IMPLAN. 1998. Calculated using IMPLAN data set (based on data from U.S. Bureau of Economic Analysis, U.S. Bureau of Labor Statistics, and U.S. Census Bureau County). Stillwater, MN. See IMPLAN Web site: <www.implan.com>.

Kristof, Nicholas. 2000. Aching heartland: A special report; As life for family farmers worsens, the toughest wither. *New York Times* (April 2): 1.

Krugman, Paul. 1997. Rat democracy: Economics explains a political scandal. *Slate* (May 16). Available on-line: <http://slate.msn.com/?id=1920>.

Lehman, Karen, and Al Krebs. 1996. Control of the world's food supply. In *The Case Against the Global Economy and for a Turn Toward the Local*, ed. Jerry Mander and Edward Goldsmith, 122–130. San Francisco: Sierra Club Books.

Leistritz, F. Larry, and Randall Sell. 2000. *Agricultural Processing Plants in North Dakota: Socioeconomic Impacts* (Agricultural Economics Report No. 437). Fargo: North Dakota State University, Agricultural Experiment Station. Available on-line: <http://agecon.lib.umn.edu/ndsu/aer437.pdf>.

————. 2001a. Socioeconomic impacts of agricultural processing plants. *Rural America* 16(1): 27–34.

————. 2001b. Socioeconomic impacts of agricultural processing plants. *Journal of the Community Development Society* 32(1): 130–159.

Lobao, Linda, and Paul Lasley. 1995. Farm restructuring and crisis in the heartland: An introduction. In *Beyond the Amber Waves of Grain: An Examination of Social and Economic Restructuring in the Heartland.* Ed. Paul Lasley, F. Larry Leistritz, Linda Lobao, and Katherine Meyer, 1–27. Boulder, CO: Westview Press.

Long, Patrick, Jo Clark, and Derek Liston. 1994. *Win, Lose, or Draw? Gambling with America's Small Towns.* Washington, DC: The Aspen Institute.

Looker, Dan. 1999. Unite for success: Value-added co-ops help families capture greater margin in the food chain. *Successful Farming Online* (special issue). Available on-line: <www.agriculture.com/sfonline/sf/1999/special/hope/coop.html>.

Losure, Mary. 1999. *Renville County's Lagoon Blues.* Minnesota Public Radio (December 15). Available on-line: <http://news.mpr.org/features/199912/15_losurem_hogs/>.

Malecki, Edward. 1991. *Technology and Economic Development: The Dynamics of Local, Regional and National Change.* New York: Longman Scientific and Technical.

McMichael, Philip. 1993. World food system restructuring under a GATT regime. *Political Geography* 12(3): 198–214.

Merrett, Christopher D., and John Gruidl. 2000. Small business ownership: The effect of gender and location on entrepreneurial success. *Professional Geographer* 52(3): 425–436.

Merrett, Christopher D., Mary Holmes, and Jennifer Waner. 1999. *Directory of New Generation Cooperatives.* Macomb: Illinois Institute for Rural Affairs.

Merrett, Christopher D., and Norman Walzer. 2001. A survey of new generation cooperatives: Exploring alternative forms of rural economic development. In *A Cooperative Approach to Local Economic Development*, ed. Christopher D. Merrett and Norman Walzer, 91–116. Westport, CT: Quorum Books.

Morehart, Mitch. 1999. *Financial Performance of U.S. Farm Businesses, 1999.* Washington, DC: U.S. Department of Agriculture.

Morrison, E. 1998. Go fish, Egyptian style: A Renville co-op grazes two million fish on the prairie. *AURI Ag Innovation News* 7(3). Available on-line: <www.auri.org/news/ainjul98/tilapia.htm>.

National Rural Economic Developers Association. 2000. *NREDA: National Rural Economic Developers Association Website.* Available on-line: <http://www.nreda.org/>

Oser, Jacob, and Stanley Brue. 1988. *The Evolution of Economic Thought* (4th ed.). New York: Harcourt, Brace and Jovanovich.

Pates, Mikkel. 2001. Wheat co-op asks members for cash. *Grand Forks (ND) Herald* (November 12). Available on-line: <http://web.northscape.com/content/gfherald/2001/11/12/agweek/1112BAKER.htm>.

Putnam, Robert. 2000. *Bowling Alone: The Collapse and Revival of American Community.* New York: Simon and Schuster.

Rich, Jennifer. 2001. U.S. farmers look back . . . and see soy growers in Brazil shadowing them. *New York Times* (July 10): Sec. C, 1.

Ridgeway, James. 1999. Mondo Washington: Broken heartland. *The Village Voice*

(52) (December 29). Available on-line: <www.villagevoice.com/issues/9952/ridgeway.php>.

Roland, Earl. 2000. There is a crisis in rural America: Producers deserve a fair return on investment. *Agweek Online* (AgLink) (May 8). Available on-line: <www.agweek.com/docs.0508/2784CD5.htm>.

Shelley, Fred. 1993. *The Wal-Mart Frontier.* Presentation made at the Conference on World Systems in Political Geography, Virginia Polytechnic and State University, Blacksburg, Virginia.

Song, Booyong, Gerald A. Doeksen, Mike D. Woods, and Dean Schreiner. 1990. *Multiplier Analysis for Agriculture and Other Industries* (Oklahoma Cooperative Extension Publication F-821). Stillwater: Oklahoma State University.

South Dakota State Department of Environment and Natural Resources. 2001. *South Dakota Soybean Back in Compliance with Environmental Permits.* Available on-line: <www.state.sd.us>.

South Dakota Soybean Processors (SDSP). 1998. *Website—Our Beginning.* Available on-line: <www.swiftel.net/sdsp/begin.html>.

Steil, Mark. 2000. *Water Welfare.* Minnesota Public Radio. Available on-line: <http://news.mpr.org/features/200007/07_steilm_water-m/>.

Tweeten, Luther, and Cornelia Flora. 2001. *Vertical Coordination of Agriculture in Farming-Dependent Areas.* Ames, IA: Council for Agricultural Science and Technology.

U.S. Census. 2000a. *Statistical Abstract of the United States, 120th edition* (32, Table No. 33, Metropolitan and Non-metropolitan Area Population by State, 1980 to 1998). Washington, DC: U.S. Bureau of the Census.

———. 2000b. *Statistical Abstract of the United States, 120th edition* (452, Table No. 716, Gross Domestic Product in Current and Real [1996] Dollars by Industry: 1990 to 1998). Washington, DC: U.S. Bureau of the Census.

———. 2000c. *State and County Quickfacts.* Washington, DC: U.S. Bureau of the Census. Available on-line: <http://quickfacts.census.gov/qfd/>.

———. 2001. *USA statistics in brief—Supplement to the Statistical Abstract of the United States.* Available on-line: <www.census.gov/statab/www/part3.html#employ>.

USDA (U.S. Department of Agriculture). 1997a. *1997 census of agriculture—State data* (Table 1, Historical Highlights—1997 and Earlier Census Years). Washington, DC: USDA.

———. 1997b. *1997 Census of Agriculture—State Data* (Table 11, Tenure and Characteristics of Operator and Type of Organization: 1997 and 1992). Washington, DC: USDA.

———. 1998. *A Time to Act: A Report of the USDA National Commission on Small Farms.* Washington, DC: USDA.

USDA–ERS. (U.S. Department of Agriculture-Economic Research Service). 2000. *Food Marketing and Price Spreads: USDA Marketing Bill.* Washington, DC: USDA–ERS. Available on-line: <www.ers.usda.gov/briefing/foodpricespreads/bill/table1.htm>.

U.S. Forest Service. 2001. *Inventory and Monitoring Institute: Economics Program.* Available on-line: <www.fs.fed.us/institute/econ_center.html>.

W.K. Kellogg Foundation. 1997. *Collection of Rural Community Development Resources.* Available on-line: <www.unl.edu/kellogg/>.

Walzer, Norman, and Mary Holmes. 2001. Case study of Southwest Iowa Soy Cooperative. In *New Generation Cooperatives: Case Studies*, ed. Mary Holmes, Norman Walzer, and Christopher D. Merrett, 55–67. Macomb: Illinois Institute for Rural Affairs.

Walzer, Norman, Christopher D. Merrett, and Mary Holmes. 1999. Agriculture and local economic development. *Rural Research Report* 10(10). Macomb: Illinois Institute for Rural Affairs.

Williams, Chris, and Christopher D. Merrett. 2001. Putting cooperative theory into practice: The 21st Century Alliance. In *A Cooperative Approach to Local Economic Development*, ed. Christopher D. Merrett and Norman Walzer, 147–166. Westport, CT: Quorum Press.

8

LEE W. MUNNICH JR. AND GREG SCHROCK

Rural Knowledge Clusters

The Challenge of Rural Economic Prosperity

The implications of globalization for economic development have been dramatic. Firms and industries are presented with a double-edged sword—they have access to global markets, but this access has come at the price of exposure to global competition. In this new competitive climate, firms and industries producing innovative, high-value products have prospered, while those producing standardized, high-volume, low-value products have not. In addition, industries historically accustomed to insulation from global competition have also adjusted less favorably to this new economic context.

The Challenge of Rural Economic Prosperity

Because of this, rural areas face formidable challenges to economic prosperity in an increasingly knowledge-based economy. Although agriculture has been and remains a key staple of the rural economy, manufacturing has also played an important role; however, the traditional sources of rural economic competitiveness—access to natural resources and relatively low costs—have been eroded by declining transportation costs and the globalization of markets. Disadvantages of both geographic (inability to achieve equivalent economies of scale and specialized division of labor) and structural natures (migration from rural communities) help to explain the underperformance of rural relative to urban economies. Since the early 1980s, the wage gap between metro and nonmetro counties has grown significantly, with average earnings in nonmetro counties at a historical low of 69.1 percent of metro earnings in 1998 (Gale and McGranahan 2001).

Rural areas as a whole have lower levels of educational attainment (a rough measure of accumulated knowledge), lower levels of patenting (a measure of ongoing, economically valuable knowledge creation), and have lower levels of venture capital investment than do metropolitan areas. Consequently, rural economies have consistently underperformed in high-technology industries and activities in which knowledge, translated into innovation, forms the only enduring source of competitive advantage. High-technology industry clusters are limited to relatively few U.S. metro areas (Cortright and Meyer 2001), and rural high-technology employment has been generally limited to production-level jobs in branch plants, showing few "clustering" tendencies (Glasmeier 1991).

In an increasingly competitive global economic climate, economic development policymakers and practitioners have actively sought ways of conceptualizing and explaining successful, high-performance economies. This is true both in urban and rural economies. By understanding the fundamental mechanics of these economies, they seek to put in place effective strategies and policies to promote the economic and community vitality of the places where they live and work.

This chapter explores "rural knowledge clusters" as a model of high-performance rural economies. It begins with a discussion of the theory and history of "industry clusters" and the application of this model to rural economies. Lessons drawn from research on rural clusters are discussed, and a synthetic model of "rural knowledge clusters" is proposed. Preliminary evidence on the application of this model to three innovative rural Minnesota economies is presented. The final section explores the economic development implications of this model, including policies and strategies for promoting rural knowledge clusters.

Industry Clusters as a Model of Regional Development

"Industry clusters" have become a popular currency in the past decade for analyzing regional economies and for organizing strategies and policies to promote regional development; yet both the popularity and the elegance of the industry cluster model belie the broad range of economic thought that precedes it.

As Edward Feser (1998) rightly points out, "There is no theory of industry clusters, per se" (19); however, economists, geographers, and regional scientists since the time of Alfred Marshall have sought to explain the complex dynamics of industrial districts. Most of this early work, including that of Allyn Young and Alfred Weber, emphasized the microeconomic benefits of industrial co-location. It was theorized that external (to the firm) economies would result from the agglomeration of industrial activity—not just from scale economies within firms, but from increased specialization and division of labor among firms, lower transaction costs, and greater access to information. The dynamic nature of these externalities promised not only lower production costs but also opportunities for innovation and cross-fertilization of technological advances (i.e., the conversion of semiconductors from military to civilian high-tech applications in Silicon Valley). This seminal work informed the emerging field of regional science and the development of industrial location theory in the 1950s and 1960s.

Deindustrialization in the 1970s and early 1980s placed renewed focus on the fundamentals of industrial location and regional competitiveness. In particular, the resilience and differential performance of successful regions and industries became the center of attention in the late 1980s. Silicon Valley and the "Third Italy" were held up as models of regional development. Silicon Valley, the emerging center of global high-tech development in California, was lauded for its free-wheeling entrepreneurship and dynamic, synergistic relationships between higher education and industry (Saxenian 1994). Meanwhile, the "Third Italy" (portion of northern Italy encompassing the region of Emilia-Romagna) was noted for its "flexibly specialized" networks of small producers in relatively low-tech industrial sectors like shoe production (Piore and Sabel 1984). Countless economic development researchers and policymakers visited these places in search of transferable ideas for regional development.

In 1990, Harvard business economist Michael Porter drew together these rejuvenated theories of regional development with elements of business strategy into a compelling and lucid work, *The Competitive Advantage of Nations*. Porter theorized that successful industry clusters could be explained in terms of a "diamond of advantage." This diamond consisted of four main elements (see Figure 8.1):

1. *Factor conditions:* A region's endowment of factors to production, including human, physical, knowledge, and capital resources, and infrastructure, which make it more conducive to success in a given industry (e.g., wood products in northern Minnesota).
2. *Demand conditions:* The nature of home demand for a given product or service, which can pressure local firms to innovate faster (e.g., Italian shoe production).
3. *Related and supporting industries:* Networks of buyers and suppliers transacting in close proximity to foster active information exchange, collective learning, and supply-chain innovation.
4. *Firm strategy, structure, and rivalry:* A climate that fosters both intense competition among localized producers, yet cooperation and collective action on shared needs, making it fertile for innovation and regional competitive advantage.

Figure 8.1   **Michael Porter's "Diamond of Advantage"**

Source: Porter 1990.

In addition, Porter conferred a peripheral role to *government* and *chance* in affecting the competitive advantage and development path of industry clusters.

Whereas Porter's work on industry clusters resembled existing theories of regional development in many ways, it also represented meaningful extensions of those theories. In addition to incorporating elements from his field of business strategy, Porter drew from emerging (or reemerging) theories of entrepreneurship and "creative destruction" (Joseph Schumpeter), institutional economics (Mancur Olson, Douglass North), and the importance of social relationships and "social capital" (Robert Putnam, Mark Granovetter). The unique synthesis reflected in the work of Porter, Piore and Sabel, and others caused even the late regional political economist Bennett Harrison to conclude that the reemergence of industrial district theory was not, in fact, merely "old wine in new bottles" (Harrison 1992).

From an economic development perspective, several important elements of the industry cluster framework stand out:

- *Endogeneity:* Successful industry clusters tend to possess dynamics, such as trust, competition, and entrepreneurship, that lay the foundation for future success.
- *Agency:* Human agency factors, in the form of collective action, industry, and regional leadership, are crucial elements of ongoing success.
- *Strategy:* The strategic decisions of local firms in competition with one another aid in "raising the bar" for all parties.

The industry cluster model has rapidly become the focus of many economic development initiatives throughout America. Several states, including Arizona and Connecticut, have initiated industry cluster strategies (Waits 2000), while countless cluster initiatives have focused on substate regions, metropolitan areas, and even rural regions. A recent primer on cluster-based

Table 8.1
Four Stages of Industry Cluster Strategies

Stage 1: Mobilization—Building interest and participation among different constituencies needed to carry out the initiative.

Stage 2: Diagnosis—Assessing the industry clusters that comprise the economy and the economic infrastructure that supports cluster performance.

Stage 3: Collaborative Strategy—Convening demand-side stakeholders (companies in each cluster) and supply-side stakeholders (public and private supporting economic institutions) in working groups to identify priority challenges and action initiatives to address shared problems.

Stage 4: Implementation—Building commitment of cluster working group participants and regional stakeholders to actions and identifying or creating an organization to sustain implementation.

Source: Information Design Associates, with ICF Kaiser 1997.

economic development prepared for the Economic Development Administration by Information Design Associates, with ICF Kaiser (1997) described the cluster strategy process as consisting of four discrete stages: (1) mobilization, (2) diagnosis, (3) collaborative strategy, and (4) implementation (Table 8.1). However, the nature of cluster initiatives has ranged from informational (e.g., analyzing the local, regional, or state economy) to strategic (e.g., organizing public policy relating to economic development), while most have incorporated some elements of both.

Rural Industry Clusters—Evidence and Implications

To some observers, the notion of a rural industry cluster seems outright oxymoronic. One of the primary elements of cluster "theory" is that agglomeration economies resulting from urbanization and sectoral division of labor within an economy help promote specialization, productivity, and competitive advantage. These advantages of scale economies are rarely enjoyed by rural areas, as evidenced by the considerable underrepresentation of producer service industries that have been associated with increased productivity and per capita incomes (Gale and McGranahan 2001).

Nonetheless, a considerable body of anecdotal and empirical evidence over the past decade has documented the existence of innovative, successful rural industry clusters. Notable examples of rural clusters frequently cited in economic development literature include the carpet industry in Dalton, Georgia; recreational vehicles in northern Indiana; furniture in Tupelo, Mississippi, and in North Carolina; and houseboats in southern Kentucky (Rosenfeld, Liston, Kingslow, and Forman 2000). Examples from the Pacific Northwest

Table 8.2
Rural Minnesota Industry Clusters Studied by SLPP

Southeast (1996)	Southwest (1998)	Northwest (1998)	Northeast (2001)
• Composites • Food processing • Printing, publishing, and software • Industrial machinery and computer manufacturing	• Computer/Electrical components manufacturing • Value-added ag cooperatives • Precision ag equipment manufacturing • Dairy processing	• Recreational transportation equipment • Value-added ag processing • Wood products • Tourism	• Forest products • Health services • Information technology • Tourism

Source: SLPP, Rural Minnesota Industry Clusters

include the fishing gear industry cluster in Woodland, Washington; bronze casting in Joseph, Oregon; and the sporting goods and apparel industry in Hood River, Oregon.[1] In each of these cases, companies in these rural areas rest at the cutting edge of their respective industries, producing differentiated, high-value products that succeed in the marketplace.

Recent work by the Humphrey Institute's State and Local Policy Program (SLPP) has also uncovered a number of successful industry clusters based in rural Minnesota. Since 1996, SLPP has conducted regional industry cluster studies in southeast (1996), southwest (1998), northwest (1998), and northeast Minnesota (2001) (Table 8.2). Each study examined four industry clusters using the Porter "diamond of advantage" framework discussed above. The diversity of industries found in greater Minnesota is quite striking. They range from traditional natural resource-based staples (e.g., food processing, forest products) to high technology (e.g., computer and electrical components) to high value-added manufacturing (e.g., recreational transportation equipment). Some are relatively mature, stable clusters (e.g., industrial machinery), whereas others are nascent and emerging in nature (e.g., information technology, software). All, however, are important drivers of their respective regional economies and are marked by innovation and regional competitive advantages.

The evidence from qualitative studies of rural industry clusters suggests that their dynamics and structural framework may differ from urban clusters. Rosenfeld and colleagues (2000) posit that rural clusters can take the form of niche "micro-clusters" (i.e., houseboats in southern Kentucky) or, alternatively, extensions of metropolitan clusters. While the latter are more responsive to traditional economic development efforts (such as industrial recruitment), the former represent more robust examples of dynamism and competitive advantage, exhibiting characteristics such as entrepreneurial "spin-off" activity, continuous product innovation, and differentiation. Alternative configurations to the Italianate (or Marshallian) model of flexibly specialized small firm networks are also likely, including "hub-and-spoke" clusters (one or two large firms surrounded by an array of smaller supplier firms) and "satellite platforms" (agglomeration of branch plants based on abundant local resources such as timber). Much the same as Ann Markusen (1996) finds with regards to industrial districts generally, the Italianate model tends to be less common among rural industry clusters.

What do industry clusters contribute to rural economic outcomes? Empirical studies of rural industry clusters have shown that, where they exist, they contribute positively to regional economic growth. Mark Henry and Mark Drabenstott (1996, 67) state that the evidence "points squarely at rural industry clusters as a major source of growth in rural areas" in the 1980s and early 1990s. Furthermore, Robert Gibbs and Andrew Bernat (1997) find that rural industry clusters are associated with higher wages for rural workers.

Even so, the evidence also suggests that specialization in rural economies is a double-edged sword. One team of investigators (Barkley, Henry, and Kim 1999, 184) found that rural industry agglomerations may provide a boost when the industry is growing locally, but come at the cost of greater employment losses when the industry declines. In other words, economic development strategies geared toward increasing industrial specialization may be tantamount to placing a region's proverbial "eggs in one basket," positioning it for cycles of boom and bust. For this reason, rural economic development strategies have traditionally emphasized diversification (usually away from agriculture) over specialization.

In addition, not all rural communities are equally positioned to adopt cluster-based development strategies (Barkley and Henry 1997). Trying to "seed" a cluster from scratch is almost always a recipe for failure; in such cases, a cluster-based strategy may be wholly unsuited to the region; however, where assets, market opportunities, or innovative activities exist that can be built upon, cluster strategies hold much more promise. In either case, the evidence suggests that industry cluster strategies should not be viewed blindly as an all-purpose means toward rural development ends.

As of now, the verdict on industry clusters and rural economies is still open to debate. A wide range of rural economies exhibit characteristics that could be classified as industry clusters, despite generally smaller scale and sectoral scope. And while both anecdotal and empirical evidence associate industry clusters with positive economic outcomes, considerable skepticism still abounds among both academics and practitioners about the utility of the industry cluster approach in rural areas. Part of this concern may be attributed to the general failure of empirical studies to make qualitative distinctions among rural industry clusters. Clusters defined in terms of industry concentration do not necessarily capture important qualitative characteristics, such as the degree of innovation, which may better predict their growth potential. The next section will address this issue and will propose a model of "rural knowledge clusters" to describe high-performance rural economies.

"Rural Knowledge Clusters"—A Better Explanatory Framework?

Dynamic, innovative, and successful rural clusters rely heavily on a base of localized knowledge about the processes, markets, or technologies relating to the products they make. Such an observation should hardly seem surprising on the face of it. Successful companies can be expected to anticipate nascent customer needs with innovative products, or meet existing needs with the newest, most efficient processes and technologies. Both require a considerable amount of knowledge and "know-how," which are embedded in the people and institutions that comprise the cluster.

How could a model of rural innovation address the role of knowledge? "Rural knowledge clusters" offer promising insights. Rural knowledge clusters are specialized networks of innovative, interrelated firms centered outside of major metropolitan areas, deriving competitive advantages primarily through accumulated, embedded, and imported knowledge among local actors.

The rural knowledge cluster framework augments the traditional industry cluster model by placing added emphasis on the instrumental role of knowledge as the engine of innovation and competitive advantage. This is especially important for rural economies, where advantages of agglomeration, scale economies, and highly articulated interindustry linkages—key ingredients of successful urban clusters—are less evident. Furthermore, this framework is consistent with the idea of knowledge as the fundamental basis of competitive advantage in the globalized economy.

Several operational challenges are involved with defining precisely what a "rural knowledge cluster" might be. Each constituent part of the phrase—rural, knowledge, and cluster—is marked by a certain degree of definitional ambiguity. Even the question of what is "rural" is open to debate. Should all areas outside of federally defined metropolitan statistical areas (MSAs) be considered rural, or are measures like the USDA's urban–rural continuum ("Beale") codes more appropriate? (Beale Codes classify counties on a rural-urban continuum. Metropolitan counties are classified by size and nonmetropolitan counties are classified by degree of urbanization and proximity to metropolitan areas. "Beale" refers to Calvin Beale, the USDA economist who developed the system. Within rural development circles they have taken on the shorthand term "Beale" codes.) Or is "ruralness" more subjective in nature, relating to disadvantages faced by the lack of urbanization economies enjoyed by major metropolitan areas? Although deciding what is "rural" is not necessarily the most crucial research question, it is illustrative of challenges inherent in social scientific research.

By comparison, defining "clusters" and "knowledge" is more fundamental (but no less challenging). The industry cluster model has been attacked regularly for its lack of definitional clarity and consistent application (Rosenfeld 2001). Generally, including SLPP's work on industry clusters in Minnesota, clusters have been measured in terms of industrial concentration (e.g., location quotients), growth, and competitive shift (e.g., shift-share analysis); however, sometimes traditional industrial taxonomies mask cluster activity—for example, the cluster of composites producers centered around Winona, Minnesota, are distributed across a host of industrial codes, making their detection through quantitative sources alone very challenging. (Composites are a matrix of one material that has been reinforced by the fibers and/or particles of another material.)

Furthermore, while the term "cluster" almost self-evidently implies the existence of multiple (and competing) firms, what about "hub and spoke" areas, where a major employer is surrounded by a host of supplier firms? This raises an important point about the potential distinctions between a "knowledge cluster" and an "industry cluster." Though this discussion has implied that not all industry clusters are knowledge clusters—the basis of competitive advantage in some industry clusters may be largely resource-based (e.g., forest products or mining)—it is also conceivable that a knowledge cluster may not exhibit characteristics of an industry cluster. To the degree that knowledge about a certain process, technology, or market is diffused and externalized among localized actors (e.g., among employees of "hub" and "spoke" firms) in a manner that creates competitive advantages, it could be considered a knowledge cluster.

Of course, knowledge is a highly intangible commodity and is not synonymous with information. Whereas technology is allowing information to disseminate across greater distances at greater speeds, knowledge continues to cluster geographically. This is because knowledge is more complex, less codified, tends to be embedded in individuals, and, hence, is less readily transferred across space. This conception of knowledge has implications for a wide range of industries. Peter Maskell and co-workers (1998) developed a model of "low-tech learning and innovation" to explain how firms in high-cost European countries compete successfully in traditional "low-tech" industries such as furniture and fish processing through a continuous process of knowledge creation. Recent attempts to quantify knowledge creation and deployment have focused on patent activity (Audretsch 1998; Cortright and Meyer 2001), although the uneven nature of patenting across industries, and the considerable time lag, limits their utility as a broad, cross-sectional measure.

What matters to rural knowledge clusters? Three things matter most of all:

1. *Competitive advantage:* To succeed, the firms within a rural knowledge cluster must enjoy some degree of competitive advantage, in the traditional Michael Porter sense (see Figure 8.1). In the case of a rural knowledge cluster, these may include a rich base of skilled workers, access to proximate market opportunities, or a locally entrepreneurial culture.

2. *History:* Rural knowledge clusters exhibit a path of historical development and evolution to the local knowledge base. Knowledge rarely, if ever, appears out of thin air. This could be the existence of one or two key companies, unique conditions (e.g., geographical), or other factors that have granted local residents the chance to be "in the know" about market opportunities relating to a particular product or technology.

3. *Institutions:* Rural knowledge clusters are marked by institutions, both formal and informal, that have fostered the creation, diffusion, and renewal of the local knowledge base. This is highly important, given the speed with which knowledge can become obsolete economically. Institutions of higher education, including both universities and technical colleges, tend to be prominent in this regard, but informal institutions can also play a role.

These three hypotheses about the nature of rural knowledge clusters drive the exploratory fieldwork conducted recently by SLPP, to be discussed in the next section.

Evidence from Three Rural Knowledge Clusters in Minnesota

In an effort to test the rural knowledge cluster model, three innovative and successful rural clusters in Minnesota were examined by SLPP. The three case studies—wireless technologies in Mankato, automation technologies in Alexandria, and recreational transportation equipment in northwestern Minnesota—were chosen based on consultation with economic development analysts knowledgeable about the rural Minnesota economy. It was believed that these three examples could provide preliminary evidence toward the rural knowledge cluster model.

For each example, the case study methodology addressed three key questions: (1) What is the history of this cluster, and how has the knowledge base relating to these activities developed over time? (2) What are the present sources of competitive advantage for this cluster? and (3) What institutions have been instrumental in the development of the knowledge base?

Mankato: Wireless Technologies

Mankato, a small city of 30,000 people located in south-central Minnesota, is the center of a diverse cluster of activities related to wireless technologies. The cluster is comprised of two regional wireless service providers, Midwest Wireless and HickoryTech (spun out of the local telephone company); several mid-sized manufacturers of electronic components for wireless and communications technologies (including both locally and nonlocally owned firms); and the Institute for Wireless Education, based out of Minnesota State University–Mankato and South Central Technical College, which provides basic and advanced informational training about wireless technologies to major wireless companies such as Nokia, AT&T, and Lucent.

Mankato's historical base of knowledge relating to wireless technologies traces back to E.F. Johnson, a manufacturer of two-way radio systems founded in the nearby town of Waseca in 1923. The presence of E.F. Johnson cultivated a strong base of local knowledge in radio frequency technologies among engineers and technicians employed by the firm. As the company's fortunes waned in the 1970s and early 1980s, several entrepreneurial E.F. Johnson employees struck out on their own to form new companies, including several that offer engineering and contract manufacturing for wireless and communications technology components. This historical knowledge base in wireless technology very likely influenced the development of wireless service providers in the area, including the early diversification of the local telephone company into wireless.

Today, Mankato's primary sources of competitive advantage in wireless technologies rest with its base of highly skilled engineers and technicians, which provides a fertile environment for both the creation of start-up companies and the attraction of outside companies in need of these skills and specialized knowledge. In addition, the local educational infrastructure has continued to produce engineers and technicians with an orientation toward wireless and communications technologies. These supply-side advantages are complemented by Mankato's proximity to industry clusters where new opportunities for wireless applications are emerging, such as the medical devices in the Minneapolis–St. Paul area. The ability of local firms to cultivate new and creative niches for wireless technologies across industries reduces the cluster's vulnerability to cyclical trends.

Both formal and informal institutions have played a role in catalyzing the development of the wireless cluster in Mankato. It is likely that the most important formal institutions have been Minnesota State University–Mankato (MSU) and South Central Technical College (SCTC), which have been instrumental in fostering the region's specialized skills base. Both MSU and SCTC have close connections with the local industry base, and they have worked together recently to eliminate overlaps and foster cooperation between complementary programs relating to wireless technologies. Also, the Wireless and Communications Technology Alliance was recently formed to provide leadership and organizational capacity to Mankato's wireless cluster; however, informal institutions like the ham radio club have also been important in facilitating networking and social capital among individuals knowledgeable in wireless technologies.

Alexandria: Automation Technologies

Alexandria, a small city of fewer than 10,000 residents nestled among the lakes of west-central Minnesota, is at the center of a cluster of firms utilizing automation and motion-control technologies. Although the primary base of this knowledge is located within the local packaging machinery cluster, this knowledge has been "cross-fertilized" into process technology for a diverse set of local manufacturers, resulting in considerable productivity gains. At the center of this cluster is the local technical college, which acts as a "broker" for these automation and motion-control technologies.

Alexandria's knowledge base in automation technology relates directly to the historical strength of the manufacture of packaging equipment in the region. Automation technologies are essential to industrial packaging machinery, which allows high volumes of products to be placed into shipping containers. The historical locational advantages for Minnesota in this industry can be understood in terms of forward linkages to the food processing industry and backward linkages to producers of paper products. Today, however, local packaging companies such as Douglas Machining and Brenton Engineering, and nearby Thiele Technologies (Fergus Falls) and Minnesota Automation (Crosby), produce equipment for use in a wide variety of industries, including automotive parts and pharmaceuticals.

The base of knowledge in Alexandria relating to automation technologies has been instrumental in its application to local companies across a broad array of manufacturing industries. The use of technologies such as programmable logic controllers (PLC) allows for the automation of a wide range of manufacturing processes, enhancing product reliability and worker productivity. For example, Alexandria Extrusion Company, a midsize contract manufacturer of extruded aluminum parts, is one of the few companies in its field that employs automation technologies. The company credits this process innovation to its proximity to sophisticated users of automation technology in the Alexandria area.

Local institutions have played a key role in promoting knowledge spillovers, however. The Center for Automation and Motion Control (CAMC) at Alexandria Technical College (ATC) serves as a broker for knowledge about these technologies. The CAMC was formed in the early 1990s from the college's long-standing competency in fluid-power technology and incorporates more recently developed programs in manufacturing engineering technology and machine assembly. Through its customized training programs, ATC has developed close and interactive relationships with local companies. These relationships are mutually beneficial—companies become exposed to new technologies (i.e., automation technologies) and can equip their incumbent workers with the skills to use them, while the technical college obtains a better, "real time" source of information about the skills needed by graduates of their programs. The college's customized training department is associated with Minnesota Technology, the state's Manufacturing Extension Partnership affiliate, allowing it to leverage additional resources for efforts at modernizing manufacturing.

Northwest Minnesota: Recreational Transportation Equipment

The sparsely populated northwestern corner of Minnesota is the birthplace of the snowmobile and the home of the only two domestically owned snowmobile manufacturers—Polaris and Arctic Cat. The two companies employ over 3,000 workers in the towns of Roseau (pop. 2,750) and Thief River Falls (pop. 8,400), respectively. A more classically defined industry cluster, Polaris and Arctic Cat share a network of suppliers dispersed throughout greater Minnesota. In addition to producing snowmobiles, both companies have expanded and diversified into the production of all-terrain vehicles (ATVs), which have effectively mitigated the cyclical nature of the snowmobile industry. And although Polaris has moved its corporate headquarters closer to the "Twin Cities" in recent years, this region remains the heart of snowmobile manufacturing, and a hub for recreational transportation equipment in general.

The history of the recreational transportation equipment cluster can be traced back directly to Edgar Heteen, an entrepreneurial producer of farm equipment in the 1940s and 1950s. Noting the practical need to get around during the long, snowy winters, Heteen and several of his colleagues began experimenting with designs for belt-driven snow traveling machines and soon thereafter founded Polaris. Seven years later, when Heteen left to start Arctic Cat in 1961, the rivalry began. Locals point out that the pasttime of snowmobile racing began as soon as the second snowmobile was built. In much the same way, the presence of these two companies a mere seventy miles away from each other has engendered a competitive spirit that exists to this day.

Without question, the region's primary source of competitive advantage in recreational transportation equipment is home demand—that is, its proximity to a demanding local customer base. While this factor was certainly important in the cluster's development, it has been equally important in its recent success. Polaris and Arctic Cat both lost considerable market share in the late 1970s and 1980s to Japanese competitors like Yamaha, Kawasaki, and Honda (in fact, Arctic Cat went bankrupt for a short period in 1981–1982). Both companies responded by focusing on innovative, high-performance machinery for the most demanding of customers—the snowmobile racing circuit. The ability to satisfy this market, which they credit to their proximity and agility in developing new ideas, has, in turn, enhanced the ability of the companies to compete on high quality within the broader snowmobile market. This demand-driven competitive advantage can also be credited for the preponderance of recreational boat manufacturers throughout greater Minnesota.

In contrast to the previous examples, formal institutions have played a less instrumental role in the historical development of this knowledge cluster. More important, perhaps, has been the "racing culture" that permeates the local communities. The racing metaphor is a rich one for understanding the forces promoting competition and innovation within the cluster; however, local technical colleges, including Northland Community and Technical College in Thief River Falls, play a vital role in promoting continuous improvement and workforce skill development for Polaris, Arctic Cat, and key local supplier firms, through customized training curricula. As the skill intensity of production jobs continues to increase in the future, the importance of local technical colleges can be expected to grow as well (Table 8.3).

Analysis: What Do These Cases Tell Us?

What can be learned from these three case studies of rural knowledge clusters in Minnesota? Several findings can be drawn:

• *Innovative companies do not exist in a vacuum—Context matters.* While many, if not most, innovative companies and clusters can be traced back to the entrepreneurial efforts of one or two individuals, there is something to be said about the context that made the climate conducive to their success. Par-

Table 8.3

Three Rural Knowledge Clusters in Minnesota:
History, Competitive Advantages, and Institutional Drivers

Rural Knowledge Cluster	History	Competitive Advantages	Institutional Drivers
Mankato (Wireless technologies)	E.F. Johnson, producer of two-way radios in Waseca, cultivated base of talent in radio frequency engineering; decline of company in 1970s and 1980s led to entrepreneurial spin-off activity among former E.F. Johnson employees; cluster currently encompasses electronic component manufacturing, wireless telephone service provision, and wireless education.	Strong base of engineers and technicians with experience and expertise in wireless technologies; proximity to market opportunities in related industry clusters such as medical devices in "Twin Cities."	Local university (MSU-Mankato) and technical college (South Central Technical College); Wireless and Communications Technology Alliance; local radio club
Alexandria (Automation technologies)	Strong local cluster of packaging equipment manufacturers; automation technology essential to product innovation in packaging equipment; local competency developed in automation technologies among workforce and local institutions.	Robust local demand for automation technology: local base of midsize manufacturers in diverse industries looking for process innovations to enhance productivity.	Center for Automation and Motion Control, customized training programs, Alexandria Technical College; manufacturing extension program
Northwest Minnesota (Recreational transportation equipment)	Snowmobile first developed in 1950s by Edgar Heteen, local producer of farm equipment; founded only two current domestically owned snowmobile producers, Polaris and Arctic Cat, which employ over 3,200 locally; expanded recently into ATV production.	Close connection to demanding local customer base (snowmobile racers); fierce competition between Polaris and Arctic Cat; both factors promote innovation.	Informal "racing culture"; local technical colleges (Northland Community and Technical College), customized training programs, continuous improvement programs.

Source: Munnich, Schrock, and Bonelli 2002, 26.

ticularly where multiple innovative, successful companies share common ties—products, workers, knowledge base, history, etc.—this context must be understood. Understanding the advantages inherent in a place is important, not just for assessing competitive strengths, but also for assessing potential weaknesses and liabilities.

• *The same knowledge base can be a driver in multiple industries.* Each of the three examples described a cluster in which knowledge accrued from one setting (industry) has been redeployed to take advantage of market opportunities in another. This is indicative of the complex nature of knowledge. Innovation frequently occurs at the intersection of knowledge from one field with knowledge from another. Economic development strategies should promote cross-fertilization of knowledge and ideas between diverse groups of successful companies.

• *Feedback loops between industry and education are highly important.* Educational institutions played a role in the maintenance, development, and diffusion of the knowledge base in each of the three cases studied. Most prominent of these were linkages between industry and educational institutions. Both universities and technical colleges have an important role to play in advancing the local knowledge base, promoting innovation and continuous improvement in the workplace, and enhancing the skill base of both the emerging and incumbent workforce (Rosenfeld 2000). The synergies are most evident where these linkages exhibit strong feedback loops that transmit real-time information from employers to educators.

Directions for Future Research on Rural Knowledge Clusters

These three case studies offer preliminary evidence supporting the rural knowledge cluster model; however, more work is needed to explore these concepts further, to develop a more robust model, and to identify workable policy alternatives. Key challenges to be addressed in future research include the following:

• *Getting beyond the "fuzzy concept" stage.*
As discussed earlier, a number of definitional issues confront the concept of "rural knowledge cluster." The preliminary work discussed here has focused on articulating the concept further and developing a conceptual model. The next step is to develop definitions that lend themselves to more rigorous quantitative analyses. This will allow for more substantive debate about the merits of this model of rural innovation.

• *The causality trap—Are local factors causes, effects, or neither?*
Any model that examines success stories is almost inevitably inclined to assume a causal link between the local circumstances and its success. While a good case study approach (i.e., one that considers more than just success sto-

ries) can help lessen these tendencies, there is still a tendency to fall into the causality trap. Can a place with history, competitive advantage, and institutional drivers fail? Can a place succeed without them? Such critical questions are important in understanding the public policy implications of this research.

• *Exploring applicability of model to underdeveloped rural economies.*
Unlike the three cases examined here, many rural communities do not enjoy a history of innovation or economic prosperity. Do the lessons from these successful rural economies offer any clues for fostering economic development in underdeveloped rural regions? More work is needed to understand the potential of the rural knowledge model as a developmental model.

Conclusion: Designing Rural Institutions for a Knowledge-Based Economy

The rural knowledge cluster approach to economic development, like the industry cluster model that has prevailed over the past decade, is fundamentally about learning from successful regional economies. Changes in the global economy have forced both urban and rural places to focus increasingly on innovation and competitiveness and to look for creative niches and specializations. This development has posed a dilemma for rural development practitioners and policymakers trying to update their economic base to the changing contours of a knowledge-based economy. What role does a region's historical knowledge base play in creating opportunities for the future? What conditions are necessary for this adaptation and evolution to take place? How do localized institutions catalyze this process? The evidence on rural knowledge clusters presented here suggests some preliminary answers to these questions. More work must be done, however, before concrete solutions can be offered to meet the challenge of rural prosperity in a knowledge-based global economy.

Note

1. We thank Joe Cortright of Impresa Consulting, Portland, Oregon, for supplying us with these examples from the Pacific Northwest.

References

Audretsch, David. 1998. Agglomeration and the location of innovative activity. *Oxford Review of Economic Policy* 14(2): 18–29.
Barkley, David L., and Mark S. Henry. 1997. Rural industrial development: To cluster or not to cluster? *Review of Agricultural Economics* 19(2): 308–325.
Barkley, David L., Mark S. Henry, and Yunsoo Kim. 1999. Industry agglomerations and employment change in non-metropolitan areas. *Review of Urban and Regional Development Studies* 11(3): 168–186.

Cortright, Joseph, and Heike Meyer. 2001. *High-Tech Specialization: A Comparison of High Technology Centers.* Washington, DC: The Brookings Institution, Center on Urban and Metropolitan Policy.

Feser, Edward J. 1998. Old and new theories of industry clusters. In *Clusters and Regional Specialisation,* ed. M. Steiner, 18–40. London: Pion Limited.

Gale, Fred, and David McGranahan. 2001. Nonmetro areas fall behind in the "new economy." *Rural America* 16(1): 44–52.

Gibbs, Robert M., and G. Andrew Bernat, Jr. 1997. Rural industry clusters raise local earnings. *Rural Development Perspectives* 12(3): 18–25.

Glasmeier, Amy. 1991. *The High-Tech Potential: Economic Development in Rural America.* New Brunswick, NJ: Center for Urban Policy Research.

Harrison, Bennett. 1992. Industrial districts: Old wine in new bottles? *Regional Studies* 26(5): 469–483.

Henry, Mark, and Mark Drabenstott. 1996. A new micro view of the U.S. rural economy. *Economic Review* (2nd qtr.): 53–70.

Information Design Associates, with ICF Kaiser. 1997. *Cluster-Based Economic Development: A Key to Regional Competitiveness.* Washington, DC: U.S. Department of Commerce, Economic Development Administration.

Markusen, Ann. 1996. Sticky places in slippery space: A typology of industrial districts. *Economic Geography* 72(3): 293–313.

Maskell, Peter, Heikki Eskelinen, Ingjaldur Hannibalsson, Anders Malmberg, and Eirik Vatne. 1998. *Competitiveness, Localised Learning and Regional Development: Specialisation and Prosperity in Small Open Economies.* New York: Routledge Press.

Munnich, Lee, Greg Schrock, and Anna Hayes Bonelli. 2002. *Rural Knowledge Clusters: Implications for Minnesota State Colleges and Universities.* Minneapolis: State and Local Policy Program, Humphrey Institute of Public Affairs.

Piore, Michael J., and Charles F. Sabel. 1984. *The Second Industrial Divide.* New York: Basic Books.

Porter, Michael. 1990. *The Competitive Advantage of Nations.* New York: The Free Press.

Rosenfeld, Stuart A. 2000. Community college/cluster connections: Specialization and competitiveness in the United States and Europe. *Economic Development Quarterly* 14(1): 51–62.

———. 2001. *Backing into Clusters: Retrofitting Public Policies.* Unpublished paper. Carrboro, NC: Regional Technology Strategies.

Rosenfeld, Stuart A., Cynthia D. Liston, Marcia E. Kingslow, and Eric R. Forman. 2000. *Clusters in Rural Areas: Auto Supply Chains in Tennessee and Houseboat Manufacturers in Kentucky.* Carrboro, NC: Regional Technology Strategies.

Saxenian, Annalee. 1994. *Regional Advantage: Culture and Competition in Silicon Valley and Route 128.* Cambridge, MA: Harvard University Press.

State and Local Policy Program (SLPP). 1999. *Industry Clusters: An Economic Development Strategy for Minnesota.* Minneapolis: SLPP, Humphrey Institute of Public Affairs, University of Minnesota.

Waits, Mary Jo. 2000. The added value of the industry cluster approach to economic analysis, strategy development, and service delivery. *Economic Development Quarterly* 14(1): 35–50.

9

BRIAN DABSON

Strengthening Local Rural Economies Through Entrepreneurship

Karl Stauber (2001), in his recent paper to a banking conference, asked "Why invest in rural America?" This is a provocative look at the way public policy is holding back much of rural America, or even driving it further into trouble. His answers to his own question suggest that the way forward could be in any or all of the following: protecting and restoring the environment; producing high-quality, decommodified food and fiber; providing laboratories of social innovation; creating healthy, well-educated future citizens; and offering a location for immigrant populations. He sees these as part of a new social contract with urban and suburban populations, in which resources are invested in rural areas in return for these kinds of services.[1]

Entrepreneurship: What Is It and Why Is It Important?

Whether Stauber is right or wrong about this future for rural America, there can be little doubt that a fresh ingredient is required—a widespread ability among rural residents to take risks, to identify new economic opportunities, to be able to break away from established ways of doing business—in other words, a new generation of entrepreneurs. Entrepreneurship is one of the main hopes for reviving and strengthening America's rural economies, yet it attracts little attention from rural policymakers and practitioners. Despite overwhelming evidence to the contrary, there is widespread belief that the continuing support of agriculture should be at the heart of rural development or that business attraction and incentives are the most effective routes to rural economic development.

Entrepreneurship comes in many forms. The National Commission on Entrepreneurship (NCOE) (2001a) focuses on what it calls "entrepreneurial growth companies"—small businesses that have the potential to grow rapidly, developing new technologies, products, and services; creating jobs; and stimulating economic growth and investment. Jay Kayne (1999, 3) at the Kauffman Center for Entrepreneurial Leadership, describes entrepreneurs as "individuals who blend innovation with sound business practices to commercialize new products and services that result in high-growth firms."

Less glamorous are microenterprises—sole proprietors, partnerships, or family businesses that employ fewer than five people. As described by Jack Litzenberg, of the Charles Stewart Mott Foundation, microenterprise programs "have the ability to reach low-income and disadvantaged populations effectively, and to raise incomes and asset levels among the poor" (Clarke and Kays 1999, v). In between is the wide array of small businesses started every year by those who are looking for a steady stream of income and employment, either as part of a search for freedom and a change in lifestyle, or out of economic necessity because they have lost their jobs through downsizing.

As a recent evaluation of the Appalachian Regional Commission's Entrepreneurship Initiative points out, "In rural, distressed areas . . . small businesses of all types are needed—those with high growth potential and also those formed for life-style purposes or self-sufficiency that primarily serve local needs" (Regional Technology Strategies 2001, 1).

Obstacles and Opportunities

Starting and growing a business anywhere is fraught with well-documented perils. These are compounded in rural America by low population density and remoteness, with their implications for access to markets, capital, labor, peers, and infrastructure, as well as the way they shape cultural attitudes toward entrepreneurship. There seems to be general agreement about the obstacles to rural entrepreneurship, although the following descriptions owe much to the characteristics of rural communities identified by Gregg Lichtenstein and Thomas Lyons (1996). They categorize the obstacles into three broad groups: (1) those associated with the small size and low densities of rural communities, (2) the social and economic composition of rural communities, and (3) the nature of internal and external linkages.

Low population size and density and, as a consequence, limited local demand make it difficult for rural businesses to achieve economies of scale or critical mass. Without such economies, products and services must be sold at higher prices, often beyond the reach of local consumers, thus limiting the rural market still further. Small firms have no choice but to sell outside their regions, often in niche markets, although for many this is now a more realistic strategy than it used to be with the advent of e-commerce. Conversely, small stores in the retail or local services sectors, which are unable to offer competitive prices, are vulnerable to the arrival of large regional and national discount stores on the edge of town—as many struggling downtowns across the country can testify.

The difficulties in achieving economies of scale are also apparent for those who provide services to small businesses. Entrepreneurs in rural communities are less likely to find the resources and services that are taken for granted in more urban locations, such as regular parcel services, high-speed Internet access, or technical advice from specialists. Suitable buildings with the right access, configuration, or utilities may be hard to find. In many rural communities, there are few lending institutions, the effect of which is to limit access to capital, restrict competition and options, and encourage risk-averse and sometimes discriminatory behaviors. Moreover, entrepreneurs are less likely to encounter peers with whom they can share ideas and problems—the absence of support networks may limit new business creation.

The social and economic composition of rural communities can also have a dampening effect on entrepreneurship. Agriculture, natural resource extraction, or a single manufacturing plant often dominate a rural economy, with most local institutions geared to serving that industry and its employees. This lack of economic diversity may not be a problem in good times, so dependency and complacency—the antithesis of entrepreneurship—become embedded in the culture; however, when farm prices collapse, when natural resources are exhausted, or when the branch plant leaves town, there is little capacity to withstand the consequences of the change in fortune.

Many rural workforces suffer from low skill levels, a lack of skill diversity, a dearth of professionals, and a structural mismatch between available jobs and people. Young and well-educated individuals tend to leave. Rural people, by force of circumstance, may be more self-sufficient than their urban counterparts, but the culture of entrepreneurship tends to be weak. The strong sense of independence, borne of necessity and experience, lessens the likelihood of seeking assistance and reduces interaction. Moreover, there is limited capacity to solve economic development problems—the pool of people and organizations on which to draw is small, and public and civic assistance is less plentiful.

Entrepreneurs rely on internal linkages that encourage the flow of goods, services, information, and ideas. The intensity of family and personal relationships in rural communities can sometimes be helpful, but they may also present obstacles to effective business relationships—business deals may receive less than rigorous objectivity, and intercommunity rivalries may reduce the scope for regional cooperation. Existing businesses might resist new business development for fear of allowing further competition in a limited market. Local politics can blur lines of authority and decision-making processes.

It is their limited connectedness to the outside world that most clearly characterizes rural communities. Remoteness from an airport or an interstate highway will limit the type of businesses that can operate in rural locations. Rural businesses have to make extraordinary efforts to access urban markets, and relationships between urban and rural economies are often unequal. Natural resources are shipped out to urban centers without opportunities for local value to be added through processing or manufacturing. Many rural assets are controlled by absentee owners, whether government or corporate, severely limiting opportunities for local entrepreneurial activity.

The seriousness of these challenges to entrepreneurship obviously varies from region to region. Perhaps the most serious are to be found in many of the remote Indian Country communities, where all of the above obstacles are to be found, but which are further complicated by issues of sovereignty, land tenure, and legal/cultural constraints. Senator Tim Johnson (D–SD) (2001), when addressing tribal leaders, called for more efforts to promote entrepreneurship: "You can go into an area that has a significant population," he observed, "but the business enterprises and job presence is a tenth of what you might expect they might be in a community of that size. You walk away wondering, where are the coffee shops, barber shops, shoe repair shops, gas stations and the hardware stores you would ordinarily expect to find?"

Therefore, we now have a picture of a complex web of barriers to rural entrepreneurship. Despite this, it is also the case that there are many opportunities to promote entrepreneurship, some of which are the converse of the previously mentioned challenges. Three examples illustrate these opportunities: (1) products are available that project traditions of quality, craftsmanship, connectedness with nature, and a sense of place and culture; (2) the quality of life and natural beauty that are inherent to many rural communities are attracting entrepreneurs to relocate from congested and pressured cities; and (3) access to faster telecommunications is spreading, which offers, with some caveats, the possibility for businesses to operate almost independently of location.

In the Pacific Northwest, Ecotrust is a nonprofit organization that helps local communities in the coastal temperate forest region create practical examples of conservation-based development. Ecotrust's founder, Spencer Beebe, vigorously promotes the concept of a conservation economy in which natural resource-based communities can harvest economic wealth while conserving and restoring natural and social capital. Beebe sees the driving force behind a conservation economy to be what he calls "conservation entrepreneurs"—small- and medium-sized business owners who not only embrace a conservation ethic, but also have a rational self-interest in the maintenance and restoration of healthy ecosystems.

Ecotrust has created a new organization, Shorebank Enterprise Pacific (SEP), in partnership with the Shorebank Corporation, a well-known Chicago-based community banking institution. SEP, whose portfolio comprises sixty borrowers and $7 million of loan originations, provides market, financial, management, and development resources to local enterprises. Its strategy is to connect local businesses to green markets and to support them with financing and technical assistance, while working to strengthen whole sectors important to rural economies such as seafood and secondary timber products.

Across the country and facing a different ocean are similar efforts to put into practice conservation-based enterprise development. Coastal Enterprises, Inc. (CEI), a long-established East Coast community economic development organization, sees the potential in developing new markets in hard-pressed natural resource communities, which, in turn, can deliver job growth and further environmental goals (Dickstein, Branscomb, Piotti, and Sheehan n.d.). For instance, CEI has invested in a company that manufactures organic compost from fish waste in Maine's poorest county. Not only did this solve a waste problem for other fishing and aquaculture businesses, but it also created a high value-added export product and jobs in the local community. Neither SEP nor CEI would suggest that this is an easy approach, but they both see harnessing entrepreneurs to achieve economic, community, and environmental goals as being the best hope for the future of rural America.

The natural attractions of rural areas, whether mountains, forests, lakes, or deserts, have become the sparkplugs of many rural economies. "Even isolated communities with relatively high costs of living can attract firms, as long as their quality of life is good enough to attract an educated workforce" (Howe, McMahon, and Propst 1997, 10). Although migration into these communities can create significant problems associated with growth, it can unlock or introduce what Thomas Power (1996, 38) calls entrepreneurial energy that "may lead to creative exploration of ways to exploit markets previously ignored or left to out-of-town business."

The jury is out on the extent to which improved telecommunications access will provide an entrepreneurial boost to rural America. William Fox and Sanela Porca (2000) suggest that its impact is likely to be greater in rural regions that are already economically more integrated with urban and global markets. Conversely, for remote areas, advanced telecommunications may be less advantageous to business although it may help considerably in delivering higher-quality education and health services, which may serve both to upgrade human capacity in these areas and to open up some niche entrepreneurship opportunities. A report by MDC, Inc. (2000), *State of the South 2000,* reinforces this point:

Within the South, the digital divide hits rural communities especially hard. Distance and low population density make digital infrastructure more expensive to build in rural areas . . . [b]ut . . . it is critical that rural businesses have access to affordable, broadband connectivity. Rural communities need the connections to do business in the new economy. (47–48)

Current State of Public Policy and Practice

Although significant shifts have occurred in public policy in recent years, the major focus remains on farming and on physical infrastructure investment. In 1995, the Rural Policy Research Institute (RUPRI) (1995), commenting on the Farm Bill as a vehicle for federal rural policy, observed,

The balance of federal rural development policies and programs consists of a fragmented constellation of programs dispersed among several agencies, with the USDA having a Congressional mandate for coordination. However, this rural development policy has been minimalist, and much less effective than possible, in assisting rural people and places as they confront the fundamental changes occurring in the national and world economies.

One of the mechanisms for focusing government attention on rural America and encouraging partnerships across state and federal government departments and agencies is the National Rural Development Partnership (NRDP). The NRDP comprises three elements: (1) some forty State Rural Development Councils, each with its own mission, structure, plan, and leadership; (2) the National Rural Development Council (NRDC), which brings together program managers from over forty federal agencies; and (3) the National Partnership Office, housed within the U.S. Department of Agriculture (USDA), which is the administrative center for the NRDP. There is no particular focus on entrepreneurship either at the state or federal level, although the Kauffman Center for Entrepreneurial Leadership has given a grant to Partners for Rural America and the Nebraska Community Foundation to work with State Rural Development Councils in Maine, Minnesota, Missouri, and West Virginia to design strategies to promote entrepreneurship.

A concern of current public policy is to avoid assisting businesses already adequately served by private institutions. This has led to a greater emphasis on the targeting of distressed communities and on the reinvigoration of technical assistance services. Recent government initiatives, such as the New Markets initiative, which seeks to mobilize capital in rural areas and tribal reservations, as well as inner cities, are leading to the expansion and refocusing of some existing business-assistance programs within the Small Business Administration (SBA) and the USDA.

Certainly, there is no shortage of government programs that, in various ways, provide support infrastructure to some of the small businesses. The single largest source of federal assistance is the SBA's 7(a) program, which guarantees loans from private lenders to small businesses unable to secure bank financing on reasonable terms. Data on financing per capita show that nonmetropolitan areas receive less than three-quarters of what their counterparts in metropolitan areas receive, which is the result both of lower levels of economic activity in rural America and of fewer private lending institutions in rural communities. The main rural beneficiaries of this nearly $10 billion annual program are counties specializing in services, retirement-destination counties, and nonmetro areas in Western states. A similar program, the USDA's Business and Industry Program, provides about $1 billion annually in loan guarantees exclusively for rural businesses.

There are direct loan programs, such as the SBA's Microloan Program, the largest source of financing for microentrepreneurship, and the USDA's Intermediary Relending Program (IRP). The IRP provides low-interest financing to private nonprofits, public agencies, and tribal groups, which then relend the money to microenterprises and small businesses:

> Such programs may be more appropriate for supporting entrepreneurship in distressed communities or among former recipients of public assistance. Nonprofit organizations have been a traditional conduit of IRP funds to ultimate recipients, and these organizations have an advantage in developing social collateral among borrowers that is key to microenterprise lending. (USDA–ERS 2000, 22)

Estimated funding for 2000 was about $40 million. The SBA and USDA recently entered into a Memorandum of Understanding to allow USDA borrowers to obtain technical assistance through Small Business Development Centers (SBDCs), of which there are fifty-eight state centers plus an extensive network of sub- and satellite centers located at universities, community colleges, and economic development organizations nationwide. These SBDCs provide counseling, training, and technical assistance in all aspects of small business management. The newly established Program for Investment in Micro-Entrepreneurs (PRIME) provides technical assistance to disadvantaged entrepreneurs through microenterprise development organizations. There are also more than eighty Women's Business Centers affiliated with the SBA that provide start-up and managerial assistance to female entrepreneurs and small business owners, although these tend to be located mainly in metropolitan areas.

Recent political changes in Washington have raised some concerns about whether some of these programs will continue. For instance, SBA, toward the end of the Clinton administration, launched a Rural Initiative as part of its efforts to better respond to the needs of rural businesses and rural development finance climate. Roundtables across the country revealed problems that were leading to a decline in SBA-guaranteed rural lending, the lack of venture capital in rural areas, and a lack of coordination with SBDCs and with other federal agencies. The Rural Initiative included a pilot program to speed up the loan approval process and provide better coordination with USDA. Unfortunately, the presidential budget called for a 43 percent reduction in SBA funding levels and fees to be charged for SBDC counseling services, both of which could have disproportionate impacts on rural areas.

The U.S. Treasury's Community Development Financial Institutions (CDFI) Fund provides capital to community development banks, credit unions, venture capital funds, and microenterprise loan funds in distressed areas. Since 1994, the fund has awarded $300 million to community development organizations and financial institutions and, as such, should be a valuable source of funding for organizations promoting and supporting rural entrepreneurship; however, only 11 percent of these awards went to rural America, reflecting the relative lack of eligible CDFIs, according to the National Association of Development Organizations (NADO). Representing some 260 rural and small metropolitan regional development organizations across the country, NADO (2000), makes the point that, although its members are often the primary, and sometimes the only, development agencies in rural areas, they, as local government-controlled entities, are ineligible for CDFI certification and support.

One of the more focused public-sector efforts to stimulate and support rural entrepreneurship has been made by the Appalachian Regional Commission (ARC) (2001). The goal of ARC's Entrepreneurship Initiative is to promote the creation and development of locally owned, value-adding firms that increase local wealth and provide employment opportunities for local residents. It focuses on five areas: (1) entrepreneurial education and training, (2) entrepreneurial networks and clusters, (3) technology transfer, (4) access to capital and financial assistance, and (5) technical and managerial assistance. Through November 2000, ARC invested over $17.6 million, funding 169 educational, business assistance, and capacity-building projects that, in turn, leveraged a further $13.9 million from other sources. Projects included one-on-one assistance for new and existing firms, adult education and training, and business networks and seminars.

The initiative encountered two major obstacles: (1) the lack of institutional capacity to support entrepreneurs and (2) the need to counter criticisms from economic developers. The ARC has sought to address the capacity issue through conferences and workshops, training scholarships, publications, and on-line resources. These have enabled community leaders to build partnerships with associations, consultants, and mentors to assist in developing local entrepreneurship efforts. As important as these linkages are, however, they require sustained effort over many years to achieve real impact on entrepreneurial activity in the region.

The second obstacle has been the belief in some states that business recruitment is the only cost-effective approach to revitalizing rural economies. This translates into resources for marketing and incentives, and also to continued expenditures on basic physical infrastructure. As critics of the initiative have commented, "[W]e cannot effectively develop and retain entrepreneurs if homes straight pipe their waste into streams, if business cannot grow when they cannot obtain clean water, and if transportation barriers increase the cost of commerce, making our firms uncompetitive" (ARC 2001, 114). The challenge facing ARC has been to argue convincingly that entrepreneurship strategies add to, and not replace, traditional approaches.

A recent evaluation of the initiative by Regional Technology Strategies (2001), offered a number of recommendations, of which three are germane. The first was that for the programs to have a substantial impact on the region's economy, they have to be expanded to a more significant scale, and with a multiyear time horizon, and, thus, enhanced resources. It is unfortunate, therefore, that the funding for the initiative has in fact been scaled back.

Regional Technology Strategies' other two recommendations focused on capacity. Building capacity among grantees is critical, they argue, as small organizations in rural areas have few places to turn to for advice and counsel, and they suggested that ARC consider creating a technical assistance budget, form learning networks, and provide staff training. At a larger scale, the evaluators recommended that ARC should build regional technical assistance capabilities—either new or within established organizations—funded to develop expertise, provide technical assistance, store knowledge and information, provide contacts and broker relationships, and conduct training sessions.

Entrepreneurship Infrastructure

What this points to is the growing interest among those engaged in rural policy in the creation or strengthening of intermediation structures. These are seen to be capable of building capacity in ways that address the challenge of diseconomies of scale and to provide the means to identify comparative advantages and market access. The PRIME initiative seeks to build the capacity of microenterprise organizations, particularly important in rural communities; the CDFI Fund invests in intermediary financial structures in places where mainstream financial institutions cannot or will not serve poor communities; and ARC is experimenting with grants to a wide array of business development, financing, and educational organizations to help them better serve the needs of local entrepreneurs.

Of course, this is not new. For years, the federal Economic Development Administration (EDA) and ARC have operated through a network of intermediaries primarily across rural America. Their Economic Development Districts and Local Development Districts, respectively, are essentially formal collaboratives of county governments and, as already noted, for many rural communities they represent the only available professional development capacity. As might be expected in large networks, the quality and scope of services varies enormously, but despite of strong recommendations from evaluators, EDA's resources have not been sufficient to invest in building their capacity and raising standards.

Nevertheless, through the activities of NADO and its research foundation, efforts are being made through research, education, and training to enable these regional development organizations to play a greater and more effective role in rural development, including entrepreneurship and business development. A new initiative takes this a step forward. With support from the Kauffman Center for Entrepreneurial Leadership, NADO has launched the Pioneer Award for Leadership in Entrepreneurial Promotion in Rural America (NADO 2001). Three awards were made in 2001 to regional development organizations that have successfully overcome challenges to promoting entrepreneurship.

The Eastern Maine Incubator Without Walls program, the first-place award winner, was recognized for adapting the business incubator concept to reach businesses in a region of low population density. The program grew out of a partnership between a regional development organization and a community action agency, and it then was extended to include three other such agencies. Now, eight incubators have been established in six Maine counties, operating as a network of service providers that includes colleges, banks, and government agencies.

Another example of intermediation is provided by Rural Local Initiatives Support Corporation (Rural LISC), which was established in 1996 to build the capacity of resident-led rural community development corporations (CDCs). Rural LISC works with seventy-seven CDCs, offering training, technical assistance, and funding, primarily in connection with affordable housing and commercial, industrial, and community facilities. Some of the CDCs provide direct support to rural businesses and entrepreneurs.

The RUPRI's Don Macke (n.d.), project leader for the Rural Entrepre-

Table 9.1
National Ranking of Key Indicators of Entrepreneurship and Urban–Rural Disparity:
Twelve Midwestern States

	Urban/ Rural Disparity	New Companies	Change in New Companies	New Business Job Growth	Private Lending to Small Firms	SBIC Financing
Illinois	44	45	35	34	46	8
Indiana	7	46	43	39	9	44
Iowa	36	50	7	16	8	31
Kansas	17	49	50	37	31	34
Michigan	20	42	46	21	19	22
Minnesota	26	39	10	30	27	18
Missouri	36	38	40	10	38	20
Nebraska	40	44	24	39	4	45
North Dakota	32	41	23	35	1	38
Ohio	3	48	34	31	21	4
South Dakota	38	36	12	42	13	37
Wisconsin	2	47	47	20	44	11

Source: Corporation for Enterprise Development 2001b.

neurship Initiative argues, that entrepreneurial infrastructure in the form of networks, intermediaries, and clusters has the potential to address the issues of economies of scale and comparative advantage mentioned earlier. Intermediaries, whether organized as nonprofit enterprises or trade associations, are "always on the lookout for opportunities, new markets, better production processes, management support, enabling technology, and ensuring a supportive environment for its member entrepreneurs."

These notions of entrepreneurial environment and infrastructure are also themes taken up by the Corporation for Enterprise Development (CFED). Its annual *Development Report Card for the States* (CFED 2001b) provides comparative benchmarking data for all fifty states across sixty social and economic indicators grouped into three main indexes: (1) economic performance, (2) business vitality, and (3) development capacity. Several of these indicators provide insights into the entrepreneurial environment in each state—the number and rate of growth of new companies, the growth of employment created by young companies, private lending to small businesses, and small business investment company financing. Table 9.1 shows how Midwest states compare by indicating their national rank. It also shows urban/rural disparity ranking as an indicator of the difference in performance of urban and rural counties within a state in terms of employment growth, unemployment, average earnings, and earnings growth.

Table 9.2
National Ranking of Competitive Performance Benchmarks and Entrepreneurial Hotspots (EHS): Twelve Midwestern States

Rank	State	EHS Index
13	Indiana	50
15	Minnesota	48
18	Wisconsin	47
19	Ohio	46
22	Missouri	44
25	Michigan	39
26	South Dakota	38
29	Illinois	36
31	Kansas	35
35	Nebraska	33
40	North Dakota	26
47	Iowa	19
U.S. Average		**50**

Source: Indiana Economic Development Council 1999.

The degree to which economic performance differs between urban and rural areas varies significantly across the Midwest. The differences are least marked in Wisconsin (the nation's number two), Ohio (third), and Indiana; whereas the greatest disparities are to be found in Illinois and Nebraska. In terms of new company formation, all the Midwest states are modest to poor performers, with Iowa ranked fiftieth in the nation. Nevertheless, the jobs created by young companies in the region are above the national average in Iowa, Michigan, Missouri, and Wisconsin. On the small business financing side, there is great variation among the states. North Dakota (first in the nation), Indiana, Iowa, Michigan, Nebraska, and South Dakota are strong in private lending, with Illinois and Wisconsin being among the nation's weakest; Illinois and Ohio are in the top ten states for financing of small business investment companies (SBIC), with Indiana and Nebraska in the bottom ten.

Overall, the Midwest region does not compare favorably in its entrepreneurial performance with other parts of the country. This is confirmed by *Indiana Benchmarks,* a periodic review by the Indiana Economic Development Council that documents and assesses the state's competitive position. The latest edition published in 1999 included an Entrepreneurial Hot Spot Index using Cognetics' rating of states based on their share of young firms in

Table 9.3

National Ranking of Small Population Labor Market Areas (LMAs) by Growth Company Index: Midwestern LMAs Performing Above the National Average

Rank (n=76)	LMA Populations 100,000–150,000	State	Growth Company Index	Strongest Business Sectors
5	Monett	MO	170	Local Market
7	Mount Pleasant	MI	165	Retail
12	Greensburg	IN	132	Retail
13	Ottumwa	IA	128	Distributive, Extractive, Manufacturing
14	Wabash	IN	128	Manufacturing
22	Columbus	IN	114	Manufacturing
27	Hibbing	MN	102	Manufacturing
29	Norfolk	NE	96	Distributive
32	Vincennes	IN	95	Distributive, Extractive
34	Hutchinson	MN	86	Distributive, Manufacturing
35	Galesburg	IL	84	Business Services, Retail
Average			**79**	

Source: National Commission on Entrepreneurship (NCOE) 2001b.

the economy and young firms experiencing significant growth. Table 9.2 lists the ranking for Midwest states.

Unfortunately, neither of these tables provides a clear picture of what is happening in the rural Midwest. A recent report from the National Commission on Entrepreneurship (NCOE) (2001b) presents an analysis of the incidence of high-growth companies by labor market area across the country. Table 9.3 shows how Midwestern labor market areas (LMAs) with populations of 100,000 to 150,000 (the smallest and most rural category) rank according to NCOE's Growth Company Index. Table 9.4 presents the same information for the highest-performing small LMA in each of the Midwest states.

Table 9.3 suggests rural Indiana, with four communities of the eleven in the Midwest performing above the national average, has a conducive entrepreneurial environment, particularly compared with the highest-performing small LMAs in North and South Dakota, Ohio, and Wisconsin, which are all significantly below the national average (see Table 9.4).

The CFED's (2001a) recent study for the Mary Reynolds Babcock Foundation took this type of analysis a stage further for ten Southern states; it found an enormous disparity between states in the depth and breadth of infrastructure in place to support entrepreneurship. North Carolina scores high with long-term

Table 9.4

National Ranking of Small Population Labor Market Areas (LMAs) by Growth Company Index: Top Performing LMA in each of the Twelve Midwestern States

Rank (n=76)	LMA Populations 100,000–150,000	State	Growth Company Index	Strongest Business Sectors
5	Monett	MO	170	Local Market
7	Mount Pleasant	MI	165	Retail
12	Greensburg	IN	132	Retail
13	Ottumwa	IA	128	Distributive, Extractive, Manufacturing
27	Hibbing	MN	102	Manufacturing
29	Norfolk	NE	96	Distributive
35	Galesburg	IL	84	Business Services, Retail
38	Salina	KS	73	Business Services, Distributive, Local Market
40	Minot	ND	68	Distributive, Local Market
52	Athens	OH	45	Retail
58	Monroe	WI	34	Distributive, Manufacturing
72	Aberdeen	SD	7	Distributive
Average			**79**	

Source: National Commission on Entrepreneurship (NCOE 2001b).

and consistent public-sector support for the full range of entrepreneurial services, and for the presence of several of the nation's leading CDFIs providing statewide coverage and targeting both rural and urban communities. In addition, there are strong trade associations for CDCs, microenterprise practitioners, and community development credit unions, and philanthropic support for institutions and initiatives promoting entrepreneurship.

In contrast, policy in states such as South Carolina is grounded in a philosophy that business attraction and incentives are the most effective routes to economic development. Little has been invested in the promotion of local entrepreneurship. The services that do exist are usually localized to the service area of a single institution that patches together funding sources to provide capital and technical assistance to entrepreneurs. These institutions are typically isolated from one another, given the absence of practitioner networks and associations, and they lack a policy voice on behalf of their interests.

The CFED study identified several aspects of infrastructure essential for creating an effective entrepreneurial development system. First, there has to be a supportive policy environment. State policy is the means by which entrepreneurial development strategies reach scale. State appropriations and tax incentives provide the seed and operating capital necessary to build the institutions that deliver products and services to low-wealth communities. Legislative rules create opportunities to redeploy existing state and federal resources in new ways to support entrepreneurial development.

A second aspect is capacity and leadership development for practitioners. Many states lack the fora for practitioners to share best practices, build new skills and competencies, or pursue an agenda of policy advocacy. Practitioner networks and trade associations at the state level are an important tool for building the field, which can be still more effective if linked to national institutions and local and state intermediaries that can provide them with access to even greater resources and opportunities.

The National Commission on Entrepreneurship (NCOE) has as its mission "to provide local, state, and national leaders with a roadmap for sustaining and expanding a flourishing economy." The NCOE (2001a) sees "[e]ntrepreneurship as the critical force behind innovation and new wealth creation, the key drivers of our country's economic growth" (inside front cover). The NCOE set out a five-point policy agenda for entrepreneurial growth companies. One common theme across this agenda is the need for an education system that produces employees with the right basic and technical skills, echoing a widely held view that all economies, and rural economies in particular, are held back by an inadequately educated and skilled workforce.

This ties in well with investments made by ARC's Entrepreneurship Initiative in REAL Enterprises and heralded in Regional Technology Strategies' evaluation as a good example of building capacity at the local level by linking into available expertise and resources at the national level. The REAL program introduces individuals, communities, schools, and rural America to hands-on entrepreneurship education; REAL is a nonprofit intermediary for a national network of individuals, organizations, and corporations committed to making entrepreneurship education available to all. It provides tools to elementary, middle, and high schools; to community and four-year colleges; and to others to increase awareness of the value of entrepreneurship as a career option and a way of thinking. There are currently twelve state REAL organizations, and the experiential curriculum is taught in schools in another twenty states nationwide.

Future Directions

Placing Rural Entrepreneurship on the Federal Policy Agenda

From a policy standpoint, rural development is still the stepchild of agricultural policy, and rural entrepreneurship is low on the list of priorities for rural development policymakers and practitioners. A priority task is to identify opportunities to bring about changes in attitudes and policies at the federal level. For instance, the Congressional Rural Caucus, with the support of the National Association of Development Organizations, the National Association of Towns and Townships, and the National Association of Counties, is calling for a White House Conference on Rural America to create a common framework for improving the nation's approach to rural policy development. Entrepreneurship has to be on the agenda.

Giving Greater Funding Priority to Programs That Support Rural Entrepreneurship

A greater focus on entrepreneurship is needed to change funding priorities within federal programs—for example, additional resources to expand upon the promising work of ARC's Entrepreneurship Initiative and to ensure that similar funds are allocated to the new Delta Regional Commission; funding to advance microenterprise activities within the SBA and especially for PRIME, which supports capacity building for microenterprise development organizations; resources through EDA (Economic Development Administration) to build capacity among staff and boards of regional development organizations; and implementation of the SBA's currently stalled Rural Initiative.

Encouraging Investment in Research, Ideas, and Action

There is considerable energy going into promoting different aspects of entrepreneurship. The Kauffman Center for Entrepreneurial Leadership has invested in a range of projects to stimulate ideas and action in addressing the challenges of rural entrepreneurship. These include the Rural Entrepreneurship Initiative referred to earlier and a partnership with the National Governors' Association to form the Governors' Academy on Entrepreneurship in ten states to focus on the factors needed to create entrepreneurial economies. These are important seeding initiatives to raise awareness and understanding at local and state levels.

Investing in Intermediary Institutions

According to NCOE (2000), "the keys to a region's entrepreneurial success are private networks and a regional commitment to entrepreneurial growth. Perhaps government's most effective tool is to stimulate and support private-sector institutions that work directly with entrepreneurs to build networks and spur regional entrepreneurial development" (26).

The way forward to achieve a real shift in entrepreneurial activity in rural America is to invest in a network of high-quality intermediaries—whether public, private, nonprofit, or some combination—that can achieve economies of scale and uncover comparative advantage for the benefit of high-growth entrepreneurs or individuals seeking economic self-sufficiency.

Building on Current Innovations

There is already considerable innovation and activity that gives hope for rural America, but it is still scattered and below the scale needed to achieve a deep and lasting impact. Some examples from which to learn, and upon which to expand, include the following:

• The state infrastructure that North Carolina has created to support entrepreneurship is worthy of more detailed examination to gauge its effectiveness and its replicability.

• There are a number of sophisticated nonprofit development organizations in rural America that are at the forefront of innovation and best practice and that combine entrepreneurship support and enterprise development, with a range of other important rural development functions. Ecotrust/Shorebank Enterprise Pacific and Coastal Enterprises were mentioned earlier; others include Mountain Association for Community and Economic Development (MACED) in Kentucky; Alternatives Federal Credit Union in upstate New York; ACEnet Ventures in Appalachian Ohio, Kentucky, and West Virginia; and The Nature Conservancy's Compatible Ventures Unit.

• The CDFI Fund has certified 452 organizations—community development banks, loan funds, venture capital funds, and microenterprise development agencies—as meeting certain standards to operate as financial services entities with a community development mission. Of the over one-third of these organizations that have received core funding from the fund, two-thirds serve both rural and urban areas, and at the last count just seventeen served rural areas exclusively. Assuming the fund will continue to attract support from Congress, there is considerable potential for expansion into rural America, including tribal communities.

• There are at least 283 microenterprise practitioner programs all across the United States. These have provided financing and technical assistance to over 250,000 microbusinesses. There is now considerable interest in creating state networks and associations to promote state policy initiatives, generate funding streams, and build capacity among practitioner programs. With funding from the Charles Stewart Mott Foundation and the Ford Foundation, CFED has provided financial support for sixteen of a total of an estimated twenty-seven emerging or existing state networks. Although there are no data on how many serve rural communities, anecdotal evidence shows that they have a significant presence serving primarily low-income individuals.

• CFED has recently launched a major new initiative, the National Fund for Enterprise Development (NFED). Based on the model provided by the Nebraska Enterprise Opportunity Network, this will provide financial products and development services to community development financial institutions operating either at a state or regional level whose purpose is to expand, leverage, or consolidate financial and technical resources for underserved micro and small business entrepreneurs. The goal of NFED is to be a catalyst and national intermediary for a new generation of state-level microenterprise intermediaries that will, in turn, focus on state-level fund-raising, best-practices adoption, delivery coordination, enhanced impact, and accountability. Some evidence suggests a latent demand for such intermediaries in twenty-five states. There are already examples operating in Montana, Nebraska, North Carolina, and Virginia. Although NFED does not have a specific focus on rural America, it seems likely that its primary investments will be in rural intermediaries.

• Through the Consortium for Entrepreneurship Education, steps have been taken to raise awareness among policymakers, especially at the state level, of the importance and value of entrepreneurship education in schools and communities. With membership that includes energetic national youth enterprise organizations such as REAL Enterprises and the National Foundation for the Teaching of Entrepreneurship (NFTE), as well as school and college educators and administrators, performance criteria have been drafted for advancing the quality of entrepreneurship education. The power of this growing movement was evidenced by enthusiastic participation at conferences and workshops across rural Appalachia in 2000, organized as part of ARC's Entrepreneurship Initiative.

Putting Entrepreneurship on the Map in Rural America

This list could be much longer, but the key point is that there is great potential to put entrepreneurship on the map in rural America. What it will take is continued efforts by organizations such as the Center for the Study of Rural America, the Kauffman Foundation, the National Commission on Entrepreneurship, the Rural Policy Research Unit, the Appalachian Regional Commission, National Association of Development Organizations, Corporation for Enterprise Development, and many others to keep raising awareness and understanding; to identify innovations and best practices; and to provide opportunities for learning and sharing among public, private, and nonprofit organizations.

What it will also take is a shift in legislative priorities at the state and federal levels to ensure that efforts to create entrepreneurial economies take their proper place alongside physical infrastructure and farm support in rural America.

Note

1. This chapter is an adaptation of Dabson's chapter in the following publication: Dabson, Brian. 2001. Supporting rural entrepreneurship. In *Exploring Policy Options for a New Rural America*, ed. Center for the Study of Rural America, 35–48. Kansas City, MO: Federal Reserve Bank of Kansas City.

References

Appalachian Regional Commission (ARC). 2001. *Entrepreneurship Initiative Approved Projects*. Washington, DC: ARC.

Clarke, Peggy, and Amy Kays. 1999. *Microenterprise and the Poor.* Washington, DC: The Aspen Institute.

Corporation for Enterprise Development (CFED). 2001a. *Infrastructure for Entrepreneurial Development: A Scan of Ten Southern States for the Mary Reynolds Babcock Foundation.* Washington, DC: CFED.

———. 2001b. *Development Report Card for the States, 2001.* Available on-line: <www.drc.cfed.org>.

Dickstein, Carla, Diane Branscomb, John Piotti, and Elizabeth Sheehan. n.d. *Sustainable Development in Practice: A Case Study Analysis of Coastal Enterprises, Inc.'s Experience.* Wiscasset, ME: Coastal Enterprises.

Fox, William F., and Sanela Porca. 2000. Investing in rural infrastructure. In *Beyond Agriculture: New Policies for Rural America*, ed. Center for Study of Rural America. Kansas City, MO: Federal Bank of Kansas City.

Howe, Jim, Ed McMahon, and Luther Propst. 1997. *Balancing Nature and Commerce in Gateway Communities.* Washington, DC, and Covelo, CA: Island Press.

Indiana Economic Development Council. 1999. *Indiana Benchmarks 1999: Indicators for Monitoring Indiana's Competitive Performance* (2nd ed.). Indianapolis: Indiana Economic Development Council.

Johnson, Tim. 2001. Quoted in Kay Humphrey. Developing economy key in boosting employment. *Indian Country Today.* Available on-line: <www.indiancountry.com/?1854>. Downloaded: April 15, 2002.

Kayne, Jay. 1999. *State Entrepreneurship Policies and Programs.* Kansas City, MO: Kauffman Center for Entrepreneurial Leadership.

Lichtenstein, Gregg A., and Thomas S. Lyons. 1996. *Incubating New Enterprises: A Guide to Successful Practices.* Washington, DC: The Aspen Institute.

Macke, Don. n.d. *Entrepreneurship in Rural America.* Available on-line: <www.nebcomfound.org>.

MDC, Inc. 2000. *The State of the South 2000.* Chapel Hill, NC: Author.

National Association of Development Organizations (NADO). 2000. *EDFS Reporter.*

———. 2001. *Taking Care of Business: The Role of Regional Development Organizations in Promoting Rural Entrepreneurship.* Washington, DC: NADO

National Commission on Entrepreneurship (NCOE). 2000. *Building Companies, Build-*

ing Communities: Entrepreneurs in the New Economy. Washington, DC: NCOE.
————. 2001a. *Five Myths About Entrepreneurs: Understanding How Businesses Start and Grow.* Washington, DC: NCOE.
————. 2001b. *High Growth Companies: Mapping America's Entrepreneurial Landscape.* Washington, DC: NCOE.
Power, Thomas Michael. 1996. *Lost Landscapes and Failed Economies: The Search for Value of Place.* Washington, DC, and Covelo, CA: Island Press.
Regional Technology Strategies. 2001. *Evaluation of ARC's Entrepreneurship Initiative.* Chapel Hill, NC: Author.
Rural Policy Research Institute (RUPRI). 1995. *Opportunities for Rural Policy Reform: Lessons from Recent Farm Bills* (Policy Paper P95–2). Available online: <www.rupri.org/pubs/archive/old/policy/P95–2.html>.
Stauber, Karl N. 2001. Why invest in rural America—and how? A critical public policy question for the 21st century. In *Exploring Policy Options for a New Rural America.* Ed. Center for Study of Rural America. Kansas City, MO: Federal Reserve Bank of Kansas City.
U.S. Department of Agriculture–Economic Research Service (USDA–ERS). 2000. Technical assistance assuming greater role in business assistance programs. *Rural Conditions and Trends* 11(1): 19–24.

10

JOHN C. LEATHERMAN

The Internet-Based Economy and Rural Economic Competitiveness

The first Internet Web browser was introduced in 1993. Today, the Internet seems ubiquitous and indispensable. We have witnessed a true phenomenon with the growth of the World Wide Web. Advances in the Internet and other telecommunications technologies have opened new frontiers in communication, commerce, medicine, politics, and almost every other aspect of private and public life. It is not an overstatement to suggest that the Internet is among the most powerful forces shaping the early twenty-first century.

So what is this likely to mean for rural communities in the Midwest and elsewhere? Will telecommunications technologies level the playing field for rural places, allowing them to overcome the penalty of distance and usher in new rural prosperity? Or will the benefits associated with these new technologies, as so many other broad economic trends of the past, work against rural places, leaving them further behind?

Concerns have already been expressed about the "digital divide" that has emerged between groups of people who have the access and ability to take advantage of Internet technologies and those who do not. The divide spans ethnic, socioeconomic, and geographic boundaries (NTIA 1999). Perhaps not surprisingly, the two places that seem to be lagging most are urban inner cities and remote rural places, including Native American communities.

Yet there are those who express at least cautious optimism on behalf of rural areas. It has been suggested that rural communities can be attractive to "lone eagles" and "high fliers," those entrepreneurs and firms that deliver services by way of telecommunications technologies (Beyers and Lindahl 1996). Others have pondered whether telecommunications may be the vehicle whereby rural places may be competitive in attracting back-office, mail order, and Internet-based retail businesses (Stenberg, Isserman, and Young 1998).

The Internet and, more broadly, advanced information technologies will, indeed, have implications for rural community viability in the decades ahead.

This chapter will explore some of what we currently know about the rapidly unfolding impacts that advanced information technologies have for economic activity in rural places. The primary focus will be the implications for private-sector economic activity and rural community competitiveness.

The chapter begins with a brief discussion of the scale and scope of information technologies in the U.S. economy together with some explanation of the benefits such technologies impart to businesses. Some of the relevant factors relating to rural community competitiveness in attracting or otherwise benefiting from this technology is then presented. Next, a few ideas relating to how rural business can maximize the use and utility of these technologies are offered. Finally, prescriptions are offered that address the adaptive strategies available to those rural communities that want to maximize their competitiveness in a new era increasingly dominated by advanced information technologies.

Overview of the Internet Economy

To begin, it will help to define the scope of our discussion of the Internet economy. Most attention has focused on the idea of Web-based retail sales. This, however, is only a small part of what advanced information technologies (IT) contribute to enhancing economic relationships. Indeed, electronic business refers to a host of applications enabled by the electronic exchange of information, goods, services, and payments (Conhaim 1998). The U.S. Census Bureau defines the "digital economy" as consisting of three components: (1) the supporting infrastructure that builds, supports, and transmits digitized information; (2) electronic business processes that govern how business is conducted; and, finally, (3) electronic commerce involving the transfer of goods and services mediated by Internet-based transactions (Mesenbourg 2001). Electronic exchanges can occur by way of the World Wide Web, or in many other ways, including intranets and extranets, smart cards, optical scanners, and a host of other technologies that digitize and transmit information. It is more accurate to be expansive when thinking about electronic business and the information economy and the myriad ways IT has influenced business and economic relationships.

The focus of this chapter will be somewhat narrower, dealing primarily with Internet-based applications. Again, the dimensions of the Internet-based economy extend far beyond the notion of Web-based retail sales. Perhaps the most widely cited conception was offered by the Center for Research in Electronic Commerce (CREC) (Cisco Systems and the University of Texas 2001), located at the University of Texas at Austin. Researchers there conceptualize the Internet economy as consisting of four layers of economic activity.

The first layer is the Internet *infrastructure* layer, which consists of the telecommunications companies, manufacturers of networking equipment and PCs (personal computers), Internet service providers, and other vendors who help make the physical system work. The second layer of the Internet economy is the Internet *applications* layer, which involves the software makers and other intermediaries that facilitate Internet-based transactions.

The Internet *intermediary* layer, the third layer of the Internet economy, includes the firms that help provide the content found on the World Wide Web. These firms develop products for using the Web, such as search engines, or broker Web-based transactions, such as on-line travel agents and brokerages. The final layer of the Internet economy is one that engages directly in the sales of products and services over the Internet, the group that CREC labels the Internet *commerce* layer. Such firms include the Internet-based booksellers, auto dealers, and subscription services.

These combined sectors accounted for over $200 billion in revenue during the second quarter of 2000, a 59 percent increase over the second quarter of 1999, according to a CREC estimate. These sectors also employed nearly 3.1 million people at the end of the second quarter 2000, a 22.6 percent increase over the previous year.

Needless to say, the growth in these sectors of the economy has been impressive. While IT-producing sectors comprise only a small percentage of overall economic activity in the United States, they accounted for a substantial proportion of the positive economic performance witnessed in the 1990s. The U.S. Department of Commerce credits these combined sectors with contributing on average 30 percent of the nation's real economic growth between 1995 and 1999, reducing overall inflation by an average 0.5 percentage points annually between 1995 and 1998, and contributing about half of the overall productivity growth observed in the United States in the latter half of the 1990s (Buckley et al. 2000). Further, the U.S. Department of Commerce projects that by 2006, almost half of the U.S. workforce will be employed in industries that are either major producers or intensive users of IT products and services.

Though U.S. governmental agencies have clearly been bullish in touting IT benefits, others have been more moderate. The McKinsey Global Institute (2001), a management consulting firm, suggested that IT played only a limited role in enhancing U.S. productivity growth. Its direct contribution to growth in productivity between 1995 and 2000 was substantial and significant for only a limited number of economic sectors. Much of the productivity growth was attributed to old-economy factors such as innovation, competition, and cyclical demand. Information technology was found to help drive productivity growth only when it enabled managerial innovation, facilitated the reorganization of functions, and applied to labor-intensive activities.

Whether a major driver or simply a mediating mechanism, IT and Internet-based exchange clearly are factors with potential to influence business competitiveness and viability. As such, any business or community not considering how these technologies might create or constrain opportunities does so at some risk.

How Electronic Commerce Benefits Business

In addition to growth associated with the industries building the Internet infrastructure and the content of the World Wide Web, the new technology enables two types of economic relationships that are beneficial to many companies. The first is hardly visible to ordinary consumers, while the second targets those very consumers.

The greatest economic value currently associated with Internet-based commerce involves business-to-business transactions (OECD 1998). Shifting many of the internal functions of business operations, such as order placement, inventory control, technical specification procurement, and product distribution, from paper-based to electronic transactions can dramatically reduce business costs and increase productivity. For example, Wal-Mart Stores, an early adopter of IT-based management systems, recently surpassed Exxon Mobil as the world's largest corporation, and is credited with driving productivity increases in the U.S. retail trade sector through its fierce competitive practices (McKinsey Global Institute 2001; Postrel 2002).

Meanwhile, Kmart Corporation, widely known for its resistance to adopting IT, could not master supply-chain technology, failed to compete with Wal-Mart on price, and ultimately filed for bankruptcy protection (Konicki 2002). Many large companies have reported significant savings and are increasingly demanding that suppliers and vendors switch to electronic systems. To some degree, this may force small- and midsize vendors doing business with larger companies to acquire technologies sooner than they otherwise might have.

Lucking-Reiley and Spulber (2001) gathered several anecdotal examples of how electronic transactions have reduced business costs:

• By moving external procurement functions to electronic commerce, British Telecom estimated it reduced costs from $113 to $8 per transaction.

• MasterCard estimated the cost of processing purchase orders fell from $125 to $40, while the time needed to complete processing went from 4 days to 1.25 days.

• According to Lehman Brothers, the costs to complete financial transactions were $1.27 for a teller, $0.27 for an ATM, and $0.01 for an on-line transaction.

• Traditional discount brokerage fees have fallen from in excess of $50 to below $5 on-line.

There are numerous ways IT has potential to enhance business productivity (Lucking-Reiley and Spulber 2001). Cost efficiencies are gained from the automation of transactions between buyers and suppliers by avoiding the need to translate computer files into paper documents, a process often involving errors, delays, and costly personnel. Search costs are also lowered, a potentially significant savings depending on the value of the product. Communication costs can also be lowered by negating the need for interpersonal communication, travel, meeting space, and the processing of paper documents. New Internet-based intermediaries can lower the costs of bringing buyer and seller together by reducing search and communication costs, certifying buyers and sellers, consolidating markets, providing product information, and providing one-stop shopping.

New exchanges are being formed by a number of larger companies to take advantage of economies of scale, especially in markets that have high fixed costs and where the marginal costs of facilitating Internet-based transactions are very close to zero. One example is the new joint venture by General Motors, Ford, and DaimlerChrysler to form an integrated supplier exchange (Bartholomew 2000). The new exchange will be a private company open to all automotive manufacturers and suppliers. Company executives project it will do a trillion dollars worth of business annually.

The final way IT should enhance business productivity may be to foster greater outsourcing of goods and services that were previously produced internally. This will save companies the cost of managing these activities and allow them to focus on their core products and services.

The second way the Internet has been utilized by business is in direct sales to the final consumer (business-to-consumer). Businesses such as Amazon, e-bay, e-Toys, and Auto-by-Tel appeared seemingly out of nowhere only a few years ago and rapidly built staggering sales figures (OECD 1998). Other businesses such as brokerage and securities trading firms have been transformed, with many now providing the bulk of their services via the Internet (Barber and Odean 2001). The Internet has allowed many merchants to open hitherto inaccessible markets at relatively low cost.

An on-line environment provides advantages to both consumers and retailers (Bakos 2001):

• Search costs for both buyers and sellers are reduced. Consumers have access to vastly expanded information resources with which to research and comparison-shop prior to making purchases, even if those purchases are from traditional retailers. Sellers are able to identify qualified buyers for their products without advertising or making sales calls.

• For many classes of items, lowered search costs will lead to greater price competition among sellers and lower costs to consumers.

• Sellers will have greater opportunity to differentiate their products from competitors. An on-line world is free of shelf space limitations, permitting an expanded product line and greater quantities of information about offerings. This may be of special benefit to small-scale sellers if they are able to establish appropriate niches for their product lines.

• Internet technologies permit greater customization of product offerings. Consumer profiling will permit sellers to offer known preferences. By combining purchasing histories and consumer demographic information, sellers can estimate the preferences of new customers with a minimum of information.

• On-line auctions open a new marketplace, facilitating business-to-business and customer-to-customer transactions or providing sellers new mechanisms of price discovery.

• Finally, the role of intermediaries is again important as new virtual shopping malls organize and make available product classes sought by buyers.

All of this discussion points to the scope and scale of what is occurring, and it begs the question of whether rural businesses and communities will participate in the benefits associated with this economic growth. The positive view suggests that the technology can help rural communities overcome the disadvantages of distance and remoteness. Critics counter that the capacity to access and use the technologies will be slow in coming to rural areas.

Economic Activity and Rural Competitiveness

There are several ways to address the question of rural competitiveness in this new business environment. Unfortunately, much of the assessment is largely speculative given the paucity of research data. Some of the available information is gleaned from Internet-business boosters or advocacy groups and needs to be evaluated accordingly. Thus, the best that might be accomplished is to raise questions about how rural areas are likely to fare.

Rural Characteristics

Rural America is a large and diverse area. Some rural places, particularly those with high amenity values and those not too distant from metropolitan communities, are doing quite well (Johnson and Beale 1999). Other rural places suffer from what is sometimes called the "rural penalty" (Malecki

1996). Actually, there seem to be three general characteristics of rural places that would affect their access to or use of IT: (1) the remote geography both increases costs associated with infrastructure diffusion and makes rural markets less attractive for outside investment; (2) the economic structure of rural places seems a detriment insofar as their industries are neither heavily IT-producing nor IT-using; and (3) the human capital found in rural areas does not seem especially attractive either as a labor market or as a consumer market.

Those industries that are either involved in the development of Internet-related technologies or are heavy users of the information that may flow through this medium are the most likely beneficiaries of Internet-based activity. Studies produced by the U.S. Department of Commerce defined critical components of the emerging "digital economy." Researchers identified the industry sectors that are the major producers of IT, including those related to the Internet (Buckley et al. 2000) and the industry sectors considered the major users of IT equipment (Henry et al. 1999), as shown in Tables 10.1 and 10.2. They documented the more rapid growth of IT-producing industries, as well as the increasing efficiency of IT-using industries relative to other sectors of the economy.

Although, while no studies providing definitive data were found, in reviewing the IT-industry lists one might speculate that urban areas are likely to possess a higher absolute number and proportionate share of these types of industries than rural areas. Rural economies tend to be dominated by traditional extractive industries, lower-skill manufacturers, local government institutions, and a relatively large proportion of retail and service proprietors (Cook and Mizer 1994; USDA-ERS 1995). Many of these economic sectors are not projected to experience especially strong growth (Hamrick 1998). Traditional rural assets that tended to lower production costs, specifically labor and land costs, may not be an advantage for IT-related industries. While these are important factor inputs for IT-related businesses just as with any other business, more critical to IT business success will be access to telecommunications infrastructure and labor with the skills that are in demand by IT businesses.

Much work remains to be done on the geography of IT. There is some indication that rural places with amenity values and good telecommunications services will capture a share of the rapidly growing producer services (Beyers and Lindahl 1996). Similarly, among catalog and direct sales firms, both of which have the potential to operate across a range of places, smaller firms catering to niche markets and not overly dependent on high-end telecommunications were found in rural areas (Stenberg, Isserman, and Young 1998).

The U.S. Department of Commerce report also considered the effects of these trends on labor markets. IT-related occupations were identified and are shown in Table 10.3 (Buckley et al. 2000). The IT jobs tend to be highly

Table 10.1
Information Technology Producing Companies

Hardware Industries	*Software/Services Industries*
Computers and equipment	Computer programming services
Wholesale trade of computers and equipment	Prepackaged software
	Wholesale trade of software
Retail trade of computers and equipment	Retail trade of software
Calculating and office machines, nec*	Computer integrated systems design
Magnetic and optical recording media	Computer processing, data preparation
Electron tubes	Information retrieval services
Printed circuit boards	Computer services management
Semiconductors	Computer rental and leasing
Passive electronic components	Computer maintenance and repair
Industrial instruments for measurement	Computer-related services, nec*
Instruments for measuring electricity	
Laboratory analytical instruments	
	Communications Services Industries
	Telephone and telegraph communications
Communications Equipment Industries	Radio and TV broadcasting
Household audio and video equipment	Cable and other pay TV services
Telephone and telegraph equipment	
Radio and TV and communications equipment	

*not elsewhere classified.

Source: Buckley et al. 2000.

skilled and require frequent updating of those skills. Correspondingly, the wages for IT workers tend to be higher than the economy-wide average. The report cautioned that the wage gap between IT workers and other workers is likely to widen (see also D'Amico 1999; Katz 1999; Meares and Sargent 1999). Here, again, to the extent urban places have a relatively greater quantity of people possessing needed occupational skills, potential employers will find urban areas to be more attractive locations (Gorman 2001).

In a related fashion, electronic commerce promises to change many existing occupations. A report by the OECD (1998) suggests that the sectors most likely to be affected by the adoption of new technologies include communi-

Table 10.2
Industries Considered Major Users of Information Technology Equipment

Telecommunications	Security and commodity brokers
Radio and TV broadcasting	Business services
Other services, nec*	Health services
Motion pictures	Holding and investment offices
Legal services	Wholesale trade
Insurance carriers	Real estate
Instruments and related products	Insurance agents and brokers
Depository institutions	Nondepository institutions
Pipelines, except natural gas	Petroleum and coal products
Chemicals and allied products	Electronic equipment

*not elsewhere classified

Source: Henry et al. 1999.

Table 10.3
Information Technology Occupations

Engineering, science and computer system managers	Computer engineers
	Computer support specialists
Database administrators	All other computer scientists
Systems analysts	Electrical and electronics technicians
Computer programmers	Duplicating, mail and other office machine operators
Broadcast technicians	
Computer equipment operators	Billing, posting, and calculating machine operators
Data processing equipment repairers	
Communications equipment operators	Data entry keyers
Electrical powerline installers and repairers	Electronics repairers, commercial and industrial equipment
Telephone and cable TV installers and repairers	Electrical and electronic equipment assemblers, precision
Central office and PBX installers and repairers	
Electrical and electronics engineers	Electromechanical equipment assemblers, precision
	Electronic semiconductor processors

Source: Buckley et al. 2000.

cations, entertainment, education, health, professional services, publishing, financial services, and the postal service. Within these sectors are travel agents, investment brokers, insurance agents, and many other occupations that facilitate transactions or broker information. Although still too early to project the effects that electronic commerce may have on these and other occupational categories, it is probably safe to assume that the nature of many of these jobs is likely to change. The OECD report concluded that, whereas electronic commerce may not cause the wholesale elimination of many of these jobs, exactly what these people do within the occupation is likely to be affected. This, of course, places a premium on individual adaptive skills.

This is relevant to the discussion of rural areas to the extent that many of these occupations represent the small businesses of rural communities. In rural areas, a high proportion of all jobs are retail and service sole proprietors. To the extent that large nonlocal firms market directly to consumers, there may be an erosion of the income earned by local providers and an increasing leakage of income from rural areas. Similarly, the challenge to many of these providers is to adapt to the changing way business is done. This will likely present a challenge to many service providers in rural and urban areas alike, with the major difference being that urban places should have greater access to new skill training and to alternative occupations if these people must change careers.

In addition to the challenges associated with geography and economic structure are the demographic characteristics of rural areas. Rural communities tend to have populations with lower levels of income and educational attainment and higher proportions of the elderly and disabled (Bowers and Hamrick 1997). All of these factors are known to influence computer access and use (NTIA 1999).

Rural Telecommunications Infrastructure

Telecommunications, however, probably will not mean the "death of distance" as some have speculated (Cairncross 1997). Several recent studies have concluded that advanced telecommunications services have disproportionately agglomerated in the largest metropolitan regions and that the bandwidth gap between the largest places and everyone else is growing (Gorman and Malecki 2000; Malecki and Gorman 2001). The reasons are relatively straightforward: external economies of scale, the ability to create and commercialize new knowledge rapidly, the availability of skilled labor, and the presence of venture capital (Moss and Townsend 1999; Zook 2000).

The situation for rural areas is not all bleak, however. The U.S. Department of Commerce (2002) reported that rural households were essentially equivalent to their urban counterparts in their rate of Internet use, at 53 and 54 percent, respectively. Even so, while there have been impressive advances in access to digital services and the Internet in all areas, Edward Malecki (2001) points out that the gains have been uneven, depending on state regulations, local demand characteristics, and the priorities of available telecommunications providers, and that rural areas continued to lag in access to broadband services. Broadband permits the transfer of very large quantities of data very rapidly, enabling many high-end telecommunications services such as teleconferencing and streaming video.

An NTIA/Rural Utilities Service (RUS) (2000) report indicated that problems of distance and low population densities hindered the diffusion of these technologies; it also noted that rural areas may benefit somewhat more with access to such services as telemedicine, electronic commerce, and distance education. Though technology exists to close the gap between urban and rural areas, service providers are moving most quickly to build the urban telecommunications infrastructure. For the most remote rural users, no existing technologies can deliver all of the telecommunications services that may be desirable.

Rural Leadership and Institutional Capacity

One of the more inscrutable but essential qualities of rural places that affects community economic viability is the quality of their leaders and institutions. These institutions include the schools, service groups, local governments, and the many other organizations that have a major influence on local quality of life. Clearly, visionary and effective leaders can have a significant impact on a community. What a single individual can accomplish, however, is small compared to the potential of organized groups banding together to achieve community goals. Thus, both the quality of local institutions and their interactions are critical to creating an environment conducive to taking action that can improve community viability (Flora and Flora 1993; Flora, Sharp, and Flora 1997).

To energize local leaders and institutions, rural communities must foster a broad-based understanding of the opportunities that IT provides. If rural communities need upgraded telecommunications infrastructure or local training programs, the demand must come from a cross section of community organizations. Among the local institutions that are well-positioned to lead the effort are schools and libraries, given the numerous government and foundation initiatives to provide Internet access. Similarly, many local social service providers are aware of the potential that communication technologies offer for information access and organizational development. Beyond these groups, however, local business organizations, local governments, and civic and service groups must grasp the potential for individual, business, and organizational benefits from IT. When there is a broad-based understanding of community need and a consensus among local institutions, there is a greater likelihood that the community will take successful action. This will be true in relation to community technology needs just as it is for local economic development, health care, or any community issue.

There may be some question about the capacity of rural institutions to facilitate community consensus building and foster adaptive strategies to bring about needed change. Socioeconomic and demographic indicators suggest that the people who make up rural institutions may lack the interest, understanding, and experience needed to make technology access and use a major community priority. Among the important predictors of Internet use among individuals are wealth, education, and age (Benton Foundation 1999; NTIA 1999). Rural areas tend to be less wealthy, less educated, and older than urban places—all factors associated with lower use of the Internet.

Also relevant in this discussion is the extent to which IT can strengthen local institutions. Indeed, there is early evidence that the Internet can be used as a tool to strengthen social institutions and other local communities of interest. Andrea Kavanaugh (1999) found that the Internet, especially e-mail and discussion lists, reinforces and even expands social networks in a community. Further, and this is important relative to the quality of interaction among groups, Internet users who are members of multiple local organizations use the technology to strengthen ties among organizations. These group ties make it easier for the community to mobilize quickly and organize to achieve common goals.

Thus, the social/organizational function of the Internet can be employed as a tool for rural community organization and goal attainment. Particularly in rural communities, where so much depends on voluntary efforts by community groups, this capacity would strengthen local institutions. The question and challenge is whether rural community leaders, for whom much of the new advanced telecommunications technology is alien, can learn to harness its potential.

Enhancing Rural Business Competitiveness

This assessment of rural community competitiveness may appear somewhat gloomy. Indeed, the evidence is fairly clear that rural places have challenges to overcome to gain advantage from IT-related trends. Thus, the focus should be to identify strategies whereby rural businesses and disadvantaged communities can meet these challenges. Discussion now will turn toward some of the opportunities for rural businesses to take advantage of IT and for communities to respond to IT-related trends.

Business Applications of the Internet

Depending on the goods or services being offered, businesses use Internet Web sites for a variety of purposes. Here, four business Internet Web applications are identified (Noonan 2001).

Customer Support

The objective of a customer support site is to provide product and related information. Among the benefits to the customer is twenty-four–hour access to instructional, troubleshooting, and value-added information through areas such as "frequently asked questions" (FAQ) and opportunities for upgrades and updated information. From the business's perspective, the advantage is to shift some of the costs of information transfer to the customer rather than via a sales or technical representative, including the savings of sometimes substantial printing costs.

A related customer support function of a business Web page is to get information to customers on short notice. Such was the case when airline carriers dealt with the tragedy of highjackings. Concerned friends and relatives of victims could go on-line for the latest information and instructions. Perhaps less consequential, many firms have used the Web to quickly address controversy or rumors.

Brochure/Catalogue

This application is the traditional commercial products site. It provides information and shows product lines in highly attractive ways, but does not perform on-line transactions. Among the benefits to customers is twenty-four-hour access to information, the ability to compare different product brands easily, and the opportunity to learn and shop absent the need to travel and deal with salespeople. The business has an opportunity to build brand recognition and loyalty.

Virtual Storefront

The virtual storefront enables actual transactions such as at Amazon.com. These sites tend to be larger and require much more complex programming and support. To succeed, these sites must be exceptionally user-friendly and easy to navigate. As on-line security improves and consumers become more acclimated to shopping on-line, sales are expected to increase dramatically. This may work best for businesses servicing specialty niche markets and for larger businesses with established and successful distribution systems.

On-Line Mall

These are Web services that aggregate large amounts of products and services into various categories. One example is the *Yahoo! Store*, where the search engine capitalized on its popularity for use in organizing Web information to serve as a broker for retail transactions.

Using the Internet as a Tool for Rural Business Managers

Not every business needs a Web site. In fact, there are many ways the Internet can help a business owner or manager as a consumer of information. The Internet can also be used to facilitate business in other ways such as customer service and product promotion through e-mail, purchasing and selling through on-line auctions, or posting classified ads on on-line bulletin boards. Rural businesses can also benefit from the Internet (Noonan 2001).

Learning About the Internet

Effective use of the Internet requires understanding its scope and capabilities. To utilize its communication potential, a business owner must learn about e-mail and data transfer. To find information on the Internet efficiently, one must know about search engines and search strategies. Thus, the first opportunity to benefit by the Internet is to learn about it, and the best place to learn about the Internet may be on the Internet itself.

Finding Business-Related Information

The Internet can serve as a gateway to find information valuable in conducting business. There are sites that offer business management instruction, and there are opportunities to track industry news and developments. The *Internet* can also help keep tabs on competitors' activities.

Government Contracting Opportunities

State and federal governments represent untapped potential markets for many rural businesses. Today, there are free services that track publications in which government requests for proposals and bids appear and then automatically send an e-mail notice of the opportunity. Similarly, many government agency Web sites include instructions about how to submit a bid and include application forms.

Managing Supply Networks

Businesses purchase many goods and services, ranging from raw or intermediate materials from suppliers and distributors to professional services from attorneys, advertising agencies, and accountants. The Internet offers the opportunity to see what types of services and support existing vendors offer online and to make making comparison shopping for potential alternative vendors much easier. Powerful encryption software and secure servers make the transfer of sensitive information less risky. New security technology and services will make future transactions even more secure.

Competitive Intelligence

Business owners can learn much from, and about, their competition on the Internet. Many companies' Web sites identify the range of goods and services the firm offers and may even include pricing information. The Internet offers the opportunity to learn not only what the competition is doing, but also how it is doing it. Opportunities exist to evaluate how the best in the industry are using the Internet to build customer relationships, market themselves, and position their products.

Finding New Ideas

Another type of competitive intelligence the Internet enables is searching the U.S. Patent and Trademark Office and the Security and Exchange Commission (SEC). A patent search can stimulate new ideas or keep a business owner up-to-date on current industry technologies. Similarly, monitoring reports provided to the SEC can offer insight about other companies' experiences with new products and marketing strategies and even some that are in the developmental stage.

Creating a Support Network

Many small business owners and managers lack ready access to peers and colleagues with whom to talk about their challenges and problems. The Internet provides the opportunity to meet others on-line and to discuss issues through specialized discussion groups. Many professional associations also enable member interaction at their Web sites. This can help otherwise isolated business owners and managers establish a support network of peers with whom to ask questions and share knowledge and experiences.

Financial Information

Financial information may be among the richest content areas of the Internet. The Internet has numerous sites that help users search for public and private financing, including grants, loans, and venture capital. State and federal tax agencies now routinely post all their instructional guides and forms on the Web. Similarly, various government regulatory agencies post their rules and guidelines for easy access.

International Marketing Opportunities

One of the benefits of the Internet is the opportunity to open distant markets. Even international marketing becomes possible. So, too, do the realities of tariffs, trade regulations, exchange rates, and language and cultural differences. Fortunately, many government agencies and other organizations are developing Web-based information resources that can help overcome these potential barriers. Thus, very real opportunities may exist to become involved in international markets.

Adaptive Strategies to Enhance Rural Community Competitiveness

Recognizing the potential that advanced IT represents, the reality remains that infrastructure deployment has lagged, and development of the human capacity to fully exploit existing technologies also may be lagging in rural communities. The question then becomes one of identifying strategies available to rural community developers, institutions, local officials, and businesses to improve the situation. Though no easy solutions exist, several ideas may help in creating adaptive strategies. Perhaps the most effective strategies will be those fostering action on multiple fronts. That is, if the challenge is to demonstrate that sufficient demand exists to justify infrastructure investments, people must understand the latent potential of the technologies they currently lack. Thus, an element of human capacity development is needed in conjunction with efforts to build the physical infrastructure. Following are some ideas that have proven beneficial to rural communities.

Strategic Planning for Rural Telecommunications

It is unlikely that a community will be able to secure all of the investments, services, and other benefits of IT instantly or simultaneously. An element of prioritization about the targets and beneficiaries of IT development is needed. This is to suggest, as with most successful rural community development initiatives, that the process of attaining relative improvements begins with collaborative action and strategic planning (Walzer 1996).

Strategic planning starts by evaluating both the existing market and the opportunities and potential future technology applications (McMahon and Salant 1999; Minnesota Department of Administration, Minnesota Department of Transportation, and Minnesota Planning 2000; Parker 1996). Such an initiative involves a broad cross-section of public and private information users and providers. Priorities must be established, such as upgrading local school infrastructure, creating a central community access point, or bringing telemedicine services to the hospital, any of which might serve as a starting point for upgrading local infrastructure. Finally, an action plan that outlines strategies, funding resources, organizational issues, and a timeline for implementation is created.

The strategies that might be included in the action plan would generally focus on how to bring outside investment into the community or how to marshal the resources found within the community to make needed investments. Attracting outside resources requires demonstrating adequate demand to justify needed investments and/or taking advantage of any of the several assistance programs that may be available. To marshal internal resources will require building coalitions within the community and a public–private partnership.

LaGrange, Georgia (pop. 26,000) is a community that tied its strategic vision to IT development (Read and Youtie 1996). Long dependent on textile manufacturing, community leaders saw the need in the mid-1990s to move aggressively toward diversifying the city's economic base. The city of LaGrange decided to work toward upgrading telecommunications infrastructure in an effort to attract "footloose" back-office operations.

The city had to negotiate with several telecommunications providers to construct a point of presence (POP) to access the Internet backbone, install digital switches for direct data transfer, lay fiber optic cables to broaden access, and take the fiber the "last mile" to connect to the user. Many of the upgrades were made when the city could demonstrate that existing IT-intensive firms would use expanded service. Other portions of the upgrade were city-financed and owned.

City officials overcame numerous obstacles, not the least of which was to educate themselves about highly complex technical issues. It will be some time before La Grange will know whether its back-office operations strategy will pay off. In the interim, however, the city has been able to attract several more IT-using industries, such as a Wal-Mart regional distribution center and a Caterpillar construction equipment plant.

Demand Aggregation

Low-income and rural communities typically suffer from similar problems when market-driven solutions are needed. That is, they lack the economic base to be attractive investment targets to profit-driven interests. The Benton Foundation (Le Blanc 1999a) suggested that the principles of cooperatives might be successfully applied to enhance the attractiveness of these communities. The notion is one of aggregating demand into something like a rural cooperative to enhance the negotiating capacity and/or buying power of participating individuals.

The most feasible cooperative-type model might function in association with existing trusted local nonprofit organizations. Churches, unions, colleges, tribal councils, agricultural organizations, and other locally based organizations may be in the best position to negotiate with technology manufacturers and providers given their strong preexisting ties with larger numbers of potential co-op members. This model could supplement access provided at public locations such as schools and libraries.

A similar strategy is to "piggyback" small users onto communications nodes created for larger users. For example, these rural area networks might bring together local businesses, health care providers, and local governments and piggyback them onto a major private-sector employer or the state educational system (Parker 1996).

Yet a third strategy in this group is to offer training and education within the community to show consumers and business owners the potential available (McMahon and Salant 1999). The more that local consumers know what is possible using telecommunications technologies, the greater the potential market. Similarly, working with local firms and institutions to create mid-range (five-year) information technology improvement plans is another way to create demand, determine future needs, and demonstrate potential demand to outside service providers.

A good example of the piggyback strategy is in Kearney, Nebraska (pop. 28,000), home of Cabela's, a major telemarketer of outdoor products (Parker et al. 1992). Cabela's needed a POP to expand its Internet-based presence; however, rather than establishing it as a proprietary telecommunications link, Cabela's permitted other users, including other telemarketing firms, to piggyback on the technology that allows them to dial directly into the long-distance network, thereby reducing access costs and permitting the use of specialized calling software. This has proven a successful strategy to diversify the city's economic base beyond traditional manufacturing to now include telemarketing and other back-office operations.

Locally Based Telecommunications Enterprises

In cases where private-sector companies have not provided high-quality, low-cost telecommunications services in rural areas, there have been a number of successful initiatives to create public or not-for-profit enterprises to fill the gap.

Following the model of public electric and water utilities, some rural communities are creating public enterprises to provide advanced telecommunications technologies. The case of Iowa is significant in this respect (Van Wart, Rahm, and Sanders 2000). In recent years, thirty rural communities in the state have voted to create municipal telecommunications utilities. Generally, these initiatives are aided in locations wherein the municipality already owns an electric utility because revenue surpluses and bond capacity can be directed to the new utility start-up. Other keys to success include creating technically sophisticated services; having in-house expertise; securing local commitment by community leaders, businesses, and citizens; having access to financial resources; and effectively marketing the available services. In some cases, cities provide the backing to help create private local telecommunications utilities.

Similar to public utilities, not-for-profit organizations have been formed to bring Internet-related services to underserved rural areas. An excellent example of this type of model is the North Central Kansas Community Network (NCKCN at www.nckcn.com) (Cyr 2000). Started in 1995 by the North Central Regional Planning Commission (NCRPC), this not-for-profit company was formed to bring the Internet to a rural area without affordable access. For an up-front investment of $6,000 in equipment costs and a monthly guarantee of $740 for line and port charges (all paid by the sponsoring local governments and other public participants), the NCRPC leased locally available circuits from area telephone providers. The NCKCN then became the area Internet service provider (ISP) and created a wide area network (WAN) linking schools, local governments, and libraries. The schools, libraries, and other participants purchased their own equipment (e.g., computers, modems, etc.) needed to connect to the ISP and created access points for low-income individuals who would not otherwise have Internet access.

Today, the NCKCN serves a nine-county rural area in Kansas, providing

Internet access to homes, businesses, and public institutions at rates vastly more affordable than the Internet service plus long-distance costs previously available. The corporation is profitable based on household and business user charges and even makes annual grants back to the communities. There is currently a waiting list of communities who want to join the network now that they have seen the potential of affordable service. These communities are actively lobbying local phone companies for the necessary equipment upgrades.

According to the NCRPC, the greatest hurdle to starting the venture was convincing local officials to view the initial investment and monthly charge guarantee as if they were public infrastructure investments. Most local officials believed telecommunications services belonged in the realm of the private sector, yet for many rural places, alternative organizational models may provide their best hope for making the types of telecommunications investments needed in an information-intensive economy.

Upgrading Local Government

Given the essential role that local governments play in supporting rural community development, helping elected policymakers understand the opportunities associated with IT is essential to bringing a needed partner into the process. This may best be accomplished by demonstrating how the application of IT can improve local public service delivery (Neff and Moulder 1998).

To foster greater awareness and use of IT for local government service delivery, state and national governments and professional service organizations can play a major role in disseminating information about successful applications. Similarly, these applications must be highlighted in publications and at conferences to help local officials move from viewing such efforts as luxuries of larger, wealthier places to seeing the possibilities of local application and the potential broader benefits of private-sector application.

Support from Broader Levels to Foster Technology Development and Literacy

There are numerous initiatives to help close the digital divide experienced by disadvantaged groups. State and federal governments are often a primary source of funding, technical assistance, and policymaking to help put the telecommunications infrastructure in place. The executive branch of the federal government placed great emphasis on issues associated with Internet technology development and dissemination and, as a result, many federal agencies have moved aggressively to develop assistance programs (FCC 1999;

U.S. Government Working Group on Electronic Commerce 1999). Beyond what broader levels of government are doing, however, is an impressive array of programs and activities by many nonprofit organizations, private foundations, and private corporations. One of the critical strategies for local communities concerned about access to IT is to take full advantage of available assistance from external sources.

Several states have begun to use requests for telephone company mergers as an opportunity to negotiate expanded technology access for community telecommunications services. In California and Ohio, state regulatory commissions use the merger review process to facilitate private company grants to create technology access and training programs in rural, low-income, and underserved communities (Goslee 1998). Similarly, state regulators control various subsidy mechanisms that help determine whether carriers invest in new technology and what rates are charged for services.

State government itself represents a major telecommunications customer. States that buy dedicated leased lines for private use should consider the rural development implications. In Oregon, for example, the state replaced leased lines used to connect lottery terminals with dedicated data networks conducive to expanding comparable capacity to rural businesses and residential users (Parker 1996). Similarly, Iowa has invested nearly half a billion dollars in a fiber optic system that operates in all of the state's ninety-nine counties, but neither local government nor the private sector is yet legally allowed direct access to the system (Van Wart, Rahm, and Sanders 2000).

Local Initiatives to Foster Technology Development and Literacy

There are too many locally based initiatives to catalogue. Several sources that catalogue such success stories are the Benton Foundation Web site (www.benton.org) and the Digital Divide Network Web site (www.digitaldividenetwork.org).

More importantly, the collective experience provides guidelines useful for improving the prospects of creating successful local programs. Among the more important elements is that successful programs tend to be *locally* designed and driven (Le Blanc 1999b). This is to say that each program needs heavy input from local institutions and their target population to create programs responsive to the needs of the underserved. Although the federal government and major private foundations have a demonstrated commitment to underserved people, a "standard template" approach is unlikely to have the desired impacts.

One way to increase the desired impact is to work through established, trusted local institutions. This is to incorporate an added element of technology access and training to places and programs where the underserved already go for education, training, or other assistance. Thus, program success is more likely when programs are built through existing community centers, service programs, and other local institutions (Kretzman and McKnight 1993).

The other major element needed for success is to emphasize training in the use of technology beyond simply providing access. Many members of underserved populations need encouragement and assistance in overcoming their ambivalence or reticence toward technology. The success of a technology access center will increase when coupled with targeted training opportunities such as after-school programs for youth, job-skills training for the poor, family communications opportunities and health care information of interest for the elderly, or business applications for remote locations.

Finally, though much has been made of the need to foster technology-related skills, others have prudently suggested the need to foster generic learning skills (Anderson and Bikson 1998). By focusing on generic skills such as learning-to-learn, analysis and problem solving, and innovation and communication, individuals can function more effectively in a changing and technology-intensive society. In most cases, specific technology-related applications can be learned with modest effort, but the life skills fostered with generic learning are applicable across any setting and in all aspects of life—both economic and noneconomic.

Conclusion

Most people today recognize the fundamental ways that advanced information technologies have changed economic relationships. In light of the importance of these trends, many have expressed concern about the "digital divide" that exists between various socioeconomic groups and regions. Among those areas currently lagging in the diffusion and use of advanced IT are rural communities. This chapter discussed some of the opportunities that electronic businesses (e-business) can create, and also some of the challenges that must be overcome if rural communities are to take advantage of those opportunities.

Both IT and e-business are not "silver bullets" that will lead to prosperity. They are but one additional factor that must enter into consideration if rural businesses and communities are to remain competitive. Businesses must continue paying attention to the "fundamentals," including focusing on competition, innovation, customer service needs, and their human capital. Yet the Internet and IT represent an opportunity for rural businesses—large and small, traditional or high-tech—that every manager and business owner should be thinking about.

Several ways that businesses have used IT to transform operations were identified, including automating transactions, reducing supply costs, lowering the cost of information delivery, improving marketing, and creating better linkages to customers' needs and wants. Other ideas about how individual managers and owners can use the technology were outlined, including discovering useful and relevant business-related information, gathering better competitive intelligence, finding new markets, and saving time by gathering information on-line.

Correspondingly, communities also must take a broad view of what it means to be competitive in an economy increasingly dependent on advanced information technologies. Local officials must move beyond a narrow emphasis on Web-based retail sales and tax policy to a fuller range of concerns, including strengthening human and institutional capacities and improving access and infrastructure.

Several ideas were outlined here that can help local officials—for example, creating public–private partnerships for strategic planning, aggregating demand, and conducting business differently. Other ideas include considering whether a community should take more aggressive action in securing infrastructure improvements as well as using the technology itself to improve operations and services delivery, and initiating local efforts to foster improved technology literacy and skills. To remain economically viable, rural communities will require both access and capacity to utilize technology for a broad range of applications related to learning, institution building, community organization, and service delivery, in addition to economic uses.

References

Anderson, Robert H., and Tora K. Bikson. 1998. *Focus on Generic Skills for Information Technology Literacy.* Paper presented in a workshop on "Information Technology Literacy," Computer Science and Technology Board of the National Research Council, January 14–15, Irvine, California. Available on-line: <www.rand.org/publications/P/P8018/>. Downloaded: March 17, 2002.

Bakos, Y. 2001. The emerging landscape for retail e-commerce. *Journal of Economic Perspectives* 15(1): 69–80.

Barber, B.M., and T. Odean. 2001. The internet and the investor. *Journal of Economic Perspectives* 15(1): 41–54.

Bartholomew, Doug. 2000. Automakers get (the same) e-ligion. *IndustryWeek.Com* (May 15). Available on-line: <www.industryweek.com/CurrentArticles/asp/articles.asp?ArticleID=816>. Downloaded: March 17, 2002.

Benton Foundation. 1999. The digital divide. *The Digital Beat* 1(8). Available on-line: <www.benton.org/DigitalBeat/db070899.html>. Downloaded: March 17, 2002.

Beyers, William B., and David P. Lindahl. 1996. Lone eagles and high fliers in rural producer services. *Rural Development Perspectives* 11(3): 2–10. Available on-line: <www.ers.usda.gov/publications/rdp/rdp696/>. Downloaded: March 17, 2002.

Bowers, Doug, and Karen Hamrick, eds. 1997. *Rural Conditions and Trends* (Socio-economic Conditions Issue) 8(2). Available on-line: <www.ers.usda.gov/epubs/pdf/rcat/rcat82/index.htm>. Downloaded: March 17, 2002.

Buckley, Patricia, Sabrina Montes, David Henry, Donald Dalton, Gurmukh Gill, Jesus Dumagan, Susan LaPorte, Sandra Cooke, Dennis Pastor, and Lee Price. 2000. *Digital Economy 2000.* Washington, DC: U.S. Department of Commerce, Economics and Statistics Administration. Available on-line: <www.esa.doc.gov/508/esa/DigitalEconomy.htm>. Downloaded: March 17, 2002.

Cairncross, Frances. 1997. *The Death of Distance.* Boston: Harvard Business School Press.

Cisco Systems and the University of Texas. 2001. *Measuring the Internet Economy.* Austin: Center for Research in Electronic Commerce (CREC), University of Texas at Austin. Available on-line: <www.internetindicators.com/>. Downloaded: March 17, 2002.

Conhaim, Wallys W. 1998. E-commerce. *Link-Up* 15(2). On-line newsletter of the Access Minnesota Main Street Program, University of Minnesota-Extension. Available on-line: <www.extension.umn.edu/mainstreet/curriculum/ecomm/conhaim1.html>. Downloaded: March 17, 2002.

Cook, Peggy J., and Karen L Mizer. 1994. *The Revised ERS County Typology: An Overview* (Rural Development Research Report 89). Washington, DC: USDA–ERS. Available on-line: <www.ers.usda.gov/publications/rdrr89/>. Downloaded: March 17, 2002.

Cyr, J., Executive Director, North Central Regional Planning Commission. 2000. Personal communication on the background and history of the North Central Kansas Community Network, July 10.

D'Amico, C. 1999. *Understanding the Digital Economy: Workforceimplications.* Paper presented at the Understanding the Digital Economy: Data, Tools, and Research conference, May 25–26, Washington, DC.

Federal Communications Commission (FCC). 1999. *Universal Service.* Washington, DC: Author. Available on-line: <www.fcc.gov/ccb/universal_service/>. Downloaded: March 17, 2002.

Flora, Cornelia B., and J.L. Flora. 1993. Entrepreneurial social infrastructure: A necessary ingredient. *Annals of the American Academy of Political and Social Science* 29 (September): 48–58.

Flora, J.L., J. Sharp, and Cornelia B. Flora. 1997. Entrepreneurial social infrastructure and locally initiated economic development in the nonmetropolitan United States. *Sociological Quarterly* 38(4): 623–645.

Gorman, Sean P. 2001. *Where are the Web Factories? The Urban Bias of e-Business Location.* Draft paper. New York: Taub Urban Research Center, New York University. Available on-line: <www.informationcity.org/research/web-factories/index.htm>. Downloaded: March 17, 2002.

Gorman, Sean P., and E.J. Malecki. 2000. The networks of the internet: An analysis of provider networks in the USA. *Telecommunications Policy* 24(2): 113–134.

Goslee, Susan. 1998. *Losing Ground Bit by Bit: Low-Income Communities in the Information Age.* Washington, DC: The Benton Foundation. Available on-line: <www.benton.org/Library/Low-Income/>. Downloaded: March 17, 2002.

Hamrick, Karen. 1998. Future job growth will benefit educated workers most. *Rural Conditions and Trends* 9(3): 11–16. Available on-line: <www.ers.usda.gov/publications/rcat/rcat93/>. Downloaded: March 17, 2002.

Henry, D., S. Cooke, P. Buckley, J. Dumagan, G. Gill, D. Pastore, and S. LaPorte. 1999. *The Emerging Digital Economy II.* Washington, DC: U.S. Department of Commerce, Economics and Statistics Administration, Office of Policy Development. Available on-line: <www.ecommerce.gov/ede/>. Downloaded: March 17, 2002.

Johnson, Kenneth M., and Calvin L. Beale. 1999. The continuing population rebound in nonmetro America. *Rural Development Perspectives* 13(3): 2–11. Available on-line: <www.ers.usda.gov/publications/rdp/rdp1098/>. Downloaded: March 17, 2002.

Katz, Lawrence F. 1999. *Technological Change, Computerization, and the Wage Structure.* Paper presented at the Understanding the Digital Economy: Data, Tools, and Research conference, May 25–26, Washington, DC. Available on-line: <http://post.economics.harvard.edu/faculty/katz/papers/lkdig2.pdf>. Downloaded: March 17, 2002.

Kavanaugh, Andrea. 1999. *The Impact of the Internet on Community Involvement: A Network Analysis Approach.* Paper prepared for the Telecommunications Policy Research Conference, Alexandria, Virginia, September 25–27. Available on-line: <www.tprc.org/agenda99.html>. Downloaded: March 17, 2002.

Konicki, S. 2002. Now in bankruptcy, Kmart struggled with supply chain. *Information Week* (January 28). Available on-line: www.informationweek.com/story/IWK20020125S00207. Downloaded: August 13, 2002.

Kretzman, J.P., and J.L. McKnight. 1993. *Building Communities from the Inside Out: A Path Toward Finding and Mobilizing a Community's Assets.* Chicago: ACTA Publications.

Le Blanc, Jamal. 1999a. Demand aggregation and the digital divide. *The Digital Beat* 1(20). Available on-line: <www.benton.org/DigitalBeat/db120999.html>. Downloaded: March 17, 2002.

———. 1999b. Resolving the digital divide. *The Digital Beat* 1(19). Available on-line: <www.benton.org/DigitalBeat/db111299.html>. Downloaded: March 17, 2002.

Lucking-Reiley, D., and D.F. Spulber. 2001. Business-to-business electronic commerce. *Journal of Economic Perspectives* 15(1): 55–68.

Malecki, Edward J. 1996. *Telecommunications Technology and American Rural Development in the 21st Century.* Paper presented at the Tennessee Valley Authority Rural Studies Conference, Lexington, Kentucky. Available on-line: <www.rural.org/workshops/rural_telecom/>. Downloaded: March 17, 2002.

———. 2001. Going digital in rural America. In *Exploring Policy Options for a New Rural America,* ed. The Center for the Study of Rural America, 49–68. Kansas City, MO: The Center for the Study of Rural America, Federal Reserve Bank of Kansas City.

Malecki, Edward J., and Sean P. Gorman. 2001. Maybe the death of distance, but not the end of geography: The internet as a network. In *The Worlds of Electronic Commerce,* ed. S.D. Brunn and T.R. Leinbach, 87–105. New York: John Wiley.

McKinsey Global Institute. 2001. *U.S. Productivity Growth 1995–2000: Understanding the Contribution of Information Technology Relative to Other Factors.* Washington, DC: McKinsey Global Institute. Available on-line: <www.mckinsey.com/knowledge/>. Downloaded: March 17, 2002.

McMahon, Kathleen, and Priscilla Salant. 1999. Strategic planning for telecommunications in rural communities. *Rural Development Perspectives* 14(3): 2–7. Available on-line: <www.ers.usda.gov/epubs/pdf/rdp/rdpoct99/>. Downloaded: March 17, 2002.

Meares, C.A., and J.F. Sargent, Jr. 1999. *The Digital Work Force: Building Infotech Skills at the Speed of Innovation.* Washington, DC: U.S. Department of Commerce, Office of Technology Policy. Available on-line: <www.ta.doc.gov/reports.htm>. Downloaded: March 17, 2002.

Mesenbourg, Thomas L. 2001. *Measuring Electronic Business* (E-Stats Research Paper). Washington, DC: U.S. Bureau of the Census. Available on-line: <www.census.gov/eos/www/papers/ebusasa.pdf>. Downloaded: March 17, 2002.

Minnesota Department of Administration, Minnesota Department of Transportation, and Minnesota Planning. 2000. *Net Plan: A Community Planning Guide for Advanced Telecommunications Services.* St. Paul: Minnesota Planning. Available on-line: <www.mnplan.state.mn.us/pdf/2000/planning/netplan.pdf>. Downloaded: March 17, 2002.

Moss, Mitchell L., and Anthony M. Townsend. 1999. How telecommunications systems are transforming urban spaces. Originally published in *Cities in the Telecommunications Age: The Fracturing of Geographies*, ed. J.O. Wheeler, Y. Aoyama, and B. Warf. New York: Routledge. Available on-line: <www.informationcity.org/research/telecom-urban-spaces/telecom-urban-spaces.pdf>. Downloaded: March 17, 2002.

National Telecommunications and Information Administration (NTIA). 1999. *Falling Through the Net: Defining the Digital Divide.* Washington, DC: U.S. Department of Commerce. Available on-line: <www.ntia.doc.gov/ntiahome/digitaldivide/index.html>. Downloaded: March 17, 2002.

NTIA/Rural Utilities Service. 2000. *Advanced Telecommunications in Rural America: The Challenge of Bringing Broadband Service to all Americans.* Washington, DC: U.S. Department of Commerce and the U.S. Department of Agriculture. Available on-line: <www.ntia.doc.gov/reports.html>. Downloaded: March 17, 2002.

Neff, D.L., and E. Moulder. 1998. *Long-Range Information Technology Plans: Strategies for the Future.* Washington, DC: International City/County Management Association.

Noonan, D. 2001. *Electronic Commerce Curriculum.* St. Paul: University of Minnesota–Extension, Access Minnesota Main Street. Available on-line: <www.extension.umn.edu/mainstreet/curriculum/index.html>. Downloaded: March 17, 2002.

Organisation for Economic Co-operation and Development (OECD). 1998. *The Cconomic and Social Impact of Electronic Commerce: Preliminary Findings and Research Agenda* (DSTI/ICCP(98)15/REV2). Washington, DC: OECD, Committee for Information, Computer and Communications Policy. Available on-line: <www1.oecd.org/dsti/sti/it/ec/prod/>. Downloaded: March 17, 2002.

Parker, Edwin B. 1996. *Telecommunications and Rural Development: Threats and Opportunities.* Paper presented at the Tennessee Valley Authority Rural Studies Conference, October 28, Lexington, Kentucky. Available on-line: <www.rural.org/workshops/rural_telecom/>. Downloaded: March 17, 2002.

Parker, Edwin B., Heather E. Hudson, Don A. Dillman, Sharon Strover, and Frederick Williams. 1992. *Electronic Byways: State Policies for Rural Development Through Telecommunications.* Boulder, CO: Westview Press.

Postrel, V. 2002. Lessons in keeping business humming, courtesy of Wal-Mart U. *The New York Times* (February 28): Sec. C, 2.

Read, William H., and Jan L. Youtie. 1996. *Telecommunications Strategy for Economic Development.* Westport, CT: Praeger Publishers.

Stenberg, P., A. Isserman, and N. Young. 1998. *Telecommunications and the Rural–Urban Economic Landscape: Mail Order and Internet-Based Retail Business in Rural Regions.* Proceedings of Telecommunications in Rural Areas Workshop, September 14–15, Washington, DC.

U.S. Department of Agriculture–Economic Research Service (USDA–ERS). 1995. *Understanding Rural America* (Agricultural Information Bulletin 710). Washington, DC: USDA–ERS. Available on-line: <www.ers.usda.gov/publications/aib710/>. Downloaded: March 17, 2002.

U.S. Department of Commerce. 2002 *A Nation Online: How Americans Are Expanding Their Use of the Internet.* Washington, DC: U.S. Department of Commerce. Available on-line: <www.ntia.doc.gov/ntiahome/dn/nationonline_020502.htm>. Downloaded: March 17, 2002.

U.S. Government Working Group on Electronic Commerce. 1999. *Towards Digital eQuality* (2nd Annual Report). Washington, DC: U.S. Government Working Group on Electronic Commerce. Available on-line: <www.ecommerce.gov/bodytext.htm>. Downloaded: March 17, 2002.

Van Wart, M., D. Rahm, and S. Sanders. 2000. Economic development and public enterprise: The case of rural Iowa's telecommunications utilities. *Economic Development Quarterly* 14(2): 131–145.

Walzer, Norman, ed. 1996. *Community Strategic Visioning Programs.* Westport, CT: Praeger.

Zook, Matthew A. 2000. *Grounded capital: The Geographic Nature of Venture Financing in the United States.* Draft paper. New York: Taub Urban Research Center, New York University. Available on-line: <www.informationcity.org/research/venturecapital/index.htm>. Downloaded: March 17, 2002.

11

RAYMOND LENZI

Financing Trends and Future Options for Rural Illinois and America

Rural areas of the United States suffer from slow economic growth and low per capita incomes. Much of this is related to the lack of higher risk debt capital and equity/venture capital (VC). This chapter documents the extent of the problem by examining banking and equity investment patterns across America from a comparative urban and rural perspective. Low bank loan to deposit ratios and the lack of active VC firms and venture investments in rural areas are critical problems. A comparative analysis of innovative approaches to "nontraditional" VC in rural areas is provided. A special focus on the Mississippi Delta Region and Illinois further illustrates the problems and potential solutions at the local and regional levels. Finally, some synthesized solutions are suggested for consideration by Midwestern and national policymakers, with an aim to increase both equity and debt investment in rural America.

Relationship Between Financing and Economic Growth

The strong relationship between business financing and economic growth can be illustrated in many ways. When the economy slows during a recession, the Federal Reserve lowers interest rates and reserve requirements to stimulate lending and hence the economy. The converse is also true. "Redlining" (not lending in minority areas) is now forbidden by law and policy precisely because the lack of lending creates unfair economic hardships. Each of these examples underscores the importance of lending and investment finance to economic growth.

Rural areas across the country suffer from lower bank-loan-to-deposit ratios than more prosperous urban areas (Lenzi 1992b; Sheshunoff Information Services 2001a). Loan-to-deposit ratios show the percentage of bank deposits that are loaned in the immediate area. Reported loan-to-deposit ratios in urban areas may be 80 to 90 percent, whereas some depressed rural areas may have loan-to-deposit ratios as low as 40 percent.

Though the strong relationship between lending and economic growth is clear, the question remains, "Which is the cause and which is the effect?" Most bankers and economists would assert that a poor economic climate is the cause of low lending rates. If there is no demand for capital, how can there be loans and investment? The prevailing view, then, is that business loan demand "demands" or creates capital supply (Barkley, Markley, Freshwater, Rubin, and Shaffer 2001a; Parkinson 2002).

There is, however, an opposite view that the lack of willing and active lenders and equity investors is also a cause of poor-performing economies. To address the problems of finance supply, public policy has developed multiple market intervention responses, including direct government programs like SBA, USDA, and HUD loan and loan guaranty programs.

State economic development agencies offer low-interest "gap" or mezzanine loans to further modify market behavior to encourage economic and business expansion. State bonding authorities not only bundle small-issue bonds but are increasingly involved in equity markets. States often have statewide VC funds. Thus, there is abundant evidence that policymakers believe that financial market interventions may be the "cause" of further business and economic expansion.

Therefore, while most economists would generally agree that the overall economic climate is the cause and financial markets the effect, plenty of examples demonstrate that innovative financial interventions may be the spark or "cause" for accelerating a slow economy. Certainly, economic and financing activities in much of rural Illinois and America definitely need acceleration.

Rural Challenges in Development Finance: Mississippi Delta, Wisconsin, and Illinois

Rural areas and small cities have experienced slower economic growth than the American economy for the past thirty years (Barkley et al. 2001a; Bluestone and Long 1989) and lag behind metropolitan communities partly because of unequal access to loan and equity finance by rural enterprises. Rural areas also lack capacity to produce an adequate quantity of good loan requests. For example, rural counties in Missouri have bank-loan-to-deposit ratios nearly 30 percent below the standard metropolitan (metro) areas. Numerous studies have implied or even charged that small city and rural banks are less cooperative in providing financing for commercial, industrial, and other loans (Barkley, Markley, and Rubin 2001b; Lenzi and Pigg 1990; Shaffer, Pulver, Rogers, Wojan, and Gerland 1989). These same studies have ana-

Figure 11.1   **Risk Return Relationship of Finance Forms**

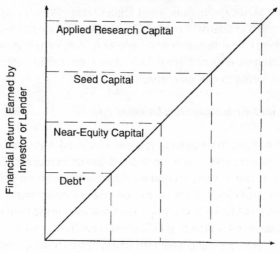

Risk Incurred by Investor or Lender

Source: Lenzi 1992b.
*Long-term and subordinated secured debt

lyzed the availability of finance capital for business expansion in rural areas with a focus on types of financing such as loans and equity capital as well as level of difficulty in obtaining financing for different types and stages of business.

This chapter identifies problems of economic development finance in rural Illinois and America; it explores various options and programs to address these problems, including initiatives from other parts of the country; and it proposes policy initiatives to improve rural economic development finance. Depending on the nature of the economic development project and the financial position of the project owners or sponsors, different types of finance are appropriate. Various forms of finance are used relative to the level of risk incurred by the investor or lender (Figure 11.1).

The higher the level of risk, the greater the rate of return expected by the lender or investor. Debt with the lowest risk is called "classic long-term collateralized fixed debt" and is typically provided to established enterprises with a proven track record at a bank market loan rate. "Near-equity capital" has a greater degree of risk in that it is often noncollateralized debt on more marginal firms or projects and often yields higher rates of returns (15% to 25%) through various instruments. "Venture and seed capital" provide important equity dollars needed for risky expansions and start-ups, often involving new products, services, or technologies that have had limited market tests. Venture and seed capital, thus, yield higher rates of return, typically 40 percent compounded annually (Cochran 2002). "Applied research capital" is capital that supports new research and invention, carries the greatest risk, and yields the highest return. Figure 11.1 shows the relationship of these various financial forms to risk and return.

Rural Banking and Economic Development

Shaffer et al. (1989) cite three general reasons why rural America has lagged behind the rest of the country in economic development in recent decades. The first is that the structure of rural economies depends more heavily on primary industries such as agriculture, forestry, and mining and end-product manufacturing. The primary industries and end-product manufacturing both have been hurt by high exchange rates affecting U.S. exports and have moved production offshore. Second, they cite inadequate information and decision-making skills and the resultant slow adaptation to changing technology and economic climate. This view also is supported by others (Sorenson and Isserman 1988).

The third reason cited by Shaffer et al. (1989) is lack of "vital resources," including "capital"—an idea supported by numerous subsequent studies (Barkley et al. 2001a; Jossi and Duncan 1998; Rubin 2000). Shaffer et al. (1989) add that, "Access to capital by non-farm firms is not a universal problem in rural areas." They do, however, identify types of firms that have problems locating financing in rural areas:

- Businesses new to rural regions (difficulty in loan evaluation)
- Firms in sectors dominant in local markets (owing to concerns over loan portfolio diversification)
- Very small businesses with small loan requests
- Large firms with loan requests that may exceed local lending limits
- Pre-venture or start-up firms needing debt capital
- High-risk firms because of limited access to equity capital and lenders' unwillingness to use participation and guarantees to spread risk
- Fast-growing companies seeking expansion loans
- Firms with insufficient collateral to secure long-term loans
- Firms outside the local geographic service area of the bank (this limits the credit options for most rural firms)

Shaffer et al. (1989, 8) conclude that, "Rural capital initiatives must be set in a total body of effective rural development policy if rural areas are to close the economic gap with urban areas."

Rural capital initiatives include community education and technical assistance to rural businesses and banks, assistance to lenders in evaluating unusual loan applications, strengthening loan-risk dispersal mechanisms such as neighborhood and correspondent bank loan sharing, regulations directing more capital to rural areas, government loan and venture funds targeted to rural areas, and target areas for interest subsidy and loan guarantees.

A problem faced by entrepreneurs in rural areas is their choice of financial institutions for loans. Studies have shown that smaller banks make 70 to 95 percent of their commercial loans within their home city or county (Lenzi 1992a; Parkinson 2002; Shaffer 1978; Shaffer et al. 1989). A study in Wisconsin found that 86 percent of rural bank lending activity was within ten miles of the bank (Taff, Pulver, and Staniforth 1984). Shaffer et al. (1989) reported in a survey of 815 Wisconsin firms that 84 percent of the bank debt was from banks within fifteen miles of the firm. A New England study of 582 companies found that 75 percent of all loans were obtained from banks within ten miles of their businesses (Markley 1990).

Shaffer et al. (1989) found urban businesses more satisfied (82%) than rural businesses (74%) with the ability of their banks to finance them. Twenty-five percent of rural businesses, compared with only 20 percent in urban areas, said they could not find capital within thirty miles. The researchers did not find statistical differences between regions categorized as nonisolated and isolated (no urban center greater than 20,000 population and distant from major banking centers). One research team (Peterson, Shaffer, and Pulver 1985) found rural and isolated firms were denied loans more often for lack of collateral, had to put more money down, and received higher interest rates and shorter maturities on long-term loans.

One of the first pieces of evidence showing problems with rural economic development finance was reported in a study of economic development finance in the Federal Lower Mississippi Delta Commission Region (Lenzi and Pigg 1990). Trends and implications of banking and other finance patterns on economic conditions and development in the Lower Mississippi Delta Commission Region (a 214–county area along the Mississippi River in seven states, extending from southern Illinois and southeast Missouri to New Orleans and the Gulf of Mexico) were analyzed. The findings have important implications for those committed to rural economic development. Recent data analysis indicates these same trends still hold true (Sheshunoff Information Services 2001b).

The Lower Mississippi Delta Region has among the poorest economic conditions in the nation (Hand 1990), similar but worse than conditions in rural America in general. Though the Delta Region lacks many major economic development essentials such as human capital and physical infrastruc-

Map 11.1   **Capital Flight from the Delta Region**

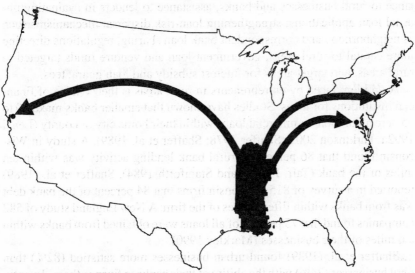

Source: Lenzi and Pigg 1990.

ture, it also lags behind in capital and finance for business start-ups and expansions. The Delta Region research examined various aspects of finance, including a detailed study of the banks and banking system, state financing programs, the Small Business Administration (SBA) loan programs, VC (venture capital), and other unique business finance programs.

The Delta Region study revealed several interesting patterns in banking within the region, including the following:

- Loan/deposit ratios within the region were well below national averages. This was due to a lower level of loan demand (owing to market conditions) combined with more conservative lending practices by many small rural banks within the region. Milkove (1985) and others found the same pattern around the country. These low loan to deposit ratios reflected "capital flight" from the region, as depicted in Map 11.1.

- Commercial loans were a smaller portion of the total loan portfolio in Delta Region's banks than for the nation as a whole, which is an indication of a lower level of loan activity in "basic" economic sectors associated with economic development and vitality.

- Rural banks had a significantly lower level of loan activity, giving fewer commercial and industrial loans.

- The Delta Region's banks were well-capitalized with low nonperforming loan rates.

Table 11.1
Large Metro Versus Balance of Region Loan/Deposit Ratios

Place	Deposits (millions $)	Loans (millions $)	Loan/Deposit Ratios
New Orleans, LA	7,649	7,078	92.53
Shelby, TN	8,552	7,318	85.57
Hinds, MS	4,694	4,007	85.36
Pulaski, AR	2,402	1,852	77.14
Delta Region	59,928	44,208	73.80
Large Metro	23,297	20,256	86.95
Balance/LMDR	36,631	23,952	65.39

Source: Sheshunoff Information Services 1989.

The region was capitalized at a higher rate than the national average, with lower than average rates of nonperforming loans. Small rural banks, especially, were characterized by a pattern of capital strength and few nonperforming loans. The pattern is indicative of small banks with relatively weak loan demand and somewhat conservative lending practices. It also indicates that the region's banking system as a whole had considerable excess capacity to finance economic development within the region if institutions and instruments can be created that (1) increase loan demand, (2) present banks with loan arrangements that are acceptable from the risk perspective, and (3) attract alternative investment opportunities that retain capital in the region to assist regional economic development.

Low loan to deposit ratios result from the "capital flight" problem. Money leaves the Delta Region for large city commercial banks and government debt instruments. This is especially true of small, more rural banks within the region. In the Delta Region, as a whole, the four largest metropolitan counties (representing New Orleans, Jackson, Little Rock, and Memphis) had a composite loan-to-deposit ratio of 87 percent, compared to 65.4 percent for the remaining 210 counties in the region (Table 11.1).

Venture Capital

Venture capital (VC) and other forms of higher risk and subordinated financing have been shown to be largely unavailable in most nonurban areas (PriceWaterhouseCoopers 1999). B.H. Daniels (1989a) has researched rural capital availability in Arkansas, Georgia, Kansas, Massachusetts, Mississippi, North Carolina, and Virginia. He found rural areas especially unwilling to provide loans to both expansions and start-up enterprises. The inadequacy included first-position loans but was even more dramatic in the cases of subordinated finance and equity and near-equity capital. Daniels and associates have been instrumental in designing and implementing funds to address rural investment needs in many of these states.

One team of researchers (Hustedde and Pulver 1989) found half of the forty Midwest venture capitalists surveyed had not invested in businesses in cities with populations under 50,000 (i.e., rural areas). The same two researchers surveyed 318 firms seeking at least $100,000 and found 62 percent of urban firms successful compared to only 37 percent of rural firms. Other investigations (Barkley et al. 2001a; Parkinson 2002) have reconfirmed these patterns.

Research on the Delta Region identified no major VC corporation. The Southern Development Bancorporation's Southern Ventures Inc. (SVI) was the only identified venture firm in Arkansas. It was also the only company identified as having definite venture investments in the region (with four modest deals). There are certainly more venture investments (especially by the SBA-sanctioned Small Business Investment Corporation [SBIC]), but venture deals in the Delta Region appear to be a scattered few and far between (Lenzi and Pigg 1990).

Equity Overview

The latest edition of Growthink's (2002) *Total U.S. Private Equity Funding Report, Fourth Quarter, 2001* aptly characterizes the paucity of VC in rural America, especially the rural Midwest. During the last quarter of 2001, more than $8.1 billion of refunds were invested in 760 technology ventures. While the report was positive regarding early signs of a rebound in the VC markets (which nosedived with the dot com crash), its implications for the rural Midwest are dismal.

Most of the investments were on the two coasts, with $2.56 billion (31.5%) of the $8.1 billion invested in the Bay Area alone and an additional $1.362 billion (16.8%) invested in the Boston/New England area. Thus, nearly half (48.3%) or $3.922 billion was invested in just two high-tech metro areas on the east and west coasts.

While Illinois is categorized as part of the central United States, this area contains everything "between the coasts," including Colorado, Iowa, Kansas, Kentucky, Louisiana, Michigan, Minnesota, Missouri, Nebraska, Ohio, Texas, West Virginia, Wisconsin, and "others." While the central United States had total investments of $1.13 billion for this period, the only Illinois investments are listed as "Metro Chicago" at $94.95 million. *No* Illinois VC investments are documented for any nonmetro Chicago location. This clearly demonstrates the lack of VC in rural America in general and in Illinois specifically (Growthink 2002).

Wilhelm, Conlon, and Associates, a Chicago firm committed to starting a rural Midwest equities fund, sees the situation unequivocally (Parkinson 2002). Tom Parkinson, fund manager for the in-process Hopewell Fund, reports that a 1999–2001 survey found only one equity investment of any kind for a three-year period in rural Illinois south of Interstate 70. Lenzi's experience in southern Illinois has documented only one venture investment in the same time period. In this case, Tampa, Florida, VC was infused, and the company has since moved to Florida with its venture "parents." While there is some activity in Champaign with the Prairie Ventures Fund, the economic landscape of rural Illinois has a serious lack of VC.

Analysis—The RUPRI Study

The Rural Policy Research Institute (RUPRI) Center for Rural Entrepreneurship so clearly recognized the problem of rural equity capital access that it commissioned a study, the RUPRI *Rural Equity Capital Initiative* (Barkley et al. 2001a). This study, now largely recognized as the seminal work on the subject of rural equity capital, like others, found the structure of rural markets lacking. While rural debt (banking) institutions were in sound financial condition, the competitiveness of rural markets was suspect.

Specifically, the RUPRI group found rural VC markets "unorganized and often nonexistent" (Barkley et al. 2001a, 9) Traditional VC is concentrated both geographically on the "coasts" (i.e., California, Boston, and New York, especially) and in high-tech sectors. Information technology dominated all other sectors. The RUPRI group found a very small share of private and public equity going to rural entrepreneurs between 1995 and 1998.

Debt capital gaps also overlapped and compounded the VC availability problem for rural entrepreneurs. The RUPRI team identified four distinct debt capital gaps: (1) borrowers with large and complex capital needs, (2) borrowers with limited or unusual collateral, (3) borrowers with a business unfamiliar to lenders, and (4) borrowers who have lost "relationship" lenders. Clearly, all but the last group represent the stereotypical high-tech entrepreneur at the heart of the new and fastest growing sectors of the economy. If these debt gaps are not addressed, rural America will continue to be left behind.

The RUPRI team also identified specific rural VC gaps. They concluded that traditional VC institutions do not invest in rural enterprises because of (1) limited deal flow, (2) higher costs per investment, (3) limited exit opportunities, and (4) lack of local business support services. Thus, they found a serious policy challenge in creating institutional capacity in rural financial markets. Many of these findings were also supported by related studies (Jossi and Duncan 1998; MacIntosh 1997).

These rural shortcomings are not surprising and, in many ways, are inherent in "rural" areas. "Rural" means lower population (and business) density than "urban," so it should come as no surprise that there is more limited deal flow (naturally leading to higher costs per investment), more limited business support services, and fewer exit (sales) opportunities for the venture investor.

Rural areas in Illinois provide a specific case in point regarding rural debt and equity finance. Economically speaking, Illinois is two states. The Chicago metropolitan area, constituting nine counties and 55 percent of the state's population, is a major economic engine. During the past century, Greater Chicago has had one of the most dynamic economies not only in the United States but also on the planet. The balance of the state is another story. While there are pockets of smaller metro areas (e.g., Peoria, Champaign–Urbana, Bloomington–Normal, and parts of St. Louis Metro East) that have enjoyed prosperity, western Illinois and southern Illinois have suffered from slow economic growth and/or high unemployment. Not coincidentally, these areas have seen a lack of economic development financing both in bank lending and VC. With that information in mind, we will examine financing trends in rural Illinois as an example of what can happen when financing is not available.

Rural Illinois Lending/Finance Patterns

Not surprisingly, rural Illinois business lending and finance patterns conform to the Mississippi Delta and national trends. The sixteen southernmost Illinois counties are part of the newly created Delta Regional Authority (DRA); they overlap the Delta Region and represent some of the worst examples of inactive capital markets in the state. These rural business finance problems extend to most nonmetro areas of Illinois, represent both debt and equity capital sectors, and are increasingly recognized as "problems" by those who recommend public policy intervention (Cochran 2002; Parkinson 2002; Rubin 2000).

Lending Patterns

The data on rural Illinois lending, while not as dramatic as the overall Delta Region situation, shows similar patterns. Data for 2000 indicate that metro county banks had average loan-to-deposit ratios of 76.01 percent, whereas rural county banks averaged only 69.92 percent (Sheshunoff Information

Services 2001a). This picture is almost certainly more positive for rural areas than the actual situation, as urban banks often lend *more* than 100 percent and then "sell" loans to rural banks, thus diluting and weakening the actual contrast in loan-to-deposit differences between metro and rural areas.

Moreover, several anomalies in the data also dilute the contrast. For example, the only bank listed in Alexander County in southern Illinois (which has the state's highest unemployment rate) has a 92.6 percent loan-to-deposit ratio. Likewise, depressed Hamilton County shows a similar 94.3 percent loan-to-deposit ratio, which is certainly not reflective of local loan activity and probably is representative of the purchased "urban" loans previously mentioned. Removing Alexander and Hamilton counties and the university and "near-urban" counties of Adams (Quincy), Coles (Eastern Illinois University), Jackson (Southern Illinois University), Knox (Galesburg), McDonough (Western Illinois University), La Salle (Ottawa/LaSalle–Peru), and Vermillion (Danville) provides a picture closer to the true trends. With these obvious adjustments, the balance of seventy-one rural counties in Illinois shows an adjusted loan-to-deposit ratio of 67.2 percent. Again, the gap between urban and rural lending patterns is still understated because the rural banks "buy" urban bank loans, as previously mentioned.

The picture is dramatized when we examine counties with loan-to-deposit ratios of less than 65 percent even though there are only three such urban counties: (1) Henry (63.6%), (2) St. Clair (63.8%), and (3) Rock Island (49.6%, also probably an exception). By contrast, there are eighteen such rural counties (Bond, Carroll, DeWitt, Douglas, Edwards, Fayette, Ford, Fulton, Hardin, Jefferson, Perry, Pulaski, Randolph, Saline, Schuyler, Scott, Stark, and Wayne). Not surprisingly, all but three of these counties are in the traditional rural Illinois slow-growth/poverty pockets of western and southern Illinois (Map 11.2). Clearly, rural areas in Illinois lag behind urban areas in debt capital activity. The picture is much bleaker when we examine equity markets.

Rural Illinois Equity/VC

Given the problems with traditional bank-lending finance, even more serious problems exist with "rural equity capital," effectively a misnomer. Except for scattered individual or "Angel" investments that can only be documented anecdotally, very little equity capital exists in rural Illinois. Venture capital funds exist in the Chicago area and possibly small funds exist in several downstate Standard Metropolitan Areas (SMAs). Funds in the St. Louis area generally do not invest outside the metro region, as was confirmed by Lenzi and Pigg's 1990 study that found no VC in rural southern Illinois. Parkinson (2002) and Cochran's (2002) subsequent investigations reaffirmed this situation.

Map 11.2 **Rural Illinois Counties With Loan-to-Deposit Ratios Less Than 65 Percent**

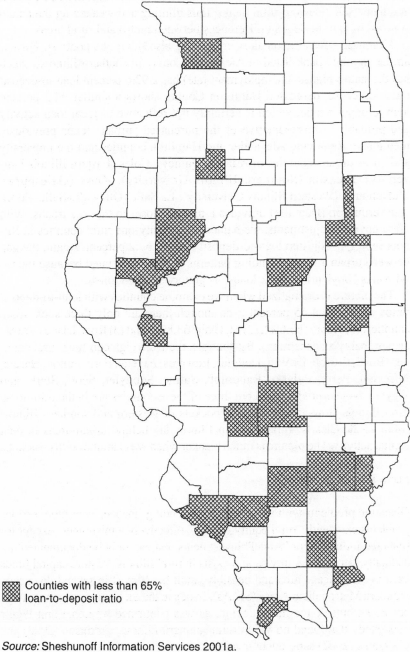

Counties with less than 65%
loan-to-deposit ratio

Source: Sheshunoff Information Services 2001a.

David Wilhelm (2002), former political consultant and now an investment banker interested in advancing social issues, recognized the implications of a lack of rural VC and has attempted remedies. He organized a regional venture fund—the Appalachian Ohio Fund—in southeastern Ohio with Ohio banks and public participation. A similar attempt to launch a fund—first titled the Southern Illinois Development Fund—was aborted despite a $5 million commitment of union pension funds and other small commitments. (The prospective fund's minimum needed to launch was $20 million.)

The major objection of banks and other hesitant institutional investors was that there was not sufficient "deal flow" (quality demand) in southern Illinois. Later, the scope was expanded to all of rural Illinois, but "deal flow" doubts still kept the fund from gathering sufficient capital to launch. This failure to launch was also related to the collapse of the dot com and VC markets (Wilhelm 2002).

Wilhelm (2002) and his associates have further revised their strategy and are now seeking capitalization of a federally certified SBIC (Small Business Investment Corporation). Not only has the structure changed, but the geographic scope has been expanded. The proposed new fund, titled the Hopewell Fund, will make equity investments in rural Iowa, Wisconsin, and Indiana, as well as in Illinois. The thought is that by expanding the target area, projected "deal flow" will be sufficient to satisfy investors. A similar SBIC, Prairie Ventures, has recently begun operations in rural Illinois and, at the time of this writing, is the only formal VC fund in rural Illinois identified in this study.

Direct and Indirect Public Intervention and Investment

One would be remiss if there was no acknowledgment of the wide range of public and quasi-public interventions in rural Illinois and America that have already been attempted to remedy both the tightness of business loan supply and the lack of equity capital in rural markets. Although no overview is exhaustive, these can be compiled in two broad categories (which sometimes overlap): (1) debt intervention and (2) equity intervention (Cochran 2002).

Debt Intervention

There are now, and have long existed, a wide range of public-policy interventions in loan markets. Some of the major interventions worthy of mention include SBA (Small Business Administration) programs, USDA Rural Development, state economic development programs, state bonding programs, and tax credit programs used in many states. These include the many SBA programs, especially the SBA 7(a) loan guarantee and the SBA 504 fixed-asset subordinate loan companies.

These programs have greatly expanded loan access in rural markets, although most rural banks in the smallest towns still participate at low levels (Cochran 2002). Loan guarantees and subordinated (junior) loans are now common tools in extending debt capital in all markets, including rural markets. Together, these two SBA programs have probably done more to extend debt capital for business expansion than any other programs in the United States. Still, these SBA programs, like other innovative finance market interventions, are vastly underutilized in rural Illinois and in America (Cochran 2002; Lenzi and Pigg 1990).

USDA Rural Development Programs

In addition to SBA, other major federal finance intervention programs are the USDA Rural Development (RD) finance options. These include loan guarantees and the Rural Business Enterprise Grant's (RBEG) loan and loan guarantee programs (Teckenbrock 2002). The RBEG allows for significant grants to small- and medium-sized businesses that create new jobs and payrolls. These grants become, in effect, equity, and they greatly extend financing.

The USDA-RD can also provide direct long-term loans at lower than market rates that can be used with other equity and debt. Finally, USDA-RD can use loan guarantees to entice banks to lend on marginal projects. All of these USDA programs are especially important to note because, as their name implies, they focus exclusively on the most rural areas.

State Economic Development Programs

Illinois Department of Commerce and Community Affairs (DCCA) programs are a major component of the current options available to extend credit and investment in rural Illinois. As such, they deserve recognition and summary reviews. Similar programs exist in the economic development departments of all states. The DCCA makes Community Development Action Program (CDAP) awards to cities, and these then become subordinate low-interest loans to Illinois businesses. The CDAPs are used extensively in rural Illinois and in America. As businesses repay these subordinate low-interest loans, they become the basis for a "local" Revolving Loan Fund (RLF) that continues to lend to small business start-ups and expansions. These "local" RLFs, usually managed by cities or counties, are among the most commonly used sources of subordinate lending in rural America, and they are supplemented by federal Economic Development Administration (EDA) RLFs (usually administered by Regional Planning Commissions) and operate in a similar manner.

Other state programs may provide interim or construction financing (Treasurer's office) or loan participations (DCCA). Although it was created by the State of Illinois, one of the most visible "state" players is now an autonomous entity—the Illinois Development Finance Authority (IDFA) (Cochran 2002). Almost all states have similar bonding and economic development finance authorities.

The IDFA is Illinois' state bonding agency. Originally established to issue Industrial Revenue Bonds (IRBs), IDFA is the official bonding authority for both for-profit and nonprofit entities. It also is a VC arm. While theoretically it could be an active player in rural Illinois, it has done relatively few deals outside Chicago and other metro areas (Cochran 2002). The VC program, for example, makes only "matching" venture investments when another venture firm has already committed to the deal. Rural Illinois, lacking any venture firms, has no "match" and, thus, has received no IDFA venture investments. Many states—Missouri, for example—also offer tax credits for investments in venture funds; this is an indirect method of public–private investment in VC.

In recent years, the Counsel for Community Development Inc. (CCD), a Boston-based firm, has developed statewide equity and near-equity funds around the country. Among these are the Massachusetts Capital Resource Company, the North Carolina Enterprise Corporation, the Arkansas Science and Technology Authority (an applied research and seed-capital fund), and the Virginia Economic Development Corporation (VEDCORP). The CCD also developed proposals for equity funds in Kentucky and Georgia. During the past several years, Virginia has put together an interesting experiment in rural economic development finance under the VEDCORP model, which is described here.

To address the growing gap in development and incomes between urban and rural Virginia, various public and private entities collaborated to create VEDCORP, which identified the need for additional financing instruments in rural Virginia. VEDCORP's final report states, "Venture capitalists do not have a cost effective network through which to identify potential rural . . . investments as they do in urban . . . centers" (Daniels 1989b). The report further states that banks are constrained from financing many "deals" because they are restricted from taking higher rates of return for riskier deals in which venture capitalists might be interested.

Banks also cannot afford the extensive management assistance needed by fast-growth and marginal firms. These conditions create an economic development financing gap in all rural areas, not just Virginia. To address this gap,

Figure 11.2 **Southern Development Bancorporation Structure**
(With equity in millions)

Source: Lenzi 1992b.

VEDCORP was created to provide "equity, near-equity and other forms of flexible growth financing" (Daniels 1989b, 2) for rural Virginia. This is an innovative and aggressive approach to the need for rural economic growth.

Southern Development Bancorporation

The Southern Development Bancorporation (SDB) in Arkansas is also a unique and aggressive new actor in rural economic development, with its operations centered in Arkadelphia, Arkansas. The SDB actively pursues loan and investment opportunities and uses equity-oriented approaches, like those associated with investment banking, as well as conventional finance methods. Personal interviews with Jeff Doose (1990), President of SDB at the home bank in Arkadelphia, revealed that SDB is based on the earlier experiment in community-based development banking at the Southshore Bank in Chicago. Taub (1988) chronicled Southshore's history in *Community Capitalism*. This in an impressive model of community development-based banking that might be characterized as banking and investment with a social conscience.

The SDB model is shown in Figure 11.2. The diagram illustrates the multiple facets of a rural finance intervention model. The SDB itself is a bank holding company. It is essentially a for-profit community development corporation (CDC) that owns ("holds") the Elk Horn Bank and Trust. This commercial bank operates in typical fashion, making secured loans for personal, residential, and commercial operations. Theoretically, bank loan patterns will be slightly more aggressive and progressive in generating economic development momentum in the area. The bank also may invest in a geographically larger area than just the local community (e.g., a Delta substate region). The SDB in Arkansas currently targets about thirty counties in southeast Arkansas. In addition to the Elk Horn Bank and Trust, SDB "holds" Opportunity Lands Incorporated, a for-profit real estate development corporation.

Opportunity Lands Incorporated targets the development of real estate projects in the area that will be profitable, helps area economic development, and improves the local investment climate. Opportunity Lands Incorporated has invested in business incubators and low- and moderate-income housing projects.

In addition to the two for-profit companies held by SDB, the holding company has a separate nonprofit corporation, Arkansas Enterprise Group (AEG), which, in turn, holds a for-profit venture company—Southern Ventures, Inc. (SVI)—and another nonprofit company—the Good Faith Fund—a loan program for micro-businesses ($1,000 to $2,500 loans). Each arm of SDB addresses a separate problem area of rural economic development finance. The AEG is financed with donations and grants and is not expected to provide a return to investors, whereas the bank and land corporation must produce returns to satisfy equity investors.

Bank CDCs

The SDB is a specific example of the Bank Community Development Corporation (CDC), a new approach which is gaining in popularity (*Bank Community Development Corporation* 1989). Bank CDCs are another finance tool for rural America (Barkley et al. 2001a; Lenzi 1992a). Normally, banks are restricted from making equity or near-equity investments and make only collateralized loans on the debt side. Bank CDCs allow lending institutions to make equity and near-equity investments indirectly through subsidiary Bank CDCs. Bank CDC programs are administered for bank holding companies by the Federal Reserve and for national bank subsidiary CDCs by the Office of Comptroller of the Currency (OCC). The OCC's allowance for Bank CDCs began in 1963 and was expanded in 1971 with the first subsidiary Bank CDC established in 1979 (Lenzi 1992a).

One main difference between regular bank lending and the Bank CDC investments for economic development is the "ability of Bank CDCs to make equity investments such as common stock . . . or participation in surplus cash flow on real estate projects" (Sower 1992). Bank CDCs allow banks to carry equity and unsecured investment on their books as assets as long as there is a social and economic benefit to the community.

The Florida Black Business Investment Fund is a state-initiated program that helped establish and supervise a half-dozen Bank CDCs in cities around the state with black populations (Lenzi 1992a). These Bank CDCs, created in response to black unrest in Miami in the early 1980s, have invested millions of dollars in new housing, shopping centers, commercial buildings, and industrial projects in black communities throughout Florida. The Southshore Bank CDC in Chicago has been given credit by Taub (1988) for "turning around" the property values and investment climate of a large minority community.

Ronald Gryzwinski (1990), past president of the Southshore Bank CDC, has been one of the most prominent leaders of the Bank CDC movement in the United States. He states the case for them strongly and with the credibility of someone with a strong track record. This CDC financed the rehabilitation of 9,000 housing units in the 1980s alone, and also financed substantial commercial ventures, including shopping malls. The CDC has also been profitable and has had very low losses. Gryzwinski identifies three conceptual components to the Bank CDC investment process: (1) replace "psychology of decline" with self-confidence in area development, (2) spur community involvement that releases the energy of local residents, and (3) attract other public and private investment to the area.

Practically, Gryzwinski stresses four steps in the community reinvestment process: (1) initiation of large-scale housing and commercial projects, (2) massive bottom-up housing rehabilitation investment (i.e., no loans just to change ownership; rehabilitation must be included), (3) job-creation investment, and (4) investment to expand local business economy (Gryzwinski 1990).

The North Carolina Nations Bank CDC in Charlotte, has invested millions in revitalizing neighborhoods and commercial areas in downtown Charlotte. In all, there are nearly forty Bank CDCs under the supervision of the OCC, with another fifteen bank-holding companies supervised by the Federal Reserve (Lenzi 1992b). The VEDCORP and SDB are the best-known rural examples. Bank CDCs have an impressive record in both rural and urban areas.

These successful, documented, and nontraditional approaches teach policymakers that creating new financial institutions can increase economic development in rural areas. Bank and traditional finance can be expanded, quality loan demand and enterprise formation can be increased, and equity and near-equity financing can be created or expanded. The added investment and business formation can greatly benefit the economies of rural areas.

RUPRI Nontraditional Venture Capital Trends/Resources

Fortunately, the Barkley et al. (2001a) RUPRI study also found a number of examples of rural nontraditional VC institutions that have uniquely addressed the rural VC gaps previously identified. These emerging rural VC institutions typically (1) operate outside regions and sectors where traditional VC is concentrated, (2) will accept lower financial returns than will traditional venture investors, (3) generally have an explicit rural geographic focus, and (4) often have a "dual bottom line" of social and financial returns.

Nontraditional VC institutions can succeed precisely because their community and regional focus helps fund managers assess risk-return trade-off in new enterprise in a broader and different context from traditional VC firms. The consideration of both social and financial returns creates more flexibility for both expected return threshold and exit strategies.

Some of the successful nontraditional rural VC funds demonstrate diverse and unique characteristics. The Community Development Financial Institutions (CDFI) Fund—a federal initiative—and the New Markets Fund have been successful because they have provided state and federal public support for nontraditional VC. Kansas Ventures, the Appalachian Ohio Fund, and the SDB have based success on strong partnerships between rural banks and their nontraditional VC institutions. The Colorado Seed Fund learned that the rural focus required relaxing other constraints. Coastal Ventures LP accepted that higher operating costs were required in a rural fund to overcome limited deal flow and lack of business support services. The Kentucky Highlands group accepted that greater resources had to somehow be provided for deal development and creation. All groups stress adequate capitalization to diversify portfolio and make "follow-on" (second or subsequent stage) investments. The Iowa Capital Corporation structured its fund to minimize political interference when public capital was utilized by creating an arms-length corporate board to make all investment decisions (Barkley et al. 2001a).

The RUPRI researchers divided the twenty-three nontraditional rural VC institutions into six groups (defined by source of investment, control, and legal structure) and citing "lessons learned" from these entities. The six "types" of nontraditional VC entities are (1) Public–Public (public investment and public control), (2) Public–Private (public investment, private control), (3) Public Incentives (tax credits, etc), (4) Community (more local or small regional), (5) Community Development VC Funds (CDVCFs—larger regional with a mix of public and private investment), and (6) SBICs (the SBA-licensed Small Business Investment Corporation that receive a 2–1 leveraged federal match to all nonfederal funds raised).

The RUPRI team learned numerous lessons from case studies of these different types of alternative rural VC institutions. Team members concluded that, whereas there is no single "best" model for nontraditional VC funds, there are commonalities. Common factors of successful funds include (1) private management, (2) public sector investment, (3) higher per deal operating costs to generate "deal flow" and provide support services, (4) hiring a skilled professional fund management team, (5) adequate capitalization for "follow-on" investments, and (6) accepting lower return-on-investment (ROI) than traditional

VC funds. This assessment provides a framework for rural Illinois and America to use as they target rural-focused VC funds to serve their needs.

The problems with the scarcity of equity and debt capital in rural Illinois in particular and rural America in general have been documented, and successful rural finance ventures exist around the country. The next question is, "What should be done now?" While a review of finance intervention options provides ideas, we propose a unique, synthesized agenda, which would be useful to Midwestern states. This "Rural Finance Agenda" is a set of action and policy recommendations for policymakers and economic development specialists, but it is also important to bankers, investors, and business owners. Though this "agenda" is not a "final word," it should prove to be a sound basis for some discussion and, it is hoped, action.

Proposed Rural America Finance Agenda

1. Establish as local, state, and federal policy goals the expansion of debt and equity capital in rural America.

2. Create a network of rural venture/equity capital pools by rural region. Scale these to geography, population, and potential economic activity. For example, three such regions in Illinois are proposed here: (1) southern Illinois, (2) northern Illinois, and (3) central Illinois. Similar regions could be identified in other Midwestern states. These should be publicly supported and geographically based pools that will link to other private venture pools such as the Chicago, St. Louis, IDFA, and Hopewell funds. They would serve as rural "hubs" or "magnets" to attract and leverage other equity capital as well as debt financing. Regions should be large enough to support an equity overhead and infrastructure.

3. Provide targeted assistance to create major regional "hub" Revolving Loan Funds (RLFs) to provide subordinate financing to enterprise start-ups and expansions in Midwestern states. The USDA's Intermediate Revolving Loan Fund (IRLF) dollars could be used to establish these funds in each rural region, as previously mentioned. These regional RLFs would, in turn, be linked to and leverage smaller RLF state and federal loan and loan guarantee programs, as well as bank debt financing.

4. Develop measurable state and regional financing targets in each of the three categories of debt and equity financing. Monitor these results on a statewide and regional basis.

5. Hold Rural Finance Summits in each Midwestern state with the state lawmakers and policymakers, bankers, economic development officials, Rural Partners, DCCA, USDA, the Small Business Development Centers (SBDC), the SBA-504 corporations, venture capitalists, community foundations, and

others to develop a detailed rural finance agenda. Hone this "agenda" to an action plan for implementation.

6. Form statewide Rural Finance Teams in each state to implement and monitor the "agenda." Meet quarterly to review progress and update and implement the action plan. Make needed and appropriate adjustments as time and circumstances dictate.

7. Enlist federal policy and funding support to create the regional debt and equity funds. Operational funding support to establish and manage the funds as well as leveraged public investment should be included. This national policy should be administered by the USDA-RD office. Provide a framework of leveraged funding to entice states and regions to create these funds.

Though this Rural Finance Agenda is broad in scope and challenging in its vision, it is a much needed call to action for the impoverished parts of rural America now left behind. Is it not time for rural advocates to raise our voices and rally to this important challenge and agenda with sustained action?

References

Bank Community Development Corporation. 1989. Springfield: Illinois Department of Commerce and Community Affairs.

Barkley, David L., Deborah M. Markley, David Freshwater, Julia Sass Rubin, and Ron Shaffer. 2001a. *Establishing Nontraditional Venture Capital Institutions: Lessons Learned.* Columbia, MO: RUPRI.

Barkley, David L., Deborah M. Markley, and Julia Sass Rubin. 2001b. Certified capital companies (CAPCOs): Strengths and Shortcomings of the latest wave in state-assisted venture capital programs. *Economic Development Quarterly* 15(4): 350.

Bluestone, Herman, and Celeste A. Long. 1989. Growth falters in most rural counties: Manufacturing both hero and goat. *Rural Development Perspectives* 5(2): 8–10.

Cochran, Marcia. 2002. Personal interview with finance officer from the Illinois Development Finance Authority, Carbondale, Illinois.

Daniels, B.H. 1989a. *Finance for the Future: Capital Markets Analysis and Action to Enhance Georgia's Economic Development.* 1989. Boston: Council for Community Development (CCD).

———. 1989b. *VEDCORP Market Research.* Boston: CCD.

Doose, Jeff. 1990. Personal interview with president of Southern Development Bancorporation; Arkadelphia, Arkansas.

Growthink. 2002. *Total U.S. Private Equity Funding Report, Fourth Quarter, 2001.* Available on-line: <www.growthink.com>.

Gryzwinski, Ronald (President, Shorebank Corporation). 1990. *Stimulating Investment in Disinvested Areas.* Keynote Address to International Community Development Society Annual Conference, July, Little Rock, Arkansas.

Hand, R.T. 1990. *Delta Council Economic Progress Report.* 1990. Stoneville, MS: Delta Council.

Hustedde, R.J., and G.C. Pulver. 1989. *Factors Affecting Equity Capital Acquisition: The Demand Side.* Unpublished document, University of Wisconsin–Madison, Department of Agricultural Economics.

Jossi, Frank, and Paul Duncan. 1998. Angels take wing. *Ventures* (October): 34–36.

Lenzi, Raymond. 1992a. *Bank Community Development Corporations (CDCs): New Initiatives For Small City Economic Development.* Paper presented at the Small Cities Conference, Kalamazoo, Michigan.

———. 1992b. Nontraditional sources of economic development financing. *Economic Development Review* 10(2): 20–24.

Lenzi, Raymond, and K. Pigg. 1990. *Lower Mississippi Delta Economic Development Finance: A Proposal for a Delta Development Bank.* Unpublished document, University of Missouri–Columbia, Office of Public Policy Resources.

MacIntosh, Jeffrey G. 1997. Venture capital exits in Canada and the United States. In *Financing Growth in Canada*, ed. Paul Halpern. Calgary, Alberta: University of Calgary Press.

Markley, Deborah M. 1990. *The Impact of Financial Deregulation on Rural Commercial Credit Availability in Four New England States: Empirical Evidence and Policy Implications.* Final Report to the Ford Foundation and the Rural Economic Policy Program of the Aspen Institute.

Milkove, D.L. 1985. Are rural banks different, or just small? *Rural Development Perspectives* (October).

Parkinson, Tom. 2002. Personal interview with manager of the Hopewell Fund, January.

Peterson, J., R.E. Shaffer, and G.C. Pulver. 1985. *Terms of Credit for New Small Businesses.* Madison: University of Wisconsin–Madison, University Small Business Development Center.

PriceWaterhouseCoopers. 1999. *National Venture Capital Survey.* Available on-line: <www.pwcglobal.com>.

Rubin, J.S. 2000. *Community Development Venture Capital: A Report on the Industry.* Available on-line: <www.cdvca.org>.

Shaffer, R.E. 1978. *Commercial Banking Activities in West Central Wisconsin: 1969 and 1974.* Madison: University of Wisconsin–Madison, College of Agriculture and Life Sciences.

Shaffer, R.E., G.C. Pulver, G. Rogers, T. Wojan, and D. Gerland. 1989. *Rural Nonfarm Business' Access to Debt and Equity Capital.* Madison: University of Wisconsin–Madison, Department of Agriculture Economics.

Sheshunoff Information Services. 2001a. *Banks and S&L's of Illinois, 2001.* Austin, TX: Author.

———. 2001b. *Bank Loan Data for Arkansas, Illinois, Kentucky, Missouri, Louisiana, Mississippi, and Tennessee.* Austin, TX: Sheshunoff Information Services.

———. 1989. *Banks and S&L's of Arkansas, Illinois, Kentucky, Louisiana, Missouri, Mississippi, and Tennessee, 1989.* Austin, TX: Author, p. 334.

Sorenson, D.J., and A.M. Isserman. 1988. *Rural/Urban Difference in Bank Lending Levels: The Importance of Management and Other Factors.* Paper presented at the SRSA Annual Meeting, Morgantown, West Virginia.

Sower, John. 1992. Bank CDCs. *Economic Development Commentary* (August): 3–5.

Taff, S.J., G.C. Pulver, and S.D. Staniforth. 1984. *Are Small Community Banks Prepared to Make Complex Business Loans?* Madison: University of Wisconsin–Madison, College of Agriculture and Life Sciences.

Taub, R.P. 1988. *Community Capitalism: Banking Strategies and Economic Development.* Boston: Harvard Business School Press.

Teckenbrock, Marvin. 2002. Personal interview with USDA official, Carbondale, Illinois, January.

Torpey, W.J. 1989. *1988 Annual Report.* Boston: Massachusetts Capital Resource Company.

Wilhelm, David. 2002. Personal interview. Chicago, IL.

12

JOHN J. GRUIDL AND RONALD J. HUSTEDDE

Key Practices in Creating a Learning Community

The effective practice of community development is critical in Midwestern rural communities facing the impacts of dramatic economic, technological, and social change. The forces behind such change have been well-documented and are extensively discussed in other chapters (e.g., Sofranko and Samy, Chapter 3; Johnson and Scott, Chapter 4; and Swanson, Samy, and Sofranko, Chapter 5). Primary among them is the phenomenon of globalization, fueled by the telecommunications revolution, which has brought rural communities into closer trade and communication linkages with the rest of the world. The agricultural sector, still the mainstay of many Midwestern rural economies, continues to decline as commodity prices hit new lows (although it is in the process of developing new opportunities through value-added enterprises). Retail businesses are confronting stiff competition from large discount stores, catalogue operations, and e-commerce to such an extent that many go out of business. These forces, together with shifting demographics that reflect significant out-migration of young people and aging of the remaining population, have altered the economic and social fabric of many communities.

Responding to this rapidly changing environment poses a daunting challenge. It seems unlikely that solutions will come from massive government programs, outside intervention, or the collapse of cities. Instead, the enormous responsibility of responding to these turbulent times will be borne by the residents themselves who live in rural communities.

An effective response requires residents and communities to be proactive in local change initiatives if the vitality of a place is to survive. Tom Bonnett (Chapter 13) points out the necessity for community residents to be constantly learning new skills so that they can adjust to new demands. He suggests that an essential part of community sustainability is the investment in human capital and the active promotion of lifelong learning among residents.

He cautions, however, that the culture of rural communities sometimes gets in the way of change. For communities to act effectively, they need a local culture that encourages innovation, learning, and broad participation.

Throughout the rural Midwest, many residents are seeking ways to effectively mobilize so they can achieve what they really want in their community. In an effort to guide rural towns in this process, this chapter presents the "learning community framework." This framework describes practices that assist communities in organizing themselves to become more flexible, adaptable, and creative within a changing environment. A word of caution is needed at this point: the learning community framework is not a tight package with a template that fits all rural areas. Each community, and the context within which it is found, is unique and requires a special approach for successful development; however, when followed over time, these practices can be shown to improve the way that residents and organizations relate, lead, and organize for community development.

The following discussion of the learning community framework draws heavily from the model of collective change advanced by Peter Senge and his colleagues, that is known as the learning organization approach (Senge 1990; Senge et al. 1994; Senge et al. 1999; Senge et al. 2000). Senge and his colleagues note that most of the organizations reported as adopting this approach are businesses, including many Fortune 500 companies.[1] In reviewing the impact on businesses, Art Kleiner et al. (1994, 22) state that "the gains from enhancing learning capacity have proven to be sustainable, cumulative, and self-reinforcing"; however, organizations other than businesses have also benefited from the learning organization approach. For example, the Sullivan Elementary School in Tallahassee, Florida, applied learning organization principles, such as creating a shared vision and identifying core values, to transform itself. This process led to greater parental involvement and a rise in teacher approval ratings by 20 percent (Kerka 1995).

The learning organization model is adapted here for use in community development. Many of the specific practices, such as shared visioning, are not new to communities and have frequently been applied to community development. Many communities have followed one or more of these practices, in most cases not identifying them as learning organization practices. Furthermore, many programs are available from universities, private organizations, and state agencies that can assist communities in implementing one or more of these practices (e.g., MAPPING the Future of Your Community through the Illinois Institute for Rural Affairs [www.mappingthefuture.org], Arkansas Vision 2010 through the Cooperative Extension Service [www.v2010.org], the Sirolli Institute [www.sirolli.com], and the Yellow Wood Associates [www.yellowwood.org]).

Despite of the fact that these practices are not entirely novel for communities, it is valuable, in our view, to present them within an integrated framework. The learning community framework allows this. Integrating the practices provides a more complete and holistic view of what communities need to do to be more successful.

In this chapter, six practices essential to creating a learning community are discussed along with examples of each practice. These practices require changes in processes and relationships within and among organizations. Furthermore, they require changes on the personal level. A call for such extensive changes is perhaps overwhelming, and it is doubtful that any community will completely master them; however, the learning community model provides an ideal, a vision of a community's optimal future. Without doubt, as organizations and citizen groups exercise the practices of the model individually and collectively, the community itself will become more adaptable and flexible in reaching its goals.

What Is a Learning Community?

Learning is not simply the act of acquiring more information; rather, it is the capacity to produce the results that are truly desired. By extension, then, whether it is a business, school, or community, a learning environment is one "in which people at all levels, individually and collectively, are continually increasing their capacity to produce the results that they really care about" (Senge et al. 1994).

A learning community is defined by its ability to learn, to seek out new knowledge and insights, to share this knowledge throughout the community, and to modify its behavior to reflect this new learning. Although this concept is related to principles of civic participation and democratization, it is distinct in its focus on changing the culture so that the capacity for learning, both individually and collectively, is maximized (Ratner 1997).

In a community that learns, people who traditionally have been suspicious of each other—business owners and union officials, environmentalists and industrial developers, government officials and ordinary residents—recognize their common stake in the future of the community and are amenable to what they can learn from one another. Furthermore, a learning community creates increased participation of its citizenry and promotes a sustainable energy so that there is better performance over the long run. A learning community is distinguished by its flexibility and, thus, is in a better position than traditional communities to respond to the rapidly changing circumstances that characterize the rural landscape of recent times.

Central to this description is the notion that a learning community does not simply target a solution to the immediate problem. Rather, it is able to recognize that immediate problems are part of a broader system and to seek long-term, systemic change. Approaches to problem-solving can be categorized into two learning types: (1) generative and (2) adaptive (Malholtra 1996). *Adaptive learning,* or single-loop learning, focuses on solving problems without examining the appropriateness of the learning behaviors. When practicing adaptive learning, people do not question the fundamental assumptions underlying the existing ways of doing work.

In contrast, *generative learning* emphasizes continuous experimentation and feedback in an ongoing examination of the very way people go about defining and solving problems. To maintain generative learning, communities must be in a state of frequent, near continuous change in structures, processes, and goals, even in the face of apparently optimal adaptation. In other words, generative learning brings about systemic change.

Although this task seems daunting, the six practices of the learning community framework discussed in this chapter can help move communities along the path of learning. All the practices are concerned with a shift away from an authoritative, top-down approach to community development toward a more participatory one. As residents are encouraged to participate more fully, they garner individual skills and abilities geared to solve problems. Furthermore, as people seek new knowledge, new mechanisms evolve within the community to apply that new knowledge in the problem-solving process. In addition, ongoing evaluation of the effectiveness of the process takes place and more learning ensues, creating a virtuous cycle of learning and change.

Table 12.1 contains some practical applications about the six learning community practices. It is not intended to be comprehensive but, rather, illustrative. It will assist communities in applying the practices as they plan and implement projects.

Practice Number 1: Engage Diverse Groups of People in Thinking Systemically

In the past, many communities focused exclusively on the goals and objectives of specific projects. It seemed foolish, costly, and esoteric to direct attention outside the framework of the project and to examine how the project fit in with a broader system. The problem is that this perspective neglects to consider the complexity of a community and how it interacts. Projects are not isolated from other community goals and visions. For example, what happens in a health-sector project can positively or adversely affect other sectors such as business or education. Project organizers and managers are realizing they can no longer afford to be isolated. They need a broader perspective.

Table 12.1

Practical Applications in Using the Learning Community Approach

Practice Number One: Thinking Systemically

Think broader than merely focusing on goals and objectives. Link new projects with broader sectors of the community, including the arts, business, civic groups, education, entrepreneurs, health care, law enforcement, religion, transportation, and other sectors that are typically omitted in planning, implementation and evaluation.

Involve those who represent the diversity of the community in the initiative, particularly those whose voices have not always been heard or may perceive they are in conflict. This may include youth, minority groups, women, senior citizens, the disabled, immigrants, and those with limited or low income. With broader involvement, the initiative is more likely to reflect the diversity of community concerns and interests and, hence, is more likely to succeed than those projects involving the "usual suspects."

Find ways to help participants view the community as a system in which all parts are interdependent and are self-adapting to a changing context.

Practice Number Two: Asset-Focused

Don't concentrate on community problems and deficits because it can lead to hopelessness and feeling overwhelmed.

Ask participants to identify the skills and knowledge that they have to make the project successful.

Identify the assets of informal groups such as bowling clubs or Bible study groups to build project success.

Identify the broader assets of the community to build project success, including civic life; formal groups (such as banks, hospitals, and places of worship); history; attitudes; the qualities of the community's leaders; and relationships with external groups, communities, and organizations.

Practice Number Three: Reflection and Shared Learning

Action without reflection doesn't lead to new knowledge about oneself or the community. Build in frequent feedback and reflection into the project.

Don't ask questions such as "Who's to blame?" for failures and unexpected events along the way. Don't concentrate on personalities or politics. Ask questions such as "What have we learned here?" or "What does it mean?"

Let feedback and reflection guide new actions.

Celebrate and recognize accomplishments through festivals, awards, or other means.

Practice Number Four: Public Deliberation

Offer participants opportunities to move from divisive questions such as "Whose side are you on?" to questions such as "What are the choices?" Use or adapt the National Issues Forums or Study Circles materials to help initiate more productive dialogue about controversial issues.

Anticipate differences and involve participants in dealing with these controversies that do not lead to debate or unproductive attacks.

Give participants basic skills in public conflict resolution and analysis.

Work towards greater consensus in order to reveal better choices for the community to accept.

Practice Number Five: Shared Vision

Involve the diversity of citizens and sectors in building a shared vision about what needs to be preserved and changed.

Involve citizens in asking what they want the community to be within the next 5, 10, or 20 years.

Lay out a practical plan for achieving the vision(s).

Re-envision when visions have been accomplished or need to be changed.

Explore whether a community vision complements or is in contrast to other organizational or group visions. Work on differences and build more inclusive visions.

Practice Number Six: Polycentric Circles of Leaders

If you don't have a county or community-wide leadership program, start one.

Make sure it has clear goals that respect the diversity of the community's citizens and sectors. Involve citizens in designing, implementing, and evaluating the leadership program.

Build trust and mutual responsibility by making government more transparent and less clannish or secretive. Engage others who have a diversity of views.

Create a climate for a critical mass of informed citizens through the use of Speak-Outs or facilitated dialogues.

Create opportunities for diverse leaders to know each other beyond the superficial level.

The first practice under discussion here is one that encourages residents to view their community as a *system*. Leonard Moffitt (1999, 240) contends that systems have three key criteria: (1) the whole is greater than, and distinct from, the sum of its parts owing to the interaction of those parts; (2) all parts are interdependent, meaning that an impact on any one part affects all other parts; and (3) a living system perpetuates itself both by reproducing and by self-adapting to an ever-changing context.

As human systems, communities share many of these criteria, in that the parts of a community are interdependent and an impact on one part of the community likely affects other parts. Furthermore, the systemic community is in a continual process of adapting to external changes so as to meet member needs and to interact successfully with other systems.

Certainly, the community system is very complex, and it may not be possible to develop a complete understanding of its behavior; however, the key to understanding the behavior of any system is to examine the channels by which its elements feed information and influence to each other over time (Senge et al. 1994). Therefore, it follows that a more critical discernment of the interdependencies of the elements within the community system is critical to understanding its behavior. Once the relationships among elements and its channels are better known, then change can be directed based on that knowledge.

Following a systemic approach necessarily means abandoning quick fixes. Under a systems approach, there is the recognition that solving one problem is likely to reveal other problems and possibly create new problems. Without considering the broader impacts, the quick fix can easily cause a decline instead of an increase in the vitality of the community. Conversely, "systems thinking shows that small, well-focused activities can sometimes produce significant enduring improvements, if they're in the right place" (Senge 1990, 63–64).

A first step in this practice is for communities to build cooperation and partnerships among local sectors and organizations such as local government, the Chamber of Commerce, private business, health care, and local service clubs. These groups need a venue at which they can communicate their activities and begin to see the interrelationships and mutual interests. For example, one small Illinois town holds a monthly "roundtable" luncheon meeting at which representatives of key community organizations report their activities and look for ways to work cooperatively on projects.

Systems thinking extends beyond cooperation and partnerships, however. Peter Scholtes (1995) agrees that collaborative relationships between organizations and sectors are prerequisites for creating systems. He contends, however, that cooperation is not enough. Instead, communities must understand systems, think systemically, create systems, lead systems, and work together in systems.

According to Scholtes (1995), when a community operates within a systems perspective, it works together to identify (1) the purpose of the community, (2) the highest priority needs of the community, (3) indicators of how well these needs are being met, (4) the system of interacting conditions and factors, (5) the interventions that are necessary to solve the problems at their source, and (6) plans for implementing these solutions and monitoring the outcomes. This requires residents willing and capable of seeing the whole, rather than just the parts, and willing to intervene to create lasting, sustainable change.

Table 12.1 contains practical examples of how the practice of engaging diverse groups of people in thinking systemically can be carried out. Unfortunately, most communities lack venues at which residents can discuss the purpose of the community, describe the systemic context of problems, and design indicators and a monitoring system. Communities should create opportunities for representatives of the various sectors (e.g., economic development, education, health, local government, union) to discuss their perspectives, goals, and activities and examine how those activities interrelate. This forum should engage individuals into an open, nonthreatening discussion of diverse perspectives and integrate those perspectives into a broad systemic view. Systems thinking is not just a solitary activity, but, instead, gains richness by having differing perspectives.

The experience of a small Illinois town illustrates the advantage in bringing people together to discuss what they want from each other and what they would like to see in the future. At a community meeting, representatives from the local hospital explained how difficult it was to recruit additional physicians. After inquiry into the reasons for the recruiting problem, hospital officials explained that physicians who visited the community were concerned about the quality of their children's education in the school district and were dissuaded from relocating into the community.

Specifically, they were concerned about the breadth and depth of course offerings for college-bound students. School district officials explained, in turn, that they were limited in their capacity to offer additional courses by financial constraints resulting from the high debt level brought on by previous school boards. The community realized that to improve their health-care system they had to strengthen the school system, which, in turn, depended on the success of economic development efforts. The interdependencies among the health, school, and economic development organizations became much clearer to the assembled residents.

The Cooperative Extension Services in Florida, Kentucky, and North Carolina practice systems thinking in their Natural Resource Leadership Institute. Each institute involves approximately thirty participants who represent various sectors in natural resource issues, including environmentalists, developers, industrialists, and regulators. They spend two days every month studying issues from each other's perspectives. They are also taught skills of systems thinking, public conflict resolution, and deliberation. In Kentucky, more than a hundred people have participated in the program. They are changing the typical culture surrounding natural resource issues from an adversarial one in which people shout at each other to one in which a critical mass of natural resource advocates, developers, and government regulators can reach a better understanding of each other and begin to explore options (Hustedde 2002).

Practice Number 2: Focus on Assets, Not Deficits

In the past, communities were encouraged by experts to assess their problems and deficits as the first step in community development. They were instructed to explore questions similar to these: "What is wrong with our community?" "What are our problems?" "What are our deficits?"

Owing in large part to the work of two researchers (Kretzman and McKnight 1993), it was discovered that this "deficit-based" approach inherently produced less than desirable results. Focusing on the negative often had the effect of discouraging residents, leading them to participate less in public processes for the betterment of the community. The deficit approach hits hardest on citizens in economically depressed areas because the problems are posed in such a way that they seem enormous and unmanageable. Instead, Kretzman and McKnight called for an "asset-based" approach to community development. The researchers had visited the poorest neighborhoods in America and had asked a different set of questions: "What do you value in your community?" "What is right here?" and "What are the assets here?" They were taken by surprise when people answered these questions with energy and enthusiasm.

Kretzman and McKnight (1993) developed interviews and other techniques that helped uncover the skills of individuals and resources of associations and institutions. Their work led to the development of a type of "asset mapping" that enabled community developers and residents to grasp the potential for generating change. Following the asset-mapping process, communities were found to be more likely to view themselves as not just a collection of isolated problems, but rather as a whole network with the diverse skills and abilities of individuals as well as the resources of organizations.

Table 12.1 contains practical suggestions about focusing on assets, not deficits. In one Chicago neighborhood, Kretzman and McKnight (1993) spoke with six single mothers who were dependent on welfare. They claimed that they were among the best soul food cooks in the neighborhood or even the city. These six women were brought together because of their cooking skills. They prepared dishes for each other and exchanged recipes. Eventually, some people in the neighborhood asked these women to cook for a wedding or a funeral. After a period of informal catering, and with some technical assistance, the women created their own catering firm. Today their business is the premier soul food catering firm in the city of Chicago. It is questionable that such a thing would have happened if the focus had been on the deficits that these women faced.

Elliott County, Kentucky, views itself differently because of its willingness to take an asset-based approach. Furthermore, the county has reaped visible results. The county is known as one of the top ten poorest counties in the United States and consistently leads Kentucky counties in unemployment. The county lost population from the 1940s until 2000. Industrial development groups told local citizens of their deficits, that the country was too remote and too distant from major highways to recruit external employers. The University of Kentucky Cooperative Extension Service agents in the county and tourism specialists and representatives of the Kentucky Department of Fish and Wildlife Service questioned whether such perspectives were very useful, however. Instead, they began asking questions about the strengths and assets of the county. They explored who might be interested in the county's protected areas, natural beauty, talented artists, strong workforce, and rich history. One tourism leader said the county has one of the most pristine creeks in the eastern United States and that its creek floor and watershed are reminiscent of a century ago. They forged strong links with regional, state, and national tourism systems.

The county's Extension agents worked closely with residents to form the

Elliott County Tourism Development Council. Over $600,000 in external grants were brought into the county to stimulate eco-tourism, and tourism revenues jumped from approximately $600,000 in 1997 to about $700,000 in 1998—a 10 percent increase in one year. At one point, traditional economic developers viewed the county's winding and twisting highways as a problem for potential manufacturers, but local groups have seen Highway 32 as an asset that links them to opportunities. They are petitioning for the route to be named as a Scenic Byway and cited in travel magazines, creating more opportunities for the county. At the same time, they are encouraging cleanups along Highway 32 to make it more attractive to tourism.

Through its planning, Elliott County is finding that the diversity of the community can be part of its tourism efforts. Storytellers, wildlife observers, trail enthusiasts, and local artists and craftspeople can be integrated into a tourism experience that is authentic and rich. Narrow thinking focused solely on deficits could have made this Kentucky county even poorer and more isolated, but thinking about assets has enabled the county to reap benefits.

As these examples illustrate, one benefit of the asset-mapping approach is that, in the process, latent, unseen talents of individuals are often uncovered, similar to the way that business organizations often discover unrecognized talent when they undertake the learning organization approach (Senge et al. 1994). An excellent starting point for communities that wish to initiate change is for residents to identify, in a realistic way, the resources and assets within their locale. They might also begin to inventory local organizations and identify each organization's goals and resources. In addition, they might identify leaders in the community, both formal and informal, to obtain a sense of leadership capacity. These assets will be key to development, and identifying them early in the process will encourage residents to adopt a positive, proactive stance in their development efforts.

Practice Number 3: Provide Opportunities for Reflection and Shared Learning

Some action-oriented community leaders have felt it was a waste of time to reflect much about what they learned from a particular initiative. The harshest critics claimed reflection was a form of "introspective navel gazing" that took citizens away from the task at hand and did not lead to many accomplishments. These views are being more frequently challenged, especially by funders who want to find out what a community or organization has learned about itself. The quest for accountability has created more opportunities for reflection and shared learning.

The third practice of the learning community is to develop a learning infrastructure that is adaptable to individual interests, allows for reflection, and facilitates the sharing of knowledge. According to Senge et al. (1994), it is the responsibility of individuals to ensure that their learning and personal development continue. Even so, communities can take steps to provide a supportive atmosphere in which residents can learn.

First, the community should establish goals that are adaptable to the emerging interests of its residents. The most effective and enduring type of learning in the community system is "learning by doing," by working on community development projects. This only occurs if it is sparked by people's own ardent interest and curiosity and is consistent with their personal vision; therefore, it is important that the vision of the community be broad enough and that there be enough give-and-take in modifying community goals over time so that local residents can find their innate curiosities satisfied within local projects.

Second, feedback and reflection should be a vital component in all development projects. Yet, in reality, it is not often that participants have the opportunity to share knowledge within the community group or to reflect on lessons learned. *Feedback* is the sharing of information about the outcome of an activity to those involved such as providing a public speaker with input as to what was effective about the just-delivered speech and what might be done to make it more effective.

At the conclusion of a project, the development group should obtain feedback from those who actively implemented the project as well as from those who were the beneficiaries. For wide-reaching projects, it is also useful to obtain feedback from groups external to the community such as the outreach unit of a local university or planning agency. Because these agencies are engaged with projects in many communities, they have a valuable perspective on what is required for success.

Feedback informs the process of *reflection*. When reflecting on the outcomes of a project, the focus should be on effectiveness, not personalities or politics. This means answering the questions "What happened?" and "What actions might have served us better?" Deliberation of such questions in a group can lead people to better understand the effectiveness of what they are doing and to use this learning in improving the management of future projects.

Thus, the process of learning in communities should follow a cycle: first, planning, then action, followed by sharing of experiences (feedback), then reflection and new action. With each revolution, this virtuous cycle will enhance the capacity of local residents. Projects will become more successful and the process of feedback and reflection will be reinforced.

Third, communities should recognize accomplishments through practical actions, such as town festivals, to support the learning infrastructure. Festivals can restore the sense of belonging and collective memory through the re-creation of historic events or other activities that have meaning for local people. Communities can give awards or otherwise honor those residents who have been instrumental to the community's success. This reinforces the solidarity of the group and keeps the attention on what has been accomplished, rather than on perceived problems.

Table 12.1 contains a few practical applications about how a community can provide opportunities for reflection and shared learning. The following example illustrates how the concept has been carried out. In rural Illinois, a group of communities located near Peoria formed the West-Central Illinois Rural Coalition on Development. The purpose of the organization is to expand the capacity of local leaders to engage in community development, to promote a regional identity among the communities, and to solve intercommunity problems that may arise. The organization has brought speakers to share information with the members, including a congressman, state economic development officials, university staff, and representatives of rural development organizations.

Coalition members also report on new developments and projects within their communities. Ever since its inception in 1999, the coalition has developed a "learning circle" of community leaders who have developed strong professional ties and increasingly see the fortunes of their communities as being connected. They are now developing collaborative efforts to enhance the area's economic well-being, such as a project to attract health professionals. The coalition has also reached out to the city of Peoria, realizing that there are many economic and social interrelationships between their small towns and the adjacent city. This is an example of the type of forum that enables learning to take place and is particularly noteworthy because of the fact that it is a multicommunity, regional initiative organized by local leaders.

Practice Number 4: Encourage Public Deliberation to Discover Common Ground

Many communities face divisive issues with strident opinions held on all sides. For example, if a choice is framed such as whether or not to build a factory on the banks of a pristine river on the outskirts of town, the community can quickly be polarized into environmentalists and pro-growth factions. Such divisions can lead to unproductive stalemates or destructive relationships that can seriously harm communities. Even if public issues are less inflammatory, it becomes very important to have a mechanism by which residents can move beyond debate to deliberation.

Deliberation is more than just an expression of opinions. The question that is asked is not "Whose side are you on?" but rather, "What are the choices?" Deliberation occurs through forums or dialogues when people are confronted by a serious problem and discuss their options. It often leads to a sense of deep understanding in terms of where common ground can emerge. Serious deliberation is marked by listening to each other's interests and concerns and then moving toward a common understanding of how to act as a public (Hustedde 2002).

David Mathews (1994) says that deliberation means to weigh. He contends that the costs and consequences of possible actions must be weighed by the public. This weighing increases the probability that the final decision will be sound. Without deliberation, the public's decisions are based on incomplete information or impulse. Having the opportunity to consider, at length, public issues and challenges helps a community to find common ground and a sense of shared purpose.

It is important to provide public forums at which varied perspectives can be openly expressed and residents can begin a nonthreatening dialogue of their commonalities and differences. Yet the opportunities for public deliberation in most communities are few and far between. Shanna Ratner (1997, 19) contends that the "typical citizen input processes are too short, too expensive, and too focused on process and outside experts to be meaningful."

Fortunately, tools are available to gain input. One noted approach to finding common ground was developed by the Kettering Foundation and the National Issues Forum, a unique entity that reframes public issues into three or four policy choices (Hustedde 1996). As residents explore the pros and cons of each policy choice, the participants move from mere opinions toward reflective and shared perspectives. Issue booklets and short videos stimulate discussion and frame the issue in neutral terms. This method is being implemented by university Cooperative Extension educators in Kentucky and Missouri and holds promise in moving residents away from shouting matches toward more rational and reflective discussions.

Communities might employ other innovative approaches to provide an opportunity for residents to find common ground—for example, public dialogue (Yankelovich 1999), public conflict resolution and understanding (Hustedde, Smutko, and Kapsa 2001), and study circles (Oliver 1987). All these approaches provide an opportunity for people to air their perspectives and listen to the views of others. In the process, they try on different perspectives like one might try on clothing in a department store. By walking in the shoes of defenders and critics of various public policy choices, participants can gain a better understanding of their own perspectives as well as those of others. The use of such approaches can lead to better decision making and more solidarity within a community.

In Oconto, Wisconsin, residents faced a difficult decision regarding development along the Green Bay waterfront. Through a deliberative process, the community integrated technical and socioeconomic information from experts with the knowledge, preferences, and values of residents. This occurred through a series of interviews, surveys, and educational events that gathered extensive feedback from Oconto residents. The process of asking, listening, analyzing, and reporting led to a greater consensus than expected about the appropriate waterfront development. The most substantial shift in the community's attitude was a change in focus from a high-cost, high-risk municipal arena option to a more affordable option that focused on relatively simple features such as walking and hiking trails (Behr, Shaffer, Lamb, Miller, and Sadowske 1998).

Practice Number 5: Create a Shared Vision of the Community's Future

Communities may have many significant project accomplishments; however, if a diverse group of citizens lacks a collective vision of the community's future, these accomplishments may be disjointed and lack meaning. Without a shared vision, no one knows where the community is headed. Its destination is unknown and prey to chance. In the fifth practice of a learning community, residents come together to create shared images of the future of the community, which results in a sense of commitment and mutuality:

> Visioning is a process by which a community envisions the future it wants and plans how to achieve it. Through public involvement, communities identify their purpose, core values and vision for the future, which are then transformed into a manageable and feasible set of community goals and an action plan. (Green and Haines 2002, 43)

Visioning is defined as being clear about the "big picture" hopes and dreams of residents. It serves to build consensus and commitment among residents. The vision can also guide the community when it comes time to make specific choices about what type of development to embrace or resist. Visioning is not a static process but, rather, a dynamic one in which community leaders must continually revision their community's future and renew their passion. In recognition of this, many rural Illinois towns have updated their initial action plans created through the MAPPING the Future of Your Community program. The "revisioning" sessions enabled these localities to assess their progress, examine new directions, and bring new energy and residents into the effort.

In the United Kingdom (UK), Hull is one of many localities aspiring to become a "learning town," the British term for a community that utilizes broad-based learning and citizen participation as key strategies for rejuvenation.

Through a shared visioning process, Hull residents co-created the vision of becoming a revitalized, successful maritime city. Four regeneration strategies were identified to help bring this vision to fruition: (1) enhancing skill levels to meet employers' needs, (2) improving the learning infrastructure, (3) raising achievement and graduation rates, and (4) pursuing lifelong learning. To implement these strategies, Hull City Learning was established as a public–private partnership with partners from the universities, other educational institutions, the media, the private sector, and the volunteer sector. Hull City Learning is founded on the notion that a broad community coalition can succeed in attaining a shared vision of raising the skills and capacities of local residents. For more information about the "learning towns and cities" movement in the UK, visit <www.lifelonglearning.co.uk/learningcities>.

One challenge for the visioning process is to represent the diversity of the community and to engage a large number of residents in supporting and implementing the vision. Table 12.1 contains some practical applications about shared visioning. Johnson County, Kentucky, addressed this challenge in an innovative way through the leadership of a Cooperative Extension educator. Rather than convene a large meeting, she asked where residents naturally met and discovered at least thirty settings, ranging from cafes to community centers. Discussion leaders were trained and led sessions in these natural meeting places. Consequently, nearly 600 people were involved in creating the community-wide vision in Johnson County. They represented senior citizens, youth, women, minorities, business, government, and many other segments of the town (Hustedde 2002).

More than 150 people were actively engaged in implementing the vision of Johnson County along with local businesses, local government, and external agencies and organizations. Although it took nearly six years, much of the vision has become a reality (Hustedde 2002). This is an outstanding example of how the strategic visioning process can lead to a sense of commitment and can strengthen the capacity of local residents.

Practice Number 6: Create Polycentric Circles of Leaders Who Encourage Team Learning

As Suzanne Morse (1998) looks to the future, she foresees a new type of leadership in successful communities. These communities will not be characterized by either centralized leadership or decentralized leadership but, rather, they will create many centers of leadership that interrelate—that is, they will have *polycentric* leadership. This organization of the future will look less like a pyramid and more like a series of circles. Each circle represents an element of the community—for example, local government or social services—and each is able to make decisions that are guided by a shared vision held by the community (as described above in Practice 5). Leaders will emerge within each circle where their particular skills and interests are most relevant.

Under this new structure of leadership, community development will be accomplished collaboratively through multiple efforts and multiple leaders. Participants will be required to take on new leadership responsibilities; they not only must be able to build effective teams, but these teams must be encouraged and supported to continually learn.

Team learning, the sixth practice of a learning community, differs from team building in that it goes well beyond traditional "team building" skills (i.e., the development or improvement of courteous behaviors, communication skills, cooperation, and strong relationships) (Roberts 1994). Instead, team learning uses skillful discussion and dialogue to enable team members to move beyond the more superficial requirements of team building. Dialogue helps people learn to think together in the sense of occupying a collective sensibility, wherein thoughts, emotions, and resulting actions belong to all members together (Isaacs 1994). William Isaacs explains that dialogue "invites us to contact what our hearts could say that our minds could not yet predict" (Toms 1998). People can then start to move into coordinated patterns of action, and the tedious process of planning and decision-making becomes unnecessary. They are then able to act in a coordinated way, each knowing what is best to do, just as a flock of birds does when it takes flight. Table 12.1 offers some thoughts on how to implement team learning with a polycentric circle of leaders.

An example of dialogue practiced on the community level occurs in the City of Lexington, Kentucky. A series of intensive discussions labeled as Speak-Out Lexington are held each year. Thousands of people come together in existing groups or they join a temporary group to take part in dialogues about difficult issues such as economic development, the environment, or diversity and race. Two fellow citizens, acting as facilitator and scribe, who have attended a brief facilitation training and orientation session, lead each group. Ideas from the groups are summarized and reported to the public through the mass media, posters, public art, and festivals. These intense dialogues create an ambience in which the public can speak out in a safe environment without fear of ridicule or derision. They can also develop a critical mass of informed residents who can act in a private or public manner on a specific issue. In such settings, there are more opportunities to form new relationships or to strengthen existing relationships.

The building of trust and mutual responsibility in teams can lead to a synergy in which the results are greater than the sum of the parts. The experience of Blue Mound, Illinois, with a population of approximately 1,200, provides an illustration of this process. In the mid-1980s, the community faced many empty storefronts in a deteriorating uptown area. A team of volunteers offered to repair several empty storefronts on the condition that a few local residents would agree to move their home-based businesses uptown. This modest start led to a rewarding outcome, beyond expectations. Within an eight-year period in the late 1980s and early 1990s, twenty businesses, mostly home grown, were started or expanded. The community was successful in attracting a dentist, building a grocery store, and renovating an old firehouse into a public library through volunteer support and community fund-raising.

Blue Mound, Illinois, also discovered that it would be necessary to raise water rates 100 percent to pay for an upgrade of pumps and mains that would enable a nursing home to expand. Although typically a controversial issue, the rate hike was supported by residents with little, if any, opposition. They had come to trust their government because the local municipal officials were part of the team engaged in revitalizing the town (Kline 1996).

Conclusion

The pace of change is rapid and continuous for today's rural communities. In the face of such chaos and complexity, it is easy for local leaders to feel overwhelmed. How can they ensure that the choices they make are sound ones that will lead to a viable and resilient community? How can they possibly keep pace with the surge of new information and the impact of external economic and social forces? Do they retain any power or influence on their community's destiny? This chapter suggests that effective adaptation is possible; however, it requires new structures and processes through which residents learn, not simply by acquiring knowledge individually, but, rather, by enhancing their capacity, sharing it throughout the community, and utilizing it to solve problems.

Using the model of a learning community, this chapter presents an outline of how communities can improve the relationships among residents and organizations and, thereby, strengthen the way that residents lead and implement development projects. An advantage of this model is that it brings together many important ideas under one holistic framework. The guiding idea is that a learning community has greater capacity to learn and, therefore, is more adaptable and flexible in a changing environment.

The practices of a learning community that are described here are not really new. In fact, decades of research and practice by communities, businesses, and nonprofit organizations support them. Organizations and communities learn more if they focus on assets, provide opportunities for reflection and feedback, offer opportunities for dialogue and deliberation, encourage team learning, share their learning, and think systemically about solutions.

These practices are not easy, however. They are not a "quick fix" of community problems; rather, they require long-term commitment because they involve fundamental changes in the community culture. As these processes are practiced, communities will find a much greater capacity to act. They will take action to create new jobs, protect the environment, improve the quality of schools, and otherwise make their community a better place. The result will be improvement not only in the residents' lives today, but also in the lives of their children tomorrow.

Note

1. Among the large corporations that have followed this approach are AT&T, Intel Corporation, Harley-Davidson, Hewlett-Packard, Toyota, Herman Miller Inc., Ford Motor Company, Royal Dutch/Shell Oil, National Semiconductor Corporation, and Merck & Co. For example, the Electrical and Fuel Handling Division of Ford Motor Company has created thirty active team learning projects involving 1,200 employees. Sales and profits have demonstrated unprecedented growth and turnaround for the company (Bierema 1997).

References

Behr, Chris, Ron Shaffer, Greg Lamb, Al Miller, and Sue Sadowske. 1998. Building community-based consensus: The Oconto experience. *Journal of the Community Development Society* 29(2): 1–22.

Bierema, Laura. 1997. Research as development: A learning organization implementation. In *Annual Conference Proceedings of the Academy of Human Resource Development*, 390–397. Bowling Green, OH: Academy of Human Resource Development.

Green, Gary Paul, and Anna Haines. 2002. *Asset Building and Community Development.* Thousand Oaks, CA: Sage.

Hustedde, Ronald J. 1996. An evaluation of the National Issues Forum methodology for stimulating deliberation in rural Kentucky. *Journal of the Community Development Society* 27(2): 197–210.

———. 2002. *The Role of the Cooperative Extension Service and Innovations in Community Development.* Unpublished manuscript.

Hustedde, Ronald J., Steve Smutko, and Jarad Kapsa. 2001. *Public Conflict: Turning Lemons into Lemonade.* Mississippi State: Southern Rural Development Center, Mississippi State University.

Isaacs, William. 1994. Dialogue. In *The Fifth Discipline Fieldbook: Strategies and Tools for Building a Learning Organization*, ed. Peter Senge, Art Kleiner, Charlotte Roberts, Richard Ross, and Bryan Smith, 357–364. New York: Doubleday.

Kerka, Sandra. 1995. The learning organization. In *Myths and Realities* (ERIC/ACVE MR 00004). Available on-line: <http://ericacve.org/docs/mr00004.htm>.

Kleiner, Art, Charlotte Roberts, Rick Ross, George Roth, Peter Senge, and Bryan Smith. 1994. The challenges of profound change. In *The Fifth Discipline Fieldbook: Strategies and Tools for Building a Learning Organization*, ed. Peter Senge, Art Kleiner, Charlotte Roberts, Richard Ross, and Bryan Smith, 21–34. New York: Doubleday.

Kline, Steven. 1996. Implementing strategic visioning programs. In *Community Strategic Visioning Programs*, ed. Norman Walzer, chapter 10, 161–182. Westport, CT: Praeger.

Kretzman, John P., and John L. McKnight. 1993. *Building Communities from the Inside Out: A Path Toward Finding and Mobilizing a Community's Assets*. Chicago: ACTA Publications.

Malholtra, Yogesh. 1996. *Organizational Learning and Learning Organizations: An Overview*. Available on-line: <www.brint.com/papers/orlrng.htm>.

Mathews, David. 1994. Afterthoughts. *Kettering Review* (Summer): 67–70.

Moffitt, Leonard Caum. 1999. A complex system named community. *Journal of the Community Development Society* 30(2): 232–242.

Morse, Suzanne W. 1998. Five building blocks for successful communities. In *The Community of the Future*, ed. Frances Hesselbein, Marshall Goldsmith, Richard Beckhard, and Richard F. Schubert, chapter 21, 229–236. San Francisco: Jossey-Bass.

Oliver, Leonard P. 1987. *Study Circles*, Cabin John, MD: Seven Locks Press.

Ratner, Shanna. 1997. *Emerging Issues in Learning Communities*. St. Albans, VT: Yellow Wood Associates.

Roberts, Charlotte. 1994. What you can expect from team learning. In *The Fifth Discipline Fieldbook: Strategies and Tools for Building a Learning Organization*, ed. Peter Senge, Art Kleiner, Charlotte Roberts, Richard Ross, and Bryan Smith, 355–357. New York: Doubleday.

Scholtes, Peter R. 1995. *Communities as Systems*. Potomac, MD: The W. Edwards Deming Institute (as presented in Ratner 1997).

Senge, Peter. 1990. *The Fifth Discipline*. New York: Doubleday.

Senge, Peter, Nelda Cambron-McCabe, Timothy Lucas, Bryan Smith, Janis Dutton, and Art Kleiner. 2000. *Schools That Learn: A Fifth Discipline Fieldbook for Educators, Parents, and Everyone Who Cares About Education*. New York: Doubleday.

Senge, Peter, Art Kleiner, Charlotte Roberts, Richard Ross, George Roth, and Bryan Smith. 1999. *The Dance of Change: The Challenges to Sustaining Momentum in Learning Organizations*. New York: Doubleday.

Senge, Peter, Art Kleiner, Charlotte Roberts, Richard Ross, and Bryan Smith. 1994. *The Fifth Discipline Fieldbook: Strategies and Tools for Building a Learning Organization*. New York: Doubleday.

Toms, Michael. 1998. Dialogue—The art of thinking together sparks spirit of aliveness in organizations, an interview with William Isaacs. *The Inner Edge* (August/September).

Yankelovich, Daniel. 1999. *The Magic of Dialogue: Transforming Conflict into Cooperation*. New York: Simon and Schuster.

13

TOM BONNETT

Looking Forward by Looking Back: State Approaches to Rural Development

For more than two centuries, states have made major public investments to promote economic development in their communities. In the early days of the republic, the states invested in harbors, bridges, main thoroughfares, and canals to facilitate the transport of food and commodities from the land to urban markets. In the mid-nineteenth century, the states chartered and assisted the development of railroads to serve these purposes (Beatty 2001).

As the web of railroads knitted regions together to form national markets and facilitated the growth of giant industries such as steel production and oil refining, the states were active in developing public education systems. By the first decades of the twentieth century, when the mass-assembly techniques of Henry Ford and others required skilled workers, the states had imposed compulsory education laws, enforced child labor laws, and established high school attendance requirements. Clearly, this emerging industrial economy needed trained workers, and the states responded by creating educational systems and institutions to achieve that objective (Conant 1959). This focus on education, health, nutrition, and related public functions is now called an investment in *human capital*.

Another feature of state development policy occurred as the agrarian nation entered the industrial age. The state land grant universities, established by the Morrill Act of 1862, were the largest research and development (R&D) investments by the public sector from 1870 to 1940—until the federal government began to mobilize to fight World War II (Mowery and Rosenberg 1998). The social benefits from these state-sponsored activities improved the productivity of agriculture and natural resource development, aiding rural economies (Nelson and Romer 1996). Similarly, the Agricultural Extension Service—a joint state–federal partnership—was instrumental in educating farmers about these innovations, which is called the "diffusion of innovation" (Rogers 1995).

These core strategies of state development policy—(1) investing in *physical infrastructure*, (2) developing human capital, and (3) applying knowledge to enhance productivity—provide the organization for this discussion of recent state innovations in rural development. A fourth core strategy of state development policy concerns fiscal policy and *social capital*, which define the capacity of rural leaders and organizations to take meaningful actions to improve their localities. From the perspective of these core strategies, how did state development policy adapt as the nation's economy shifted from agriculture to industry? Furthermore, how might it continue to adapt as work is transformed by the contemporary digital economy—based on knowledge, electronic networks, and global linkages (Bonnett 2000)? This context provides a historical perspective for interpreting recent state policy innovations and suggests future directions for reform.

Investing in Physical Infrastructure

Colonial governments invested in their seaport harbors in the eighteenth century to facilitate commerce with the Old World. Most of their revenues came from the tariffs imposed on imported goods (Beatty 2001). Following independence, the states continued to make public investments in transportation systems, beginning with bridges and the main thoroughfares between the larger towns and cities, called "post roads." The opening of the Erie Canal in 1825 launched a revolution in transportation. Financed by New York State, De Witt Clinton's Big Ditch lowered "the cost of shipping a ton of grain from Buffalo to New York City from $100 to $10, and the time from twenty to six days" (Beatty 2001, 60). Other state governments followed this example. Of the $188 million invested in canals before the Civil War, approximately 73 percent came from state governments (Beatty 2001, 60).

By the mid-nineteenth century, the states were chartering and promoting railroad construction. Lacking private-sector initiatives, Virginia, the Carolinas, and Georgia began directly financing the construction of their railroads in the 1840s (Beatty 2001, 114). Early settlements in the Midwest and West lobbied hard to get the railroad routes built through their communities, linking them to the Eastern cities and ensuring their own prosperity (or so they thought). Brigham Young, the Mormon leader, was eager to get the first transcontinental railroad, completed in 1869, to pass through Salt Lake City (Bain 1999).

State investments in transportation systems during the past century have been essential to rural development, and continue to be. The state–federal Interstate highway system of the twentieth century, like the nineteenth-century railroads, facilitated the flow of rural commodities to urban markets, improved mobility for rural workers and firms, and linked rural economies to regional and national markets. Following the economic deregulation of the airlines in the 1970s, many smaller cities in the Midwest and the Plains states have subsidized daily air service to regional commercial centers because they understand the importance of this link as an important economic development objective (Bonnett 1993).

Public investment in physical infrastructure is "a necessary, but not always sufficient condition to stimulate economic development" (Bonnett 1993, 135). Infrastructure is defined as "the permanent physical installations and facilities supporting socioeconomic activities in a community, region or nation" (Sears, Rowley, and Reid 1990, 1). The term *infrastructure* conventionally includes telephone systems, highways, airports, schools, hospitals, water treatment facilities, fire stations, parks and recreation facilities, libraries, museums, and cultural institutions.

The states make substantial public infrastructure investments in rural communities, including transportation systems, water and sewer facilities, schools, libraries, hospitals, and other community facilities. These state expenditures are extremely important to rural development for several obvious reasons. Rural residents and businesses value quality public services. Rural communities often have limited fiscal capacity with which to finance these infrastructure investments on their own (Swanson 2001), and the transformation of the national economy from goods production to a knowledge-based information economy has accented *the portability of work* (Bonnett 2000). In this context, the effort to improve the quality of life in rural communities has become both an economic development objective and a social objective. Retaining existing firms and recruiting new ones to rural communities requires quality public institutions and services.

Rural advocates often contend that state budgets are tilted toward urban projects and systems. In Kansas, the phrase is "Not much state money comes west of 135" (a north-south Interstate highway in the center of the state). Georgia Governor Roy Barnes is one recent state leader who has acted boldly to address this concern. Disturbed by the allegations that there are two Georgias—a thriving, prosperous urban Georgia and a rural Georgia left behind—Governor Barnes developed a state program to address the problem of uneven development. Following his leadership, the state legislature enacted a program called OneGeorgia. Funded in part by the funds from the tobacco settlement, this initiative is designed to make strategic public-sector investments in rural areas of the state (OneGeorgia 2001).

Most states have not engaged in this debate as directly as has Georgia. On a general level, the states have been very active in the past decade in developing information technologies to improve service delivery systems for rural communities. Early experiments with telemedicine in West Virginia, for example, suggest videoconferencing via a T1 line to an urban hospital could substantially improve rural access to quality health care, overcoming the rural problems of isolation and distance. (A designated T1 line has a transmission capacity of 1.544 megabits per second.) A Rural Health Telecommunications Network in Pennsylvania "uses video conferencing to link patients at 12 remote, rural sites with specialists at four major teaching hospitals" (Bonnett 1996, 42).

In the mid-1990s, Texas developed a widely dispersed system of video kiosks that provided job listings and other information about state services. Similarly, most states are developing distance-learning networks that can provide specialized instruction to rural students. Indeed, in 1998, the Western Governors' Association launched a "virtual university" to provide higher-education classes to citizens in the eleven-member states via the Internet and other distance-learning systems (Baer 1998). Washington state has become the first state to provide extensive social services information on a website available to all of its citizens, and most states have invested in libraries and other community facilities to provide public access to the Internet (Patterson 2001).

These state-funded efforts to use information technologies to improve service delivery will benefit all citizens. Rural communities could benefit the most of all because electronic networks can overcome the traditional distance barrier that hinders rural development (Parker, Hudson, Dillman, Strover, and Williams 1992); however, rural communities will benefit only to the extent they have sufficient telecommunications infrastructure, the skills with which to use these information technologies well, and a willingness to embrace innovation.

Embracing Innovation to Engage in the Digital Future

The term *digital divide* is used frequently to emphasize the relative lack of access to information technologies by many identifiable groups compared to the early adopters, who are well-educated and affluent. More than two-thirds of households earning more than $50,000 had Internet connections in the summer of 2000 (61% of households earning between $50,000 and $75,000; and 78% of households earning more than $75,000), according to a federal survey (NTIA 2000). This report found that more than half of all American households had a computer, and slightly less than half had Internet access (as of August 2000, 51% and 41.5%, respectively). The digital divide has diminished in recent years as the cost of computers and communications has declined, and as more Americans at every income level are gaining access to the Internet.

Two important distinctions must be emphasized. First, the digital divide is not just about having access to the latest digital toy. It is about a willingness to employ digital technologies and develop a new set of skills that will become essential in this emerging knowledge-based economy (Bonnett 2000). An entry-level office worker whose skills include mastery of Microsoft's packages—*Word*, *Excel*, and *PowerPoint*—earns a wage premium in most labor markets today (Bonnett 2001).

Second, the digital divide remains a special problem for rural America because its geography, low density, and isolation reinforce its cultural resistance to change. A smaller percentage of rural households own home computers and have Internet access than the national average. While access is improving for rural residents, their success in taking advantage of the opportunities of an information-based society requires more investment. To bridge the digital divide successfully, rural residents must have a commitment to improving e-literacy (Tscheschlok 2001), as well as an understanding of the potential of electronic networks to overcome the traditional distance barriers that thwart rural development.

This cultural resistance to change, which poses a challenge to rural development leaders, was expressed in this motto, mounted in a local government office:

> Make it Do,
> Wear it Out,
> Use it Up, or
> Do Without.

Most local public officials in rural areas are behind the social learning curve in using the Internet. A survey of nonmetropolitan communities in Illinois in 2000 found that "[e]-mail has not yet transformed small town government operations. . . . It has yet to even penetrate local government in the majority of communities that responded to the survey. . . . Only in the largest communities, with populations over 10,000, has e-mail begun to facilitate interaction between residents and government" (Hammel 2001, 19). Clearly, some are learning how to use e-mail to communicate with constituents, and many smaller communities in the Midwest are beginning to develop Web sites that present information about their communities:

> Only 16 percent of the communities with web sites have sought assistance from government agencies or other non-profit firms. . . . While communities have a variety of reasons to create web sites, for nearly 40 percent of the respondents, the web site exists because a resident knew how to de-

velop it and was willing to do so for free. The Nebraska plan to train college students in the design and creation of web sites, and then send them home during the summer to help their communities, would seem to facilitate this tendency to rely on local talent quite effectively. (Hammel 2001, 15–16)

Rural leaders should be concerned that they are being left behind as information technologies, and the skills to use them well, transform the national economy.

The digital divide in rural America is often presented as an inadequate telecommunications infrastructure or lack of hardware. Compounding these presenting conditions is a deeper problem: a traditional culture that is reluctant to embrace innovation. Though not an easy task, searching for the best way to entice telecommunications infrastructure investment in a rural community demonstrates a commitment to engage in the digital future. These broad challenges for the leaders of rural localities are inexorably linked.

Stimulating Investment in Telecommunications Infrastructure

Unlike the traditional public infrastructure of roads and schools, the telecommunications industry in the United States has been largely built and managed by private firms. The notable exceptions are rural telephone cooperatives and about 200 municipally owned telephone companies.

Before the Telecommunications Act of 1996 was enacted, these privately owned telephone companies enjoyed an exclusive franchise to provide services, even though their rates were regulated by public agencies. The 1996 federal legislation ended the era of having a monopoly provider for local telephone service. The current policy enables choice and competition in local telephony (Bonnett 1996).

Rural subscribers have been subsidized by the old system. Some obtained telephone services from rural telephone companies that received universal service funds from the regulating agencies, which kept rates affordable. The rates of most rural telephone subscribers have been based on geographic averaging throughout a large service area, which pooled the lower-cost urban areas and higher-cost rural areas together. As the existing providers begin to face competition for business customers in many metropolitan areas, they may seek to rebalance their rate structures. One might expect the providers to lower the business rate and urban residential rates to match those offered by their competitors. Consequently, some providers have tried to increase residential rates in their highest-cost areas.

Rural telephony, owing to the low population density and large distances, is much more expensive to provide than urban telephony. Many states created universal service funds during the 1990s to mitigate the anticipated increase in basic telephone rates on rural subscribers (Bonnett 1999). If increasing competition in local telephone service forces rate rebalancing, which has occurred in Europe at a much faster pace than in the United States, rural advocates will become focused on the scope and funding for state universal service programs to keep rural telephone service affordable.

Rural development leaders should understand, however, that the current policy of allowing choice and competition in local telephony provides opportunities to encourage new private-sector investment in the telecommunications infrastructure in their localities. This would serve an important economic development objective. The emerging consensus among economic development practitioners is that the telecommunications capacity of a community is becoming an increasingly important consideration in business retention and site location decisions. Russ Kesler of GTE observed, "Eighty-two percent of relocation businesses list telecommunications capacity as a key factor in selecting a new site" (Bonnett 1996, 32).

Quality telecommunications services can help existing companies remain competitive and may help recruit new firms to a community. Achieving both objectives would improve the employment prospects of local residents and enhance the economic prosperity of the community. A report by the National Governors' Association (NGA 1994, 4) offers an example:

> Already the emergence of advanced communications has reversed outmigration and declining job opportunities in many nonmetropolitan areas. In 1989 Premium Standard Farms (PSF), a pork-production facility, chose to locate near Princeton, Missouri, a community of 3,600 residents 90 miles northwest of Kansas City. PSF selected Princeton for its facility in part because the local, independent phone company could offer electronic, fully digital communications. Initially employing only three people, the PSF workforce grew to 700 employees within five years. The company's need for high-technology telecommunications continues to grow. This year the local telephone company will install a direct fiber-optic link between its facilities and PSF.

The State Role in Broadband Deployment

The explosive popularity of the Internet in the past decade has stimulated a growing appetite among consumers and businesses for broadband connections. Cable operators, which serve residential markets, have taken an early lead in this broadband market by providing cable modems. Incumbent telephone companies are promoting DSL, a digital subscriber line, which also provides a broadband connection. The problem with this, however, is that DSL only works for those who live within 18,000 feet of a central office. Competing in this market for broadband connections are competitive local exchange carriers (CLECs—pronounced SEE-lecks), which also sell DSL. Finally, various firms are promoting wireless Internet connections, using satellites or unlicensed spectrum. Indeed, some contend that the forthcoming third generation of wireless technologies (3G), which are being developed now in Europe and Japan, could transform the communications sector in this country (i.e., if appropriate spectrum can be obtained for their use) (Gohring 2001).

The Federal Communications Commission's broadband report in 2000 provided a fair snapshot of broadband deployment. At the end of December 1999, approximately 1.8 million consumers subscribed to high-speed services. Also, approximately 1 million high-speed lines provided service to large business and institutional consumers. Deployment was not uniform throughout the nation: "[P]opulation density is highly correlated with the availability of facilities necessary to support advance services" (FCC 2000, 6). The FCC report concluded, "[M]arket forces alone may not guarantee that some categories of Americans will receive timely access to advanced telecommunications capability. We identify certain categories of Americans who are particularly vulnerable to not having access to advanced services. These include low-income consumers, those living in sparsely populated areas, minority consumers, Indians, persons with disabilities, and those living in the U.S. territories" (FCC 2000, 6).

The FCC (2000) defines advanced telecommunications capability as "the availability of high-speed, switched, broadband telecommunications that enables users to originate and receive high-quality voice, data, graphics, and video using any technology platform." In its third inquiry, the FCC (2002, 16–17) estimated there were 9.6 million high-speed (services with over 200 kilobytes per second (kbps) capacity in at least one direction) subscribers in June 30, 2001. This measures an extraordinary growth rate nationally, a 250 percent increase from the December 1999 data reported in the second FCC report on this topic. Rural areas with sparse populations, nevertheless, remain below the national average in the percentage of households who subscribe to these high-speed services and the number of providers in their communities (FCC 2000, 19–20).

Rural officials should understand the questions facing their state governments: Is broadband capacity essential to economic development in their rural communities? Would market forces provide sufficient investment to develop broadband capabilities without public intervention? What should the states do to promote broadband development in those localities in which market conditions may not prompt sufficient private investment?

Advanced telecommunications capacity enables businesses and their customers to exchange data over long distances rapidly, efficiently, and securely.
The fastest growing sectors of our economy require modern telecommunications infrastructure to transmit voice, data, and video quickly and reliably
throughout the world (Bonnett 2000). The "new growth economics" developed by Paul Romer, Robert Barro, Robert Lucus, and others emphasize
knowledge and intellectual capital as the sources of social wealth in this
new knowledge economy (McCraw 1997). Regions containing clusters of
firms in these sectors that are networked to each other and the rest of the
world will enjoy *first-mover* and competitive advantages in the global
economy (Porter 1998).

As with the more traditional forms of public investment, telecommunications infrastructure may be a necessary but not sufficient condition for economic development. Its most important complement is a well-trained
workforce that can manipulate and exploit these information technologies to
create new forms of wealth. Jobs in the rapidly growing information technology sector have salaries almost 80 percent higher than the average private-
sector wage (Working Group on Electronic Commerce 2000).

Does the value of broadband deployment for regional economic development justify public intervention by the states? Those with the greatest faith
in markets are not sure. Economists, for example, maintain that private-
sector investment will follow clear expressions of demand for advanced telecommunications services. It is, they contend, much too early in development
of the market for these advanced services to begin changing or removing
regulations that single out certain population groups for different treatment
(Furchgott-Roth 2000).

Yet many state government experts doubt private investment will finance
broadband deployment in the most disadvantaged communities for reasons
such as the infrastructure is expensive, the demand is low, and disadvantaged communities have populations of low density, low income, or both.
Notice how they have defined this problem with a sense of urgency: "As the
Internet revolutionizes our economy, inner cities and rural America face
a potentially alarming and disastrous future. These areas could lose jobs
and investment from industry that they desperately need because affordable broadband Internet services are passing them by" (NASIRE/NASTD
2000, 5).

Others have speculated that the affluent urban and suburban areas attracting most of the private telecommunications investment will enjoy PANS
(Pretty Amazing New Services), while most remaining communities will be
left with POTS (Plain Old Telephone Service). Gloria Tristani, then a member of the FCC, expressed this sentiment in the fall of 2000:

While broadband deployment is occurring in some small cities and rural areas, I am concerned that it may not be happening as quickly or ubiquitously as it should. No single top-down solution is going to work in all rural locations. The solutions need to emerge from local communities themselves with supporting help from state and federal governments. (Wohlbruck and Levy 2000/2001, 5)

Edwin Parker (2000, 12), a telecommunications expert testifying before the U.S. Senate, asserted, "Communities not connected to our emerging broadband network will suffer the same economic fate as many communities that were bypassed by the telephone network, the railroad or the Interstate highway system." Warns a foundation official, "Nobody will move to your town if you are not connected to the Internet" (Doug Brown 2000, 26).

States do not want to commit public funds to support functions that can be provided as well as or better by the private sector, unless these early investments can serve as a powerful catalyst for regional economic development. That reasoning has stimulated preliminary initiatives to promote the development of broadband capacity. The examples below represent some of the strategic policy options available to the states.

Leveraging Public Investment to Expand Services

Massachusetts requested bids from all providers for T1 services to its many municipal governments and schools. Using the power of the state's large purse, bidders were required to offer the same price for T1 service to any customer, regardless of location. The winning contract, according to the FCC (2000, 72), "cut T1 costs in Massachusetts nearly in half, and guaranteed access to T1 services to all towns, villages, and schools in the state." Colorado and Montana have also used this strategy to expand services to underserved areas. (See also the Michigan example below.)

Constructing a Public High-Speed Network

Iowa built the first statewide, state-administered, fiber optics network. Illinois is building a high-speed statewide network in partnership with its public school system and with higher educational institutions. Minnesota has attempted to use the public right of way along Interstate highways for 2,000 miles of fiber optics cable, which will serve as a telecommunications backbone. Approximately sixteen states are building public networks or are leasing capacity from private vendors to provide capacity for public purposes (Bonnett 2001).

Investing State Resources to Target Underserved Areas

Virginia has a program that equalizes the cost of broadband access for citizens and businesses throughout the state. North Carolina has established a Rural Internet Access Authority (RIAA) to work in partnership with telecommunications providers in order to expand high-speed, affordable Internet access to all citizens. Arizona has committed $100 million on a new program called TOPAZ (Telecommunications Open Partnerships of Arizona) to stimulate broadband development in 167 rural communities with populations of at least 500.

Creating Tax Incentives to Firms

Montana and Colorado are two of the states granting tax credits to firms that accelerate the growth of high-speed telecommunications infrastructure in their states.

Developing a Strategic Plan

LinkMichigan (2001) is a comprehensive plan that includes aggregating the collective purchasing demand of all public-sector agencies in the state, requiring providers to "build and maintain a high-speed backbone infrastructure that extends to most regions of the state to serve these customers," and winning bidders must sell "excess network capacity on a non-discriminatory wholesale basis to increase competition and encourage investment in regions that might not otherwise attract new service providers." As a strategic objective, this plan seeks to establish tax equity in the telecommunications industry and streamline right-of-way permitting procedures. To achieve these broad goals, the plan requires more information from providers, establishes quality-of-service standards, and offers local community planning grants to coordinate and leverage local strategies to the statewide backbone initiative.

Following the blueprint of LinkMichigan, Governor John Engler proposed legislation in 2001 to establish a new state Right of Way (ROW) fee, which preempts local authority over ROW and would generate state funds to provide loans and grants for broadband deployment projects in underserved areas. This legislative initiative, which passed the Michigan State Senate in February 2002, is the most direct effort by any state to finance advanced telecommunications infrastructure capacity in its rural communities (Kirchhoff 2002).

Community Planning for Telecommunications

Rural leaders can advocate for state policies to upgrade telecommunications networks that serve their localities. They can also begin community planning efforts to stimulate private-sector telecommunications infrastructure investment. McMahon and Salant (1999) have developed a strategic planning model that has been successful in northeast Wyoming and Morgan County, Colorado. This model provides the following benefits to rural communities seeking improved telecommunications services:

- Identifying gaps in existing telecommunications infrastructure by pinpointing problems that limit economic development, service delivery, or quality of life
- Helping people decide which problems are most important to address first
- Creating opportunities for partnerships by identifying common interests
- Building more broad-based support for new telecommunications applications
- Providing a mechanism to coordinate multiple strategies

This planning approach begins with a needs assessment to take stock of the local telecommunications environment, including basic use by businesses, public agencies, and households as well as the potential demand for additional infrastructure and services. This assessment also identifies financial resources and potential partnerships. The next step in working with local leaders is to identify priority goals and help participants understand the potential benefits if these goals are met. This process clarifies what is needed and the local commitment in place to make it happen. The third step is to create an action plan charting a course that, if followed, could meet the priority goals for the region and enhance telecommunications services (McMahon and Salant 1999).

Bonnett (2001) presents a more detailed community planning model, which emphasizes building alliances and forming partnerships to aggregate community demand in order to leverage private-sector investment. The example of Berkshire Connect in western Massachusetts demonstrates how community planning can lead to aggregating demand and subsequent telecommunications investments. Formed by community leaders, a project task force sought to enhance its telecommunications infrastructure. That planning initiative led to a competitive selection process for a company to build a partly publicly funded network. A private-sector firm, Equal Access Networks (EAN), won the contract but declined the use of public funds. Instead, EAN served as a broker to aggregate demand by local businesses and cultural institutions and simultaneously contracted with a large telecommunications provider for these advanced services (NRC 2002).

Aggregating community or regional demand for telecommunications services has long been the most effective strategy in convincing firms to make substantial infrastructure investment in rural communities. Congress, understandably, lacks interest in revisiting the contentious issues embedded in the Telecommunications Act of 1996. If it should ever demonstrate an appetite for this, rural advocates and the states should press hard for a change in Section 254 to allow communities to aggregate demand for advanced services by creating virtual private networks. Section 254 ensured access to advanced telecommunications services to schools, rural health care facilities, and libraries. As administered by the FCC, the "E-rate" program provides subsidies to the schools and libraries; a separate fund assists rural health care facilities. Unfortunately, the services subsidized by these funds cannot be included as part of a rural community's aggregate demand for advanced telecommunications services. The intent of Section 254 is laudable, but the effect of this accounting restriction has been to remove a huge chunk of the aggregate demand for advanced telecommunications services in rural localities (Parker 2000).

Developing Human Capital

The second broad strategy in state development policy is best illustrated in its long-standing engagement in public education, which preceded the economist's term of "human capital." Since Horace Mann's time in the nineteenth century, state reformers have fought for public education to promote citizenship, assist urban immigrants in assimilating to American culture, and prepare young people for jobs that require skill and patience. At the beginning of the nineteenth century, twenty-eight states had child labor laws and thirty-eight states had compulsory education statutes (Sawhney and Jayakar 1999). During that period, just 4 percent of American youth attended college, and only 35 percent of all seventeen-year-olds attended high school; by the mid-twentieth century, 35 percent attended college and 70 percent of all seventeen-year-olds were in school (Conant 1959). The states were active in designing, promoting, and managing public education systems as the Industrial Revolution of the late nineteenth century demanded trained workers. Government reforms associated with the Progressive effort, social norms, and other institutions served to socialize adults to work in structured environments. Baseball, which became the nation's most popular sport in the 1880s, taught rural boys how to follow rules.

A brief look back on the state role in public education during the twentieth century reveals a different theme relevant to the discussion of rural development. What happens to rural institutions when the state assumes a larger policy role in shaping the public education system?

The rationalization of public education, led by reformers and educators, initiated a school district consolidation movement. Bill Kauffman (2001) reports that the number of school districts in the United States declined from 127,531 in 1932, to 83,718 in 1950, 40,520 in 1960, and 17,995 in 1970, leaving fewer than 15,000 today. Small towns and rural communities lost control of their most important social institutions.

Small schools were closed. New, much larger, ones were built. Comprehensive high schools, following James Conant's (1959) advice, became the blueprint—the one best way to build high schools across America. "The policy makers deferred to the professional educators; the educators won. It was the best of intentions. They got most of what they wanted," yet the products of reform were physical plants so large, so impersonal that they resemble the Toyota factory in Lexington, Kentucky, that produces the best-selling Camry (Bonnett 2000, 99).

Diane Ravitch, an educational historian, offers this critique of what resulted from following Conant's (1959) advice for five decades:

> The *shopping mall high school* . . . offers something for everyone, cafeteria-style, but it cannot provide the individual support and nurturance that most of these young people need. The typical comprehensive high school is large and impersonal, with a studied air of neutrality toward all students. But that is exactly what these children do not need. They need schools that work closely with each student and his or her family; they need schools that are designed to be intensely engaged with each child as a unique person. Children need schools where there are many adults who know their names and care about them, know when they are absent, know when they have a problem, think about their futures, and expect to talk frequently to their parents or guardians. (Ravitch 1997, 255)

The modern regional high schools are vastly superior in every physical dimension to those they replaced, and they offer much greater variety of instruction than the small high schools could have provided. Only in recent years have prominent educators posed the counterargument—that "enrolling no more than 400 students in high school may provide better education than their large counterparts, as a function (at least in part) of their small size" (Kauffman 2001, 50). This revisionism becomes more poignant in light of recent educational trends: the growth of homeschooling and charter schools, more magnet schools to appeal to gifted students, and the advance of distance-learning technologies that enhance instructional choices in any setting. These current trends undermine the prevailing conventional wisdom, which dominated the second half of the twentieth century—that bigger schools were better schools.

Following the "bigger is better" philosophy promoted by the state educators might not have been the best choice for the children, the parents, or the rural communities (Sher 1977). Closing small schools destroyed the major social institutions that held many rural communities together (Hobbs 1991).

The third phase in rationalizing public education was the state's growing share in school financing, which began in the 1970s. This was done for a variety of reasons. It was good policy and good politics. Many states were complying with court rulings that determined school spending should not rest solely upon local property wealth. More state spending on education served to ease property tax burdens, which was popular with voters. In addition, educators had become perennial lobbyists in the state capitols. The states currently spend more than 30 percent of their annual budgets to support public education (U.S. Bureau of the Census 1999).

The consequence of this state policy shift has been significant. John Brandl (1998, 31) reports that "In barely a generation, the third of a century between 1960 and 1990, per student spending on elementary and secondary education in the United States, in 1990 dollars, rose from $1621 to $4960." Despite this steady increase in total educational spending, the state share of elementary and secondary education expenditures jumped from 39 percent during the 1960s to 47 percent during the 1990s (NCES 2001).

Rural students and taxpayers have been the primary beneficiaries of the increased state aid to public education. More state aid flowed to rural school districts, improving educational opportunity and, in theory, easing the property tax burden on rural property owners. Ironically, relatively few rural advocates have praised this enlightened social policy. Why?

The closing of small schools and the loss of community control of their school systems may have distanced the more recent social gains from the expanded state funding. To many rural officials, these trends were bittersweet victories of educational reformers. As this reflection suggests, a greater state role in addressing rural needs represents opportunities for progress and, if imposed in a heavy-handed way, threats to valued institutions.

Human capital represents more than elementary and secondary education. In his 1961 book, *Investing in Ourselves,* Nobel Laureate economist Theodore Schultz coined the term *human capital* (Bonnett 1993). Gary Becker (1997), another economist who received the Nobel Prize for his work on human capital, explains, "Wealth in the form of human capital consists of present and future earnings because of education, training, knowledge, skills, and health." Becker (1997, 26) continues, "Human capital is estimated to be three to four times the value of stocks, bonds, housing, and other assets." Management expert Peter Drucker (1977, 94) provides a similar interpretation of the concept: "The basic factor in an economy's development must be the rate at which a country produces people with imagination and vision, education, theoretical and analytical skills."

Understanding this concept of human capital prompted the governor of Iowa to launch an unorthodox campaign to recruit Iowa natives to return to their home state. Iowa, like all the states, recruits firms to locate within its borders, but it has also been very sophisticated in developing innovative ways to recruit urban professionals to add to its stock of human capital (HRRC 2001). Some rural communities have attempted similar efforts to lure native sons and daughters back from the cities. Those who return have gained valuable work experience and skills, and often become community leaders and entrepreneurs in their hometowns.

Some rural experts lament that social investment in human capital has not always been a successful rural development strategy. They cite persistent rural poverty despite social investments in these populations and their rising educational attainment levels. Quite pointedly, the Task Force on Persistent Rural Poverty (1993, 41) asks, "Do poverty and unemployment result from a 'skills gap' between rural workers and the jobs available to them? Or does poverty stem from the lack of good jobs available to rural workers? This is a classic debate."

These questions reflect traditional views of a stagnant economy, not contemporary perspectives on a dynamic economy. For rural leaders and development practitioners committed to improving the economic prospects of their communities, investing in human capital must be viewed as a necessary, but not sufficient condition for economic development. To compete and progress in this knowledge economy, rural communities must promote lifelong learning as a social and economic objective. This means using social institutions, including schools, to provide more instruction to rural adults. Governor Tom Vilsack of Iowa appointed a commission in the summer of 2000 to promote lifelong learning. State policy discussions should focus on how to serve all citizens with educational and training opportunities.

During the industrial era, high school was the endpoint of formal education for most workers. Today, it is simply the foundation for future learning. In today's knowledge-based economy, the most important thing any high school student can learn is how to learn. Skill sets erode overnight as new technology emerges, jobs churn quickly and without warning, and new responsibilities will require constant learning (Bonnett 2000). Rural communities that cultivate lifelong learning and adapt social institutions to provide more instruction for adults of all ages will be better able to integrate their local economies with regional, national, and global markets.

Stan Davis and Jim Botkin (1998, 163–164), writing in *The Knowledge Economy,* present an important assessment of how knowledge is transmitted as society changes:

> Learning in agricultural economies is often church led, focuses on children between 7 and 14 years of age, and is sufficient to last all the years of a working life. In industrial economies, learning has been government led, and the age range of students is between 5 and 22. In knowledge economies, the rapid pace of technological change means that learning must be constant and that education must be updated throughout one's working life. People have to increase their learning power to sustain their earning power.
>
> Knowledge is doubling about every seven years, and in technical fields in particular, half of what students learn in their first year of college is obsolete by the time they graduate. In the labor force, the need to keep pace with technological change is felt even more acutely. For companies to remain competitive, and for workers to stay employable, they must continue to learn.

Applying Knowledge to Enhance Productivity

The states' long-standing support of their land-grant universities illustrates the third state development strategy. American agriculture became the most productive in the world because farmers substituted capital for labor, used new hybrid seeds and fertilizers, learned about crop rotation, and applied new knowledge to every part of the production process. The role of the land-grant universities in this transformation cannot be overstated. To cite just one example, "The investment in agricultural research that produced hybrid corn generated benefits that were about seven times larger than the costs" (Nelson and Romer 1996, 17). As mentioned, the Agricultural Extension Service, a joint state–federal partnership, was instrumental in educating farmers and diffusing innovation (Rogers 1995).

Most of what local governments and the states spend on economic development is for industrial retention and recruitment—another legacy from the industrial era (Fisher and Peters 1998). For a variety of institutional and policy reasons, economic development agencies cannot drop "smokestack chasing" from their arsenal (Bartik 1991). Beginning in the 1980s, though, many economic developers began a series of new initiatives to strengthen local economies from within. They have been called the "second wave" in economic development: "States established venture capital pools, created small business incubators, and initiated workforce training programs in an attempt to support 'homegrown' enterprise" (Radin et al. 1996, 58).

In recent years, economic developers have become much more sophisticated in understanding their local and state economies (Redman 1994). Strategic economic development plans try to identify value creation and linkages about economic actors in a region. Michael Porter presents the intellectual argument for crafting a new wave of economic development strategies based on clusters and business networks:

> The competition among locations has shifted from *comparative advantage* to the broader notion of *competitive advantage*. Comparative advantage due to lower factor costs (for example, labor, raw materials, capital, or infrastructure) or size still exists, but it no longer confers competitive advantages in most industries nor supports high wages. Globalization now allows firms to match comparative advantages by sourcing inputs such as raw materials, capital, and even generic scientific knowledge from anywhere and to disperse selective activities overseas to take advantage of low-cost labor or capital. (Porter 1998, 322–323)

Porter (1998) contends that traditional locational advantages cannot be assumed. This suggests a paradigm shift for many active in rural development. Middle-aged professionals have spent half their lives thinking about the inherent value of place and the obvious barriers of distance. Thinking about business relationships and linkages, and how to strengthen them, is a new analytical challenge. Economic developers in rural localities should look closely at the clusters of local businesses and suppliers to the region to determine how to build on local assets, strengthen existing businesses, and develop better linkages with neighboring urban economies. One practical application of this approach is to form public–private ventures to design skills training programs in order to meet the needs of local employers (Bonnett 2000).

Michael Farmer and Gordon Kingsley (2001, 174–175) present a model of interviewing existing firms to develop social networks. Borrowing network theory from sociologists, they observe: "Programs that increase interactions increase innovation by building trust, norms, and cohesion within a social network (Fountain, 1998). This, in turn, reduces the transaction costs and perceived risk associated with investing in an innovation (Ostrom, 1990)." Hence, Farmer and Kingsley (2001, 176) contend that "firm visitation is one of the fastest-growing applied methods for designing and implementing a community rural development effort." Business visitation programs could achieve more than the identification of community resources. These interviews could, they argue, "[r]eveal a great deal about the relationship between the amount of *social capital* that firms possess and efforts to learn new skills and secure resources" (177).

Former Governor Tom Ridge of Pennsylvania explained that this new approach is not based on industrial recruitment and tax incentives, but, rather, on attracting talent and promoting networking. He observed, "Before the Internet, companies had to find allies where they arose naturally. It used to be 'location, location, location.' Now I think it's more 'Network, network, network.' And we can network from any location" (Gruman 2000, 126). Governor Ridge also said, "One of the things the government can do is to help . . . the academic world and the existing technology world expand their environment" (Gruman 2000, 129).

Applying network theory to economic development strategies explains the trend of developing value-added products from agriculture and natural resource commodities. Not content with exporting logs to Canada, Maine officials work closely with small businesses to develop value-added wood products. Iowa's Value-Added Agricultural Products and Processes Financial Assistance Program (VAAPFAP) serves as another example. Ever since its inception in 1994, VAAFPAP, administered by the Iowa Department of Economic Development, has awarded nearly $25 million to 200 innovative, value-adding agricultural ventures (Iowa VAAPFAP 2001).

Employment in rural areas is surprisingly similar to the national figures. Two-thirds of the jobs in nonmetropolitan counties in 1987 were in the service sector: retail and wholesale trade; hotel and tourist operations; and financial, health, legal, and government services. Manufacturing employed one in six rural workers, similar to the national average. Fewer than 10 percent worked in agriculture (Bonnett 1993). The share of U.S. gross domestic product (GDP) in agriculture and mining fell to below 4 percent at the beginning of the 1990s (Radin et al. 1996). Rural communities must build on their economic strengths, form links to external markets, and learn how to apply knowledge to work to improve productivity. Clinging to the old ways will not enhance their economic prospects.

Strengthening Fiscal Capacity and Social Capital

States make substantial investments that benefit rural communities. They invest in physical infrastructure, in human capital programs such as schools, job training, and higher education, and in other mundane program areas as well (e.g., public safety, disease control, and criminal justice programs).

State fiscal policy over the last three decades has helped rural communities. As mentioned above, the increase in state aid to education has led to better educational opportunities for rural students and lower property taxes for rural homeowners. Thirty-five states increased the state share of total local–state revenues from 1970 to 1994. This fiscal centralization enabled states to assume some of the traditional responsibilities of the local governments, or to increase aid to local communities, or both (Mackey 1998). As has been said in more than one state capitol, "decisions follow the dollar." Some states are better than others in providing fiscal assistance to rural communities without imposing tiresome mandates.

A related development called "tax-sharing" gave increased authority to local governments to levy sales and income taxes. In 1970, twenty-three states authorized local sales taxes and just ten states allowed local income taxes. By 1997, local governments in thirty-three states could impose a local sales tax and in sixteen states levy local income taxes (Mackey 1998).

Progress in these areas may not be sufficient to satisfy rural advocates who claim their communities lack the *fiscal capacity* to make necessary investments to build a better future, or who claim that rural communities should receive a larger share of state resources. Unlike Georgia's new program to support rural development, most states fund programmatic budgets (such as economic development, housing, and education) and grants-in-aid to local governments (Radin et al. 1996). Perhaps local officials should lobby for additional taxing powers, or perhaps rural advocates should form coalitions to seek more state funding for rural development.

This provokes a seminal policy question: Why should the state devote special attention to the rural portion of its economy? Sears et al. (1992) suggest four reasons: (1) to improve the efficiency of the state's economy, (2) to make best use of fixed investments, (3) to improve rural–urban equity, and (4) to preserve the rural way of life. Some assert as a moral claim that state governments bear a responsibility to ensure the provision of essential public services to all communities (Bonnett 1993). In addition, Robert Reich (1988, 5) suggested that revitalized rural economies would ease the "social costs of crowding. There is a social value to dispersing population across the land. That's why all of us urban dwellers have a long-term stake in an economically sound rural America."

Similar arguments have been made on behalf of a rural development policy for the federal government (Christenson and Flora 1991). Indeed, the federal government has a glorious history in promoting rural development during the first two-thirds of our nation's history. Bonnett (1993) offers this summary:

> Early actions of the infant federal government such as the Northwest Ordinances of 1787, which provided public land for schools and roads for the newly settled territories, and the Louisiana Purchase (1803), which more

than doubled the size of the nation, established what could be called the first rural development policy. . . . The Homestead Act of 1862 provided public land to encourage the rapid settlement of the prairie and mountain West and to achieve widespread ownership of rural resources. The Morrill Act also in 1862 created the land grant universities. The national government provided public lands and generous financial support to develop railroads throughout the nation. . . . The Hatch Act of 1887 created a system of agricultural research and the Smith-Lever Act of 1914 created the extension program. The New Deal programs included the Rural Electrification Administration to bring electricity to the farms and the Resettlement Administration to help farm laborers to move to more promising locations (both in 1935), as well as a system of price supports to bolster farm incomes. (33–36)

James Bonnen (1992, 190) agrees. The federal government "invested in the basic infrastructure of agriculture, developing institutions and programs for rural free delivery of mail, rural roads, common market standards for farm products, and later for rural electrification, soil conservation, and long-term, intermediate, and short-term farm credit—all through national policy." Schwartz (1994) contends that the development of the South and West was a deliberate strategy of the F.D. Roosevelt administration from the New Deal through World War II. The last significant federal initiative on that scale was the National Defense Interstate Highway System, begun in the 1950s, which enabled manufacturing activity to relocate—often to rural areas. Recent farm bills have included modest attention to rural development, but federal agricultural policy is no substitute for rural development policy (Browne, Skees, Swanson, Thompson, and Unnevehr 1992).

Indeed, the trend since the mid-1970s has been a decline in place-based expenditures by the federal government. In 1978, under the Carter administration, 26.5 percent of total local and state spending came from the federal government. In contrast, between 1990 and 1995, 21.5 percent of local and state government spending came from the federal government (Bonnett 1998). John Donahue (1997, 29) confirms this trend: "Overall transfers from Washington to state and cities, which had surged from about 1.5 percent of the overall economy in the mid-1960s to about 3.5 percent in the mid-1970s, retreated to around 2.5 percent of GDP." The federal government spends a much larger percentage of its budget now on people (Social Security and Medicare, for example), wherever they live, than on localities. Bold initiatives to invest in rural America may not hold great promise before Congress now that a majority of the nation's voters reside in suburbs.

One important federal initiative merits praise. Beginning in 1990, the George H.W. Bush administration launched an initiative to "coordinate rural development efforts among federal departments and agencies and establish collaborative relationships with states, local governments, and the private sector" (Radin et al. 1996, 1). The diversity of rural interests and constituencies has frustrated those seeking to organize them, collaborate with others, or form effective coalitions. Many of the State Rural Development Councils (SRDCs) have provided effective leadership for rural development. Some of the SRDCs have been focused on specific projects (e.g., economic development, housing, community facilities), whereas others are committed to the process of improving rural communities. The SRDCs have provided support for both project and process approaches to rural development.

Robert Putnam (2000) uses the phrase *social capital* to describe the connections among individuals—social networks and the norms of reciprocity and trustworthiness that arise from them. Obviously, many rural communities are blessed with an abundance of civic virtue—volunteer fire departments, bake sales for good causes, and a host of activities that build and sustain community spirit. Others, of course, lack these valuable community assets.

Rural communities must have the *will to act,* which means strong leadership, and the *power to act,* which means the capacity to make meaningful decisions about how to improve the community. Chester Newland (1981) defines *capacity building* as "increasing the ability of people and institutions to do what is required of them" (iv). David Brown and Nina Glasgow (1991) soberly observe, "Local governments, especially in small towns and rural areas, tend to be conservative, consensus-seeking, nonconfrontational bodies" (198).

Summary

Today, rural communities face challenges quite different from those of the past. The immediate challenges are not limited to improving transportation systems to get farm commodities and natural resource products to the best markets in a timely fashion; nor are they limited to ensuring that rural children get the best possible education to prepare for an uncertain, demanding future.

Rural leaders must act judiciously to preserve what is best about their rural communities and invest prudently to enhance the future prosperity of their localities. Because many rural communities are constrained by their lack of fiscal resources, their leaders should be open to forming coalitions with neighboring communities, partnerships with leading firms and regional institutions (such as hospitals and colleges), and alliances with others. Aggregating community demand for advanced telecommunications services, the most promising example of this strategy, may be the best way to stimulate private–sector telecommunications infrastructure investment.

The policy challenges for the states include making strategic investments in physical infrastructure (especially in broadband telecommunications), human capital, and applying knowledge to be used in a variety of ways. More state investment in rural communities is necessary, justified, and appropriate, yet recall the bittersweet lesson of the last century: the larger state role in education forced school consolidation. More state dollars often means more state control. Rural leaders will need to work closely with state officials to devise governing structures that can be flexible in meeting the current and future needs of rural communities.

Local autonomy is laudable, except when it locks out innovation and keeps the community isolated from a fast-paced world. Continued prosperity in many rural places will rest on their ability to provide an enviable quality of life—to recruit and retain knowledgeable workers able to work anywhere—and enable them to be linked electronically with others throughout the world. Traditional approaches cannot achieve that lofty objective.

Finally, this chapter has discussed how state development policy changed to respond to pressing social needs and economic demands as the agrarian nation became an industrial giant. Now, however, knowledge has emerged as a factor of production, and rural leaders and organizations must learn how to apply knowledge to work to create value for themselves and their communities. Perhaps state policymakers can learn from the past as they prepare for the future.

References

Baer, Walter S. 1998. Will the Internet transform higher education? In *The Emerging Internet*, 81–108. Queenstown, MD: Institute for Information Studies and the Aspen Institute.

Bain, David Haward. 1999. *Empire Express: Building the First Transcontinental Railroad.* New York: Penguin Books.

Bartik, Timothy J. 1991. *Who Benefits from State and Local Economic Development Policies?* Kalamazoo, MI: Upjohn Institute for Employment Research.

Beatty, Jack, ed. 2001. *Colossus: How the Corporation Changed America.* New York: Broadway Books.

Becker, Gary S. 1997. Why a crash wouldn't cripple the economy. *Business Week* (April 14): 26.

Bonnen, James T. 1992. Why is there no coherent U.S. rural policy? *Policy Studies Journal* 20(2): 190–201.

Bonnett, Thomas W. 1993. *Strategies for Rural Competitiveness: Policy Options for State Governments.* Washington, DC: Council of Governors' Policy Advisors.

———. 1996. *TELEWARS in the States: Telecommunications Issues in a New Era of Competition.* Washington, DC: Council of Governors' Policy Advisors.

————. 1998. *Is the New Global Economy Leaving State–Local Tax Structures Behind?* Washington, DC: National League of Cities.

————. 1999. The new state role in ensuring universal telecommunications services. In *Making Universal Service Policy: Enhancing the Process Through Multidisciplinary Evaluation*, ed. Barbara A. Cherry, Steven S. Wildman, and Allen S. Hammond IV, 215–235. Mahwah, NJ: Lawrence Erlbaum.

————. 2000. *Competing in the New Economy: Governance Strategies for the Digital Age.* Philadelphia: Xlibris.

————. 2001. Starting a telecommunications plan in your community. *Rural Research Report* 12(8): 1–11. Illinois Institute for Rural Affairs, Macomb.

Brandl, John E. 1998. *Money and Good Intentions are Not Enough.* Washington, DC: Brookings Institution.

Brown, David L., and Nina L. Glasgow. 1991. Capacity building and rural government adaptation to population change. In *Rural Policies for the 1990s*, ed. Cornelia B. Flora and James A. Christenson, 194–208. Boulder, CO: Westview Press.

Brown, Doug. 2000. USDA seeds the net. *Interactive Week* (December 11): 26.

Browne, William P., Jerry R. Skees, Louis E. Swanson, Paul B. Thompson, and Laurian J. Unnevehr. 1992. *Sacred Cows and Hot Potatoes: Agrarian Myths in Agricultural Policy.* Boulder, CO: Westview Press.

Christenson, James A., and Cornelia B. Flora. 1991. Rural policy agenda for the 1990s. In *Rural Policies for the 1990s*, ed. Cornelia B. Flora and James A. Christenson, 333–337. Boulder, CO: Westview Press.

Conant, James B. 1959. *The American High School.* New York: McGraw-Hill.

Davis, Stan, and Jim Botkin. 1998. The coming of knowledge-based business. In *The Knowledge Economy*, ed. Dale Neef, 157–164. Boston: Butterworth-Heinemann.

Donahue, John D. 1997. *Disunited States.* New York: Basic Books.

Drucker, Peter F. 1977. *People and Performance: The Best of Peter Drucker on Management.* New York: Harper and Row.

Farmer, Michael C., and Gordon Kingsley. 2001. Locating critical components of regional human capital. *Policy Studies Journal* 29(1): 165–180.

Federal Communications Commission (FCC). 2000. *Deployment of Advanced Telecommunications Capacity: Second Report* (August). Washington, DC: FCC. Available on-line: <www.fcc.gov/broadband>.

————. 2002. *Deployment of Advanced Telecommunications Capacity: Third Report* (February). Washington, DC: FCC. Available on-line: <www.fcc.gov/broadband>.

Fisher, Peter S., and Alan H. Peters. 1998. *Industrial Incentives: Competition Among American States and Cities.* Kalamazoo, MI: Upjohn Institute for Employment Research.

Fountain, J.E. 1998. Social capital: Its relationship to innovation in science and technology. *Science and Public Policy* 25(2): 103–115.

Furchgott-Roth, Harold. 2000. Concurring statement. In *Deployment of Advanced Telecommunications Capacity: Second Report*, ed. FCC, 1–2. Washington, DC: FCC. Available on-line: <www.fcc.gov/broadband>.

Gohring, Nancy. 2001. 10 myths of wireless. *Interactive Week* (August 6): 22–24.

Gruman, Galen. 2000. A governor's tech crusade. *Upside* (February): 125–132.

Hammel, Daniel J. 2001. *Internet Use Among Local Governments in Illinois' Nonmetropolitan Communities.* Macomb: Illinois Institute for Rural Affairs.

Hobbs, Darryl. 1991. Rural education. In *Rural Policies for the 1990s*, ed. Cornelia B. Flora and James A. Christenson, 151–165. Boulder, CO: Westview Press.

Human Resource Recruitment Consortium (HRRC). 2001. *Advance Your Careers and Lifestyle in Iowa.* Available on-line: <www.smartcareermove.com>.

Iowa Value-Added Agricultural Products and Processes Financial Assistance Program (VAAPFAP). 2001. Material from Iowa Department of Economic Development, Des Moines.

Kauffman, Bill. 2001. The road to Columbine. *The American Enterprise* (September): 50.

Kirchhoff, Herb. 2002. Michigan senate passes key broadband bills. *Washington Internet Daily* (February 22), 2.

LinkMichigan. 2001. Michigan Economic Development website. Available on-line: <http://medc.michigan.org/>.

Mackey, Scott. 1998. *Critical Issues in State–Local Fiscal Policy.* Denver: National Conference of State Legislatures.

McCraw, Thomas K. 1997. Retrospect and prospect. In *Creating Modern Capitalism,* ed. Thomas K. McCraw, 531–542. Cambridge, MA: Harvard University Press.

McMahon, Kathleen, and Priscilla Salant. 1999. Strategic planning for telecommunications in rural communities. *Rural Development Perspectives* 14(3): 2–7.

Mowery, David C., and Nathan Rosenberg. 1998. *Paths of innovation: Technological Change in 20th Century America.* New York: Cambridge University Press.

National Association of State Information Resource Executives (NASIRE) in partnership with the National Association of State Telecommunication Directors (NASTD). 2000. *Closing the Digital Divide with Broadband Internet Access.* Lexington, KY.

National Center for Education Statistics (NCES). 2001. *Digest of Education Statistics, 2001* (Table 157) (pp. 76–77). Available on-line: <http://nces.ed.gov/pubs2002/2002130.pdf>. Downloaded: April 26, 2002.

National Governors' Association (NGA). 1994. *Telecommunications: The Next American Revolution.* Washington, DC: Author.

National Research Council (NRC). 2002. *Broadband: Bringing Home the Bits.* Washington, DC: National Academy Press.

National Telecommunications and Information Administration (NTIA). 2000. *Falling Through the net: Toward Digital Inclusions.* Washington, DC: NTIA. Available on-line: <www.ntia.doc.gov>.

Nelson, Richard R., and Paul M. Romer. 1996. Science, economic growth, and public policy. *Challenge* (March 13): 9–23.

Newland, Chester A. 1981. Local government capacity building. *Urban Affairs Papers* 3(1): iv–v.

OneGeorgia. 2001. OneGeorgia Web site. Available on-line: <www.onegeorgia.org/>.

Ostrom, Elinor. 1990. *Governing the Commons: The Evolution of Institutions of Collective Action.* New York: Cambridge University Press.

Parker, Edwin B. 2000. Closing the digital divide in rural America. *Telecommunications Policy Online.* Available on-line: <www.tpeditor.com/contents/2000/parker.htm>.

Parker, Edwin B., Heather E. Hudson, Don A. Dillman, Sharon Strover, and Frederick Williams. 1992. *Electronic Byways: State Policies for Rural Development Through Telecommunications.* Boulder, CO: Westview Press.

Patterson, Darby. 2001. State of the digital state. *Government Technology* (June): 31–61.

Porter, Michael E. 1998. *On Competition.* Boston: Harvard Business School Publishing.

Putnam, Robert D. 2000. *Bowling Alone: The Collapse and Revival of American Community*. New York: Simon and Schuster.

Radin, Beryl A., Robert Agranoff, Ann O'M Bowman, C. Gregory Buntz, J. Steven Ott, Barbara S. Romzek, and Robert H. Wilson. 1996. *New Governance for Rural America*. Lawrence: University of Kansas.

Ravitch, Diane. 1997. Somebody's children: Educational opportunity for all American children. In *New Schools for a New Century*, ed. Diane Ravitch and Joseph P. Viteritt, 251–273. New Haven, CT: Yale University Press.

Redman, John M. 1994. *Understanding State Economies Through Industry Studies*. Washington, DC: Council of Governors' Policy Advisors.

Reich, Robert B. 1988. The rural crisis, and what to do about it. *Economic Development Quarterly* 2(1): 1–6.

Rogers, Everett M. 1995. *Diffusion of Innovations* (4th ed.). New York: The Free Press.

Sawhney, Harmeet, and Krishna Jayakar. 1999. Universal service: Migration of metaphors. In *Making Universal Service Policy: Enhancing the Process Through Multidisciplinary Evaluation*, ed. Barbara A. Cherry, Steven S. Wildman, and Allen S. Hammond IV, 15–37. Mahwah, NJ: Lawrence Erlbaum.

Schwartz, Jordan A. 1994. *The New Deal: Power Politics in the Age of Roosevelt*. New York: Vintage.

Sears, David W., John M. Redman, Richard L. Gardner, and Stephen J. Adams. 1992. *Gearing Up for Success: Organizing for Rural Development*. Washington, DC: The Aspen Institute.

Sears, David W., Thomas D. Rowley, and J. Norman Reid. 1990. Infrastructure investment and economic development: An overview. In *Infrastructure Investment and Economic Development: Rural Strategies for the 1990s*, 1–18. Washington, DC: USDA–ERS.

Sher, Jonathan P., ed. 1977. *Education in Rural America: A reassessment of Conventional Wisdom*. Boulder, CO: Westview Press.

Swanson, Louis E. 2001. Rural opportunities: Minimalist policy and community-based experimentation. *Policy Studies Journal* 29(1): 96–107.

Task Force on Persistent Rural Poverty. 1993. *Persistent Poverty in Rural America*. Boulder, CO: Westview Press.

Tscheschlok, Christian. 2001. Rising to meet the digital challenge in rural communities: A growing divide? *Rural Research Report* 12(3): 1–11. Illinois Institute for Rural Affairs, Macomb.

U.S. Bureau of the Census. 1999. *1997 Census of Governments, Vol. 1*. Washington, DC: U.S. Government Printing Office. Available on-line: <www.census.gov/prod/gc97/gc971-1.pdf>.

Wohlbruck, Aliceann, and Melissa Levy. 2000/2001. Bridging the digital divide. *Economic Development Digest* (December/January): 1–5. Washington, DC: National Association of Development Organizations Research Foundation.

Working Group on Electronic Commerce. 2000. *Toward Digital eQuality*. Washington, DC: U.S. Department of Commerce. Available on-line: <www.ecommerce.gov/annrpt.htm>.

About the Contributors

Tom Bonnett has had an extensive career in public policy. He has worked as a state legislator, a policy analyst, and as an advisor to public officials and nonprofit organizations. His 1996 book, *TELEWARS in the States— Telecommunications Issues in a New Era of Competition*, continues to be used as a supplemental text in college courses. His most recent book, *Competing in the New Economy: Governance Strategies in the Digital Age*, was published in October 2000. Bonnett has been an independent public policy consultant since 1997. His consulting practice provides assistance to nonprofit organizations, local and state governments, and corporate clients.

Brian Dabson is president of the Corporation for Enterprise Development (CFED), a national nonprofit organization based in Washington, D.C. The CFED promotes asset building and economic opportunity strategies, primarily in low-income and distressed communities, that combine community practice, public policy, and private markets. His specific interests are in the fields of entrepreneurship and environmentally compatible economic development. He is an experienced facilitator of community and organizational strategic planning processes, and a frequent speaker and writer on economic development issues. Dabson is the president of the OECD Forum on Social Innovations and chair-elect of REAL Enterprises, Inc.

Steven C. Deller is a professor of agricultural and applied economics with the University of Wisconsin–Madison and a community development economist with the University of Wisconsin–Extension. His work focuses on modeling the economic structure of rural areas with attention paid to local policies that affect local economic growth and development. His work has appeared in *The Review of Economics and Statistics, American Journal of Agricultural Economics*, *Rural Sociology*, and the *Journal of the Community Development Society.*

John J. Gruidl is a professor in the Illinois Institute for Rural Affairs, Western Illinois University. He directs an internship program in which returned Peace Corps volunteers earn graduate degrees while assisting small Illinois towns with local development projects. His research focuses on effective development policies for local communities, and he has published in the *Journal of the Community Development Society*, *Growth and Change*, and the *Review of Regional Studies*, among others.

Margaret Hanson works in Census Services housed in the Department of Sociology at Iowa State University. Her principal role is focused on Census data analysis and dissemination to various client groups throughout the state. Hanson is coauthor of *Iowa Counties: Selected Population Trends, Vital Statistics and Socioeconomic Data, 2001*, Iowa State University. Her work is directed toward helping communities and groups understand the implications of changing demographics for the state and helping improve public policy decisions based upon relevant and current population and housing data.

Ronald J. Hustedde is an associate professor of sociology and a rural development specialist at the University of Kentucky. He is also co–research director of the University of Kentucky Appalachian Center. His specialties include public issues education, public conflict analysis and resolution, leadership education, and rural community economic analysis and development. He is a past president (1998–1999) of the Community Development Society, and he is also on the Board of Directors of the International Association for Community Development based in Edinburgh, Scotland.

Thomas G. Johnson is Frank Miller Professor of Agricultural Economics and a professor of public affairs at the University of Missouri–Columbia as well as the director of the Community Policy Analysis Center. He teaches and conducts research in rural economic development, economic impact analysis, local government finance, rural education, and transportation economics. Johnson has served on the editorial boards of the *American Journal of Agricultural Economics* and the *Southern Journal of Agricultural Economics*, and as president of the Southern Regional Science Association.

Paul Lasley is a professor of sociology at Iowa State University. His research, teaching, and extension work focus on farm and rural issues at the state and national levels. His principal areas of inquiry include rural development, community studies, and social-demographic patterns and the consequences of these social and economic changes. He is the author or coauthor of more than a hundred professional journal articles, book chapters, and extension publications.

John C. Leatherman is an associate professor in the Department of Agricultural Economics at Kansas State University and a local government specialist with Kansas State University–Extension. He is the director of the Office of Local Government, an extension program providing educational outreach and technical assistance services for local governments in Kansas. His programming and research interests include local economic development policy and practice, local public finance and service provision, and natural resource management. He first joined the Cooperative Extension Service in 1984 and has served as a county extension agent and state specialist.

Raymond Lenzi is professor and associate chancellor for economic development and directs the Office of Economic and Regional Development at Southern Illinois University (SIU) at Carbondale. He is also currently the Strategic Research Initiative (SRI) leader for the Illinois C-FAR Rural Community Development/I-FARRM Project and chief executive officer for the Southern Illinois Research Park, a hi-tech focused development adjacent to the SIU–Carbondale campus.

Christopher D. Merrett is an associate professor of geography in the Illinois Institute for Rural Affairs, where he conducts research on public policy issues. Recent research publications include articles, reviews, and two books on a range of topics, including rural planning and economic development, cooperatives and community development, the role of value-added agriculture in the rural economy, nonprofit organizations and welfare reform, and the impact of free trade on local communities.

Lee W. Munnich Jr. is a senior fellow and director of the state and local policy program at the University of Minnesota's Hubert H. Humphrey Institute of Public Affairs. Munnich has thirty-five years' experience with local and state government, including serving as deputy commissioner of the Minnesota Department of Trade and Economic Development, research director for the Minnesota Business Partnership, manager of Midwest Research Institute's Center of Economic Studies, and executive director of the Minnesota Tax Study Commission. He also was legislative policy analyst and elected member of the Minneapolis City Council.

Mohamed M. Samy is a visiting scholar in the Department of Agricultural and Consumer Economics, University of Illinois–Urbana–Champaign. He is currently involved in a large study on "Improving Farm Incomes and Rural Communities Through Specialty Farm Products." Recent faculty positions have included Menoufia University in Egypt and the United Arab Emirates University, Al-Ain, U.A.E.

Greg Schrock is a graduate research assistant with the State and Local Policy Program, and a master's of urban and regional planning candidate at the Hubert H. Humphrey Institute of Public Affairs, University of Minnesota. Before attending the Humphrey Institute, Schrock was a research fellow with the Indiana Economic Development Council, the state's public–private economic development planning and research entity.

James K. Scott is interim director of Policy Programs and a research associate professor in the Harry S. Truman School of Public Affairs, University of Missouri–Columbia. He has published numerous articles and research reports on rural policy, community policy, and the future of local governance. He has worked with dozens of community groups and local and state government officials to assess the economic, fiscal, and social impacts of proposed or expected changes. Scott's current research focuses on technology and the changing nature of local governance, and on public participation in community decision making.

Andrew J. Sofranko is a professor of rural sociology in the Department of Human and Community Development, University of Illinois–Urbana–Champaign. For the past twenty-five years his research and teaching have focused on rural economics and demographics and small communities. He is currently involved in research on the effects of a changing age structure on small towns and farming. He has published extensively on demographic trends and their impact on rural areas.

Burton E. Swanson, professor of rural development, Department of Agricultural and Consumer Economics, at the University of Illinois–Urbana–Champaign, currently directs the C-FAR–funded *Value Project*, which seeks to improve Illinois farm incomes and rural communities through value-added agriculture. He joined the University of Illinois faculty in 1975 and has carried out assignments in thirty-five countries. Most recently he has worked extensively in China and India on major World Bank projects that seek to intensify and diversify local farming systems into high-value commodities.

Norman Walzer is a professor of economics and directs the Illinois Institute for Rural Affairs at Western Illinois University. He has worked on numerous projects with local and state government and has published on local public finance and economic development issues in the *National Tax Journal*, *Land Economics*, *Review of Economics and Statistics*, *Labor and Industrial Relations Review*, and other outlets. His most recent book, *A Cooperative Approach to Local Economic Development*, is coedited with Christopher A. Merrett and was published in 2001.

Kimberly A. Zeuli is an assistant professor in the Department of Agricultural and Applied Economics at the University of Wisconsin–Madison and associate director for the University of Wisconsin Center for Cooperatives. Her research, teaching, and extension programs focus on the cooperative model, especially its relevance and application to rural community development.

Index